Enforcement at the EPA

Enforcement at the EPA

High Stakes and Hard Choices

REVISED EDITION
JOEL A. MINTZ

University of Texas Press ◆ *Austin*

Support for this book comes from an endowment for environmental studies made possible by generous contributions from Richard C. Bartlett, Susan Aspinall Block, and the National Endowment for the Humanities.

Requests for permission to reproduce material from this work should be sent to:
    Permissions
    University of Texas Press
    P.O. Box 7819
    Austin, TX 78713-7819
    www.utexas.edu/utpress/about/bpermission.html

♾ The paper used in this book meets the minimum requirements of ANSI/NISO Z39.48-1992 (R1997) (Permanence of Paper).

The Library of Congress catalogued the first edition as follows:

Mintz, Joel A., 1949–
Enforcement at the EPA : high stakes and hard choices / by Joel A. Mintz
    p.   cm.
Includes bibliographical references and index.
1. Environmental policy—United States.   2. United States. Environmental Protection Agency. I. Title
GE180.M56   1996
363.7′56′0973—dc20

                                           95-13922

ISBNs for the revised edition:
978-0-292-72840-0 (cloth : alk. paper)
978-0-292-73711-2 (e-book, library)
978-0-292-74281-9 (e-book, other)

Contents

Acknowledgments

While researching and drafting this book I amassed an enormous volume of debt. It is a great pleasure to discharge it here.

The 190 professionals who graciously participated in my study gave generously of their time and knowledge. Their names are listed in Appendix A, along with the date(s) and place(s) of my interviews with them. The government service job titles of the present and former government employees whom I interviewed are included in Appendix B.

Particular thanks are due to Jim McDonald, Mike Smith, Rich Smith, and Shannon Davies, to Professors Meri-Jane Rochelson, Frank Grad, Arthur Murphy, and Subha Narasimhan, and to former congressman and presidential candidate John Anderson, for reading my manuscript (in one version or another) and advancing valuable suggestions. I owe special thanks as well to seven of those whom I interviewed, Ed Reich, Rett Nelson, Jon Cannon, Tom Gallagher, Gail Ginsberg, Dave Ullrich, and David Buente, who spent especially long periods of time with me sharing their keen insights.

I am thankful for the President's Faculty Scholarship Award and the President's Faculty Research and Development Grant that I received from Nova Southeastern University, for the research grants and reduced teaching schedule provided by Nova Southeastern University's Shepard Broad Law Center, and for the encouragement and support given to me by my faculty colleagues. I remain most grateful to my friends Rana Segal and Mike Smith, Gail and Bob Ginsberg, and Noel and Roger Wise, for their kind hospitality in inviting me to stay in their homes as a guest during my research travels around the United States. I also benefited greatly from the first-rate typing and clerical work of Jesse Monteagudo and the late Pat Crossman, and the skillful research and proofreading efforts of Joe Fried, Scott Alexander, and Doris Raskin.

This project was improved enormously by the highly professional work of the editorial staff of the University of Texas Press, with whom it has been a pleasure to work. I must also mention that some portions of Chapters 1, 3, 4, and 5 were initially published, in somewhat different form, in Mintz, "Agencies, Congress and Regulatory Enforcement, 1970 to 1987," 18 *Environmental Law* 683 (1988); Chapter 7 was first published in much the same form in "Neither the Best of Times Nor the Worst of Times: EPA Enforcement During the Clinton Administration," 35 *Environmental Law Reporter* 10390 (June 2005); some segments of Chapter 8 appeared in "Treading Water: A Preliminary Assessment of EPA Enforcement During the Bush II Administration," 34 *Environmental Law Reporter* 10912 (October 2004); and significant portions of Chapter 10 were previously published in "Has Industry Captured the EPA? Appraising Marver Bernstein's Captive Agency Theory after Fifty Years," 17 *Fordham Environmental Law Review* 1 (2005). The consent of the editors of each of those journals to republish some or all of those pieces in this volume is acknowledged with my thanks.

Finally, my deepest debt is to my family. Their boundless love and support, at all times and in every way, was absolutely crucial to the completion of both editions of this book.

Fort Lauderdale, Florida
October 2010

Enforcement at the EPA

CHAPTER I

Introduction

A critical actor in the federal regulation of pollution in the United States, the U.S. Environmental Protection Agency ("EPA" or "the Agency") is a governmental body charged by Congress with immense responsibility for implementing more than fourteen statutes respecting environmental quality and the public health.[1] From modest beginnings during the Nixon administration,[2] EPA's workload has increased dramatically to encompass such diverse and complex environmental issues as hazardous waste management, asbestos in schools, acid rain, and the quality of drinking water. Public support for accomplishment of the Agency's challenging mission has remained strong, widespread, and consistent.[3]

This book examines a difficult and often overlooked part of EPA's responsibilities: the enforcement of federal environmental standards established by Congress in detailed legislation and by the Agency itself in regulations that conform to congressional mandates. The book is at once a chronicle of EPA's enforcement history from the Agency's beginnings through the George W. Bush (Bush II) administration and an analysis of some important questions regarding EPA's institutional performance and environment that are suggested by more generalized writings on regulatory enforcement, congressional oversight, the federal service, and the captive agency theory of administrative agencies.

The practical and theoretical significance of EPA's institutional environment—and of its enforcement activities and structures—has been recognized by scholars, congressional leaders, and executive branch officials alike. As Christopher H. Schroeder has observed,

> When environmental policy moves from legislation to implementation, it enters a complex institutional environment, one shaped by internal and

external incentives and pressures. Without a sufficient appreciation of EPA's institutional environment, substantive environmental policy decisions can be deflected, stalled or altered in unintended ways.[4]

Environmental enforcement is clearly a crucial component of EPA's implementation work. The work of monitoring enforcement and compliance now represents approximately 25 percent of the Agency's total budget,[5] and it engages the efforts of approximately 3,200 full-time employees.[6] Furthermore, as Peter Yeager has noted,

> To the public mind, enforcement is the centerpiece of regulation, the visible hand of the state reaching into society to correct wrongs. . . . Both symbolically and practically, enforcement is a capstone, a final indicator of the state's seriousness of purpose and a key determinant of the barrier between compliance and lawlessness.[7]

Enforcement is critical both as a control on firms and individuals who violate environmental standards and as a defense of the legitimacy of the governmental intervention that sustains voluntary compliance.[8] Without it, in the words of Senator Joseph Lieberman, "most of the rest of environmental protection lacks meaning, lacks teeth, lacks reality."[9]

The enforcement aspects of EPA's work considered here include the Agency's historical evolution, its institutional setting, and its current strengths and shortcomings. In the remainder of this first chapter, I identify a set of questions suggested by the recent writings of other scholars, although not directly examined in them. These questions form the major focus of this study. I also discuss the methodology I used.

Chapter Two describes the enforcement process at EPA, both generally — in the implementation of such federal statutes as the Clean Air Act, the Clean Water Act, and the Resource Conservation and Recovery Act (commonly known as RCRA) — and as a critical component of a program that has received considerable attention from Congress, the press, and environmental organizations: the Comprehensive Environmental Response, Compensation and Liability Act (commonly known as CERCLA or Superfund). The description incorporates the insights of students of EPA's programs whose consideration of the Agency's enforcement efforts is incidental to the main thrust of their work, in addition to the pertinent observations of those whose work focuses on regulatory enforcement. To create a more detailed portrait of EPA enforcement, these analyses are supplemented by interviews with numerous EPA enforcement officials and my own professional experiences with the Agency.

Chapters Three through Eight recount the institutional history of EPA's enforcement programs. Chapter Three deals with the Agency's initial attempts at enforcement in the early 1970s, as well as the "major source enforcement effort" that was a feature of the Carter administration. Chapter Four considers the upheavals that beset EPA's enforcement work during the tenure of Anne Gorsuch as EPA administrator at the beginning of the 1980s, and the powerful congressional reaction that led to her ouster from the Agency. Chapter Five focuses on EPA's attempts to restart its enforcement programs in the face of persistent criticisms from Capitol Hill during the balance of the Reagan administration. Chapter Six reviews the key trends in EPA enforcement during the George H. W. Bush (Bush I) administration. Chapter Seven considers the major events and trends in EPA enforcement in the period in which William J. ("Bill") Clinton was president; and Chapter Eight examines the difficulties and successes of Agency enforcement during the eight years of the administration of George W. Bush (Bush II).

Because, as we shall see, EPA's administration of the Superfund Program has been at the vortex of a series of important disputes between the upper echelons of EPA's management and interested members of Congress, the Agency's enforcement of RCRA and CERCLA liability standards receives considerable emphasis in this book. That component of EPA's enforcement work is not my sole focus, however, and this study also considers the Agency's attempts to enforce the other major regulatory statutes that govern it.

Few American academics to date have focused primarily on EPA's implementation of its enforcement responsibilities. For the most part, studies of regulatory enforcement in the United States and of congressional oversight of regulatory agencies tend to be general in nature, with little or no specific references to EPA. With few exceptions, examinations of EPA—including those that consider its strained relationships with congressional oversight bodies—generally consider the Agency's enforcement work only indirectly, or as one small component of a more broad and generalized analysis. A close reading of the pertinent literature suggests several as yet unaddressed questions which careful examination of EPA's enforcement activities can help to resolve. Analysis of those issues, in light of the history and development of EPA's enforcement program, may be found in Chapters Nine through Eleven. It is a central task of this book.

The first question addressed concerns the style and nature of EPA's enforcement programs as they have evolved to date. Is EPA's enforcement process a "compliance system," in which agency personnel eschew legalistic enforcement tools in favor of a more informal system of bargaining and bluffing, or is EPA enforcement a "deterrence system," in which emphasis is placed on formal legal processes in the hope of punishing wrongdoers and deterring future noncompliance? The answer to this inquiry has implications for the agency's relationship with industrial corporations subject to its regulations, as well as its relationships with Congress, environmental organizations, and other divisions of the executive branch. It may also serve as a basis for comparing the enforcement work of EPA with that of other federal agencies as well as the regulatory activities of state and local governments.

Another set of inquiries concerns oversight of the Agency's enforcement performance by congressional committees, as well as such legislative branch investigators as the Government Accountability Office (GAO). Has congressional oversight had a significant impact on the nature and direction of EPA's enforcement work? Have congressional overseers contributed to what one observer describes as "regulatory failure" in the enforcement aspects of EPA's implementation of federal environmental laws? Or (as another scholar suggests we should generally expect in such congressional investigations) has congressional oversight of EPA enforcement merely "improved policy at the margins"? To what extent have other aspects of Congress's organizational structure and relationship with EPA, including its decentralized subcommittee system and its control of the Agency's budget, affected the Agency in its enforcement work?

These questions are the focus of Chapter Nine. That chapter also considers the broader implications of two major reorganizations that took place in EPA's enforcement office headquarters in 1981 and 1993–1994. In addition, it describes ways in which key EPA political appointees as well as the Agency's enforcement staff can and (in some instances) do contribute to and support the Agency's enforcement efforts.

Chapter Ten focuses on EPA enforcement in the context of what Professor Paul Light has described as a general decline in the capabilities of the federal service. It analyzes the extent to which EPA's enforcement experience does (and does not) support Light's diagnosis of the problems of the federal civil service, and it assays his provocative suggestions for institutional improvement.

Finally, in Chapter Eleven, I examine the extent to which EPA's enforcement program has been "captured" by the industries it is charged with regulating. After an exploration of the captive agency theory of administrative agencies, I consider the extent to which that theory may fairly be said to apply to the enforcement component of the Agency's work.

The research for this study included a review of the body of academic literature that directly or peripherally concerns EPA enforcement and its oversight by Congress. In addition, in preparing this book I reviewed EPA enforcement policy documents prepared at the Agency between 1970 and 2009, as well as a variety of other EPA files, reports, and records on enforcement activities. I also examined congressional hearing records, newspapers, trade journals, training course materials, and the reports of relevant case studies by congressional committees and subcommittees, industrial associations, private consultants, environmental organizations, nonprofit foundations, the GAO, the Congressional Budget Office (CBO), and the Office of Technology Assessment (OTA).

During the summer of 1984 and much of 1986, the winter of 1991, the spring of 1992, the spring of 2003, the winter and spring of 2004, the winter of 2005, and the spring, summer, and fall of 2009, I interviewed 190 present and former government officials—from EPA, the U.S. Department of Justice (the Justice Department or DOJ), the GAO, and the professional staffs of several congressional committees and subcommittees—to obtain their recollections of the critical trends, developments, and events in EPA enforcement programs.[10] I questioned these individuals with respect to the various sets of intra-, inter-, and extra-governmental relationships that exist in the federal environmental enforcement field, the management and working milieu of EPA enforcement programs, and their own notions of the ingredients of an effective environmental enforcement effort. I selected the interviewees on the basis of the breadth of their experience in the federal government and the likelihood that they would have been involved in or knowledgeable about EPA hazardous waste enforcement. I sought interviews with present and former officials who had diverse professional backgrounds and perspectives. For the most part, respondents held top or mid-level managerial positions with EPA or were attorneys or scientists and technical experts on the Agency's enforcement staff.

Because of the importance of EPA's regional offices in implementing the Agency's enforcement program, I conducted interviews with present and former officials in EPA Regions I (Boston), III (Philadelphia), IV (Atlanta), V (Chicago), and IX (San Francisco), as well as in the agency's National Enforcement Investigations Center (NEIC) in Denver, Colorado, and its headquarters office in Washington, D.C. I also held interviews with upper- and mid-level managers in the Justice Department's Washington, D.C., headquarters, and with counsel to several of the congressional committees and subcommittees responsible for oversight of EPA enforcement activities.

Regardless of their past or present institutional affiliations, I asked respondents a standard set of questions, which was furnished to them in advance whenever possible, along with a brief description of the purposes for the study and its methods. Beginning in 2003, I shortened my list of standard questions to eliminate previously asked questions regarding the management and working environment of EPA enforcement programs and the elements of an effective enforcement program. This modification was made in order to streamline the interview process and to focus to a greater extent on gathering the information that I realized was most central to my study. (The two sets of standard questions I asked—before and after 2003—may be found in Appendix C and Appendix D.)

I asked most respondents all of the standard questions. In a few isolated instances, a respondent completed only portions of the standard interview due to limitations of time or circumstances or because the interviewee's pertinent views had elsewhere been made part of the public record. I did not omit any items from the standard set of questions in any interview.

To help capture the complexity of the respondents' perceptions and attitudes, I posed open-ended questions. In addition to the questions included in the standard interview format, I frequently asked spontaneous follow-up questions.

In some instances, respondents specifically requested that the substance of their interview be "off the record" in the sense that their remarks not be attributed to them by name. In a few other conversations, interviewees asked that brief segments of their remarks be afforded similar treatment. These requests have been respected. In all of the other interviews, after having been told that I might quote or paraphrase what they told me, the respondents raised no objections to being identified as the source of their remarks.

One methodological issue that arose in the course of my research concerned the relative weight to be given the results of my interviews with present and former government officials, as compared with primary documents written during the period of this study. Although such documents (e.g., EPA enforcement policies and official correspondence) are referred to and occasionally quoted from at pertinent points, I have on balance tended to place more emphasis on the comments gathered from participants in (or governmental observers of) EPA's enforcement efforts. Where these comments contradict one another or conflict with contemporary written documents, I have noted the contradiction.

Emphasis on the results of oral interviews stems in part from impressions formed during my own professional work with EPA. In particular, I learned firsthand that a great many guidance documents on enforcement policies and other matters generated by the managers at the Agency's headquarters, are drafted with the overriding goal of winning the political support of one or more constituencies. Such constituencies may include other officials within the executive branch, congressional committees and their staffs, environmental organizations, regulated industries, and state and local government officials. Although such primary EPA documents are not devoid of historical significance, relying on them too heavily would be analogous to making judgments about the efforts and products of a private enterprise based solely on its public advertising. In contrast, I believe, the interviews I conducted provide a less distorted picture of the most significant trends, developments, and events in EPA's enforcement history. The results are more in keeping with my goal of presenting the warp and woof of EPA's enforcement work, as well as EPA's relationship with Congress.

Finally, a few words are in order about my own career with EPA. For approximately six years, from July 1975 to June 1981, I held several positions with EPA in its Region V and headquarters offices. I was a staff attorney in the EPA Region V air enforcement program in 1975 and 1976 and a chief attorney in the Region V water enforcement program during 1977 and 1978. In 1979 I served on the staff of the Region V regional administrator as state relations coordinator and policy advisor. I then transferred to EPA's Washington, D.C., headquarters where, in 1980 and early 1981, I participated in enforcement litigation as a senior staff attorney on the agency's Hazardous Waste Enforcement Task Force (HWETF).

I was not employed by EPA during most of the period that is the focus of this book. Thus, I was generally not in any meaningful sense a "participant observer" of the historical events that this study recounts. The major exception to that is what I have referred to as the "Task Force Phase," the 1979–1980 period during which EPA initiated its hazardous waste enforcement work. With respect to that era, I have attempted not to incorporate my personal perceptions unless they were confirmed by several others who were directly involved. I have also attempted to overcome any biases, limitations, and a priori assumptions stemming from my involvement as an EPA attorney by obtaining and closely considering the views of

EPA enforcement technical people, regional enforcement attorneys, DOJ managers, and congressional staff counsel with respect to both the periods of my service with the government and my impressions of the general nature of EPA's enforcement process.

Notwithstanding the self-imposed limitations and constraints outlined above, my own EPA enforcement experience was relevant to the preparation of this study. In addition to shaping my perceptions of the functions and historical significance of EPA enforcement policies and records, my background enabled me to prepare a preliminary list of people to interview, a list that changed and grew considerably as my research progressed. Furthermore, I used my EPA experience to frame the standard interview format and provide some working hypotheses about the development and nature of EPA enforcement activities. I altered these hypotheses considerably during the course of my research. I substantially modified my conclusions regarding several matters as I synthesized the differing perceptions of others and the voluminous information in EPA's files.

I have been engaged, challenged, and fascinated by the enforcement activities of EPA for more than thirty-five years. This book is an attempt to share what I have learned and to suggest, with respect, some ways in which those who do enforcement work at EPA—and those who oversee, support, and critique that work—might better foster its success.

"Where the Rubber Hits the Road and Everything Else Hits the Fan": A Brief Description of EPA's Enforcement Process and the Superfund Program

Enforcement occupies a central place in the administration of regulatory requirements. This is particularly so with regard to federal environmental laws. Laborious, technical, time-consuming, and suffused with tensions, the enforcement process of the U.S. Environmental Protection Agency is, in the words of one skillful, experienced participant, "where the rubber hits the road and everything else hits the fan."[1]

For well over a century, following enactment of the Interstate Commerce Act of 1887, federal administrative regulation of economic activities has become an established fact of American life. In a variety of substantive areas (from aviation to securities to labor relations) Congress has culminated prolonged struggles for reform with the passage of broad legislation aimed at redressing significant public problems. Frequently, however, that culmination is more apparent than real. As students of federal regulation have noted, the first statutes that emerge from agitation for regulatory legislation are often imprecise compromises between social forces that favor regulation and powerful interests that oppose it.[2]

Because regulatory legislation is generally broadly drafted, considerable discretion is often vested in federal administrative agencies. Those agencies are often charged with important responsibilities for establishing specific rules consistent with the general policies and purposes of the regulatory statutes themselves and enforcing those specific rules in administrative and judicial proceedings. According to one knowledgeable observer, "They are like armies of occupation, left in the field to police the rule won by the victorious coalition."[3]

From the perspective of some regulated industries, the enforcement of federal environmental laws represents another, perhaps final, opportunity to put into effect their long-standing policy preferences and views. Part of the reason for this is the sometimes indeterminate nature of environmental regulations. As Marc K. Landy and his coauthors have discovered,

> [R]egulations only reveal their true meaning through the enforcement process. The inevitably ambiguous language of the rules is defined only as decisions are made about what constitutes a violation in specific cases. In that process, arcane technical specifications that spell out what [pollution control] devices are to be installed and how their operation is to be measured often have specific public policy implications. Given the variety of processes and settings that must be dealt with, even rules written in meticulous detail will not eliminate the need for case by case enforcement.[4]

In view of this, firms who are subject to EPA enforcement actions will often attempt to persuade the Agency to adopt general or case-specific interpretations of enforceable EPA regulations that are consistent with their own perceived needs, aims, and regulatory philosophies. At the same time, the enforcement process represents a continuing test of the effectiveness and vitality of the nation's environmental laws. Its outcome determines whether the lofty aims and purposes of federal environmental statutes will ultimately be realized and the public's interest served. In the insightful words of Marver Bernstein,

> The attitude of [an administrative agency] toward its enforcement responsibilities affects its entire regulatory program. Unless it demonstrates a capacity to enforce its regulations, they will be more honored in the breach than in the observance. Those who discover that violations go undetected and unpunished will have little respect for the [agency] and will violate regulations with impunity if it is to their financial or commercial advantage.[5]

In a general sense, the enforcement activities of regulatory agencies can be seen as a sequential series of filtering operations. As Colin Diver has characterized it,

> The initial task is to identify . . . that set of activities involving an apparent violation of the underlying regulatory command. From this set of apparent violations, the enforcement agency must select those appropriate to serve as the basis for a demand for remedial action. The agency fur-

ther distills this sub-set into a group of offenses warranting the imposition of punitive sanctions.[6]

At EPA, enforcement cases typically go through three phases: inspection and information gathering, administrative case development, and (if the matter has not yet been resolved) formal litigation. In noncriminal cases, the agency has several primary sources of compliance information: self-monitoring, record keeping and reporting by individual sources of pollution, inspections by government personnel, and the specific complaints of concerned citizens.

Most EPA inspections are announced to the pollution source ahead of time to ensure the presence of vital plant personnel. Inspections may be either "for cause," that is, based on a reasonable suspicion that the inspected source is in violation, or else routinely conducted pursuant to a "neutral inspection scheme." Perhaps surprisingly, of the approximately 1,600 individuals who perform EPA inspections, more than 75 percent do so less than 20 percent of the time.[7]

When the Agency conducts an investigation on the basis of citizen information, that information may have come from a variety of individuals. Citizen informants often include, for example, disgruntled employees of suspected violators, neighbors, state or local inspectors, environmental citizens' organizations, and suspected violators' economic competitors. In potential criminal matters, these sources of information may be replaced—or supplemented—by targeted inspections, sometimes conducted under color of search warrant, by EPA criminal investigators, as well as by grand jury proceedings under the auspices of the DOJ.

Once EPA or DOJ investigators (or both) have completed their information gathering, they must determine whether the source in question is in violation of applicable standards and, if so, what type of enforcement response the Agency will make. Under most of the relevant federal environmental statutes, EPA has a range of options available to it. It may begin enforcement by issuing a notice of violation to the allegedly violating source, describing the violation and inviting the source to confer informally with agency enforcement personnel.[8] Alternatively, EPA may issue the source an administrative order requiring compliance with applicable requirements and, in some cases, an assessed civil penalty. In addition, EPA is generally authorized to refer enforcement matters to the DOJ for civil action or criminal prosecution. If it deems the circumstances appropriate, the Agency may defer to a planned or ongoing enforcement action by state or local environmental officials.

Since the late 1980s, in order to make more effective use of its limited enforcement resources, EPA has undertaken a series of nationally led, targeted enforcement initiatives that are directed at particular national firms and industries with high rates of noncompliance, whose pollution has an especially significant impact on public health and the environment. These targeted initiatives are planned at the Agency's headquarters following research into the compliance record of a variety of companies and local governments. They involve coordinated efforts by enforcement personnel from EPA headquarters and regional offices.

EPA's headquarters, in consultation with the Agency's regional offices and state and tribal officials, also prepares an annual "National Program Managers Guidance," a strategic planning tool which sets forth national enforcement program priorities.

Within the general parameters of that document, EPA decisions as to which of its various enforcement options to pursue are typically made at the regional level by technically trained personnel working in cooperation with enforcement attorneys. These determinations frequently take into account a number of factors. Regional officials typically consider, among other things, the degree to which the source's discharge or emission exceeds the maximum level established in applicable legal requirements, the duration of the violation, the number of previous enforcement actions that have been taken successfully against the same source, any relevant national EPA enforcement policies, the potential deterrence value of the case, the resources available to the Agency and the DOJ at the time of the decision, EPA's working relationship with interested state and local officials, and the Agency's estimation of the enforcement capability of those officials.[9] These calculations, which are usually made with little public knowledge or participation, have great administrative significance. As Colin Diver has written,

> Persons making these decisions—prosecutors, in the broad sense—
> occupy a very significant gate keeping position in the regulatory process.
> Not only must they ration their own scarce resources of time and energy
> among competing caseload demands, but they must also ration access to
> other institutions involved in the adjudication of violations.[10]

One final factor is also of immense importance in the regulatory enforcement work of EPA and other administrative agencies: the clarity and legal enforceability of the written standards and regulations that provide the underpinning for all enforcement actions. Marver Bernstein and other observers have noted that in order to be enforceable, regulations must be understood by persons and firms subject to them. Such standards must set forth clearly what the individual or firm must do in order to comply.[11] This conclusion has particular application to the voluminous set of requirements enforced by EPA, requirements designed to govern the conduct of hundreds of thousands of individuals, firms, and government entities. Regrettably, however, the performance of Agency regulation writers has not always been adequate. In a number of instances, imprecise or incomprehensible regulatory drafting has precluded the successful initiation and completion of EPA enforcement activity.[12]

In his provocative study of EPA implementation of the Clean Water Act, Peter Yeager has observed: "The (EPA) enforcement process is a deeply textured one. At subsurface levels, it is an uncertain mix of professional ambitions of (usually young) litigators, bureaucratic politics and changing priorities, and virtually constant negotiations with a host of recalcitrants."[13] This complex process creates a number of inherent constraints for the Agency's cadre of top and mid-level managers.

At the regional office level, enforcement duties are generally divided among senior career civil servants who head divisions that have responsibility for regulatory matters in one specific environmental medium (air, water, hazardous waste, etc.) as well as regional counsel. These officials report to more than one superior. On the one hand, they are all supervised by relatively autonomous regional administrators, senior officials whose appointments and outlooks are often considerably influenced by state governors and environmental officials. On the other hand, these same regional counsel and division directors are accountable to particular assistant administrators in EPA's headquarters who are appointed to their positions and subsequently confirmed by the U.S. Senate, with different kinds of political support. In view of their divergent power bases, it is not unusual for regional administrators and assistant administrators to disagree on particular matters of enforcement policy. When this occurs, regional division directors and regional counsel are often placed in an uncomfortable and difficult situation for reasons that are self-apparent.

These internal EPA conflicts are not the only constraints that regional managers must face as they carry out enforcement responsibilities. The same officials must maintain effective working relationships with managers and supervisors at the DOJ, an institution that, as we have seen, has primary responsibility for litigation of civil and criminal enforcement matters referred to it by EPA.[14] They must also work cooperatively with state and local officials to encourage state and local enforcement actions consistent with Agency policies and preferences. At the same time, they must occasionally initiate supplementary federal enforcement proceedings when a state or local government has taken an action that the Agency deems grossly inadequate.

EPA headquarters executives face a separate set of managerial constraints. Since most EPA enforcement activity is carried out by regional office personnel, the Agency's headquarters enforcement officials require the cooperation of regional managers (including regional administrators, regional counsel, and division directors) whose approaches to enforcement may conflict with the preferences of headquarters managers. In addition, headquarters executives must communicate effectively with their counterparts at the DOJ. Moreover, they must be responsive to the demands and criticisms of two frequently opposing institutions: members of Congress (and the staffs of congressional oversight and appropriations committees) and executive branch entities, such as the White House Office of Management and Budget (OMB).

All EPA enforcement managers, whether they work in headquarters or a regional office, have a multitude of other responsibilities and concerns as well, ranging from hiring, training, overseeing, evaluating, and retaining their staffs to preparing and justifying budget requests, relating to other managers at a peer level, responding to inquiries from investigative entities (such as the EPA Office of Inspector General and the GAO), and keeping abreast of the frequent changes in law, science, and policy that may have an impact on their enforcement work.

Finally, all EPA executives and managers with enforcement responsibilities face one additional constraint: the enforcement process itself is intrinsically and unavoidably difficult to supervise. As Marc K. Landy and his co-authors have observed,

> Because it involves such substantial discretion at the operational level, enforcement is notoriously hard to manage. . . . The great detail involved makes it difficult for bureaucratic superiors, even those with technical training, to know whether the requirements their staff proposes are adequate (or necessary) to meet cleanup objectives. It is equally difficult for them, as supervisors of an ongoing relationship, to know whether initiating coercive measures is defensible or wise. In addition, if enforcement decisions are to be technically appropriate and survive judicial review, engineers and lawyers must work together in their formulation. This creates immediate problems in managing the necessary integration.[15]

In view of these various circumstances and constraints, EPA's enforcement managers face immense challenges. Under conflicting pressures, they must work effectively with a wide range of individuals to accomplish their missions in a timely, defensible way. Given their heavy workloads and the case-by-case nature of enforcement work, they must often rely extensively on the judgment, dedication, and skill of their professional staffs.

At EPA, as at many regulatory agencies and departments, enforcement work involves considerable bargaining. In most instances, bargaining serves the interests and goals of both the Agency itself and the regulated enterprises that are subject to enforcement action. From EPA's point of view, the time and energy of its enforcement staff is limited. To accomplish its objectives, it is usually to the Agency's advantage to resolve acceptably as many enforcement matters as possible, without resorting to expensive and resource-intensive litigation. Another consideration for Agency officials is the bureaucratic wish to retain control over decisions within one's area of responsibility. When compromise is not possible and EPA refers a matter to the DOJ for litigation, some of that control is inevitably relinquished to judges and DOJ attorneys and managers.

From the regulated enterprise's perspective, negotiation and compromise are equally useful. Vicki Masterman, an attorney who represents many private companies in EPA enforcement matters, explains:

> It's an unusual set of circumstances that need to be in place for a company to decide that it makes sense to litigate fully in defense of an [EPA] enforcement action. Even if you think you have a good case, even if you think the equities are in your favor, sometimes you just can't afford the team of lawyers and the years it would take to litigate, especially given the [other] implications it has for your business. Your lenders might require that some additional financial facilities be created to anticipate a loss in litigation. Your SEC [Securities and Exchange Commission] reporting might need to be changed. . . . And that's not to even mention the cloud that hangs over your [manufacturing production] processes if you think you're going to have to change one of [them] entirely.[16]

Although a number of EPA enforcement cases implicate minor, routine violations that are amenable to prompt resolution, in other matters the enforcement process is laborious and time consuming.[17] For all concerned, these more complex cases involve high stakes and hard choices.

For regulated enterprises, the risks of enforcement sanctions—including the possibility of monetary penalties, mandatory pollution control measures that may be expensive to install and maintain, and even, in some criminal cases, jail time for responsible corporate officials—are very great. As Vicki Masterman has observed, "Enforcement [by EPA] is a very real problem for industry. Threats of imprisonment and high penalties strike the deepest chords of fear in corporate environmental managers. . . . From industry's perspective enforcement is key."[18]

Moreover, as mentioned, from a defense litigator's perspective, settlement of environmental enforcement cases is also typically the prudent course. As another experienced defense attorney noted:

> In the vast majority of [civil environmental enforcement] cases, litigation is risky and settlement is by far the best approach. The discovery is mostly focused on the defendant and not the plaintiff. Things often get worse during discovery, rather than better, because the government is just going to find out more [damaging] information. You have statutory maximum penalties that are off the charts. The government is digging to find other violations and even the most responsible companies have countless compliance points where they'll just find things. . . . As long as the government is reasonable in its settlements demands, all of the pressure [on regulated firms] is for cases to settle.[19]

Beyond avoiding or minimizing sanctions, regulated industries also have an interest in dispelling uncertainties about their future environmental responsibilities and the costs those responsibilities will entail. In many cases, they are concerned with preserving (or repairing) their public image as responsible corporate citizens and in reassuring lenders, shareholders, and potential investors of their good faith and freedom from impending open-ended liability. At the same time, regulated enterprises must take care that any settlements they enter into with EPA enforcement officials not harm their firm's competitive standing within its industry. Monies expended on pollution control measures and environmental penalties will not be available for investment in productive manufacturing equipment that can increase corporate profits. As they negotiate with regulators, representatives of industrial firms are thus often mindful of individuals within their companies who focus mostly on the bottom line and see little need for or benefit from corporate environmental expenditure.

For EPA's representatives there are difficult choices as well in enforcement negotiations. Any attempt at standardized decision making by EPA is confounded by the enormous variety of conditions and circumstances that individual cases involve. The Agency's enforcement engineers and attorneys frequently face sensitive decisions with respect to the pollution control measures they will accept, the penalties they will assess, the amount of time they will allow a violator to come into compliance, the legal prerogatives and safeguards they will insist upon, and the appropriateness of avoiding or terminating negotiations and referring a matter to the Justice Department for civil or criminal action. These judgments are complex and demanding. As one of my former colleagues at EPA once confided, "You know, we really have to be very reasonable when we're in the enforcement business. The problem is that a lot of times it's just damned difficult figuring out what being reasonable *means*."[20]

From the Agency's point of view, one factor in the successfulness of enforcement staff work is the extent to which enforcement attorneys and engineers work together as a coordinated team. Two senior EPA managers, Dale Bryson and David Ullrich, have discussed this knowledgeably:

> Engineers and attorneys are often of different personality types and they "speak a different language." They have different approaches to problem-solving and perspectives on the issues. They bring very different skills to the enforcement process. . . . [T]he key for the enforcement managers and attorneys and engineers themselves is to overcome their differences and integrate their skills.[21]

In addition to interdisciplinary coordination, successful EPA enforcement staff work also demands persistence, patience, and tact. It requires an ability to communicate with a range of interested individuals and to keep higher-ranking officials (as well as DOJ attorneys) informed and supportive of negotiating strategies and positions. Moreover, it requires firm and principled dedication to the public interest and good judgment born of experience. As one former Justice Department manager observed:

> What is very important in enforcement is good judgment. [Environmental enforcement staff must resist] the temptation to chase every little technical problem. They need to really keep their eye on the ball, accomplish overall meaningful results, and do it in a way that has an aspect of fairness. That kind of judgment generally takes years to develop. . . . It is a really big challenge.[22]

EPA's administration of CERCLA (commonly known as the Super-fund Program) has been immersed in controversy during almost all of the program's history. (CERCLA was enacted in 1980.) The Agency's work in this area (of which enforcement is a central component) has been roundly criticized by congressional investigators, citizens' organizations, insur-ers, scientists, scholars, and representatives of affected private enterprises alike. EPA's approach to the Superfund Program has been critical to the history of EPA's enforcement programs and it has been a reason for the Agency's often acrimonious relationship with Congress.[23]

CERCLA, which was initially enacted in the lame-duck period of the Carter administration (and subsequently amended in 1986), was intended to bring about the cleanup of inactive hazardous waste disposal sites and to provide a basis for emergency response when hazardous substances are released to the environment. The statute required EPA to expand, and subsequently to revise, a National Contingency Plan, to include, among other things, methods for inventorying, investigating, and evaluating haz-ardous releases and criteria for determining whether cleanup activities are appropriate and what priority they should receive. Based on this plan, the Agency had to prepare a ranked National Priorities List of those in-active hazardous waste disposal facilities that require long-term cleanup measures.[24]

CERCLA provides EPA with broad authority to undertake necessary actions to deal with hazardous substance releases. Consistent with the National Contingency Plan, the Agency can conduct immediate, short-term cleanup operations—known as removal actions—as well as longer-term efforts—termed remedial actions—to repair the damage from re-leased hazardous wastes.[25] Initially, the Agency can pay for these activities from the proceeds of a trust fund that is allocated by Congress from pub-lic funds.[26] The costs of these EPA cleanup actions can later be recovered by civil lawsuits, known as cost recovery actions, from what are generally referred to as potentially responsible parties (PRPs), that is, any persons who disposed of, transported, or arranged with a transporter for the treat-ment or disposal of the hazardous materials in question.[27] The Super-fund statute also empowers EPA to issue unilateral administrative orders to PRPs that require abatement actions necessary to protect the public health from "imminent and substantial endangerments" created by haz-ardous substance releases.[28] Violators of such orders are subject to treble damages.[29] In addition, EPA can ask the Justice Department to initiate a civil action against PRPs to secure necessary abatement measures.[30]

In implementing the Agency's legal authorities under Superfund, EPA personnel generally follow a standard set of procedures that evolved over the 1980s and early 1990s. Once the Agency becomes aware of the existence of an inactive hazardous waste disposal site, EPA's regional office will dispatch an on-scene coordinator (OSC) to perform an initial investigation (known as a preliminary assessment) at the site. The OSC reviews all existing technical information at the site and prepares a brief report that determines whether any further pre-remedial response (such as a further investigation or a removal action) is required. If an immediate removal action is recommended to abate a public health emergency, it is usually accomplished promptly, using trust fund monies. If the OSC recommends further investigation of the site, a two-phase site investigation is performed; the magnitude and severity of the hazard posed by the site are evaluated in greater depth, and a decision is made whether (and, if appropriate, where) to include the site on the National Priorities List. After a problematic site has been placed on this list, EPA regional personnel (or their contractors) will generally perform a PRP search, to identify all responsible parties who may be subject to a Superfund enforcement or cost recovery action. The Agency will then typically send PRPs notice letters that, among other things, inform them of their potential liability for response costs (as well as of the development of an administrative record), request further information about the site, and release the names and addresses of other PRPs who have also received notice letters.

EPA will also commence preparation of a remedial investigation/feasibility study, or RI/FS. This document analyzes in some detail the extent of the actual or threatened release of hazardous substances at the site; it also identifies, screens, and evaluates the alternatives proposed to affect a permanent remedy at the site, taking account of cost effectiveness, ability to implement the remedy, and the level of protection afforded the environment. Once this is complete, the Agency issues a formal Record of Decision (ROD) that selects the principal remedial actions to be taken at the site.[31]

Before, during, and/or subsequent to the preparation of an RI/FS and a ROD, EPA often participates in time-limited and intensive negotiations with PRPs. From the Agency's point of view, these discussions have the goal of securing private PRP funding for all administrative and remedial expenditures at the site in question. EPA may also issue unilateral administrative orders with the same end in view.

When the Agency reaches agreement with some or all PRPs, that understanding is usually memorialized in a formal, written consent decree, sent to the Justice Department for lodging (and subsequent filing) in an appropriate U.S. District Court. If a PRP meets certain statutory criteria, designed to assure that its contribution of hazardous wastes to the Superfund site was only minimal, the Agency may enter into a *de minimis* settlement. In such a case, the *de minimis* responsible party is typically released from further liability. In exchange, it must tender a "cash out" payment of money that exceeds, by a given percentage, that party's volumetric share of the total response costs incurred at the site.

After an ROD has been issued, EPA will then embark on what is known as a remedial design/remedial action (RD/RA). In this phase, the Agency will design, construct, and implement the remedy selected in the ROD.[32] Finally, once all necessary response action at the site has been completed, EPA will reevaluate any continuing hazards the site poses and, if appropriate, delete it from—or reposition it on—the National Priorities List.

These are the procedures most commonly followed by EPA personnel in enforcing federal environmental regulations and in implementing the Superfund Program aspect of EPA's enforcement program.

CHAPTER 3

Heavy Seas before the Maelstrom: EPA Enforcement in the 1970s

On July 2, 1970, President Richard M. Nixon notified Congress that he planned to reorganize the executive branch to create two new independent agencies: the National Oceanic and Atmospheric Administration (NOAA) and the U.S. Environmental Protection Agency. Months of increasing public concern about the declining quality of the American environment preceded President Nixon's notice.

In January 1969, a dramatic oil well blowout near Santa Barbara, California, coated many miles of beachfront with heavy oil, killing thousands of fish and waterfowl. This and similar incidents focused public attention on the presence and dangers of water and air pollution, problems that had been only peripherally addressed by the federal government before then. The Earth Day celebrations of April 1970 also dramatized the nation's environmental difficulties and intensified public pressure to address them.

President Nixon had decided to accept the recommendations of a presidential council on government reorganization (known as the Ash Council after its chairman, Roy Ash) that the NOAA and EPA be established to centralize federal responsibility for antipollution activities.[1] The president's July 2, 1970, message met with wide approval from both Congress and the rapidly growing conservation community. It was followed by an executive order, "Reorganization Plan No. 3," in which EPA was formally created on December 2, 1970. Shortly thereafter, Nixon appointed William D. Ruckelshaus, an assistant attorney general at the DOJ, as the agency's first administrator.

In the enforcement area, the fledgling EPA faced profound challenges. The programs which had been transferred into EPA from other federal departments under "Reorganization Plan No. 3" had little to do with enforcement work. The country's pollution problems were widespread, growing, and uncontrolled. The federal environmental laws in effect at the time contained few enforceable substantive provisions. Environmental enforcement, as limited as it was, had been the exclusive preserve of state and local governments.

At the outset, the leadership of the new Agency determined that it was extremely important to establish that EPA was serious about enforcing the relatively few environmental standards that then existed. The Agency adopted the phrase "fair but firm" to characterize EPA's enforcement policy. Under this approach, emphasis was placed on "thorough preparation and consideration of all facts pertinent to a case, combined with an unflinching readiness to take whatever enforcement action might be required to deter recalcitrance or foot dragging and to compel needed abatement efforts."[2]

To convey a tough enforcement message to industrial and municipal sources of pollution, the Agency directed many of its initial efforts against large national corporations and big cities. Administrator Ruckelshaus announced EPA's initial enforcement actions, which received extensive media coverage. Under the authority of the Rivers and Harbors Act of 1899 (popularly known as the Refuse Act), enforcement conferences were held at which polluters were required to devise an acceptable cleanup plan within a 180-day period. For example, EPA Region V held Refuse Act conferences in Cleveland, Detroit, Duluth, and other cities to discuss heavily polluted waterways such as Lake Erie, the Cuyahoga River, Lake Michigan, Lake Superior, and the Wisconsin River. These conferences focused on rivers and lakes whose contamination problems EPA and its predecessor agencies had studied. A wide variety of industries (including steel, chemicals, pulp and paper, and others) were targeted for enforcement action with the goal of establishing a strong enforcement presence and a sense of momentum. As part of this effort, the Agency attempted to use its limited statutory authority to bring civil and criminal actions under the Refuse Act. In its first two years, EPA took Refuse Act enforcement actions against various Fortune 500 corporations. The Agency also initiated a handful of enforcement cases under other environmental statutes.[3]

During this initial period, the Agency's top managers decided to delegate the responsibility for enforcement cases and strategies to regional administrators and enforcement division directors in EPA's ten regional offices. These offices expanded rapidly. Overall, in its first two years, EPA's enforcement staff grew by nearly five times, to a force of almost 1,500 persons (including water pollution permit personnel).[4] As the regional offices grew, they received an increasing degree of autonomy in the enforcement field. Although EPA headquarters officials maintained an intense interest in pressing forward with an assertive enforcement approach, they increasingly supported and encouraged regional efforts, rather than directly involving themselves in the enforcement fray.

For many participants in EPA's newly established enforcement program, the first two years were an intensely exciting yet a hectic time. Congress and certain "outspoken and demonstrative" environmental organizations pressured the agency for prompt enforcement results. The agency's activities were carried on in the glare of intense publicity—a fact that "helped immensely" in getting EPA's enforcement effort off the ground.[5] Moreover, the goals of the agency were widely supported by the public. As EPA enforcement manager Richard Wilson recalled: "It was a glory day. EPA was a new agency and everyone was for it. You couldn't do anything wrong."[6]

Though many individuals contributed to EPA's inaugural enforcement thrust, two people in particular played critical leadership roles. One was James O. McDonald, the first enforcement division director in EPA Region V. A strong-willed, pragmatic, and inspiring manager, with an extraordinary talent for complex negotiations and a bold willingness to seize the initiative, McDonald made a crucial contribution to building a credible EPA enforcement effort. Under McDonald's guidance, EPA Region V took more than 50 percent of the Agency's enforcement actions in its first two years, an achievement which earned him EPA's two highest awards, its gold medal for exceptional service and its gold medal for distinguished service.

In addition to McDonald, John Quarles, the Agency's first assistant administrator for enforcement and general counsel, played an important part in launching the Agency's enforcement program. Then an outspoken and effective advocate of a firm enforcement approach, Quarles won the respect of those who worked for him, as well as the support of the Agency's administrator and other government officials.[7]

The Agency's first two years were a formative time for its enforcement programs. It devoted energy to hiring new staff and building an enforcement organization in headquarters and the ten regional offices, and it generally succeeded in establishing a reputation as a no-nonsense enforcer of environmental laws. Despite this achievement, the Agency's initial enforcement programs were still limited and rudimentary in a number of respects. As noted, EPA began its enforcement push at a time when many of the basic pollution control standards and requirements had not yet been set. Though the Agency was willing to enforce, there was not that much law that it could enforce. Moreover, the state of the art of pollution control was relatively primitive. While air and water pollution problems were generally recognized and fairly well measured, the technical solutions to these problems were still months and even years away in some cases. In addition, EPA enforcement faced another formidable barrier during this preliminary phase: resistance to the initiation of federal environmental enforcement activity from state pollution control agencies. Although the states were invited to and did participate in EPA's Refuse Act conferences and other enforcement proceedings, they were often reluctant to support EPA's initial enforcement efforts.

Most state officials bitterly resented the involvement of the EPA's young staff—particularly its growing cadre of attorneys—in what they still viewed as their own domain. A number of state pollution control managers viewed EPA's assertive new enforcement program as unnecessarily stringent and overly aggressive. As the frequent objects of intense pro-industry pressures from elected officials at state and local levels, state environmental agencies viewed themselves as defenders of industry's position in early enforcement meetings and openly resisted EPA's enforcement advances.[8] This situation did not halt EPA's budding enforcement program. However, it occasionally posed a "major obstacle" to environmental cleanup during those beginning years.[9]

Finally, this formative period saw the beginning of a trend that was to have profound implications for EPA's enforcement work at later times: detailed and largely critical oversight by congressional committees. In 1971 and 1972, the Subcommittee on Conservation and Natural Resources of the House Committee on Government Operations held a series of hearings that focused on interference by White House officials with pending DOJ enforcement actions under the Refuse Act against alleged discharges of mercury. These hearings succeeded, for many years, in establishing the Justice Department's environmental enforcement activities as off-limits to those who would have preferred to subject them to interest group pressures. Along with oversight investigations of EPA's Clean Air Act implementation by Senator Edmund Muskie's Air and Water Pollution Subcommittee of the Senate Committee on Public Works, the hearings arose in the context of a general upsurge in congressional oversight of the executive branch, as well as open disparagement, by some members of Congress, of early decisions by EPA that proved politically unpopular.[10]

As EPA's enforcement program grew, so did its statutory authority. In 1972 Congress enacted a host of major environmental legislation. The

Federal Water Pollution Control Act (FWPCA) of 1972 established a range of measures to "restore and maintain the chemical, physical and biological integrity of the Nation's waters,"[11] including the National Pollutant Discharge Elimination System (NPDES), a massive permit program concerning the discharge of industrial and municipal wastes to surface waters. The Marine Protection, Research and Sanctuaries Act (otherwise known as the Ocean Dumping Act or MPRSA) created new requirements to safeguard marine waters.[12] The Federal Insecticide, Fungicide and Rodenticide Act (FIFRA) was significantly amended to achieve safe use of products.[13] The Clean Air Act, which had been enacted two years earlier, established a panoply of requirements for action to abate various types of air pollution.

Under each of these laws, EPA was entrusted with major responsibilities for both setting and enforcing regulatory standards. Armed with a full complement of legal authorities, the young Agency sought to follow up its dramatic entrance into the environmental enforcement field with a continued emphasis on vigorous action.[14] Despite stiffening resistance to environmental regulation in some sectors of the business community, Russell E. Train, who succeeded William Ruckelshaus as EPA administrator in September 1973, determined that the Agency would maintain the enforcement momentum it had established in its pre-statutory years. Though Train lacked Ruckelshaus's flamboyance, his attitudes toward enforcement were similar.

The 1973 to 1976 period in EPA enforcement was characterized by three general trends. First, the Agency continued and further expanded the autonomy accorded to enforcement units in the regional offices. Although headquarters enforcement managers issued policy guidance to the regions (and continued to exhort them to pursue numerous enforcement actions), the day-to-day responsibility for enforcement cases was turned over to regional enforcement officials to an increasing extent. Some EPA officials saw this development as a mixed blessing for the Agency's overall enforcement success. Although a number of EPA regional offices, including Regions III and V, were particularly efficient and assertive in their enforcement efforts, others experienced problems in both motivation and the development of enforcement expertise.[15]

Second, the Agency's enforcement programs began to experience some of the problems that rapid initial growth often brings to organizations. As David Kee, one of EPA Region V's initial enforcement managers, later recalled, "There was definitely a maturing. We got much bigger. We had some of the problems of a large organization, certainly from a management standpoint. We had to deal with problem employees and a lot of things that weren't so much fun. Also we became more bureaucratic."[16]

Although staff-level enthusiasm for enforcement work remained generally high, the relatively freewheeling, informal style of the Agency's earliest days was gradually replaced by a somewhat more formal situation. Enforcement procedures and routines became established, and the enormity of the regulatory tasks that Congress had placed upon EPA became increasingly evident to the Agency's career staff.

Third, EPA's enforcement relationship with state pollution control agency personnel slowly but perceptibly improved as the states themselves enacted new environmental laws and reorganized their agencies. Although some states remained highly resistant to federal enforcement efforts, others began to develop an appreciation of the value of vigorous enforcement to improved environmental quality. Spurred in part by the provision of EPA operating grants and federal delegation of primary responsibility for managing the NPDES program within their borders, some states embraced a more aggressive approach in the enforcement area as well as a new willingness to cooperate with the Agency's regional enforcement staff.[17]

In the air pollution field, EPA began its first program for enforcing the Clean Air Act. As was the case earlier in the water enforcement area, EPA's first air enforcement thrust was largely an attempt to establish a federal "enforcement presence."[18] EPA initiated information-gathering procedures, including written requests for compliance information under section 114 of the Act, opacity inspections, and a limited number of stack tests.[19] The Agency issued its first formal notices of violation and administrative orders to identified sources of air pollution and began to enforce the limitations on automobile-generated pollution.

At the outset, however, Clean Air Act enforcement was hampered by several problems. One set of obstacles sprang from the first state implementation plans (SIPs), which were hastily drafted by the states and quickly approved by EPA to comply with the strict regulatory deadlines the statute had imposed. Although many states had a good deal of air quality data when the standards were prepared, they often lacked specific knowledge about the sources of pollution in the state and the type and amount of air pollution those sources were emitting. Many of the first SIPs were thus very general in nature and lacked meaningful reference to the particular kinds of industrial facilities they ostensibly controlled.

Once the SIPs became enforceable, EPA devoted a good deal of its staff's time to determining how to apply these requirements to the numerous industrial and municipal sources that caused pollution. The Agency worked with state and local governments to establish inventories of air pollution emitters. EPA responded to a plethora of information requests from industries that were uncertain whether SIP requirements were meant to be applied to their plants. The Agency also reviewed the acceptability of proposed SIP compliance schedules for many individual facilities.[20]

Other problems emerged in the form of sharp disputes between the Agency and industrial concerns about the precise types of air pollution control technology that had to be installed at production facilities and the time by which those controls had to be in place. For example, some state SIPs established stringent requirements for curbing sulfur dioxide emissions for electric power plants that could only be complied with through the use of expensive and then relatively untried SO_2 scrubber technology. In the steel industry many SIPs called for technology-forcing measures at some air pollutant emission points, including costly controls on pollution from coke batteries. These requirements engendered widespread controversy.[21] Their enforcement consumed a great deal of EPA's time and effort.[22]

Another nettlesome issue that arose during this period was the so-called jobs-versus-environment question. In several instances, firms subject to Clean Air Act requirements began to claim that compliance with those standards would be economically impossible for them to achieve and that strict Clean Air Act enforcement would inevitably result in plant closures and local unemployment. Though most of these claims lacked validity, they proved at times to be a potent weapon for industry in the enforcement context.[23] While few industrial facilities were actually closed as a result of environmental enforcement, EPA spent considerable political energy defending a strong enforcement stance in those relatively few cases where employment claims played a role.[24]

In the water enforcement area, EPA ran into problems when it attempted to implement the FWPCA. Throughout much of 1973, an internal debate over a variety of technical and policy-related issues that the newly enacted statute had left unresolved consumed EPA. Chief among these was the question of the basis for the best practicable technology standards to be included in dischargers' NPDES permits. Although the statute seemed to call for EPA to establish industry-specific effluent limitation guidelines before attempting to set enforceable discharge limitations in individual permits, it soon became apparent that the technical work needed to develop such guidelines properly would be difficult and time-consuming. If permit insurance and enforcement were to get under way, the agency would have to find an acceptable substitute for the guidelines as a basis for permit requirements. Toward the end of 1973, EPA decided to press forward with NPDES permits written on the basis of the Agency's best engineering judgment as to what constituted best practicable technology. This controversial decision opened the door for a massive EPA effort to issue NPDES permits to industries and municipalities that discharged water pollutants.

During the latter part of 1973 and all of 1974, EPA virtually suspended its other water enforcement work and concentrated its staff's energies on processing the permit applications of industrial facilities. In a laudable effort, the Agency issued 2,699 NPDES permits to major industrial dischargers, as well as 11,459 permits to so-called minor industrial waste sources, by December 31, 1974.[25] This spate of new permits later gave rise to a wave of requests by dischargers for adjudicatory hearings before administrative law judges. Yet it also prompted many urgently needed water pollution control programs in the private sector and ultimately the new permits led to a significant decrease in the discharge of common industrial pollutants such as biological oxygen-demanding (BOD) wastes, suspended solids, oil and grease, phenol, and chromium.

Throughout the 1973 to 1977 period, EPA preferred to proceed on the basis of administrative, as opposed to judicial, enforcement of air and water act violations. In many EPA regions administrative orders were not issued under the Clean Air Act or the FWPCA, as a matter of policy, unless the industrial or municipal party that would be bound by those orders consented in advance to their terms. While this approach prevented EPA from becoming embroiled in litigation, it also created an unanticipated difficulty: in many cases the Agency's negotiations with polluters over the terms of administrative orders took months or even years to complete. As some EPA officials saw it, some companies in the regulated community were treating these negotiations as a kind of game that could delay compliance with environmental standards and the expense that compliance would entail.[26]

Cognizant of this, the enforcement divisions of some EPA regional offices moved increasingly toward civil litigation as a means of resolving enforcement cases against regulated parties that were viewed as particularly resistant to lesser enforcement sanctions. This trend was gradual. In fact, it did not occur at all in most EPA regions, and even when it did, the predominant enforcement tool remained the administrative order.[27] Nonetheless, the Agency's first, sporadic attempts at judicial enforcement of federal environmental legislation helped to lay the groundwork for the immense litigation program that the Agency was soon to undertake.

President Jimmy Carter's inauguration in January 1977 marked the start of a significant shift in the operation of EPA's enforcement programs. The new president had committed himself to a strong federal role in environmental protection during the course of his election campaign. To fulfill that commitment, Carter chose top managers for EPA with environmentalist backgrounds and perspectives.

Douglas Costle, the former director of Connecticut's pollution control agency, became the Agency's new administrator. Barbara Blum, who had worked in the president's campaign in Georgia, was appointed its deputy administrator. Marvin Durning, a particularly ardent environmentalist from the state of Washington, became EPA's new assistant administrator for enforcement. Through the efforts of these individuals, the Agency's enforcement activities received relatively generous funding in the late 1970s, notwithstanding a general fiscal stringency that affected most of EPA's programs of that time.[28]

One critical change that took place during this period was the initiation of a civil litigation approach to environmental enforcement. Immediately upon assuming office, Marvin Durning perceived the administrative enforcement efforts of the preceding EPA administration as unduly time-consuming and generally ineffective. Determined to redirect the Agency's enforcement work, Durning announced the creation of a major source enforcement effort, epitomized by the slogan "file first and negotiate later." Under this strategy, the Agency was to identify major violators of the Clean Air Act SIPs and the FWPCA's July 1, 1977, deadline for the achievement of effluent limitations based upon best practicable technology. The Agency was then to refer each of these violators to the DOJ, with a recommendation that it institute a civil action against them in an appropriate federal district court for injunctive relief and civil penalties. While any or all of these suits might be resolved subsequent to their being filed, EPA enforcement officials were discouraged from entering into negotiations with any parties subject to enforcement action until after litigation had commenced.

During 1977 and 1978, this strategy was put into effect. In conjunction with the Justice Department, EPA filed a considerable number of civil suits, most of which were ultimately resolved by consent decree. Where enforcement litigation had once been the exception at EPA, it now became the rule. The Agency's headquarters placed strong pressure on its regional offices to produce litigation referrals. Each region was expected to produce a quota of referrals within a given time period. In contrast, administrative orders, formerly the mainstay of EPA's enforcement activities, became insignificant.[29]

In tandem with this lawsuit-based approach, the Carter administration's managers introduced a Civil Penalty Policy and a National Penalty Panel to administer it. The Civil Penalty Policy applied to settlement of enforcement actions. Under its terms, state and federal enforcement officials were forbidden to negotiate settlement of the civil penalty aspects of any major air or water enforcement case for less than the amount of money that the defendant had saved by delaying compliance with applicable requirements. The Civil Penalty Policy required that additional penalties apply to alleged violators that exhibited lack of good faith. The policy permitted enforcement personnel involved in case settlement negotiations to discuss and consider a proposed civil penalty offer that was lower than the economic savings amount.[30] However, EPA could not accept such offers unless the National Penalty Panel reviewed and approved the offers.[31]

Another significant innovation was the creation of a Senior Executive Service (SES) of EPA's top management personnel. Under this arrangement, devised by EPA Assistant Administrator William Drayton, the Agency's ten regional enforcement directors were required to reapply for their own positions. If rehired, they would be admitted to the SES. In that capacity they would be afforded executive status and have the potential to earn a higher salary. However, they would also be required to agree in advance to be transferred to a similar position in another organizational unit, including a position in another city, if and when the agency's top managers ordered such a change.

Though intended as a means of developing EPA's internal management structure, this policy shift had several unforeseen and unfortunate results. Many of the Agency's regional enforcement directors, already unhappy with the new litigation referral system which undercut the autonomy they had enjoyed, viewed the institution of an SES as a further attempt to undermine their positions. Although most regional enforcement directors did ultimately reapply for and retain their positions with SES status, the experience engendered considerable resentment among the directors, because they considered the SES unnecessary, seriously traumatic, and "hopelessly mishandled." James O. McDonald resigned his position to protest the insensitive and ill-conceived way in which the SES was instituted.[32]

Along with these new policies came significant changes in the allocation of responsibility for environmental enforcement matters. In June 1977 Administrator Costle and Attorney General Griffin Bell entered into a controversial memorandum of understanding under which the DOJ's attorneys were afforded substantial control over the conduct of environmental enforcement litigation. Costle, a former DOJ attorney, was widely criticized by EPA's regional enforcement divisions for relegating EPA attorneys to a secondary role in the litigation process. The memorandum required the regional divisions to prepare a detailed litigation report to accompany each enforcement matter they referred for civil litigation. This report was to include a summary of the legal theories upon which the proposed action rested and a summary of the evidence that was available to prove the government's case.

Whereas previous litigation reports could be sent directly from EPA's regional offices to the appropriate U.S. Attorneys, all litigation reports now had to be sent to the Agency's headquarters for staff review. If headquarters enforcement personnel deemed it necessary, this referral package could be returned to the regional office for further development. If and when EPA headquarters gave its approval, however, the matter was then transferred to the DOJ for a second round of review. The DOJ in turn had the authority to seek further information from regional enforcement personnel. Like EPA headquarters, DOJ could reject the regional official's litigation recommendation if it believed the enforcement case in question was flawed or unpersuasive. If and when DOJ approval was secured, however, the matter was referred to the office of the local U.S. Attorney for another round of review. Finally, after all of the relevant governmental organizations had given their concurrence, the U.S. Attorney filed the proposed enforcement case as a civil action in the appropriate U.S. district court.

These enforcement policies and procedures had a number of consequences, both within EPA's enforcement program and outside it. Within EPA, the Carter administration's bold enforcement approach had profound effects. One of these was a general increase in the influence of EPA headquarters in the Agency's enforcement work, accompanied by a proportionate reduction in the near-autonomy that EPA regional enforcement divisions had hitherto enjoyed. No longer mere policy writers and supporters of regionally based enforcement efforts, the headquarters staff was now directly involved in reviewing, and in some cases vetoing, regional recommendations as to specific cases. Beyond that, headquarters officials assumed primary responsibility for certain types of enforcement matters, and concurrence from headquarters became a requirement in a growing number of settlement negotiations.[33] These changes caused great consternation in the Agency's regional enforcement offices and resulted in continuing disaffection and protest.

Another consequence of the new procedures was a dramatic expansion of the DOJ's enforcement responsibility. This change brought with it considerable conflict between the Agency's regional enforcement staff and DOJ attorneys and managers. While the DOJ's increasing involvement may have lent some litigation expertise and institutional credibility to the government's environmental enforcement effort,[34] it also led to significant discord at the staff level. In a number of instances, EPA regional enforcement attorneys became concerned with the length of time the DOJ took to review litigation referrals. Serious professional disputes also arose over the amount of evidence the government needed to have available before an enforcement suit could be initiated, and some Justice Department attorneys came to be viewed as "nit-picking," "arbitrary," and "high-handed" in their relationships with the Agency's regional staff.[35]

Among regulated companies, the Agency's "file first" approach was widely viewed as unnecessarily harsh and unduly rigid. Though many suits were resolved and considerable cleanup achieved, industry resentment of EPA's enforcement techniques gradually increased. The jobs-versus-environment issue, which had first surfaced in the mid-1970s, continued to receive attention in the media in the early Carter years. To an increasing extent, EPA's managers and staff were publicly criticized as ineffective bureaucrats and antibusiness zealots.[36]

EPA's strong enforcement approach also aggravated the disenchantment felt by state officials. Many states resented the Agency's attempt to subject them to a uniform policy regarding civil penalties and some flatly refused to abide by its terms. Resistant to further federal encroachment upon their enforcement domain, a number of state officials once again perceived EPA's enforcement managers as insensitive to state concerns and needlessly inflexible in their views.[37] Impervious to these criticisms, however, the Agency and DOJ persisted in their assertive civil litigation efforts.

This trend was supplemented by public expressions of support for the application of criminal sanctions to environmental violations. In a February 1978 speech to the American Law Institute–American Bar Association course of study on environmental law in Washington, D.C., James Moorman, then assistant attorney general for the Justice Department's Division of Land and Natural Resources, announced that the DOJ would prosecute "willful, substantive violations of the pollution control laws of criminal nature." He stated that "for these transgressions, the Department of Justice has begun to invoke grand jury investigations against both corporations and against individuals" and that "the Department of Justice will prosecute criminal conduct in this area." Similarly, in a May 1980 speech to graduating seniors at the University of Michigan, Attorney General Benjamin R. Civiletti emphasized the intention of the DOJ to prosecute both individuals and corporations who willfully violate environmental laws.[38]

Despite this enthusiastic rhetoric however, the Carter administration took few concrete steps to set a criminal environmental enforcement program in motion. Although the creation of a separate environmental criminal prosecution unit was seriously considered within the Justice Department during that time, a spirited bureaucratic dispute between the department's Criminal Division and its Division of Land and Natural Resources as to where such a unit should be housed effectively forestalled its realization.[39] After much delay, in January 1981 EPA Deputy Administrator Barbara Blum signed a memorandum directing the creation of an EPA Office of Criminal Enforcement and instructing each of the Agency's regional offices to hire two or three professional criminal investigators, depending upon need.[40]

However, Blum's memo, which called for the new EPA criminal investigators to report directly to the Agency's headquarters Office of Enforcement, met with strong resistance from regional enforcement personnel, who sought greater control over the investigators' work. As a result of this "turf battle" (and subsequently the wariness of Reagan administration officials) only a handful of criminal investigators were actually hired prior to the middle of 1982. Thus, in contrast to its vigorous and active environmental civil enforcement efforts, criminal environmental enforcement during the Carter years produced only a few prosecutions that were "local, sporadic, and in response to disastrous events, rather than a particular enforcement policy."[41]

How should the enforcement efforts of the Carter administration EPA be assessed? In contrast to earlier enforcement regimes at EPA, the Agency's enforcement efforts during the Carter years appear, at first glance, unerringly consistent, assertive, and effective. On closer examination however, it is evident that the litigation approach that dominated EPA enforcement work during the Carter administration yielded imperfect results.

Supported by top EPA managers and a talented group of mid-level officials, the Carter model of enforcement invigorated the Agency's efforts.

It eliminated the delays that had characterized some of EPA's prior administrative enforcement negotiations. It also reinforced and strengthened the perception, which had begun in earlier years, that EPA was serious about enforcing environmental statutes and determined to take assertive measures to compel compliance and deter intentional violations.

On the other hand, as we have seen, the Agency's "file first, negotiate later" strategy, its Civil Penalty Policy, and its litigation referral procedure had some unfortunate repercussions. Internally, the Agency created a cumbersome and often time-consuming system for considering and acting upon cases that regional enforcement professionals believed were appropriate matters for litigation. This strategy gave rise to a relatively high level of rivalry among EPA regional offices, the Agency's headquarters, and the DOJ. To some extent, these conflicts diminished the effectiveness of the government's overall enforcement effort. Also, as noted above, the perceived rigidity of EPA's new enforcement initiatives engendered hostility from both regulated industry and state environmental officials. This resentment, and the backlash it created, placed EPA, and to some degree the environmental movement as a whole, under increased political stress as the Carter years continued.

In retrospect, it could be argued that EPA's top managers would have been more successful if their litigious approach to environmental enforcement had been supplemented by a balanced and judicious use of administrative orders and pre-filing negotiations with potential defendants. Their approach might also have benefited from a selective laissez-faire attitude toward those EPA regional enforcement divisions that already had strong and assertive enforcement programs in place. That strategy was not adopted however, and as a result the Carter administration's ambitious enforcement program did not fulfill its potential. Nevertheless, the general enforcement policies of the Carter administration provided the soil in which an ambitious and largely successful hazardous waste enforcement effort was nourished.

In 1977 and 1978, several incidents occurred that served to awaken the American public to dangers posed by the past improper disposal of hazardous wastes. The spotlight of media attention was directed at the "Valley of the Drums" in Brooks, Kentucky, where more than 17,000 corroding drums of toxic and hazardous wastes were strewn about a poorly maintained landfill, contaminating a stream that flowed into the drinking source for a highly populated area. Considerable publicity was also given to the degradation of the James River near Hopewell, Virginia, with ketone, a highly toxic and nondegradable industrial waste, as well as the disastrous chemical contamination problems at the Love Canal in Niagara Falls, New York, which caused 237 families to be permanently evacuated from their homes. Additionally, intensive media coverage was given to the illegal dumping of acutely toxic wastes into a sewage treatment plant in Louisville, Kentucky, an act which forced a lengthy closure of that plant and resulted in the discharge of billions of gallons of raw or poorly treated sewage into the Ohio River.[42]

As public awareness of the hazardous waste problem grew, so too did public pressure for vigorous governmental measures to deal with the situation. Several congressional committees initiated investigations into hazardous waste dumping and EPA's response to it. These committees noted that EPA had not yet proposed any of the hazardous waste regulations it was mandated to promulgate under subtitle C of RCRA. The Agency's leaders felt an urgent need to demonstrate, by prompt and effective action, that EPA was concerned about the hazardous waste dump situation and intended to combat it. Under these circumstances, a group of EPA's top managers decided upon a two-pronged strategy for addressing the hazardous waste issue. Persuaded that the Agency's legal authority to require cleanup at abandoned hazardous waste sites was fundamentally inadequate, these officials concluded that it would be necessary to ask Congress for a new statute specifically aimed at correcting contamination from inactive dumps."[43] At this time, however, the Carter administration was focused on ways to trim the cost of government operations. There was, in the words of one key participant, "considerable resistance within the administration" to proposing any legislative initiatives in this field.[44] To overcome internal administration resistance, EPA managers decided to increase and, to the extent possible, orchestrate growing public and congressional concern about haphazard waste dumping.

On October 2, 1978, Thomas C. Jorling, then EPA's assistant administrator for water and waste management, requested that the Agency's regional offices submit their "best professional estimate" of the total number of abandoned hazardous waste sites existing within their regions. Regional officials were also asked to report on the number of sites that might contain "significant quantities" of hazardous wastes. Because no specific criteria were provided for determining which dump sites should be placed in each category, each EPA region used its own methodology to comply with Jorling's request. As a result, the first EPA estimates of the number of hazardous waste sites were highly unreliable.[45] Despite the imprecision and internal confusion resulting from this approach, however, by November 2, 1978, the Agency was able to release publicly the results of its "preliminary inventory." In congressional testimony, EPA managers stated that they believed 32,254 sites might contain hazardous wastes and 838 sites contained significant quantities of waste.[46]

The announcement of this information, combined with continuing disclosures regarding incidents of contamination from abandoned waste dumps, set off what one former Justice Department manager later described as a "firestorm of interest."[47] Amid the continuing public and media demand for firm and immediate action, EPA's managers pressed forward with their plan to propose a new abandoned waste site statute, which they began to refer to as Superfund, in reference to the expanded pool of monies that would be sought for use in a major site cleanup effort.[48] To further bolster its argument that such Superfund legislation was urgently needed, as well as to deflect mounting congressional criticism of the Agency's tardiness in promulgating hazardous waste regulations under RCRA, EPA's top leadership put into place the second part of its strategy. With the cooperation of the Department of Justice, EPA's managers took preliminary steps toward establishing a new enforcement campaign to compel known owners and operators of abandoned hazardous waste dumps to remedy endangerments that those dumps created.

On March 28, 1979, Barbara Blum, EPA's deputy administrator, wrote a memorandum to the Agency's regional administrators stating that an "aggressive program" was needed in this area. Blum indicated that the Agency's top management considered the hazardous waste site issue to be of high priority. She announced that a committee would be formed, under the leadership of Gary Dietrich, EPA's associate deputy administrator for solid waste, and Leslie Carothers, the director of the Agency's Region I Enforcement Division. This committee was to "[coordinate] activities related to inactive sites" and to develop a "cohesive, dedicated national effort" with respect to hazardous waste enforcement. Regional administrators were asked to appoint one technical coordinator and one enforcement coordinator "to jointly manage the program activities in your region and to work with Leslie and Gary."[49]

At the end of April 1979, the Agency held an imminent hazard workshop in Denver, Colorado. The meeting was attended by the newly appointed regional coordinators as well as over one hundred key staff members from the Department of Justice, EPA headquarters, and the NEIC. At the gathering, during which internal procedures for launching a hazardous waste site enforcement effort were intensively discussed, Barbara Blum reiterated the extremely high priority that EPA's top leadership placed on this program. She promised to seek additional budgetary resources for hazardous waste enforcement and to divert existing Agency resources to implement the program. Blum also made a pledge, ultimately fulfilled by EPA and the DOJ enforcement staff, that within one year at least fifty hazardous waste "imminent hazard" actions would be filed in U.S. district courts.[50]

On June 27, 1979, Barbara Blum notified the Agency's regional and assistant administrators that a Hazardous Waste Enforcement Task Force (HWETF) was being established at the Agency's headquarters. The HWETF was to be chaired at the outset by Jeffrey Miller, EPA's acting assistant administrator for enforcement. The HWETF was responsible for providing "national management" of the enforcement component of the Agency's hazardous waste program, which included development of a hazardous waste site reporting and tracking system, establishment of hazardous waste enforcement policies, and increased participation by headquarters staff and the DOJ in developing hazardous waste cases.[51] Within a short time, the task force began a vigorous effort to recruit a small cadre of experienced staff to carry out its responsibilities. A conscious attempt was made to gather EPA's "top enforcement talent,"[52] and task force managers were given a free hand to offer positions to any member of the Agency's enforcement staff who they believed would contribute meaningfully to its success.[53] Jeffrey Miller soon chose Douglas MacMillan, a former management division director in EPA Region I who was working with a congressional committee on special assignment, to be Miller's successor as task force director. Lamar Miller, a seasoned chemical engineer who had served briefly as enforcement division director in EPA Region VII, was appointed technical director of the task force. Edward Kurent, previously a headquarters water enforcement attorney and a special assistant to the assistant administrator for enforcement, was chosen task force legal director. A full complement of task force staff members was selected shortly thereafter, and EPA's initial hazardous waste enforcement program began to take shape.

At the time that the HWETF was formed, EPA had few specific legal standards to enforce under RCRA, a situation largely of the Agency's own making. In subtitle C of the act, Congress had required EPA to promulgate specific regulations, within eighteen months, with respect to the active generation, transportation, and disposal of hazardous wastes. The Agency had not met this deadline. It thus lacked the regulatory means to redress important aspects of the nation's rapidly reemerging hazardous waste problem.

In the fall of 1979, the Department of Justice created a small headquarters group of attorneys, paralegals, and secretaries under the leadership of Anthony Roisman. This unit, termed the Hazardous Waste Section, was assigned to work with EPA in developing hazardous waste enforcement cases. Because of a paucity of relevant legal authority, this newly created DOJ section and the HWETF decided to rely primarily on section 7003 of RCRA, the so-called imminent hazard provision of that statute, as their primary enforcement tool. It was decided, in the absence of a systematic understanding of hazardous waste site problems and the technology required to resolve them, that the appropriate course was to seek issuance of injunctions that would require the parties responsible for contamination problems at hazardous waste sites to study those problems and to prepare detailed cleanup plans, which EPA would then review and approve. As Lamar Miller remembered it, the task force's basic litigation approach was: "Get the most you can. Don't let anybody tell you that this is the most a judge would give you. Restore [the contaminated groundwater underneath each site] to its original condition."[54]

To bring this new enforcement strategy into effect, the litigation referral system initiated in the early Carter years was modified in several respects. The task force leadership adopted a suggestion by Jane Schulteis and Bill Constantelos, then mid-level managers in EPA Region V, that litigation reports be supplanted by case development plans, which more briefly outlined the evidence available to support the government's case.[55] The task force initiated a series of monthly meetings at the regional offices during which HWETF and DOJ personnel would "encourage, chide and in some cases direct" regional hazardous waste enforcement activities.[56]

As Douglas MacMillan recalled, EPA headquarters managers put enormous pressure on regional officials to produce a steady stream of new enforcement referrals. On several occasions, Deputy Administrator Barbara Blum, a strong supporter of the task force effort who devoted a good deal of time to its implementation, asked her headquarters staff for a series of "regional report cards." These evaluations identified regions whose enforcement efforts were viewed as ineffective by the task force staff. Upon receipt, Blum telephoned regional administrators and other key officials to "really lean on them very directly and bluntly about performance."[57]

The task force also worked to develop a national site tracking system that would identify the universe of abandoned hazardous waste dumps and systematically address the relative damages particular sites posed. Recognizing that their initial information about hazardous waste sites was "totally spotty and anecdotal,"[58] task force members spearheaded an effort to provide a more accurate site inventory. In pursuing this goal, the task force relied in part on data supplied by the Subcommittee on Investigations and Oversight of the House Committee on Interstate and Foreign Commerce, which had conducted a comprehensive survey of inactive waste sites.[59] Using this and other information, the Agency developed a preliminary site inventory of 9,600 sites, a listing that later formed the raw material from which the Superfund National Priorities List and the MITRE model—that EPA used to assess the severity of health and environmental risks at the particular sites—were molded.[60]

For those involved in the task force effort, the initiation of a hazardous waste site enforcement program was a time of hard work, excitement, and camaraderie.[61] Enthusiasm abounded and dedication to the task at hand was widespread. As James Bunting, a former task force attorney and manager, remembered the era, "There was a certain sense that you were really being a pioneer."[62] The task force itself was insulated from routine bureaucratic encumbrances that might have slowed its progress.[63] Its efforts were actively and enthusiastically supported by the Agency's top managers, including Barbara Blum and Jeffrey Miller, and public interest in the outcome of its work was exceptionally high.[64]

Though short-lived, the HWETF effort resulted in several significant accomplishments. Within a year, EPA and the DOJ had filed fifty-four judicial enforcement actions to compel cleanup of abandoned dumps, a striking achievement in view of the government's still meager knowledge and resources. Furthermore, as task force legal director Edward Kurent later observed, these lawsuits, and the hard-nosed negotiations that they engendered, "gave notice to the general public, to industry, and to the Congress that the Agency was on the job, that it had clearly identified the problem and was intent on doing something about it."[65] By its streamlined case referral system, the task force program eased some of the time-consuming red tape burdens that the Carter administration's litigation referral system had generally imposed on EPA regional enforcement officials. Finally, in establishing a national site tracking system and a set of preliminary site assessment procedures, the work of the task force laid much groundwork for the ultimate establishment of the Superfund Program.

To be sure, EPA's initial hazardous waste enforcement program had its shortcomings. Because of the relative newness of the hazardous waste site problem, the Agency's staff was ignorant of some of the complexities of hazardous waste site contamination and groundwater restoration. In their haste to establish a strong federal presence, EPA and DOJ filed some hazardous waste enforcement actions that later proved difficult to pursue.[66] Moreover, the Agency did little planning for the extensive drain on its resources that occurred when the lawsuits it filed in 1979 and 1986 spawned extensive discovery and motion practice in the months and years that followed.[67]

Notwithstanding these difficulties, however, EPA's first attempt at hazardous waste enforcement must be judged an overall success. In little time, and with relatively few resources, it established hazardous waste enforcement as a functioning and important part of the Agency's enforcement work.

In December 1980, on the eve of President Reagan's inauguration, the leadership of both EPA's HWETF and the DOJ's Hazardous Waste Section anticipated an expansion of the government's hazardous waste enforcement program. The Superfund Act had at last been enacted by a lame-duck Congress. In the act EPA had been given the explicit authority to take enforcement action with respect to inactive hazardous waste sites, as well as access to a $1.6-billion trust fund, which promised expanded resources for a redoubled enforcement effort. EPA's RCRA hazardous waste management regulations had at long last reached an enforceable stage. Congress had modestly amended that statute to augment EPA's ability to gather information regarding hazardous waste dumps and to issue administrative orders to redress any danger that they caused.[68]

Despite some misgivings, the top hazardous waste enforcement managers at EPA and the DOJ were guardedly optimistic that the Reagan administration would not attempt to slow the development of an active hazardous waste enforcement program. As former task force director Douglas MacMillan recalled: "Given the political pressure that was building around the issue, I felt that it would be simply suicidal for the new administration to attempt to stand in front of the hazardous waste bulldozer."[69] A number of MacMillan's colleagues agreed with that assessment.[70]

For the individuals who had worked to build EPA's initial hazardous waste enforcement program, the interregnum between the Carter and Reagan administrations was a time of cautious hope. Within a matter of months, though, that hope turned to anxiety, bitterness, and despair. As Anthony Roisman, the Justice Department's Hazardous Waste Section chief during the task force period, recalled: "To see that potential cut off when the Reagan people came in was incredible, just incredible. We never really recovered from it, I think."[71]

Destruction, Confusion, Confrontation, and Disarray: EPA Enforcement and Congressional Oversight in the Gorsuch Era

The arrival of the Reagan administration in January 1981 heralded a dramatic change in the tone, structure, and operation of EPA's enforcement program. The two years that followed would see a sharp decline in the initiation of new enforcement cases, a precipitous drop in career staff morale, and a drastic loss of public credibility for EPA in general. To appreciate the reasons for these trends and the pervasiveness and profundity of their impact, one must first appreciate the manner in which EPA's new top managers were selected by the Reagan administration, the attitudes they held upon taking office, and the specific ways in which they approached EPA's enforcement responsibilities.

The Reagan administration's search for a new set of top EPA managers proceeded at a deliberate pace. Almost all EPA officials who had been political appointees in the Carter administration resigned from their positions before Reagan took office on January 20. Anne McGill Gorsuch,[1] the new administration's choice to succeed Douglas Costle as EPA administrator, was not nominated for that position until February 21, 1981, and her formal confirmation was delayed until May 5. Most of the other Reagan administration appointees to high-level EPA positions were also installed in the mid- or late spring. Rita M. Lavelle, an EPA official whose attitude and activities were ultimately to have an important effect on the administration of the Superfund Program, did not assume the office of assistant administrator for solid waste and emergency response until March 31, 1982, more than fourteen months after the Reagan administration had begun.[2]

The administration's method of choosing EPA's new management team emphasized the selection of individuals with an ideological affinity for the conservative wing of the Republican Party. According to one former high-level EPA civil servant, "The White House personnel office was extremely powerful and it was obsessed with getting those with definite political views, regardless of qualifications, into their place[s]."[3]

Some chosen for high-level management posts had no specific interest in enforcement. William Sullivan, for example, the administration's choice for enforcement counsel and deputy associate administrator for enforcement, stated, "I handled Reagan's stop in Youngstown as a candidate and when they were recruiting they asked for my resume. The EPA was the last agency I wanted to go to, and enforcement was the last job I wanted at the Agency."[4] Furthermore, in selecting EPA's leadership, little thought was given to the manner in which those chosen would relate to one another once they assumed office. Anne Gorsuch, the Agency's new administrator, had little influence over the selection of EPA's regional administrators and senior headquarters managers, many of whom she had not known before taking office.[5]

The initial attitude of EPA's new leadership toward the Agency's enforcement program was, like a number of things during this period, controversial. In an interview five years later, Anne Gorsuch indicated that she had favored an effective enforcement program at EPA from the outset of her administratorship.[6] William Sullivan, who led EPA's national enforcement program during the first year of Gorsuch's tenure as administrator, stated that "to think there was a conspiracy to defeat enforcement is crazy."[7]

Conspiracy, in its technical, legal sense, may be too strong a word. Nonetheless, there is *very* considerable evidence that the initial enforcement attitude of a number of the Reagan administration's first set of political appointees was far more negative to environmental enforcement than the remarks of Gorsuch and Sullivan suggest. For example, Sheldon Novick, the regional counsel of EPA Region III at that time, later stated:

> [T]here were plainly people in the administration, within EPA, who believed that the EPA itself should be dissolved, that the statutes that it implemented were senseless, and that the federal government had no business in environmental management. Those people, who found enforcement of federal law particularly distasteful, expressed that the EPA should be dismantled, beginning with its enforcement functions. . . . Political appointees at senior levels [other than Anne Gorsuch] began saying things like that.[8]

Novick's recollections with respect to the Reagan administration's first enforcement attitudes find support in an article that appeared in the *Washington Post*. In it James C. Miller III, at that time director of the Vice President's regulatory task force, was quoted as saying, "[T]here is a strong feeling on the part of the White House staff that we ought to be decentralizing regulatory enforcement." The article also indicated that "[f]inal decisions on the roles of OSHA and the Environmental Protection Agency have not yet been made within the Administration . . . but the agencies' enforcement activities will necessarily be cut back, assuming the budget cuts proposed by President Reagan are enacted."[9]

Valdas Adamkus, the regional administrator of Region V recalled that "when [Gorsuch] came into power, her attitude to enforcement in general was negative; there was no question."[10] Edward Kurent, the Agency's water enforcement division director and associate general counsel for waste enforcement during the Gorsuch era, went so far as to suggest that Gorsuch-era political appointees implemented what was "very obviously a deliberate plan to paralyze if not totally dismantle the enforcement program."[11]

Gorsuch subsequently indicated that she and her colleagues had not entered the Agency with any negative predisposition toward the career staff.[12] However, a number of EPA's permanent enforcement staff left the Agency with an entirely different sense. One headquarters enforcement attorney and manager stated, "They came in with the feeling that the existing career enforcement staff probably weren't the type of employees they would want. They didn't approach them as a professional staff who were competent and who were trying to do their jobs. They came in, I think, with a bias."[13]

Whatever their initial attitudes, motivations, and intentions, it is clear that, toward the beginning of their tenure, EPA's new enforcement leadership made several important changes in EPA's enforcement program and personnel policies. Concerned that the Agency's previous enforcement efforts had become unnecessarily litigious and antagonistic,[14] they adopted what became known as a "non-confrontational" approach to enforcement.[15] The "file first, negotiate later" attitude of the Carter administration was replaced by the notion that, as one EPA enforcement attorney stated it, "[Y]ou were to talk first and file later only if it was absolutely necessary and only if you could clear it with headquarters."[16]

Informal attempts at encouraging voluntary compliance became the enforcement procedure of choice. At least one EPA regional administrator was directly informed by William Sullivan, the Agency's enforcement counsel, that every enforcement case referred to headquarters by his region "will be considered a black mark against you." That individual, who took the view that Sullivan was "one of the level-headed and professional individuals who wanted to do a good job and was only following instructions from others," stated that he considered Sullivan's statement to him the "strongest indication" that federal environmental enforcement was being "dismantled."[17] Additionally, considerable emphasis was placed upon deferring federal enforcement activities in favor of state enforcement.[18]

Beyond these enforcement policies, EPA's new managers carried out a series of reorganizations of the Agency's enforcement structure. On June 1, 1981, Anne Gorsuch sent a memorandum to all EPA employees in which she announced that the Office of Enforcement was "abolished" and that its components would be transferred to various media programs (e.g., air, water, and hazardous waste). An Office of Legal and Enforcement Counsel also was established. This office reported directly to the administrator on the activities of the general counsel and in regard to Agency-wide enforcement.[19]

On September 15, 1981, Gorsuch formally eliminated EPA's regional enforcement divisions. The legal functions of those divisions were transferred to the Offices of Regional Counsel, which reported directly to the Office of General Counsel at EPA headquarters. Members of the technical staff of the regional enforcement divisions were transferred to various media-operating divisions in the regions.[20] Then, in late December 1981, headquarters *legal* enforcement activities were centralized in a new Office of Enforcement Counsel. The headquarters *technical* enforcement staff, however, remained with the various media offices; thus the legal enforcement and technical staffs were permanently divided into separate organizations.[21] A number of these changes were implemented over objections made by some of the Agency's senior career enforcement managers, who argued that the reorganizations would have a disruptive and counterproductive effect on the Agency's overall enforcement efforts.[22]

In addition to these reorganizations, a number of other trends and developments in the early Reagan days played an important role in EPA's enforcement work. On his first day in office, President Reagan issued a "Memorandum for the Heads of Executive Departments and Agencies," which imposed "a strict freeze on the hiring of federal civilian employees to be applied across the board in the executive branch."[23] This action, described as a "first step towards controlling the growth and size of government and stopping the drain on the economy by the public sector," effectively prohibited EPA's mid-level supervisory management from replacing any staff members that left the Agency.

Beyond this, EPA's enforcement program was impaired by budget reductions, as well as rumors of plans to discharge or reduce in force ("rif") the enforcement staff. With the exception of the Superfund Program, which was supported by dedicated monies, between 1980 and 1983 EPA's budget as a whole declined, in constant 1972 dollars, from $701 million to $515 million, and the number of full-time positions at the Agency, excluding Superfund, declined by 26 percent, mostly through attrition.[24] Indeed, as two scholarly observers have concluded, "There is ample evidence that the Reagan administration's adoption of an administrative presidency strategy did result in significantly lower levels of EPA expenditures and in dramatic shifts in internal program priorities away from abatement, compliance, control and enforcement."[25]

Though EPA's enforcement personnel were only minimally affected by rifs during Gorsuch's tenure as administrator, there is evidence that significant cuts in EPA's enforcement force were seriously considered. As Richard Wilson, an EPA career manager, remembered:

> There were certainly people looking at major budget cuts in EPA [enforcement]. In fact, we saw proposed budget cuts from OMB that the only way to accomplish them was to rif. In that sense it was real. . . . What you didn't know from day to day was whether or not they were going to bite the bullet and in fact rif down to those levels or [just] let attrition take its toll.[26]

Ultimately, no major termination of career enforcement staff actually occurred during the Gorsuch era. However, various enforcement programs, elements, and innovations were eliminated as a result of budget reductions, and funding for staff travel and training was significantly cut.[27] Moreover, EPA's enforcement effort was impaired by a relatively high rate of attrition.[28]

Deeply concerned about actual and possible budget cuts and effectively sealed off from the decision-making process, a number of career enforcement managers and staff members began to perceive that ideological and partisan political considerations were playing an increasing role in the evaluation of their professional work.[29] In part this notion resulted from a statement by William Sullivan at a meeting of the entire headquarters enforcement staff in late December 1981. During the month or two before this meeting, several staff attorneys had been hired (at relatively high salaries), notwithstanding the continuing EPA hiring ceilings.[30] As Richard Mays, then a career enforcement manager at EPA, remembered:

> Sullivan made the announcement about the latest reorganization and then following that had a question-and-answer series. Some member of the staff asked him about the hirings of attorneys and whether political affiliation had played any role in these hirings. Sullivan's response was that essentially this was "a political world." The Republicans were the administration in power and, all things being equal, he would rather hire a Republican than someone who was not a Republican. The staff didn't like that too much, obviously, because this is a group of people who believe, and I think rightly so, that politics and ideology should have little to do with environmental protection or qualifications in terms of hiring staff.[31]

Other events also contributed to the career staff's sense that the Agency's enforcement program was becoming "politicized." Peter Broccoletti, whom Sullivan had selected to be his deputy enforcement counsel and whose approach to the career staff was seen as "domineering and intimidating,"[32] conducted a series of interviews with EPA enforcement attorneys in which at least some of them were asked questions about their memberships in environmental organizations.[33]

Broccoletti allegedly told EPA attorney and manager James Bunting that all of the EPA enforcement attorneys' original job application forms were under political review. Broccoletti subsequently denied this.[34] Nonetheless, Bunting specifically recalled: "People were being evaluated on the basis of what it was they had said there. If someone had listed a Democratic congressman as a reference, then that particular individual . . . was going to be viewed with suspicion."[35]

In addition to politicization, some EPA managers and staff members had the impression that the leadership of the Agency had regular contact with representatives of potential candidates for enforcement action outside of the presence of EPA staff members assigned to their cases. As William Hedeman stated, "[B]ehind the scenes, in the Sullivan-Burford era, industry was getting to these individuals quietly and having a major influence on how the enforcement policy took shape."[36]

An extreme but politically significant instance of this arose in EPA's negotiations with representatives of Inmont Corporation concerning a California hazardous waste disposal site. In early September 1981 Thornton ("Whit") Field, then special assistant to the administrator for hazardous waste, had a series of conversations with Inmont's attorney regarding Inmont's responsibility for site cleanup which were not reported to the Agency's designated negotiators. During one of those conversations, Field revealed EPA's bottom-line settlement figure to Inmont, an event which had a critical effect on the outcome of those negotiations.[37]

More generally, during this time some of the regulated parties that were involved in settlement discussions with the EPA's enforcement staff sought meetings with higher-ranking Agency officials in the hope that they might receive a more sympathetic hearing.[38] As a result, from one attorney's perspective, "there never was any certainty that the deal you felt you had negotiated above board [and] across the table was going to be something that you could carry through when it came back to headquarters [for approval]."[39] A number of EPA enforcement staff members also developed the perception that the people they reported to—the Agency's career enforcement managers—had little influence on setting enforcement policy. Two incidents served to reinforce that notion.

In November 1981 the entire hazardous waste management staff had a meeting in Denver, Colorado. During the course of this meeting, Douglas MacMillan, EPA's highest-ranking career official with specific responsibility for hazardous waste enforcement, made a presentation about the Agency's enforcement policy. He indicated that EPA would be using administrative orders to redress RCRA violations. He also stated that when state agencies took RCRA enforcement actions against a regulated party that EPA officials perceived to be inappropriate or inadequate, the Agency would, in some instances, be prepared to pursue its own enforcement case against the same party. Shortly thereafter, at the same meeting, Thornton ("Whit") Field explicitly rejected the policies that MacMillan had announced. Stating, "I don't buy that and I don't think Anne Gorsuch does either," Field indicated that a formal enforcement approach was "too confrontational for this administration."[40] MacMillan later scarcely remembered this event,[41] but several enforcement staff members perceived Field's statements as a strong signal. His remarks appeared to indicate not only that MacMillan's pronouncement no longer represented the Agency's policy but also that the former task force director had been "slapped down very publicly."[42]

Another critical incident occurred seven months later when Rita M. Lavelle, EPA's assistant administrator for solid waste and emergency response, removed Lamar Miller from his position as chief of the technical component of the hazardous waste enforcement program. Miller, whom most staff members viewed as an outspoken advocate of firm enforcement, had been less successful than his counterpart, William Hedeman, in gaining Lavelle's confidence. As one former member of Miller's staff recalled:

> They announced the change on a day when he was going into the hospital for some sort of surgery. At the time it was really pretty strange. He wasn't for it. Lavelle said that Lamar was going to head up some sort of a groundwater-monitoring branch in OSW [Office of Solid Waste and Emergency Response] which didn't exist at the time and never subsequently materialized. When he came back, they gave him a task on some sort of a "sludge project."[43]

In the minds of a number of EPA's headquarters enforcement staff, Miller's abrupt removal marked an important turning point. Following Miller's removal, one knowledgeable official recalled, the staff "pushed less hard" and negotiated with regulated parties by "taking deals because they were there.[44]

If the authority of the Agency's top career enforcement managers had been dramatically undermined, however, it was not at all clear who was actually in charge of EPA enforcement work. Almost from the outset of the Reagan administration, EPA's enforcement program was marked by intense rivalries among the new political appointees. As one seasoned civil servant put it: "In eighteen years in government, I have never seen a group of people as intent on doing one another in as that crowd was."[45]

During the early months of the Reagan administration, Anne Gorsuch relied heavily on William Sullivan in enforcement matters to the relative exclusion of Sullivan's superior, associate administrator Frank Shepherd, and Robert Perry, the Agency's general counsel. A competition for authority grew among these three attorneys.[46] Within a few months, Shepherd resigned, leaving Sullivan and Perry, two strong-willed individuals, to vie for influence in the enforcement field. In the end, Perry prevailed. He assumed complete control of EPA's legal operation in April 1982. Perry's ascendancy did not end the rivalry within the upper echelons of EPA's enforcement program, however. As Anne Gorsuch told me, there was "almost a constant conflict" between Perry and Rita Lavelle over the strategy to be followed in hazardous waste enforcement cases.[47] There was also considerable disagreement among the Agency's regional administrators on a variety of enforcement issues.[48]

With respect to hazardous waste enforcement in particular, the first two years of the Reagan administration saw the institution of several new policies and trends. It is notable, however, that despite the bevy of new policy questions that arose from EPA's initial attempts to implement the Superfund Program, the Agency's headquarters provided little written guidance to its regional enforcement personnel.[49] Furthermore, those few Superfund policies that did emerge were sometimes changed with great rapidity.

In general, the Superfund approach that was followed during this period was based on the preference of EPA's top management for strict conservation of the $1.6-billion CERCLA trust fund. This approach was intended to strengthen the argument that the Superfund Act, and the corporate taxes that support it, should not be renewed after the Act's expiration on October 1, 1985.

To implement the Superfund approach, EPA's leadership adopted a strategy that has been described as "lawyers first, shovels later."[50] In fact, this label is misleading. It implies that a tough, litigious approach to Superfund enforcement preceded any use of the CERCLA trust fund for site cleanup activities. In reality, with the exception of hazardous waste enforcement matters that were already pending, EPA's earliest Superfund enforcement effort was anything but litigious. Rather than "lawyers first, shovels later," the slogan "ineffectual negotiation first, shovels never" is a more apt description.

The Agency placed heavy emphasis on providing the potentially responsible parties at inactive hazardous waste sites with the option of voluntarily cleaning up those sites. The expenditure of trust fund monies for remedial actions at Superfund sites was not permitted unless and until it had been demonstrated, to the satisfaction of the Agency's top headquarters officials, that responsible parties at those sites had been identified, that they had been notified of their potential liability for site cleanup expenditures, and that they had voluntarily and intentionally declined to carry out measures on their own.[51]

Other EPA policies and procedures also contributed to a sparing use of the CERCLA trust fund. In March 1982 the Agency required states to contribute 10 percent of the cost of RI/FS preparation as a condition to the use of Superfund monies for planning and designing hazardous waste site cleanups. Because most states had limited resources to come up with this 10 percent match, this policy significantly inhibited the use of the Superfund for cleanup activity.[52] In addition, the Agency began to interpret the "imminent and substantial endangerment" language of CERCLA section 106 (and RCRA section 7003) as requiring that the Agency demonstrate a present public health emergency, as opposed to the mere threat of one, in order to obtain relief.[53] Because of the difficulty of making this showing in many cases, EPA's use of the CERCLA and RCRA imminent hazards sections to redress contamination problems at inactive hazardous waste sites was significantly curtailed.[54]

The Agency's leadership placed other restrictions on EPA's use of its emergency or "immediate removal" authority under CERCLA. This was accomplished by the promulgation of a set of regulations, incorporated as part of the Agency's National Contingency Plan, which were consistently more restrictive than the statute required.[55] It was also affected by a policy that forbade EPA's regional offices from expending trust fund monies in excess of $50,000 for removal actions without the personal approval of the agency's assistant administrator for enforcement.[56]

The Reagan administration's first EPA managers centralized decision making in other ways as well. Authority over expenditures, case-specific enforcement strategy, and the wording of documents filed in enforcement litigation was retained in the Agency's Office of Solid Waste and Emergency Response and its Office of Enforcement Counsel. Regional officials were given little autonomy in implementing these vital aspects of the Superfund law.[57]

Finally, the Reagan administration's initial approach to RCRA enforcement continued the high level of inattention and inaction that had characterized RCRA enforcement during the Carter years. As one former EPA enforcement official expressed: "[V]irtually nothing was done in terms of writing guidance, making policy decisions or establishing an RCRA enforcement program."[58] State environmental agencies, which in many cases had "minimal training and too few resources," were delegated total responsibility for RCRA enforcement, with little federal guidance or oversight.[59] The Agency's RCRA enforcement program was afforded few resources, and many RCRA hazardous waste management regulations were placed in limbo by the Agency's plans to reconsider and revise them extensively.[60]

The cumulative impact of these innovations on EPA's enforcement policies was dramatic and pronounced. The number of new civil enforcement actions forwarded by EPA regional offices to Agency headquarters fell by 79 percent in 1981, compared with the previous year, and the Agency's civil referrals to the Justice Department fell 69 percent. In the Superfund area, EPA referred no new enforcement cases to the DOJ from January 20, 1981, until April 1, 1982, and only three such cases were filed between the latter date and September 29, 1982. With respect to RCRA civil enforcement actions, EPA filed no cases in 1981 and only three cases during the first nine months of 1982, a sharp contrast to the forty-three RCRA civil cases the agency had initiated during 1980.[61]

In addition to a drop in its workload, EPA's enforcement staff was faced with considerable confusion. As William Sullivan candidly admitted: "The poor regional attorneys were left in a position where they didn't know who the hell they worked for. They couldn't even tell what the procedures were from day to day."[62] Apparently, the continuing reorganizations of the Agency's enforcement programs significantly contributed to the enforcement staff's confusion. Some present and former EPA officials saw clear organizational advantages in the demise of EPA's preexisting structure.[63] Nonetheless, a large number of those I spoke with viewed this series of organizational changes as harmful to the enforcement effort. In particular, they believed that the reorganization created barriers to effective communication among the Agency's interdisciplinary enforcement staff, giving rise to turf battles and red tape that had not existed previously.[64] In the face of these changes and uncertainties, a number of the Agency's mid-level managers became unwilling to make firm policy decisions, fearing that any position they took would be reversed at higher levels.[65]

Not surprisingly, enforcement staff morale declined precipitously in this period, notwithstanding Gorsuch's later recollection that the Agency had been "fun" and "jumpin'."[66] As one regional enforcement manager described it: "There was this feeling that the EPA was kind of a ship adrift in the water and that if we wanted to do anything it was time to leave, move on."[67] Staff members "feared for their jobs and for their reputations."[68] In the view of a former headquarters enforcement manager:

> You spent a lot of time figuring out ways to get around obstacles which were internal [to EPA] now, rather than external. You were trying to survive, trying to continue to do your job, while most of your days were spent worrying about whether you would actually have a job, in some cases, or whom you would be working for and whether that person would be a rational human being.[69]

With few exceptions, the Agency's political appointees were the objects of intense resentment from the enforcement staff. Their motives were distrusted, their enforcement policies were disliked, and the professional competency of some was questioned. Out of anger and despair, some headquarters enforcement staff members cultivated informal relationships with members of congressional committees, relationships that were to have increasing significance as the Gorsuch years wore on.[70]

In addition to internal disarray, EPA's relationships with various elements outside the Agency began to deteriorate. Fearful that budget cuts would result in lost federal grants, a number of state pollution control agency managers also began to mistrust EPA's new approach.[71] In addition, the Agency lost considerable credibility with the press.[72]

EPA's weakened enforcement effort also met with increasing disenchantment from some elements of industry. During this period, a number of regulated firms became concerned that the decline in EPA enforcement was contrary to their interests. They feared that this trend would disadvantage companies that had already expended money to comply with environmental requirements. They were also concerned that weak enforcement would lead to a public backlash in which EPA would be forced to subject industry to draconian measures.[73]

With respect to the Superfund Program, the staff became involved in what one enforcement scientist and manager referred to as "interminable negotiations" with PRPs.[74] In some instances, it was unclear who had responsibility for various aspects of the Superfund Program.[75] As a result, the site cleanup effort was marked by struggles between those organizational components with responsibility for expending CERCLA trust fund monies and those units charged with enforcing the Superfund Act.[76]

Slowly, almost imperceptibly at first, Congress and the public became concerned about the difficulties emerging in EPA's enforcement efforts. This concern was partly the result of informal analyses by congressional committee staff of enforcement statistics and other information provided by the Agency and its staff. It was also affected by the efforts of Save EPA, a committee of former EPA officials headed by William Drayton which had been formed to lobby against the administration's proposals for drastic decreases in EPA's budget.

In the second half of 1981, Congressman John Dingell (D-MI), then the politically influential chairman of the Subcommittee on Oversight and Investigations of the House Committee on Energy and Commerce (the Dingell Committee), was supplied with information from EPA documenting the decline in new civil enforcement cases. Additionally, Congressman Dingell took note of the failure of EPA to establish a criminal enforcement program, a step that was first recommended in 1979 by James Moorman, the DOJ's assistant attorney general for lands and natural resources. Additionally, two attorneys on Dingell's subcommittee staff, Richard Frandsen and Mark Raabe, learned informally from members of EPA's career enforcement staff of the confused and demoralized state of the Agency's enforcement efforts.[77]

In the fall of 1981 the Dingell Committee held a series of hearings that focused on EPA's need to hire criminal investigators.[78] Although these hearings resulted in a commitment from Gorsuch to initiate a criminal enforcement program, Congressman Dingell and his staff remained privately critical of other aspects of EPA's enforcement work. They began to prepare for additional subcommittee hearings to air their concerns and to press the Agency for a more vigorous enforcement approach in the hazardous waste area.

In the meantime, several events took place that served to heighten public awareness of the problems EPA's new enforcement approach had created. During the week of January 25, 1982, *Doonesbury*, the syndicated comic strip by Garry Trudeau, ran a series in which Ted Simpson, a mythical EPA employee, was portrayed as sitting on an office window ledge to protest Gorsuch's purported plans "to dismantle the whole enforcement team." After eliciting a promise from the EPA administrator "to reinstate the enforcement division" and to let the enforcement staff prosecute pollution violators "until such time as the President can gut the laws," Simpson was shown returning from his window ledge only to be told, "I lied. You're fired."[79]

This series of cartoons, which appeared in many newspapers, including the *Washington Post*, increased the visibility of the Reagan administration's EPA enforcement failures. Among other things, it prompted Gorsuch to send a memorandum to all EPA employees on February 5, 1982, in which she denounced "windowsill politics" and "countless press reports and rumors of massive personnel reductions planned for this agency." Gorsuch pledged that "there will be no involuntary separations due to reductions-in-force at the Environmental Protection Agency during the remainder of fiscal year 1982" and stated, "I expect to continue the same policy . . . through fiscal year 1983."

Shortly after the Ted Simpson *Doonesbury* cartoons appeared, Russell E. Train, EPA's second administrator, published a guest column in the *Washington Post* in which he sharply criticized the management of EPA and warned of disastrous consequences if proposed budget cuts in the Agency's staffing levels were permitted to occur.[80] Because of Train's prominence in the environmental field, his Republican credentials, and his credibility with moderate elements in the business community, his written remarks were seen to weaken the EPA administration's political credibility significantly.

In addition, approximately three weeks later, EPA began a series of actions that, though not directly related to its enforcement program, brought EPA's approach to hazardous waste regulation into sharp focus. On February 25, 1982, the Agency formally proposed to reverse rules that had prohibited the burial of hazardous liquids in landfills for a period of at least ninety days on the basis that these prohibitions had been unworkable and unnecessarily costly.[81] This proposal gave rise to vehement protests from environmental organizations, so-called high-tech waste disposal companies, and congressional critics of EPA, including Congressman James Florio (D-NJ), whose Subcommittee on Commerce, Transportation and Tourism held public hearings with respect to the liquids-in-landfills proposals. Within several weeks, EPA withdrew its proposal, establishing instead an interim rule that prohibited the burial in landfills of any container in which liquid toxic chemical wastes were "standing in observable quantities."[82] Although this action quieted the immediate controversy and won guarded praise from some of EPA's leading congressional critics, including Congressman Toby Moffett (D-CT), the chairman of the environmental subcommittee of the House Committee on Government Operations, the entire incident served to further tarnish EPA's reputation with respect to its regulation of hazardous wastes.

Shortly thereafter, the Dingell Committee opened its second set of hearings into the Reagan administration's enforcement approach. Administrator Gorsuch, Enforcement Counsel Sullivan, and other high-ranking EPA officials were called to testify and were subjected to pointed and embarrassing questions with regard to EPA's hazardous waste enforcement program.[83] The Agency's site cleanup negotiations with Inmont Corporation were spotlighted, along with the dramatic decrease in its civil enforcement case referrals and the continual reorganization of its enforcement structure.

These hearings were widely publicized. They provided much of the basis for a subcommittee report, ultimately published in December 1982, which contained sharp criticism of EPA's Superfund and RCRA enforcement efforts.[84] In response to the political pressures that the Dingell hearings generated, EPA's leadership continued to institute a series of management and policy changes that they hoped would place the Agency's enforcement work in a more favorable light.[85]

In late March 1982 William Sullivan was relieved of his leadership role in EPA enforcement matters. In Sullivan's stead Robert M. Perry, the agency's general counsel, was given expanded responsibility in the enforcement area. Seeking to distance himself from Sullivan's informal "voluntary compliance" approach to environmental enforcement, Perry, with the support of Gorsuch, initiated several measures designed to bolster the Agency's faltering efforts. Perry appointed a committee of five experienced career managers to review all aspects of EPA's enforcement program and to suggest improvements.[86] He also appointed Michael Brown, a forceful and dynamic attorney and manager with considerable prior experience in the Consumer Product Safety Commission, to replace Sullivan as enforcement counsel.

In response to congressional criticisms of excessive industry influence on EPA enforcement policies and of the alleged execution of sweetheart deals in particular hazardous waste enforcement cases, Perry instituted a policy prohibiting Superfund enforcement agreements with PRPs unless the government obtained all that it sought in negotiation. This policy effectively forbade settlements in Superfund enforcement matters unless PRP defendants agreed that (1) they would enter into a formal written agreement, usually in the form of a consent decree; (2) they would not be formally released from future liability, even if they fully complied with the terms of the agreement; and (3) they would assume all costs of site cleanup. Few PRPs actually agreed to settle on these extremely stringent terms.[87] Perry also began to place pressure on regional enforcement officials to generate large numbers of new enforcement actions.[88] This last initiative resulted in what one former DOJ official described as a "blitzkrieg of referrals" in late September 1982, at the end of the Agency's fiscal year.[89]

Beyond this, during this time the Agency and DOJ took small yet meaningful steps toward the establishment of a permanent criminal enforcement effort. In the summer of 1982 sixteen full-time criminal investigators were hired from a pool of nearly three hundred applicants from other law enforcement agencies. The addition of these individuals— all of whom had served as criminal investigators for a minimum of five years and some of whom had more than twenty years of investigative and supervisory experience—raised to twenty-three the Agency's total number of investigators. This was soon followed by the creation of small environmental crimes units within the Justice Department's Criminal Division and its Land and Natural Resources Division.[90]

In a political sense, these modifications to EPA's enforcement approach were too little and too late. Most of the administration's critics, both on

Capitol Hill and within the Agency, remained unpersuaded that EPA's enforcement program had become truly aggressive or effective. On June 15, 1982, Congressmen Dingell and Florio sent Anne Gorsuch an eleven-page, single-spaced letter in which they requested "actual data, rather than unsupported estimates" concerning some 144 indicators of enforcement activity over a three-and-a-half-year period.[91] This letter, which gave rise to an intensive and time-consuming search of EPA's enforcement records and statistics,[92] was supplemented by a second Dingell-Florio letter to Gorsuch on August 31, 1982, in which seventy-three specific requests for additional information were also submitted to the Agency.[93]

Other congressmen began to pursue parallel investigations. On September 15, 1982, staff attorneys for the Subcommittee on Investigations and Oversight of the House Committee on Public Works and Transportation, under the chairmanship of Congressman Elliot Levitas (D-GA) (the Levitas Committee), traveled to EPA's Region II office in New York to examine enforcement files pertaining to certain Superfund cases. Upon their arrival, these attorneys learned, to their surprise and distress, that the Agency would not permit access to the documents they sought. On the Justice Department's advice, the Reagan administration had decided to rely upon the executive privilege doctrine as a basis for withholding from congressional investigators enforcement files that the Agency deemed "enforcement sensitive" in content.[94] There is considerable evidence that this decision was made by the Department of Justice and imposed upon skeptical EPA officials. In a carefully documented report, the House Judiciary Committee concluded that before executive privilege was claimed, the Justice Department was aware of at least nine different incidents which demonstrated that EPA was willing to turn the disputed documents over to Congress.[95]

Notwithstanding its genesis, however, the decision to claim executive privilege proved a fateful one for most of EPA's top managers. On November 22, 1982, after EPA General Counsel Robert Perry had reiterated the Reagan administration's position in correspondence with Congressman Levitas, the House Committee on Public Works and Transportation formally subpoenaed Anne Gorsuch to appear before the Levitas Committee on December 2, 1982, and to bring with her enforcement-related documents regarding some 160 abandoned hazardous waste sites.[96] Gorsuch appeared before the Levitas Committee on December 2, but rather than supply the requested documents, the EPA administrator testified that President Reagan had instructed her to withhold those papers from the House. Later that day, the Levitas Committee voted to hold Gorsuch in contempt of Congress,[97] an action that was reiterated by the full House of Representatives on December 14, 1982, by a vote of 259 to 105.[98]

During the same period that the Levitas Committee encountered resistance to its requests for EPA Superfund documents, the Dingell Committee, which had begun an investigation of the possible allocation of Superfund monies for partisan political advantage, met with similar administration intransigence. On September 17, 1982, Congressman Dingell sent a letter to Anne Gorsuch requesting EPA documents with respect to three Superfund sites. These documents were formally subpoenaed by the Dingell Committee approximately one month later. As she had done in response to the Levitas Committee's subpoena, Gorsuch appeared before the Dingell Committee on December 14, 1982, and expressly refused to provide a number of the subpoenaed documents on the grounds of executive privilege. The Dingell Committee voted to hold Gorsuch in contempt on the same day.[99]

These actions set the stage for a major constitutional confrontation between Congress and the executive branch. On December 16, 1982, the Department of Justice brought suit against the House of Representatives in the U.S. District Court for the District of Columbia. The department sought to enjoin enforcement of the Levitas Committee's subpoena and to have that document declared invalid and unconstitutional. Attorneys for the House promptly moved to dismiss the DOJ's suit, a motion that the District Court took under advisement.[100]

In the meantime, the controversy over the documents, the attitudes and record of Anne Gorsuch and other high-ranking EPA officials, and virtually all aspects of the management of EPA since the advent of the Reagan administration became the focus of intense media scrutiny. Believing the "EPA scandal" to be the beginning, at least potentially, of a Watergate-style cover-up, the media provided prominent coverage of the management of the Superfund Program by Anne Gorsuch, Rita Lavelle, and others. This extensive publicity lasted for a period of several months.[101] During that time, EPA's top leadership developed what one civil servant later described as a "bunker mentality."[102] Besieged by the press and Congress, EPA's leaders became isolated from their staffs and increasingly uninvolved in matters not pertaining to the documents controversy.

EPA's enforcement staff was deeply immersed in the executive privilege dispute as well. Enforcement attorneys in EPA's headquarters and its regional offices were asked to respond to Congress's information request by reviewing all of the Agency's enforcement files to determine which of the documents contained therein were "enforcement sensitive." This was an extremely time-consuming task, involving the review of thousands of letters, memos, records, and reports.[103] In addition, approximately thirty members of the Agency's career enforcement staff were subpoenaed to testify before executive sessions of the Dingell Committee as part of its continuing investigation into Superfund abuses.[104] Many other staff members devoted a good deal of their time to responding to inquiries by the press and individual members of Congress concerning EPA's handling of particular Superfund matters.[105]

On February 3, 1983, U.S. District Judge John Lewis Smith Jr. granted the motion of the House of Representatives to dismiss the DOJ's executive privilege suit. Judge Smith stated, "The difficulties apparent in prosecuting Administrator Gorsuch for contempt of Congress should encourage the two branches to settle their differences without further judicial involvement. Compromise and cooperation, rather than confrontation, should be the aim of the parties."[106] With this judicial admonishment, high officials of the Reagan administration decided to enter into serious compromise negotiations with their congressional adversaries. On March 9, 1983, Congressman Dingell and White House Counsel Fred Fielding executed a written agreement under which the Dingell Committee was to be furnished all of the documents it had sought regarding Superfund sites.[107] A similar understanding was reached between the DOJ and the Levitas Committee approximately two weeks later.[108]

As part of the Reagan administration's plan to limit the political damage created by the documents controversy, Anne Gorsuch was compelled to resign as EPA's administrator.[109] She left office on March 9, 1983. Immediately preceding or shortly following that event, some nineteen other top-level EPA officials left their posts, resulting in a nearly complete turnover in the Agency's highest leadership.[110]

In other fallout from the congressional investigations, Rita M. Lavelle was indicted by a federal grand jury for providing false testimony to some of the congressional committees that investigated her administration of the Superfund Program. On December 1, 1983, Lavelle was convicted by a jury of most of the felony charges made against her. She was sentenced to six months' confinement, five years' probation (during which time she was required to perform community service), and a $10,000 fine.[111]

By almost any measure, the period from January 1981 until March 1983 was a devastating time for EPA's enforcement work. The number of new civil actions initiated by the EPA fell dramatically during those years. Additionally, the Agency's enforcement programs during this period experienced unprecedented levels of disorganization, demoralization, and internal strife. Although there is disagreement about whether the Agency's political leadership specifically intended those results, there can be little doubt that it was their actions and omissions that caused them.

It seems inevitable that every incoming administration will place its own political appointees in positions responsible for implementing regulatory requirements. The approach of the EPA's early Reagan administration managers, however, led to an almost complete politicization of the enforcement process. This politicization interfered with the Agency's remedial application of hazardous waste statutes and its enforcement of other federal laws, objective tasks requiring persistent professional effort and institutional stability. Beyond this, the EPA managers of the early 1980s failed from the outset to enunciate a clear and defensible approach to EPA's enforcement work. In this respect, their efforts stand in sharp contrast not only to the litigious EPA enforcement strategies of the Carter administration but also to enforcement regimes of the Nixon, Ford, and George H. W. Bush administrations. Indeed, in the words of four congressmen from the Reagan administration's own party: "[T]he poor performance of the Superfund program [in the 1981 to 1983 period] resulted from a lack of expertise, inexperience, incompetence and mismanagement" by those responsible for implementing the program.[112]

If the stormy history of EPA's enforcement efforts in the Gorsuch era demonstrates that the political leadership of administrative agencies has a practical ability to inhibit or forestall vigorous enforcement, what can it teach us with respect to Congress's effectiveness in restoring enforcement vitality? Here, the answer appears somewhat more sanguine. In many respects, congressional pressure on EPA's leadership to reverse the failings of the Gorsuch era was effective. Through oversight hearings, extensive requests for information, publicity, and informal attempts at persuasion, Congress appears to have motivated EPA's top management in the summer and fall of 1982 to stem the decline of the Agency's hazardous waste enforcement programs. In addition, aggressive congressional oversight activity during the 1983 documents controversy led to the replacement of Gorsuch and her colleagues with new managers who had different enforcement attitudes and management techniques.[113]

In view of these evident congressional successes, it might be surmised that our government has created a check on the enforcement failings of administrative agencies. On that theory, ineffective administrative agency enforcement programs—particularly when they involve regulatory legislation that enjoys broad public support—will invariably be identified by concerned members of Congress and their staffs. These ineffective enforcement efforts will be brought to light at oversight hearings and by other means, and top administrative managers—fearing unwelcome publicity and congressional displeasure—will necessarily be forced to energize and reform their agency's enforcement efforts or face dismissal and political disgrace.

On the surface, this hypothesis has some plausibility. However, upon closer examination, it is clear that it fails to grasp some of the larger implications of this phase of EPA's enforcement history. Congress's "victory" in its confrontations with EPA's top managers had a number of critical components, none of which in retrospect seems the natural or inevitable result of EPA's enforcement shortcomings. First, the congressional oversight effort was led by an experienced and influential legislator, Congressman John Dingell, who had a reputation for assertive, thorough, and detailed oversight work. No matter how politically self-interested his efforts may have been, without Dingell and the skillful work of his subcommittee staff, the congressional investigation of EPA's enforcement programs would probably not have been as successful as it was.

Second, the dispute between EPA and Congress over the Agency's hazardous waste enforcement efforts was marked by a number of costly tactical errors on the part of administration officials. For example, the decision of administration officials in February 1982 to permit the landfill burial of liquid hazardous wastes led to an intense, damaging, and entirely avoidable public controversy, a dispute that lowered the Agency's credibility in the hazardous waste area during a critical time. Similarly, the Reagan administration's decision to withhold subpoenaed documents from the Levitas and Dingell Committees converted what had been a simmering dispute over EPA's enforcement record into a major constitutional confrontation. It seems far from inevitable that Congress would have achieved the level of dominance in the area of EPA waste enforcement that it did if the Reagan administration had avoided these damaging errors.

Third, the competition between EPA and Congress with respect to enforcement questions was played out in the spotlight of intense national publicity. This situation, which resulted partly from the constitutional dimensions of the documents dispute and partly from the fact that the dispute appeared to the media to parallel the Watergate scandal of the 1970s, served to raise the political stakes for all concerned. Had the press chosen to pay less attention to the "EPA scandals" of the early Reagan administration (particularly during the autumn of 1982 and the winter of 1983), the March 1983 resignation of the Agency's top leadership would not, in retrospect, appear unavoidable.

Rather than demonstrating that it is inevitable that congressional reaction will effectively reverse poor regulatory enforcement performances by federal administrative agencies, EPA's 1981 to 1983 disputes with Congress concerning enforcement appear to yield a much more modest conclusion. They indicate that, at least in some instances, congressional investigation and oversight of weak administrative agency enforcement have the potential to effectively force a non-enforcing agency into a more vigorous enforcement posture. When the congressional opposition to agency non-enforcement is well publicized, when it is spearheaded by influential and determined legislators, and when it is aimed at administration officials unable to project a politically credible image of moderation and managerial competence, that opposition can indeed create a climate in which ineffectual enforcement practices must and will be reversed.

CHAPTER 5

"Away from the Brink"—But Not Out of the Woods: EPA Enforcement from 1983 to 1989

In July 1988, David Andrews, a private attorney who had served in EPA during the Carter administration wrote:

> There is no question that Bill Ruckelshaus moved the [Environmental Protection] Agency away from the brink of disaster and put it back on the road to recovery. Lee Thomas has kept the Agency on that road, but the Agency continued to suffer from a perception that it is not fully committed to meet its environmental and public health responsibilities. Therefore there is still some distance to travel before Congress and the public will view EPA as an agency operating with a full commitment to meeting its responsibilities.[1]

Andrews's words aptly described the circumstances of the Agency—in its enforcement efforts and otherwise—during the final six years of Ronald Reagan's presidency. As we have seen, EPA enforcement in the Gorsuch era was characterized by considerable confusion, disorganization, and discontinuity. The Agency's relationship with Congress and the press was fraught with discord and confrontation. The number of new enforcement actions initiated by the EPA declined precipitously, and enforcement staff morale was low. The appointment of William D. Ruckelshaus to be EPA's administrator once again marked the start of a different approach to the Agency's enforcement responsibilities.

Having decided to alter many of the policies and procedures of his unpopular predecessor, Ruckelshaus and his new management team initiated several well-publicized changes. In confirmation hearings before a Senate committee, Ruckelshaus publicly pledged that he would operate his Agency "in a fishbowl." He stated, "We will attempt to communicate with everyone, from the environmentalists to those we regulate, and we will do so as early as possible."[2] Ruckelshaus also committed himself to a renewed emphasis on effective enforcement. The hiring ceiling that had been applied to all EPA positions, including enforcement-related jobs, was lifted for the first time in the Reagan administration.[3] There was a gradual increase in the amount of money allocated for enforcement training and travel.[4] In addition, the Superfund enforcement staff was significantly increased, particularly in technical and scientific areas. Beyond this, Ruckelshaus and his colleagues displayed a willingness to consider the recommendations of EPA's career enforcement staffs.[5] This new approach to the permanent staff's concerns helped improve morale.[6] In the view of one former enforcement attorney: "The employees were once again viewed as being a valued part of the Agency. This improved the situation immeasurably. It instilled new life."[7]

Despite these reforms, in many quarters of the Agency skepticism prevailed regarding the new administrator's true intentions with regard to enforcement. That skepticism was deepened by the decision of Alvin Alm, EPA's new deputy administrator, not to re-create EPA's pre-Gorsuch Office of Enforcement and regional enforcement divisions.[8] This decision may well have been based on a genuine belief that further tinkering with the Agency's basic enforcement structure would only compound the shortcomings of the prior EPA administration's enforcement approach.[9] Nonetheless, it was viewed by the Agency's enforcement staff as an indication that EPA's new top management was less than serious in its commitment to reinvigorate the enforcement campaign.[10]

Concerned with the Agency's lack of progress in restoring its enforcement efforts and with the very real possibility of renewed criticism from Capitol Hill, Ruckelshaus decided to dramatize his preference for an effective enforcement program. He chose as his forum an EPA National Compliance and Enforcement Conference in January 1984. Before a large audience of nearly all of the Agency's top- and mid-level managers with responsibilities in the enforcement field, the administrator announced, "I am nervous about what I perceive to be an apparent lack of action and serious commitment to ensuring that these [environmental] laws and regulations are enforced." Chiding the Agency's managers for their poor enforcement performance, Ruckelshaus declared:

> What I was concerned about, frankly, in coming back here was that we
> had a bunch of tigers in the tank, and the minute we took the lid off
> the tank and said, "Go get them," the problem might well be an over-

reaction—that we might start treating people unfairly, just to show everybody how tough we are. Well, I think we opened the tank all right. But on the basis of what I see here the past few months, there may be more pussycats in the tank than tigers.[11]

This speech, delivered with passion and followed by sustained applause, had something of a catalytic effect. Many of EPA's enforcement staffers began to believe that they had finally received the clear signal they had sought. They were, for the first time, persuaded that the Agency's new top managers had an interest in building the credible and effective enforcement effort their immediate predecessors had failed to achieve.

That signal was reinforced, in several respects, in the months that followed. As a supplement to Ruckelshaus's speech, the Agency's deputy administrator, Alvin Alm, spearheaded a top management effort to pressure EPA's regional offices into meeting their enforcement commitments. Alm's monthly telephone calls and semiannual visits with regional administrators were intended to be a reminder that EPA's top leaders once again viewed enforcement as a priority and that regional managers would be held accountable if their regions did not increase enforcement output.

Beyond this, Ruckelshaus and his staff made efforts to improve the efficacy of EPA's fledgling criminal enforcement program. In July 1983 the Agency formally requested that the Department of Justice appoint EPA's small staff of criminal investigators as special deputy U.S. marshals. This request was designed to provide the investigators with legal authority to make arrests, execute search warrants, and carry firearms.[12] Initially, the Justice Department balked at this request. However, the DOJ was soon taken to task by Congress for its intransigence. In a September 1983 oversight hearing before his House Subcommittee on Oversight and Investigations, Congressman John Dingell pointed out that a number of the targets of EPA's criminal investigations had criminal records, operated clandestinely, and carried weapons. Without the authority to carry firearms and execute warrants, EPA's newly hired investigators were placed in a position of disadvantage and, in some instances, personal danger in carrying out their duties.[13] Notwithstanding strong congressional pressure, the Justice Department continued to resist EPA's deputization request. In April 1984, however, the DOJ finally reversed its position. It approved the Agency's deputization of its criminal investigators for a trial period, a period that lasted nearly four years.[14]

In the area of civil enforcement, Ruckelshaus and Alm took steps to improve EPA's relationship with the states and to clarify the Agency's policy respecting civil penalties. In June 1983, a task force of senior managers was established to develop a set of options outlining state and federal roles in implementing environmental programs. After a brief study, this group recommended that EPA develop an oversight program which recognized that direct program administration and enforcement were primarily state responsibilities, and that the Agency foster more trust and mutual respect in EPA-state relationships.[15]

Several months later, EPA issued a policy framework for individual EPA-state enforcement agreements. This document, formally effective in June 1984, set forth the Agency's methods for overseeing state enforcement programs. It established a set of criteria to be used for assessing good enforcement program performance and called for semiannual EPA reviews of state enforcement programs, quarterly state reporting on key performance measures, and regular EPA evaluations of state progress in addressing significant violations.[16] While far from a permanent resolution of the Agency's often tense relationships with state enforcement officials, this policy, and the individual state-EPA enforcement agreements it spawned, helped to improve intergovernmental communication and to define better the expectations and roles of federal and state enforcement officials.

EPA's evolving civil enforcement policies were further clarified in February 1984 by the issuance of a Uniform Policy on Civil Penalties. This policy required EPA program policies and regional office enforcement actions to recover the economic benefit of noncompliance from violators of environmental standards.[17] Although the Agency's inconsistent implementation of the policy was to prove an embarrassment in later years, its promulgation was an important step forward in defining EPA's formal approach in a particularly controversial area of enforcement case negotiation.

As a result of its significance in the events that led up to Anne Gorsuch's resignation as administrator, as well as its continuing importance in the minds of many members of Congress and their professional staffs, EPA's implementation of the Superfund Program was afforded a high priority by Ruckelshaus and his colleagues. In this area the new administrator chose to delegate a great deal of authority to Lee M. Thomas, who replaced Rita Lavelle as assistant administrator of the Agency's Office of Solid Waste and Emergency Response. Thomas, who began his career as an official of the state government of South Carolina in the field of criminal justice, had gone on to become executive deputy director of the Federal Emergency Management Agency (FEMA). In that capacity he had headed the federal government's efforts to provide relief to the residents of Times Beach, Missouri, who had been imperiled by improperly disposed hazardous wastes. An able manager, Thomas quickly impressed his staff with his intelligence and decisiveness. The comments of Michael Kilpatrick, an EPA manager in the Superfund enforcement program, typify the views of many of the agency's career staff: "In my mind, Lee Thomas was the reason why things got back on a smooth track here. The guy just works incredibly hard and is extremely bright. He very quickly learned what the issues were."[18]

Under Thomas's leadership, a number of changes were made in EPA's Superfund approach. The Agency's strict limitation of expenditures from the CERCLA trust fund was abruptly ended, replaced by an emphasis on attempting to clean up abandoned hazardous waste site problems as promptly as possible. This was to be accomplished primarily through accelerated use of the trust fund, as well as through renewed Superfund enforcement activities. Thomas increased the use of the CERCLA trust fund to finance preliminary assessments and site investigations and to conduct RI/FSs at dumpsites on the Superfund's National Priorities List.[19] The "lawyers first, shovels later" approach was transformed into "shovels first, lawyers later," a resolve not to allow cleanup activities to be slowed by lengthy enforcement negotiation or litigation.[20]

Lee Thomas also committed himself to the notion that enforcement had significance for the Superfund effort. Although the Agency's primary focus in that period was on the cleanup of hazardous waste sites with public funds, Thomas also emphasized the need to initiate more enforcement actions, including administrative orders, consent decrees, lawsuits, and cost recovery actions. With the cooperation of a sympathetic Congress, he expanded the Agency's Superfund enforcement resources, adding new staff, especially technically trained staff, in EPA's regional offices as well as its headquarters program components.[21] Moreover, Thomas joined with other EPA and DOJ managers in insisting that the Superfund statute be construed to create strict, joint, and several liability for responsible parties in Superfund litigation.[22]

This last stance had significant consequences. Beginning in 1983, the able efforts of attorneys for the Justice Department and EPA resulted in a number of important victories for the federal government in Superfund litigation. In a series of landmark decisions, federal district courts in various parts of the United States upheld the government's strict interpretation of the liability and causation provisions of CERCLA with remarkable uniformity. This trend, which continued through 1985 and beyond, had great influence on the substance of the Superfund Amendment and Reauthorization Act (SARA) that Congress enacted in 1986. The act established a set of ground rules for subsequent EPA negotiations with PRPs in individual Superfund cases that gave the government immense discretion to shape the terms and conditions of settlement agreements.[23]

To implement their push to reinvigorate the Superfund effort, Ruckelshaus, Alm, and Thomas delegated responsibility for day-to-day hazardous waste management to the Agency's regional offices.[24] As one veteran regional official stated, "The top EPA headquarters people began to trust the regions again."[25] The stringent concurrence requirement for regional initiation of emergency removal actions was lifted.[26] EPA's regional offices were accorded more autonomy to initiate RI/FSs and to negotiate agreements for studies and cleanup measures by private parties.[27]

Along with augmented regional authority came a gradual increase in written policy guidelines on Superfund issues. Over a period of thirty-six months, the Agency issued comprehensive guidance memorandums concerning such critical matters as the specific basis on which EPA could settle Superfund enforcement actions against PRPs, participation of responsible parties in development of RI/FSs, issuance of notice letters to PRPs, use and issuance of administrative orders under CERCLA section 106, and the preparation of Superfund cost recovery actions.[28] In addition, a hazardous waste site planning system was instituted. Under this system, regional offices were required to project their Superfund activities over given time periods and to create tentative management plans for all priority hazardous waste sites.[29]

Taken as a whole, these trends and changes moved EPA's languishing enforcement efforts—both in the Superfund area and outside of it—in the direction of renewal and revitalization. Though relatively brief, William Ruckelshaus's second term as EPA administrator did succeed in pulling the Agency's implementation of Superfund and other environmental statutes away from what David Andrews has aptly termed the "brink of disaster."

Nonetheless, the success of the administrator's efforts was constrained and incomplete. Throughout both Ruckelshaus's and Thomas's tenures, EPA's enforcement programs were viewed with intense suspicion by congressional oversight committees, environmental organizations, and certain representatives of the media. This lasting residue of mistrust, and the response to that mistrust by EPA's top managers, played a critical role in determining the substantive content of much of the environmental legislation of the 1980s. It also molded EPA's efforts to carry out Congress's mandates.

A crucial focus of congressional concern during Ruckelshaus's second term was EPA's deficient administration of RCRA. While the Reagan administration's second set of EPA managers paid considerable attention to restoring the Agency's Superfund Program, federal RCRA enforcement efforts continued to languish. Stymied by a chronic shortage of resources, particularly among attorneys in the offices of regional counsel,[30] and still the subject of comparatively little top-management attention,[31] EPA's RCRA enforcement effort continued to operate in the shadow of the partially revived Superfund campaign.

This situation did not go unnoticed by EPA's congressional critics. In November 1984 Congress modified RCRA by enacting the Hazardous and Solid Waste Amendments (HSWA), a comprehensive piece of legislation. As two EPA officials noted in a candid law review analysis: "[B]etween 1980 and 1983, Congress perceived EPA as an agency unwilling or unable to fulfill its mandate of environmental protection. Almost every section of the RCRA Amendments might be read as expressing a sense of frustration over the pace and scope of EPA action."[32]

Congressional dissatisfaction with EPA's implementation of RCRA gave rise to vigorous investigations into the Agency's enforcement of the HSWA. In December 1984 the Dingell Committee conducted a survey that revealed high levels of noncompliance with the groundwater monitoring and financial assurance requirements of EPA's RCRA regulations.[33] This survey found that, of the 317 hazardous waste facilities with inadequate groundwater monitoring wells, 26 percent had no compliance action taken against them and 26 percent received only an informal enforcement action—a notice or a warning letter. Furthermore, of 188 facilities with no groundwater monitoring wells at all, formal enforcement action had been initiated only at 89 facilities (approximately 47 percent of the total number).[34]

Dingell's survey formed the basis of a hearing by the Dingell Committee on April 29, 1985, during which the Agency's RCRA enforcement record was singled out for pointed and embarrassing criticism. As one trade journalist described the proceeding, the EPA officials who testified before the subcommittee were "left grasping at straws as they attempted to defend their apparent inaction in the face of massive noncompliance since the [RCRA] rules took effect in 1981."[35]

Now highly sensitive to the potential consequences of congressional wrath, EPA's managers responded by giving RCRA enforcement a higher priority. Groundwater monitoring and financial assurance requirements, along with RCRA's loss of interim status requirements, began to receive increasing attention from EPA's enforcement staff. The Agency launched a loss of interim status (LOIS) initiative against certain land disposal facilities. It targeted facilities that were required to lose their interim status (and thus to close down their operation) if their owners or operators had failed to submit a final permit application and certify compliance with applicable groundwater and financial responsibility requirements. This EPA initiative resulted in the filing of a significant number of civil judicial actions by the Department of Justice and the closure of approximately one thousand non-complying facilities.[36]

In February 1985 Lee Thomas succeeded William Ruckelshaus as EPA administrator. A former Ruckelshaus assistant who had received his predecessor's political support in his bid to become the Agency's top manager, Thomas promptly pledged to continue the reforms that Ruckelshaus, with Thomas's own input and support, had initiated. This was particularly true in the enforcement field. In his first major speech as administrator, Thomas promised a national conference of EPA and state enforcement officials that the Agency would pursue a rigorous enforcement effort that would place new emphasis on the pursuit of criminal cases. Specifically, he stated, "[T]here won't be any letup, as long as I'm [EPA] administrator, in any time and attention you heard Bill Ruckelshaus give enforcement last year."[37] In addition, in the Agency's annual Operating Guidance for fiscal year 1987, a document intended to guide EPA's development of annual plans, the new administrator listed ensuring "a strong enforcement presence in all of our Agency programs" as one of his six highest policy priorities. At a February 1987 senior management forum for EPA executives, Thomas set forth, as one of his "priority themes" for improving agency management, the notion that "[w]e will enforce environmental laws vigorously, consistently, and equitably, to achieve the greatest possible environmental results."[38]

In the summer of 1986 Thomas appointed Thomas L. Adams Jr. to succeed Courtney Price as assistant administrator for enforcement and compliance monitoring. Adams had previously served for three years as EPA's deputy general counsel for regional coordination. Before that he had been an appellate attorney in the Justice Department's Division of Land and Natural Resources and, from 1977 to 1983, assistant director for government relations at Republic Steel Corporation.[39] During Adams's two contentious years as assistant administrator, EPA's general enforcement efforts began to evolve in several new directions. That evolution continued—and in some respects received more emphasis and definition—in the period that followed his tenure.

One important trend was the gradual development of a multimedia enforcement focus. As the volume of EPA enforcement activity once again expanded, career enforcement professionals in several sections of the Agency's organizational structure began to realize that EPA's strict segregation of enforcement activities by environmental medium (air, water, hazardous waste, toxic substances, etc.) was inefficient and counterproductive. Ways were needed to integrate the Agency's enforcement work at particular industrial facilities and in specific categories of industry and geographical regions in order to provide greater clarity and consistency and to increase EPA's overall leverage in case-by-case enforcement negotiations.

This insight appears to have occurred to several Agency officials independently. In EPA's Midwest regional office, Michael G. Smith, a branch chief in the office of regional counsel, recommended a crosscutting multimedia enforcement strategy for a heavily industrialized portion of northwestern Indiana that won the enthusiastic support of regional administrator Valdas Adamkus.[40] At approximately the same time, Thomas Gallagher, the director of EPA's Denver-based National Enforcement Investigations Center who had recently been given responsibility for overseeing the Agency's budding criminal enforcement program, began to lobby other Agency officials for the initiation of a coordinated approach to enforcement inspections and case development.[41] In EPA headquarters, Senior Enforcement Counsel Richard Mays, with the support and encouragement of F. Henry Habicht III, the Justice Department's assistant attorney general for lands and natural resources, as well as the backing of the Agency's Office of Administration and Resources Management, drafted a formal multimedia enforcement strategy. That innovative approach was to be implemented at waste disposal facilities subject to RCRA and the Toxic Substances Control Act at which violations of the Clean Air and Clean Water Acts were also found.[42]

Despite these developments, multimedia enforcement, as a meaningful component of EPA's enforcement efforts, played a small role during the mid-1980s. For the most part, as Thomas Gallagher observed, EPA enforcement of that period was divided into "four EPAs: the water, the air, the hazardous waste, and the toxic substances EPA. It was very, very difficult to get a measure of crosscutting cooperation among all of these."[43] Nonetheless, the sporadic multimedia efforts that developed during the tenure of Lee Thomas and Thomas Adams ultimately gave rise to a more significant attempt to integrate EPA's media-based enforcement programs during the presidency of George H. W. Bush.

Another important development during this time was the advent of multi-case enforcement initiatives in designated priority areas. For the first time, the Agency and the Department of Justice attempted to streamline referral and filing procedures for similar civil judicial actions and to publicize these efforts as a way of enhancing their deterrent effects. Thus, in fiscal year 1985 (i.e., the period between October 1, 1984, and September 30, 1985) the Justice Department filed eleven cases nationwide on EPA's behalf against violators of Clean Air Act requirements regarding asbestos control during building demolition. The Agency also targeted for civil suit publicly owned municipal sewage treatment plants that had not submitted approvable local pretreatment programs, as required by the Clean Water Act. It issued thirteen administrative complaints to redress violations of Toxic Substances Control Act pre-manufacture notification requirements."[44] Similarly, in March 1986 EPA announced the filing of fifteen lawsuits against municipalities that were in violation of Clean Water Act requirements other than the pretreatment rules. In the same year, the Agency and the DOJ initiated coordinated civil actions against ten violators of Safe Drinking Water Act underground injection control regulations, eight metal-coating facilities in the Los Angeles basin, and twenty-seven electroplating plants located in the New York City metropolitan area.[45]

Beyond this, the Agency placed renewed emphasis on an enforcement technique upon which it had briefly relied in the early 1970s: the debarment of government contractors who were persistent violators of environmental standards by publicly listing them in the *Federal Register*. In 1986 EPA revised its regulations to facilitate contractor listing and established a separate staff in the Office of Enforcement and Compliance Monitoring to work with regional personnel in carrying out this program. These efforts yielded at least modest success. Between January 1986 and October 1988 the number of facilities on the Agency's Violating Facility List grew from three to seventeen, and the realistic possibility of such listing actions improved EPA's position in negotiating settlement of additional enforcement cases.[46]

EPA's enforcement work during this period was also characterized by increased levels of measured formal activity, a fact that the Agency sought to publicize by the periodic release of statistics that lauded its enforcement accomplishments. Thus, in April 1986 EPA reported that fiscal year

1985 had been a "record year" for the Agency with respect to the number of its civil and criminal referrals to the Department of Justice. In addition, it indicated that the Agency had issued 2,785 administrative orders during the same twelve months, the second highest number of orders issued by EPA in a fiscal year since 1981.[47] One year later, an EPA report on enforcement accomplishments stated that "in fiscal year 1986, state and federal environmental civil, criminal and administrative enforcement actions continued to be undertaken at record levels . . . the Agency referred 342 judicial actions to the Department of Justice, compared to 276 last year. . . . The Criminal Enforcement Program experienced its most successful and productive year since the program commenced by referring an all-time high of forty five criminal cases to DOJ."[48] In April 1988 the Agency indicated that "in fiscal 1987, EPA and the states achieved record levels of environmental enforcement, using the full range of enforcement authorities. The Agency referred 304 civil cases to the Department of Justice. . . . The Agency established an all-time record for the largest amount of civil penalties imposed in a year . . . over $24 million."[49]

Of particular significance during the concluding portion of the Reagan administration was the growth of criminal environmental enforcement. Under prodding from Congress, this program gradually increased in size and importance, both within the Agency and at the Department of Justice. This trend was carefully monitored in the private sector.[50] As one attorney who represents regulated corporations told me: "The willingness of the administration to bring criminal actions against corporate officials has enhanced their interest in supervising their lower-ranking personnel to pay attention to environmental values. Reading in the paper about criminal actions being brought against one's industry or one's company is a great motivator, I would think."[51]

Two other general EPA enforcement trends from the latter part of the Reagan administration are also worthy of mention: a continuing attempt by the Agency's Washington, D.C., headquarters, and some EPA regional offices, to promote cooperative enforcement relationships with state and local officials, and the steady decentralization, to EPA regional personnel, of authority to initiate and settle enforcement cases. Under Thomas and Adams, the Agency made an effort to implement its state-EPA agreement guidance by entering into enforcement agreements with relevant officials in individual states. This effort did succeed in increasing federal-state cooperation in a number of instances and in improving intergovernmental consultation and advance planning concerning certain enforcement cases.

At the same time, however, federal-state controversies continued to arise with regard to EPA's occasional practice of overfilling, i.e., initiating a separate federal enforcement action when the Agency determines that the terms on which a state government has resolved a particular enforcement matter are "grossly deficient" and inadequate.[52] In addition, certain EPA regional offices and states continued to differ with respect to the acceptability of the definitions employed by the states in assessing and reporting on their own enforcement achievements.[53]

While decentralization had been a feature of earlier EPA administrations, it was given new impetus under the leadership of Lee Thomas and Thomas Adams. These managers saw increased regional autonomy as an effective means of streamlining the Agency's overall enforcement effort. Despite determined and at times bitter resistance from career professionals at headquarters and key players on Capitol Hill, Thomas and Adams gradually expanded the independence of regional enforcement officials in the management of particular enforcement cases.[54]

This trend toward regional decentralization was especially pronounced in the Superfund Program. In the spring of 1987 EPA regional offices were delegated the authority to implement a number of important aspects of Superfund, including studies and investigations relating to cost recovery, special notices, demand letters and unilateral administrative orders to PRPs, and both de minimus agreements and administrative orders on consent.[55] The following year, regional Superfund authority was further extended in a series of memorandums from Thomas Adams to regional officials. On January 14, 1988, Adams provided the regions with guidance respecting the implementation of an agreement between the Agency and the Department of Justice that expanded the categories of civil judicial enforcement cases that were to be referred directly from regional offices to DOJ without the prior concurrence of EPA's headquarters.[56] The following month, Adams formally informed the Agency's regional administrators that "a fundamental premise of our efforts is that the Regions have the lead in the Agency in case selection, consistent with Agency priorities, and in case development and case management."[57] On May 2, 1988, that "premise" was acted upon further in a memorandum that listed only eight relatively narrow categories of enforcement cases in which the involvement of headquarters staff attorneys was deemed warranted.[58] One month later, Thomas Adams and J. Winston ("Win") Porter, assistant administrator of EPA's Office of Solid Waste and Emergency Response, jointly issued a memo expanding the authority of regional administrators by waiving the requirement of headquarters concurrence in CERCLA settlements and agreements, pursuant to Superfund sections 106 and 107, where total claims did not exceed $30 million.[59]

The Superfund Program, which continued to receive considerable attention from top EPA managers during the Thomas and Adams years, underwent other changes as well. The most significant of these were a direct or indirect result of SARA. As one EPA (and former Justice Department) official described the period preceding the enactment of this act, "SARA had a very difficult birth process. There were two years of legislative debate leading up to the Superfund Amendments of 1986. The legislation came late and the funding mechanism for Superfund had lapsed. As a result . . . it took some period of time for Superfund to come back to speed. The program suffered accordingly."[60]

Once in place, however, SARA engendered a somewhat more systematic and uniform approach to EPA's implementation of Superfund, particularly in the area of enforcement.[61] The Agency increased its reliance on unilateral administrative orders to PRPs[62] and established a standard process for negotiating cleanup agreements, by pre-established deadlines, on specific terms favorable to government negotiators.[63] "Model packages" were also developed for RI/FSs and for the documentation to support successful cost recovery litigation.[64] A planning process was established to monitor regional CERCLA activities and progress.[65] EPA put greater emphasis on private, rather than public, funding of Superfund cleanups.[66] All in all, in the words of one key Justice Department employee of that time, following SARA "the Superfund process became regularized, at least to the extent that things now moved in some discernible, organized time frame through the system."[67]

With standardization and increased responsibility came additional resources. On February 4, 1985, the Reagan administration asked Congress to increase EPA's operating budget for fiscal year 1986 by 3 percent, including a 45 percent increase in funding for CERCLA activities, as compared with the previous year.[68] Congress, anticipating passage of SARA the following year, raised the Agency's appropriation for Superfund enforcement activities from $39 million to $52 million. That funding level rose again over the next two fiscal years—to $100 million in fiscal 1987 and $125 million in fiscal 1988.[69] EPA increased the size of its Superfund enforcement staff during the Reagan administration's final two years from 765 to 1,027 full-time employees, including 103 new attorneys in the Agency's offices of regional counsel.[70]

Notwithstanding the salutary trends and events described above, EPA's enforcement programs were beset by a number of significant problems during Lee Thomas's tenure as EPA administrator. Some of these difficulties were internal to the Agency's administrative structure, and some were engendered by criticism of EPA from outside. Some were a result of errors and inconsistencies in the approaches of the Agency's top managers; others were merely a continuation of troubles that had arisen at earlier phases of EPA's development. Whatever their origins, however, in their totality these problems diminished the genuine progress that characterized EPA's enforcement work in the Thomas years. Because of them, EPA enforcement in the mid to late 1980s cannot be said to have been "out of the woods."

Internally, the Agency's enforcement work in this period was marked by prolonged and intensive squabbling for influence and decision-making authority among the various offices within EPA's headquarters that had been given enforcement mandates and responsibilities.[71] The scope and intensity of these disagreements varied with the substantive issues and personalities involved. Nonetheless, in a number of instances, internal EPA headquarters disputes had the effect of prolonging the development of Agency policies and negotiating positions. As one headquarters manager during that time later stated:

> [EPA] didn't have people [in headquarters] who could give answers quickly. [In matters of case development strategy] you couldn't move from point A to point B without getting everyone in the Western Hemisphere to agree. . . . On any particular issue you might have three or four different [Agency] positions, but it was never consistent. . . . It was the worst management nightmare you could think of.[72]

These problems were particularly acute in the Superfund Program, where headquarters policy-making authority was widely distributed. In March 1989 the Environmental Law Institute concluded:

> Responsibility for developing and implementing an enforcement strategy for the Superfund Program is diffused, on the national level, among four EPA offices—the office of waste programs enforcement, the office of emergency and remedial response, the office of enforcement and compliance monitoring and the office of general counsel. As a result of this diffusion of responsibility, it is unclear who has ultimate responsibility for

a national enforcement strategy. Each office tries to shape the Agency's direction, and the Agency's position and performance may be weakened in consequence.[73]

In addition to interoffice rivalry, EPA's enforcement programs experienced continuing shortages of resources during the mid to late 1980s. To many observers, this problem reflected general budget shortfalls that detrimentally affected the Agency as a whole.[74] It was particularly acute in the RCRA enforcement program and with respect to full-time EPA criminal investigators. Even in the Superfund Program, however, resource problems persisted in certain areas, notwithstanding the increases in staffing that occurred at this time.[75]

EPA's shortage of enforcement resources contributed to two other persistent and interrelated problems: noncompetitive salary scales for professional staff members and a relatively high level of staff attrition. In October 1987 the GAO reported that the annual pay for federal attorneys, chemists, and engineers—three key EPA enforcement occupations—trailed salary levels in the private sector by $7,800 to $41,300, or 25 to 60 percent.[76] This gap, which was merely an extreme version of a general—and continuing—disparity between governmental and private pay scales for professional employees, contributed to persistent turnover among EPA enforcement attorneys and technical personnel. The attrition problem was especially acute among hydrologists, chemists, toxicologists, and attorneys in the agency's growing CERCLA program.[77] However, staff turnover was not limited to Superfund. In fact, as one seasoned congressional observer noted, in all of EPA's enforcement programs "[p]eople go there at a relatively young age, relatively inexperienced. Then, just as they get over the learning curve and hit their stride, they get hired away [by employers in the private sector]. This happens to everyone from inspectors to attorneys.[78]

In addition to attrition, EPA enforcement managers faced difficulties in recruiting qualified and experienced staff members from outside the federal government, particularly technical experts with relevant experience in universities or agencies of state government. This was a result of excessively rigid civil service classification standards, which overemphasized the importance of federal agency experience in the rating of job candidates. It was also caused by time-consuming requirements for posting notices of vacant positions and for screening and rating applicants. As one EPA regional office noted in exasperation: "Sometimes the procedural aspects of it get to be overwhelming. Often, by the time you've completed all the required procedures, the [experienced] candidate you really wanted to hire has accepted a position someplace else."[79]

EPA enforcement during the Thomas period was also characterized by significant inconsistencies in the approaches of different regional offices.[80] In part, these discrepancies were a result of differences in the attitudes and preferences of the Agency's regional administrators, who were often appointed with the political support of state environmental officials within the regions. As the regulatory historian Alfred A. Marcus has written, after EPA's regional offices were established in the early 1970s,

> [t]he regional administrators perceived issues not only in terms of their own obligation to headquarters, but also in terms of their commitments to the states. In fact, if a regional administrator became aligned with the states' interests, he or she could block decisive Agency action by refusing to carry out national policy. Headquarters could do little to compel a regional administrator to change his or her ways because, once appointed, a regional administrator quickly became entrenched. EPA in Washington could risk firing a regional administrator only if it was willing to alienate his or her local supporters.[81]

Regional enforcement differences were also a result of variations in the enforcement attitudes of state officials. Thus, EPA's own inspector general, in testimony before a subcommittee of the Senate Committee on Environment and Public Works, gave the following candid response to a question posed by Senator Harry Reid (D-NV):

> [EPA oversight of state enforcement programs] varies from region to region and state to state. Some states have, apparently, a stronger commitment on their own to enforcement activities. And so, it is easier for EPA to deal with them because they're more in tune with what EPA wants to accomplish. Others are more difficult. . . . There is a fragile relationship. On the one hand, EPA has got to seek the cooperation of the states, yet on the other hand it's got to beat them over the head if they're not doing a good job. That's a difficult thing to pull off. And we think there are regions [that] are falling short of being able to pull that off effectively.[82]

Whatever its precise causes, EPA's enforcement efforts in the Thomas years were characterized by regional disparities in the significance, formality, and assertiveness of enforcement activities—a phenomenon which predated Lee Thomas's terms as the Agency's administrator and continues to some extent to this writing.

Another shortcoming of EPA enforcement in the second half of the Reagan administration was the inadequacy of much of the formal guidance provided by the Agency's headquarters to regional enforcement personnel. One regional enforcement supervisor spoke for many when he stated: "The [headquarters] guidance that comes out is not that helpful to [regional] people who practice every day. It's relevant, but it doesn't really wrestle with the hard questions. It's almost obvious. It doesn't get to the fine distinctions you need to make."[83]

In some respects, the enforcement guidance from EPA headquarters was too extensive. Its remarkable volume led one headquarters attorney to complain: "We in headquarters develop so many guidances that we cannot keep track of them."[84] On the other hand, the Agency's guidance failed to address certain important questions of national enforcement policy, including, most notably, the basis for distinguishing civil and administrative enforcement cases from matters in which criminal prosecution would be appropriate.[85] In other instances carefully constructed national enforcement policies, widely acknowledged to be equitable and sound, were ignored or implemented in the breach by regional enforcement officials.[86]

Another set of enforcement problems that were particularly acute during this period concern the EPA's collection and use of data regarding the compliance status of industrial and municipal sources of pollution. For the most part, the Agency's enforcement information support systems were established as media-specific tools for headquarters oversight of regional and state enforcement activities. The systems were designed with little attention to data quality. They also required regional and state compliance personnel to enter a great volume of information into systems that had little operational benefit to them. As a result, according to an outside computer consultant employed by EPA's Office of Information Resources Management:

> Poor quality and timeliness of data plague several of the centralized [EPA enforcement] data bases, limiting their reliability and usefulness even as headquarters tools for oversight and external reporting. . . . Further, just the inability to answer basic questions . . . frequently causes numerous staff to be diverted from their regular duties, and often leads to unnecessary friction among Congress, the Agency and various states.[87]

These information management weaknesses posed a particular problem during the Agency's initial attempts to institute multimedia enforcement. Incompatibilities of design and content, combined with indifference and resistance from some regional enforcement personnel, severely restricted the utility of EPA's numerous enforcement data systems in cross-media initiatives.[88]

Federal environmental enforcement of the mid to late 1980s was also inhibited by a recurrence of the institutional rivalry between EPA and the Department of Justice that had unsettled enforcement efforts in the late 1970s. In an article in early 1989 one former Justice Department manager described the situation in these words:

> The environmental enforcement program is further plagued by constant turf fights between the DOJ and EPA over who will actually litigate the cases in court. The tension from these turf battles is always simmering, and frequently affects the relationship between the DOJ attorney and his EPA counterpart. Unfortunately, such tension is an unnecessary drain of energy that could be better spent on developing and prosecuting enforcement cases.[89]

While discord between Agency and Justice Department attorneys affected enforcement in all environmental media, it was particularly acute in the growing and resource-intensive Superfund Program. The essence of the problem there was aptly described in a study by the Environmental Law Institute:

> [S]ome EPA and DOJ personnel have expressed dissatisfaction with each other's performance in handling Superfund enforcement cases. Complaints that DOJ delays approval of settlements (sometimes attributed by EPA to bureaucratic delay, sometimes to a line attorney's inability to perceive and resolve supervisors' concerns early in the process) are countered by criticism of EPA's preparation of cases. Some EPA personnel complain that DOJ is risk averse and unwilling to file certain cases, while DOJ officials express reluctance to file certain inadequately prepared or inappropriate cases because they fear weakening the enforcement program. These tensions inevitably weaken the program.[90]

Other difficulties between EPA and the Department of Justice were caused by resource limitations within the DOJ itself rather than by avoidable frictions in working relationships among professional staff members.[91] One regional enforcement attorney I interviewed stated:

> Frankly, [the Department of] Justice is swamped. They're working as hard as they possibly can, but they just don't have the people to do all the work that has to be done. There is a problem just moving paper through DOJ. It's not unusual for it to take six months for a consent decree that's been negotiated and signed by the defendants to be entered. Things are really slowing down. They're good attorneys. I have a lot of respect for them. I just wish there were more people there.[92]

During this period, the work of many EPA enforcement personnel also suffered because of a situation that, like interagency rivalry with DOJ, had its roots in the 1970s: extraordinarily inadequate physical working conditions. This problem was not universal within the Agency. In fact, the office facilities that housed professional enforcement staffs in many EPA regions were entirely adequate and, in some instances (at least by federal government standards) relatively luxurious. In other EPA regional offices however, the Agency's enforcement staff worked in small, cramped, noisy offices with few windows and battered furniture.

The situation was most extreme in EPA's Waterside Mall headquarters complex. This building, designed in the 1960s as an apartment complex, was remarkably ill-suited for housing government offices. Its narrow and confusingly arranged corridors, tiny and overcrowded offices, periodic security problems, and general physical isolation from most of the rest of official Washington were a persistent source of irritation and resentment among the Agency's overworked staff.[93]

This situation was made far worse in the mid-1980s by the emergence of severe indoor air pollution problems that caused serious illnesses for several members of the EPA's headquarters enforcement staff.[94] In fact, the Agency did relocate some of its enforcement staff to better quarters in Crystal City, Virginia (at some cost compared to the physical compactness and efficiency of its headquarters operations), and other steps were also taken to ameliorate the problem. Nonetheless, one EPA enforcement manager told me at the time: "It's a real blight on the Agency that its people have to labor in conditions like this and feel that they have to jeopardize their long-term physical well-being in order to serve the United States."[95]

In addition to (and in some cases as a result of) these varied internal problems, during the last quarter of Ronald Reagan's first term as president—and the entirety of his second term—EPA's enforcement program experienced recurrent difficulties in its relationship with Congress, the press, and certain national environmental organizations. Notwithstanding the improvements the Agency had made in the nature and volume of its enforcement activities, throughout this period the relationship between top EPA officials and Capitol Hill was harsh and adversarial. As one observer has noted, Agency officials were called to testify at "frequent, acrimonious oversight hearings."[96] EPA enforcement programs were repeatedly criticized in studies prepared by the GAO and the Agency's own inspector general, and many of their criticisms were noted, repeated, or supplemented by journalists or environmental citizens groups.

Some of the mistrust and conflict that characterized EPA-congressional relations in this era were undoubtedly a remnant of controversies in the Gorsuch years. The stark breakdown of the Agency's enforcement efforts between 1981 and 1983 did severe damage to the Agency's reputation on Capitol Hill. In retrospect, it seems unlikely that *any* efforts by top EPA managers—no matter how skillful or well intentioned—could have *fully* restored the trust of interested representatives and senators and their staffs for the remainder of the Reagan years. Nonetheless, at least some of the continuing tensions that pervaded EPA-congressional relations in the enforcement area from 1985 through 1988 can be attributed to the Agency's own political leaders. Their inability to anticipate and avoid criticism from Capitol Hill and to cultivate informal channels of communication with key congressional staff members undoubtedly exacerbated the difficulties they faced in obtaining Congress's approval and support.

One incident that took place very early in Thomas Adams's term as assistant administrator for enforcement and compliance monitoring served to focus and intensify congressional suspicions. In September 1986 Adams decided to institute several changes in the management of EPA's headquarters enforcement organization. Among these was the transfer of Frederick P. Stiehl, then the Agency's associate enforcement counsel for hazardous waste enforcement, to the position of associate enforcement counsel for pesticides and toxic substances. As Adams later recalled the event, his decision was motivated by a desire to replace Stiehl with a manager who "knew how to make things work politically within the Agency." He viewed Stiehl as "worn down" and maintained that the transfer would benefit Stiehl's career.[97] Stiehl, on the other hand, remembered the incident differently. He stated that, rather than being worn down, he had been quite excited at the prospect of grappling with the challenges he anticipated in implementing the soon-to-be-enacted SARA. Stiehl viewed his transfer as "disruptive to the staff" and "the wrong decision, made in the wrong way, at the wrong time."[98]

Whatever its appropriateness, Stiehl's impending reassignment, which became effective on October 12, was promptly made known to Congress by concerned EPA staff members. On October 6, 1986, Representative Dingell wrote a letter to EPA Administrator Lee Thomas questioning the legality of the Stiehl transfer. Describing this personnel action as a matter "of some urgency and concern" which had had "a serious impact on employee morale," Dingell wrote:

> Mr. Stiehl is a career member of the Senior Executive Service (SES) and, as such, is afforded the protection of 5 U.S.C. § 3395(e). The . . . statute prohibits, in pertinent part, the involuntary reassignment of a career SES appointee within 120 days after the appointment in the agency of the career appointee's most immediate supervisor, who is a non-career appointee and has authority to reassign the career appointee. In this instance the [Thomas] Adams-instigated reassignment of Mr. Stiehl is scheduled to occur approximately 50 days after he [Adams] became the assistant administrator.[99]

Lee Thomas responded to Dingell in a letter dated December 9, 1986. He asserted that, after carefully reviewing the matter, the Agency believed that it had acted in "full compliance with statutory requirements," since Stiehl's transfer had been formally instituted by another EPA official, rather than Thomas Adams.[100] However legally defensible, the reassignment of Frederick Stiehl harmed the Agency's enforcement efforts in two ways. First, the incident occurred when all of the decisions and policies of the newly appointed assistant administrator for enforcement and compliance monitoring were likely to be closely scrutinized. It also came at a time when Stiehl, who had participated in the Agency's hazardous waste enforcement efforts from their inception, had an established and cordial working relationship with congressional committee staff members and a reputation among them as a dedicated, no-nonsense enforcement official. Stiehl's abrupt transfer was thus viewed with concern by members of Congress, already skeptical of the EPA's publicly announced commitment to a vigorous enforcement effort. Second, together with the incipient decentralization of enforcement authority to regional officials, Stiehl's reassignment caused anxiety to many of the Agency's headquarters Superfund enforcement staff. One trade journal noted that Adams's organizational changes had "sparked fear among some Agency staff that a 'less confrontational' style is being developed in the enforcement office, that will result in headquarters becoming less willing to oppose the regions over controversial enforcement actions."[101] Several present and former members of the EPA enforcement staff later confirmed that the Stiehl transfer contributed to a decline in headquarters staff morale, a decline that increased with the passage of time.[102]

Rather than being an isolated incident, the congressional response to Thomas Adams's transfer of Frederick Stiehl set the stage for a chilly — and at times openly hostile — relationship between the Agency and Capitol Hill in the enforcement area. Over the next few years, congressional committees and subcommittees conducted frequent, intensive, and often adversarial oversight hearings on such diverse aspects of EPA enforcement as PCB disposal under the Toxic Substances Control Act, the organization of EPA's criminal enforcement program, "sham recycling" of hazardous wastes, implementation of the Superfund Program, hazardous waste site closure, and the enforcement of environmental requirements at federally owned and operated facilities.[103] These investigations were supplemented by a number of reports by the GAO, usually prepared at the request of congressional committees or individual senators or members of the House of Representatives, that found fault with different components of the Agency's enforcement program.[104] EPA was also taken to task in reports compiled by its own independent office of inspector general.[105]

Of all the external castigation that EPA's enforcement programs received in this period, the most passionate and sustained outcry came in the spring and summer of 1988. Once again the focus was the Agency's implementation of the amended Superfund statute. On April 11, 1988, the Subcommittee on Energy, Environment and Natural Resources of the House Committee on Government Operations held a hearing in Crystal City, Texas, at the site of a hazardous waste disposal facility that EPA had earlier placed on its National Priorities List. The opening statement of Representative Mike Synar (D-OK), the subcommittee's chairman, typified the criticism leveled at the Agency throughout the hearing:

> Two years after the [SARA] Amendments became law, the prospect for swift and permanent cleanup of these hazardous waste sites is not good. We are spending lots of money; we are fattening the pocketbooks of a lot of contractors; and we are also subsidizing the development of lots of thick, detailed technical documents. But . . . somewhere in these lengthy,

technical Superfund processes we have lost sight of the ultimate goal, and that is the protection of the environment and public health from hazardous waste.[106]

Similar sentiments were expressed two months later by Representative Dennis Eckart (D-TX) at a hearing of the Dingell Committee:

> Is the Superfund Program, in fact, on a course headed for success, or is it struggling for a passing grade? From the information we have gathered in preparation for this hearing, it appears that all is not well, particularly in the pace of remedial activity, the vigor of the enforcement program, and the selection of cleanups that emphasize treatment of the waste and permanent solutions.[107]

While acknowledging some EPA successes, especially with regard to the initiation of preliminary assessments and RI/FSs and the development of a "good, solid" removal program, Eckart decried the Agency's inconsistency regarding the remedies chosen at Superfund sites and its inattention to CERCLA cleanup standards and permanent treatment requirements.

These concerns found support in two outside assessments of the remedial aspects of the Superfund Program that were released on the very day Eckart's subcommittee met. The first of these, *Right Train, Wrong Track: Failed Leadership in the Superfund Cleanup Program*, was the seventy-three-page product of a joint effort by the Hazardous Waste Treatment Council and six national environmental organizations.[108] It analyzed and critiqued EPA's Superfund site remedy selection processes by reviewing all seventy-five RODs prepared by the agency in calendar year 1987. The report found that EPA had emphasized capping and containment of hazardous wastes at abandoned dumps to the near exclusion of permanent treatment technologies. It accused the Agency of setting cleanup goals unscientifically, ignoring natural resource damage, and exempting Superfund sites from applicable environmental standards. Based on these findings, the authors of *Right Train, Wrong Track* concluded:

> In rewriting Superfund in 1986, Congress provided EPA with the engine and resources to run a program sorely in need of strengthening. While it is difficult to imagine a more specific or better funded statute, the Agency has set its program on the wrong course, a course of repetition of past mistakes. Congress has provided the right train, but EPA has chosen the wrong track. Unless Agency approach, policy, and attitude to the new

statute [are] changed in the immediate future, the Agency will derail the statute.[109]

Equally critical—and even more damaging to EPA—was a report by the congressional Office of Technology Assessment (OTA) titled *Are We Cleaning Up? 10 Superfund Case Studies*.[110] This study focused on RODs and RI/FSs prepared by EPA regional personnel at ten Superfund sites across the United States. It found that the Superfund Program had been inconsistent in its selection of treatment remedies at similar sites and that permanently effective treatment technologies were being employed too infrequently. The OTA noted that hazardous waste cleanup technology was still a new and fast-changing field and that the Agency's Superfund workforce was relatively young and inexperienced. It criticized EPA for failing to use central management controls to further the Agency's collective understanding of common site characteristics and common cleanup problems and solutions; and it concluded that, as a result of that shortcoming, the site cleanup decisions made by EPA at the ten sites upon which OTA had focused were "questionable."[111]

These reports, which received prominent coverage in the media, were seen by many in Congress as independent confirmation that their suspicions about poor Agency implementation of CERCLA were soundly based. At EPA, on the other hand, they were viewed with consternation. Almost immediately, the Agency's top managers initiated a public campaign to discredit the OTA and Hazardous Waste Treatment Council reports and defend EPA's Superfund performance. In a June 18, 1988, interview with the *New York Times*, Win Porter referred to OTA's report as "a limited, superficial study" that drew "global conclusions" from inadequate data. He said that the study had been performed by a few officials sitting in Washington "while I have 3000 people out there working hard to make the program a success." He also stated, "I really resent them undermining our credibility with the communities we work with."[112]

Two days later, in remarks to an annual conference of the American Pollution Control Association in Dallas, Texas, Administrator Thomas took a similar tack. He stated that he resented that the OTA had made such broad allegations although it examined only ten sites and had "only minimal contact" with the EPA's Superfund workforce.[113]

At a July 21, 1988, seminar sponsored by the Congressional Environmental Study Conference, two other agency officials, Lloyd Guerci and Walter Kovalick, reiterated the Agency's defense. Guerci accused the authors of both *Right Train, Wrong Track* and the OTA study, who were present at the conference, of being "deliberately misleading and unfair." He contended that many of the remedies chosen at Superfund sites were an inevitable result of the poor financial condition of both the hazardous waste site PRPs and the governments of the states involved. Kovalick emphasized that, in selecting site remedies, the Agency had tried to focus on all nine of the remedy selection criteria that Congress had included in the statute. He accused EPA's critics of choosing only one or two of those criteria and insisting that the Agency apply them to the exclusion of the other factors.[114]

Whatever impact these countercharges may have had on the Agency's Superfund staff, they did little to assuage EPA's congressional critics. In fact, they seem to have heightened the legislators' distrust. The controversy over EPA's enforcement performance in general—and the Superfund Program in particular—continued to the end of Ronald Reagan's presidency. It provided both a peril and an opportunity for the EPA leadership appointed by his successor.

Modest Progress and Renewed Suspicion: EPA Enforcement in the Bush I Administration

Environmental protection was a significant issue in the presidential election of 1988. To the surprise of many environmentalists, who expected a continuation of Ronald Reagan's public conservatism on environmental issues, candidate George H. W. Bush attacked the environmental record of his Democratic opponent, Michael Dukakis, on the cleanup of Boston Harbor and pledged that he (Bush) would be an "environmental president" who would take firm measures to halt the greenhouse effect and stop the destruction of wetland areas. Over the course of Bush's administration, this more pro-environmental attitude resulted in beneficial changes in EPA's enforcement efforts, particularly in the early years. Nonetheless, those efforts continued to be bedeviled by a range of difficulties and, over time, by revived congressional mistrust.

Bush's post-election appointments to high-level positions at the EPA were generally consistent with the conservationist tone of his campaign. He began by choosing the president of the World Wildlife Fund and the Conservation Foundation, William K. ("Bill") Reilly, to be the Agency's new administrator. Reilly had served as a senior staff member of the Council on Environmental Quality in the early 1970s and was considered a protégé of former EPA administrator Russell Train. F. Henry ("Hank") Habicht II, who had been assistant attorney general for lands and natural resources at the Department of Justice during the Reagan years, was selected as deputy administrator. Both choices were generally well received by environmental advocates and were confirmed by the Senate without significant dissension.

However, the establishment of a new top management team at EPA had little immediate impact on the controversy that had surrounded EPA enforcement in general—and the Superfund Program in particular—at the close of the Reagan administration. In the spring of 1989, two further detailed and critical assessments of the Agency's implementation of CERCLA were publicly released. Although the first of these, a 210-page report by the Environmental Law Institute (ELI) titled *Toward a More Effective Superfund Enforcement Program* (the ELI Report), had been prepared by its authors at the request of EPA itself, which had been asked by the Appropriations Committees of both houses of Congress to commission a study of CERCLA enforcement, the report's conclusions were far from complimentary.[1]

The ELI Report found a number of flaws in the existing Superfund Program that, in its opinion, prevented the program from achieving "effective enforcement," which was defined as a regular, prompt, and efficient inducement for private responsible parties to clean up Superfund sites completely and at their own expense. The Agency was criticized for failing to communicate a national enforcement strategy to regional personnel, for declining to recognize or rely upon the potential power of its statutory enforcement authorities, for conducting ineffective PRP searches, and for perpetuating a duplicative and inefficient organizational structure at the headquarters level. Its institutional arrangements for measuring performance and allocating resources were also seen as obstacles to efficient enforcement.[2] In a critical passage of the ELI Report, the Agency's leaders were exhorted to provide clear and consistent support for Superfund enforcement:

> A sense of urgency and commitment should accompany the pronouncements of Agency leaders in order to promote support for program goals and foster cooperation between managers, especially between those at headquarters and those in the regions. Clearly stated missions build strong cultures and strong cultures drive and control the program.[3]

Further doubts about EPA's approach to Superfund implementation were expressed in a 214-page critique issued in May 1989 by Senators Frank R. Lautenberg (D-NJ) and David Durenberger (R-MN), the chairman and ranking minority member of the Subcommittee on Superfund, Ocean and Water Protection of the Senate Committee on Environment and Public Works.[4] The Lautenberg-Durenberger Report, which was drafted by professional staff members Seth Mones and Jimmie Powell, summarized many of the criticisms of EPA's post-1986 Superfund Program that had been raised at five public hearings the subcommittee had held during 1987. It noted inconsistencies in regional approaches to cleanup remedies and in the screening of sites for inclusion on the National Priorities List, delays in the accomplishment of various cleanup steps, "failure to oversee and prevent state noncompliance with EPA requirements, and conflicts of interest by the Agency's Superfund contractors." Like the ELI Report, Lautenberg and Durenberger's study found that the Agency had underutilized its full range of enforcement tools by being unwilling to enhance its negotiating posture through initiation of enforcement actions, such as unilateral administrative orders, during negotiations. "In fact," Lautenberg and Durenberger concluded, "EPA has allowed negotiations to continue beyond the time period the Agency itself deems acceptable."[5]

Some of the Lautenberg-Durenberger Report's harshest criticisms concerned the Agency's proposed deferral policy, the suggestion by some EPA officials that Superfund sites not be placed or maintained on the National Priorities List if they could be addressed by PRPs or other federal or state programs:

> Deferral of sites with rankings sufficient for inclusion on the Superfund cleanup list could deprive these sites of the many comprehensive requirements and authorities applied at other Superfund sites. . . . EPA's attempt to limit the size of the Superfund list through a deferral policy threatens to be an exception capable of swallowing a good portion of the law.[6]

These alarms did not go unheeded by the Agency's new set of top managers. At his January 1989 confirmation hearing before the Senate Committee on Environment and Public Works, Bill Reilly committed himself to an assertive EPA enforcement effort. He told the assembled senators:

> I want to stress before this committee that I understand and accept as my duty, first and foremost, to implement the environmental laws of this land as Congress has written them. . . . [E]nforcement must be inspired by a sense of vigor and urgency, for the aim of the enterprise is no less than the protection of human health, of life, and of the natural order that sustains civilization. So I pledge to take aggressive and timely enforcement action, whenever it is warranted, to safeguard public health or environmental quality.[7]

Deputy Administrator Habicht made similar statements in testimony before Congress.[8]

Aware that the criticisms that were being made were principally directed at policies and approaches established by their predecessors in office, Reilly and Habicht viewed the situation as an opportunity to streamline the Superfund Program and establish the sincerity of their pledge to invigorate the EPA's enforcement efforts.

In one of his first acts as administrator, Reilly directed a task group of EPA managers and professionals to undertake "as thorough a review of the [Superfund] program as could be completed in about ninety days."[9] This review, conducted under the supervision of Lewis Crampton, a special assistant to the administrator who later became the Agency's associate administrator for external affairs, was intended to respond to EPA's outside critics and acknowledge the need for improvement.[10] The report it produced, which came to be known as the Ninety Day Study, contained detailed recommendations concerning the Agency's implementation of CERCLA, a number of which "crystallized" ideas that had been discussed within the Agency in the closing years of the Reagan administration.[11]

The Ninety Day Study began with a candid admission:

> In the often contentious debate that has developed over Superfund policy, EPA has operated without its most valuable asset, the benefit of the doubt. Though the program has picked up speed, Superfund continues to fall short of public expectations. Whether fairly or not, debate centers around the program's flaws, both real and perceived—at all levels from national policy to local site management.[12]

To help restore public confidence, the Ninety Day Study recommended a number of measures that promoted consistency in the selection of Superfund site cleanup remedies. The report also suggested specific steps for accelerating and improving remedial actions, bringing innovative techniques to bear on pollution at Superfund sites, giving interested citizens a greater role in the Superfund Program, improving CERCLA management and administrative support, and communicating program results to the public.

In the enforcement area, the Ninety Day Study adopted many of the suggestions that had been made in the ELI Report. It recommended that EPA increase its use of unilateral administrative orders, take prompt enforcement measures against viable and recalcitrant non-settling PRPs, and conduct response actions at all sites with viable PRPs before using the trust fund, except in emergencies. The study also urged the Agency to maximize regional office flexibility in shifting funds among sites, improve its documentation and recovery of removal action costs, improve its coordination with the Justice Department, and undertake a formal study of the organization of the Superfund Program to evaluate whether a reorganization among headquarters offices would be appropriate.

The Ninety Day Study was publicly released, with Administrator Reilly's endorsement, on June 13, 1989. In its preface, Reilly endorsed all of the report's recommendations. Two days later, at a hearing before a subcommittee of the Senate Committee on Environment and Public Works, Reilly responded to a question from Senator Lautenberg by stating that he would refrain from implementing the Agency's proposed deferral policy, unless and until it was specifically reauthorized by Congress.[13] He also pledged a large increase in the budgetary resources the Agency would request from Congress to implement the Ninety Day Study's suggestions.[14]

On Capitol Hill these developments were seen as salutary and encouraging. In the minds of interested members of Congress and their staffs, the new administration's approach effectively disassociated Reilly and Habicht from the unpopular policies of their predecessors.[15] While not uniformly endorsed, it substantially succeeded in boosting the Agency's credibility while generating what Lewis Crampton referred to as a "rhetorical cease-fire" with Congress and other critics.[16]

Fortunately for the Agency's new leadership, this budding improvement in EPA-congressional relations in the enforcement area was accompanied and strengthened by the appointment of a forceful assistant administrator for enforcement and compliance monitoring with established contacts and credibility on Capitol Hill. James M. ("Jim") Strock's nomination was announced on August 4, 1989, and he was confirmed soon afterward with little opposition. Strock had been a special assistant to the EPA administrator from 1983 to 1985. For the following two years, Strock had been a member of the staff of the Senate Committee on Environment and Public Works. Then, after a two-year stint as a senior associate with a Washington, D.C., law firm, he had served from 1988 to 1989 as general counsel and acting director of the U.S. Office of Personnel Management.[17]

Strock's background as a Senate committee staff member proved helpful to him in improving the frequency and tone of communications between the Agency and its congressional overseers. In contrast with the approach of his predecessor Thomas Adams, Strock devoted a good deal of his time to holding informal dialogues with interested congressional committee staff members. Those meetings, together with his existing reputation on Capitol Hill as an advocate of strong and effective EPA enforcement, helped restore the faith of at least some congressional ob-servers in the Agency's commitment to a vigorous enforcement effort.[18]

Internally, Strock saw a need to overcome the fragmentation of en-forcement authority at the EPA headquarters level by extending the re-sponsibility and influence of the office he headed. In that endeavor, he won the support of Administrator Reilly and Reilly's deputy, Hank Habicht.

On April 18, 1990, the Agency's Office of Enforcement and Compli-ance Monitoring was formally reorganized and renamed the Office of En-forcement. A new multimedia Office of Federal Facilities Enforcement was created within this new entity. It included both the former Federal Facilities Hazardous Waste Compliance Office (part of the Office of Solid Waste and Emergency Response) and the Office of Federal Activities that had previously been a part of the Office of Enforcement and Compliance Monitoring. The jurisdiction of the Pesticides and Toxic Substances En-forcement Division was expanded to cover enforcement actions under the community right-to-know provisions of CERCLA Title III. As a way of encouraging a stronger emphasis on RCRA enforcement, the former headquarters Hazardous Waste Enforcement Division was divided into two new units: a Superfund Enforcement Division and an RCRA En-forcement Division. The latter was headed by Kathie Stein, an aggressive attorney who had been recruited from the staff of the Environmental De-fense Fund. In addition, regional counsel, whose offices handled all legal aspects of the enforcement work of EPA regional offices, began to report to the assistant administrator for enforcement rather than to the Agency's general counsel. Regional administrators and deputy administrators were required to be rated periodically by the EPA administrator and his deputy as to their job performance on enforcement activities.[19]

These organizational changes were accomplished despite the vigorous opposition of certain regional counsel. These officials viewed the admin-istrators of their regions as their primary clients. They viewed Strock's proposed reorganization—and his pro-enforcement position generally—as a potential threat to those clients' interests. In addition, the Office of Solid Waste and Emergency Response objected to losing control over some aspects of federal facilities enforcement. Other headquarters and regional officials also resisted various components of Strock's reorganiza-tion plan. As one headquarters enforcement attorney bluntly assessed it,

Strock pushed hard for a stronger role for the office of [enforcement] vis-à-vis other [headquarters] offices within the Agency and vis-à-vis the regions. I think he has pissed some regional people off. I know he's pissed some program office people off. . . . But I think there's been more of a trend to make this office more powerful and more important.[20]

In the civil enforcement area, Strock established a new set of priorities. With the firm and active support of Deputy Administrator Habicht, he stressed the development of a regional screening process to judge the strategic value of individual enforcement cases, coupled with a renewed emphasis on multimedia enforcement. As Strock envisioned it, the case-screening process should be designed to "aid the decision whether a single-media or multimedia response is warranted and what form of authority should be used to address the violation." The process "should involve coordination among the program directors, regional counsels and criminal enforcement agents to assure that the best remedy is selected for a particular case."[21]

With regard to multimedia enforcement, Strock endorsed the development of special enforcement initiatives that would more fully concentrate enforcement efforts and resources toward "resolving specific environmental compliance problems that might fall through the cracks of the traditional statute-specific, media-specific enforcement process."[22] These initiatives would include geographic-based approaches, in which one or more EPA programs would identify all polluting facilities in a given ecosystem (such as Chesapeake Bay) and then inspect those facilities to determine their compliance status and take any enforcement actions necessary to redress noncompliance. Multimedia initiatives would also include compliance-based approaches, in which the Agency would identify patterns of noncompliance by particular corporations or their subsidiaries within and across media. Several EPA programs or regions (or both) would then cooperate in a coordinated enforcement response to resolve noncompliance across all relevant environmental media.[23]

Strock's advocacy of this multimedia approach was endorsed in an important memorandum, dated February 19, 1991, from Deputy Administrator Hank Habicht to the Agency's top managers. Noting that on September 25, 1990, Administrator Reilly had established an overall goal of "twenty-five percent enforcement with multi-media efforts," Habicht stated that that goal "is part of the overall 'integrated' direction in which we are trying to move the Agency." He directed each EPA regional office to prepare an "end of the year report" on its efforts to achieve the administrator's 25 percent multimedia enforcement goal and on how successful these efforts had been. He also asked each region to draft a short transition plan that mapped out "the base program, program-specific and multi-media targeting and enforcement initiatives, and other multi-media enforcement initiatives." He directed the Office of Enforcement to create an Agency work group of headquarters and regional enforcement officials to develop recommendations for multimedia enforcement and "maintain an awareness of the progress of the regions and share results."[24]

This directive coincided with an attempt to establish, within the Agency's Office of Enforcement, an integrated method for obtaining cross-media information. The general concept was that an automated system would be employed to compile a list of the different identification numbers used in the Agency's major enforcement databases to refer to particular regulated facilities. That information would then be employed to access data on regulated facilities.[25]

In addition to multimedia activities, Strock's approach also emphasized better communication of EPA's goals and achievements. In an article published in August 1990 he explained his preferences in that area in this way:

> To get its enforcement message across to Congress, the media, the pub-
> lic and the regulated community, EPA plans to develop better explana-
> tory measures of enforcement improvement—beyond "the numbers"
> when possible—and to communicate such information accurately, clearly
> and concisely. Because no single measure, taken alone, can provide an
> accurate "thumbs up" or "thumbs down" assessment of the enforcement
> program, the Agency is working to develop a series of useful indicators
> of environmental improvement from enforcement. Such indicators will
> range from disseminating compliance rates within targeted industries
> or sectors, to expanding the deterrent impact of large penalties through
> public announcements, to promoting pollution prevention activities in-
> cluded in settlement agreements.[26]

Strock's new enforcement agenda contained several other items, such as assisting state agencies to develop their own cross-media targeting and case-screening capability, developing a comprehensive enforcement training capability with an emphasis on multimedia casework, reviewing existing permits and regulations with a view to enhancing their preci-sion and enforceability, and developing the right mix of EPA adminis-trative, civil, and criminal enforcement cases.[27] In the criminal area he favored more resources, improved training of investigators, and the fostering of a team approach among special agents, enforcement attorneys, and technical staff. He also saw a need to attribute proper emphasis to large, resource-intensive criminal prosecutions in the Agency's management tracking and budget systems.[28]

One of Jim Strock's most innovative EPA enforcement projects was actually completed after his tenure as assistant administrator was over. At Strock's request, six work groups of experienced EPA enforcement professionals prepared a set of reports that analyzed the effectiveness of the Agency's enforcement programs and offered detailed recommendations for improving the enforcement process. This effort, which came to be known as the Enforcement in the 1990s Project, was based on five guiding principles that closely reflected the enforcement philosophy Strock had developed in informal consultation with interested members of Congress and their staffs:

1. Agency/state relationships represent the key to more effective enforcement activity in the future.
2. In targeting enforcement cases, EPA's management system should be sufficiently flexible to encourage multi-media cases.
3. As a means of measurement, and as a medium of communication to the public, the counting of cases, referrals, convictions, penalties and the like, which constitutes "an established and important part" of the enforcement process, should be supplemented by "alternative measurements" which reflect "tangible improvements in environmental quality."
4. Environmental regulations should be developed in such a way that their enforceability is assured from the outset.
5. Positive behavior modifications in the regulated community, and more effective enforcement, can be promoted by the use of innovative approaches, different incentives, and leveraging actions.[29]

The project resulted in a balanced and thoughtful report, finally released in October 1991, that addressed critical areas of EPA enforcement policy.

With the active support of the Agency's two highest officials and other appointees within the Bush I administration, Strock's strong-willed pursuit of his enforcement priorities appears to have had some beneficial impact. In February 1990 the Agency's *Enforcement Accomplishments Report for Fiscal Year 1989* touted "record or near-record levels in virtually every category of enforcement activity."[30] During the first year of the Bush administration, EPA made 364 civil judicial referrals to the Department of Justice and more than four thousand administrative actions. Superfund settlements and judicial enforcement actions increased significantly, as did the value of civil penalties assessed against violators of environmental laws.[31]

While the significance of these numerical indicators can be overstated, they do serve as at least a crude indication of success for the Agency's civil enforcement efforts in this period.

EPA's renewed emphasis on criminal enforcement also bore fruit in the early Bush years. This approach received consistent public and private support from Deputy Administrator Habicht. In testimony before a Senate subcommittee Habicht described criminal enforcement as "critically important." He stated that one of its most important results was "to encourage companies and executives to put systems in place . . . so that they know what's going on, and they know they can't look the other way and think everything will be all right."[32]

Justice Department environmental enforcement statistics for fiscal year 1989 showed a 70 percent increase in the number of pleas and convictions obtained, an 80 percent rise in the value of assessed criminal fines, and a 35 percent increase in jail time imposed on convicted environmental offenders compared with the previous fiscal year.[33] The same set of records reflected further increases the following year. On November 15, 1990, the Department of Justice announced it had brought a "record number" of environmental prosecutions in fiscal year 1990. The 134 indictments returned in that period against alleged violators of federal environmental statutes represented a 33 percent increase over the preceding twelve-month period.[34]

The environmental criminal enforcement efforts of EPA and DOJ received an additional boost from the enactment, in October 1990, of the Pollution Prosecution Act of 1990. Introduced by Senator Joseph Lieberman (D-CT), the legislation called for a 400 percent increase in the number of EPA criminal investigators, as well as the addition of fifty new civil investigators for the Superfund Program.[35] Congress subsequently appropriated the funds necessary to augment the Agency's staff of criminal investigators. However, it declined to provide monies for additional civil investigators.

Another advance during this period was the issuance of a more stringent civil penalty policy for RCRA violations that called for the assessment of substantially increased forfeitures. The new policy established a matrix with three penalty classifications based upon the seriousness of the violations in question. It required EPA regional offices to provide documentation to support the penalties they assessed against RCRA violators and to justify any assessments that were inconsistent with policy guidelines.[36] The Agency continued (and intensified) its reliance on state enforcement efforts in this period, a trend that improved EPA's institutional relationship with some, but not all, state environmental agencies. It also made incremental progress in enforcing environmental standards against certain federal agencies and facilities,[37] although such progress was uneven.[38]

Despite these gains, however, significant problems continued to plague EPA enforcement in the early years of the Bush I administration. Although, as mentioned previously, the organizational structure of the Agency's enforcement efforts underwent a formal reorganization in the spring of 1990, those changes failed to overcome a continuing fragmentation of enforcement authority within EPA headquarters. Recognizing this, Jim Strock sought, ultimately without success, to strengthen further the responsibilities of the office he headed. In a closed December 5, 1990, meeting with Bill Reilly and Hank Habicht, Strock presented a plan to move technical enforcement personnel from all other EPA headquarters offices (with the exception of the Office of Solid Waste and Emergency Response) into the Office of Enforcement. This plan, which was outlined in a briefing book presented to the administrator, was intended to create a more rational chain of command for enforcement policy decisions. It contemplated no changes in the prevailing organizational arrangements within EPA's ten regional offices. Reilly and Habicht made no commitment to Strock at the December 5 meeting. They thanked him for raising the question of the workability of the Agency's organizational arrangement and promised to give his proposal further consideration. Anticipating this response, however, Strock emerged from the meeting guardedly pleased about the prospects for his reorganization plan.[39]

Strock's cautious optimism was soon to prove unfounded. On January 11, 1991, *Inside EPA*, an environmental trade journal, published a front-page article describing Strock's proposal and noting the substance of his recent meeting with Reilly and Habicht.[40] The article, which was based on information that had apparently been leaked by an individual with access to the briefing materials Strock had presented to the administrator, contained language certain to catch the attention of any affected EPA official:

> Several EPA staff say that the plan is a power play by Strock, motivated more by his wish to command additional resources and policy authority than by environmental need. . . . An EPA staffer warns that by expanding his power over EPA enforcement decisions, Strock would be able to drive policy and priorities for every office. "He is becoming everyone's boss," laments one EPA staffer.[41]

Publication of this article ignited a brief but bitter dispute. Caught by surprise, other EPA assistant administrators and their allies promptly made very plain their fervent opposition to Strock's reorganization proposal. Arguing that the plan would undermine their ability to establish priorities within their own areas of competence and that it would disrupt recent advances in the Agency's enforcement work, these individuals prevailed upon the administrator and his deputy to reject any further enforcement reorganization.[42]

Soon after these events, Strock resigned as EPA's assistant administrator for enforcement to assume the newly created position of secretary of the California Environmental Protection Agency.[43] After a six-month interregnum, during which Deputy Assistant Administrator Edward Reich served as acting assistant administrator, Strock was permanently replaced by Herbert Tate, a former prosecutor for Essex County, New Jersey, with close ties to New Jersey's former governor Thomas Kean.[44] Although the question of EPA's ineffectual enforcement structure was subsequently reviewed by the GAO,[45] no further changes were made to that organizational arrangement during the remainder of George H. W. Bush's term as president, a situation that hampered the efficiency of EPA's enforcement work. Moreover, despite the enthusiasm of the Agency's top managers for a multimedia approach to EPA enforcement, this worthwhile effort ran into two significant difficulties: inadequate information-management capability and internal resistance from single medium-oriented enforcement personnel.

In 1989 the Agency's Office of Enforcement began to develop an integrated method for obtaining cross-media information from the databases of the fourteen separate national information systems EPA had previously created to support its enforcement work. The new method, known as the Integrated Data for Enforcement Analysis (IDEA) system, was dependent upon another automated system, the Facility Index System (FINDS), whose primary aim was to compile lists of the different identification numbers used in the Agency's major databases to refer to particular regulated facilities and to access data, with respect to individual facilities, in nine of the pertinent databases. Unfortunately, these systems were poorly designed and deployed without sufficient field testing. As a result, they were far from user-friendly. In some instances, IDEA and FINDS required EPA enforcement personnel to refer to manuals that took up to six feet of shelf space in order to formulate inquiries and interpret results. They reflected other deficiencies as well, including incomplete listings of the names different EPA programs employed to refer to particular industrial facilities, facilities that lacked any FINDS identification number, and multiple FINDS identification numbers for the same facilities. Furthermore, to compound these problems, the Agency failed to budget for proper redesign of the software.[46]

In view of these difficulties, a review by the GAO concluded:

> EPA's efforts to bring together data from different environmental programs to accomplish its cross-media enforcement mission and correct its material internal control weaknesses are jeopardized by systems development deficiencies, insufficient maintenance plans and inadequate data quality. The cross-media enforcement system does not provide all the capabilities users need to assess environmental risks, target and prioritize enforcement actions, develop enforcement cases or plan strategically on a cross-media basis at the state and regional levels. As a result, EPA cannot assure that it can identify the most important cross-media enforcement priorities.[47]

EPA's fledgling multimedia enforcement program was also plagued by a paucity of cooperation from officials at both the headquarters and regional levels whose primary responsibilities concerned only one environmental medium. As one headquarters enforcement attorney described it:

> One of the problems you get into when you start trying to get the lawyers multimedia is that you get some resistance from their clients, the program offices, who are much less willing to look at things from a multimedia perspective and are not really happy about having their lawyers working on several different areas as well as their area. That's something that's going to have to be worked out.[48]

Although these difficulties were not enough to thwart the multimedia enforcement effort entirely, they did meaningfully limit its effectiveness in certain EPA regions.[49]

In implementing RCRA, EPA and its state agency counterparts largely ignored certain important categories of violations. As one Agency study frankly admitted:

> Substantially increased compliance and enforcement presence is needed for [hazardous waste] generators and non-notifiers [i.e., those who have failed to notify the EPA that they are managing a regulated hazardous waste site]. . . . Because generators and non-notifiers have consistently been a low priority, only about one third of all generators have had even one RCRA inspection, and pro-active efforts to deter non-notifier activity have been limited.[50]

Additionally, in many instances EPA and the states failed to take "timely and appropriate" enforcement actions regarding other RCRA infractions.[51]

Beyond this, EPA's enforcement work in all areas continued to suffer from a shortage of personnel,[52] as well as other chronic problems that predated Bill Reilly's tenure as EPA administrator. Those long-standing problems included inconsistencies in the enforcement approaches of EPA regional offices, difficulties in recruiting qualified staff as a result of inappropriate civil service limitations, inadequate headquarters guidance, poor working conditions in certain Agency facilities, and periodic frictions between EPA personnel and the Department of Justice.

Although the relationship between EPA and its congressional overseers concerning enforcement issues improved significantly at the beginning of the Bush administration, that trend did not continue indefinitely. While not as strident or sustained as it was during the Reagan years, criticism of the Agency's enforcement efforts by members of Congress and the GAO did increase in intensity over time, especially in the period following the departure of Jim Strock as assistant administrator for enforcement.

As in previous years, a major focus of congressional investigators was EPA's administration of the Superfund Program. In December 1990 the Dingell Committee held a hearing with regard to oversight of Superfund contractors by the Agency's Office of Inspector General. Six months later the committee issued a report concluding that EPA's Office of Inspector General was plagued by "serious leadership deficiencies" that prevented it from "effectively [pursuing] waste, fraud and abuse by the Environmental Protection Agency's major contractors." The committee cited what it characterized as "a number of disturbing problems" relating to failures by the Inspector General's Office of Investigations. It recommended that the Agency "develop and implement a comprehensive plan to investigate potential fraud in the Superfund Program."[53]

From Superfund contractor abuses, the attention of Congressman Dingell, as well as Senator Lautenberg and other interested congressional overseers, turned to the pace and consistency of cleanup activities at Superfund sites. On June 19, 1991, in an effort to respond to growing congressional concerns, Administrator Reilly directed the Agency's Office of Solid Waste and Emergency Response to investigate EPA's options for accelerating the rate of CERCLA remedial actions and determine whether the Superfund Program was using realistic assumptions to evaluate and manage environmental risks. Reilly also appointed an Agency task force to study EPA's Superfund contracting systems.[54] One month later, Don Clay, the Agency's assistant administrator for solid waste and emergency response, sent the administrator a detailed set of recommendations that came to be known as the Thirty Day Study.[55] His suggestions were ultimately adopted by Reilly and publicly released on October 2, 1991, two days before an important oversight hearing that had been scheduled by the Levitas Committee.[56] Among other things, Clay suggested that EPA's CERCLA remedial investigation and remedy selection process be standardized through the development of a "technology-based approach to remedies," guidelines for certain contaminated soils and groundwater contaminants, and regulations that designated particular cleanup technologies as appropriate for specific categories of sites. He also urged that the Agency issue a national policy encouraging PRPs to begin remedial design work prior to the entry of consent decrees requiring them to do so and that it resolve various intra- and interagency disputes that were delaying site cleanups.[57]

Clay's Thirty Day Study was supplemented by an EPA Alternative Remedial Contracting Study that was also approved by the administrator and made public on October 2. The report found that managerial and administrative expenditures by Superfund contractors were, in many instances, excessive. It recommended stepped-up EPA audits of contractor bills and charges, as well as other measures.[58]

To implement the recommendations contained in these two studies, the administrator appointed Richard Guimond, EPA's deputy assistant administrator for solid waste and emergency response, to oversee Superfund procurements and budgeting and assure uniformity among cleanup decisions. Guimond was assigned a national staff of twenty troubleshooters to assist him with these tasks.

Appropriate as they were, these actions by EPA failed to mollify the Agency's overseers on Capitol Hill. On October 4, 1991, Senator Lautenberg told a House subcommittee hearing that the Agency had made little progress in implementing the reforms it had promised two years earlier when it issued the Ninety Day Study. Lautenberg opined that EPA had been treating the Superfund Program like an "unwanted stepchild" and dismissed the Agency's Thirty Day and Alternative Remedial Contracting Studies by stating: "The disturbing thing . . . is that it hasn't already been done. . . . It's time to stop issuing reports and start implementing the law."[59]

Congressman Dingell took a similar stance. In a prepared statement he indicated that the Alternative Remedial Contracting Study showed only that "EPA has a firm grasp of the obvious." In Dingell's view, the report was "merely acknowledging what everyone else has known for months. . . . [M]any of the EPA's proposals embrace recommendations contained in a July 1991 subcommittee report, in GAO reports dating back to 1988, and in a forthcoming GAO report requested by this subcommittee."[60]

While Congress's criticisms of EPA's Superfund efforts received much attention, other aspects of the Agency's enforcement performance were also given negative reviews by congressional investigators, including, most significantly, the GAO. In a series of reports, GAO cast doubt on the efficacy of EPA's compliance and enforcement programs in such diverse areas as inland oil spills, Clean Water Act pretreatment standards, air pollution control, and NPDES permits.[61] In addition, in a study released on June 17, 1991, that was widely read by interested members of Congress and their staffs, GAO castigated the Agency and its state counterparts for failing to follow EPA's penalty policy, which requires assessment of civil forfeitures at least as great as the amount by which a company has benefited by not complying with applicable environmental standards.[62] GAO's report, which owed much to earlier studies on the same topic that had been performed by EPA's Office of Inspector General, found that in nearly two out of three penalty cases concluded in fiscal year 1990 (by EPA's air, water, hazardous waste, and toxic substances enforcement programs), there was no evidence that the economic benefit of violators' noncompliance had been calculated or assessed. Moreover, it concluded, notwithstanding the applicability of state-EPA agreements, state and local enforcement authorities adhered to the Agency's Civil Penalty Policy in an even smaller percentage of cases than did the Agency's own regional officials.[63]

These continuing congressional investigations were carried out against the backdrop of intensifying rivalry, within the Bush I administration itself, over questions of environmental policy. On a host of issues— including EPA's implementation of the Clean Air Act's permit program, the definition of wetlands for purposes of the Clean Water Act, and the administration's approach to international treaties on global warming and biodiversity—EPA Administrator Reilly clashed with the Council on Competitiveness, headed by Vice President Dan Quayle, which advocated the relaxation of environmental requirements as a means of reviving the flagging national economy. These disagreements resulted in several painful and significant defeats for Reilly during the spring and summer of 1992.[64]

These events—and the national publicity they gave rise to—contributed to a public perception that, contrary to some of its earliest positions, the Bush I administration had tilted against environmental protection. This view, which was at least partially reinforced by congressional criticism of EPA's enforcement activities, led to a further questioning of the administration's goals and intentions. Within the Agency, the morale of the enforcement staff again declined.[65] Among EPA's congressional overseers, the closing months of George H. W. Bush's presidency were a time of renewed suspicion and mistrust.

"Neither the Best of Times nor the Worst of Times": EPA Enforcement during the Clinton Administration

The election of William J. ("Bill") Clinton as president of the United States, in November 1992, gave rise to high hopes among environmental advocates. Among environmental organizations, EPA staff members, pro-environmental representatives, senators and their staffs, some state and local officials, and others who favored effective environmental regulation, the coming to power of Clinton's administration—coupled with the continued dominance of Congress by the Democratic Party—created a very real prospect that environmental matters would once again be afforded a high priority in Washington, D.C. Redoubled EPA enforcement, together with vigorous rule making (especially under the 1990 amendments to the Clean Air Act) and the prompt passage of additional federal environmental legislation, all seemed realistic and within view.

That rosy assessment, however, was soon abandoned in many quarters.[1] New, inexperienced in federal regulation, and facing an apparent anti-regulatory, anti-environmental backlash (among some leading Democrats as well as Republicans) on Capitol Hill, the Clinton administration's EPA team took a more cautious and deliberate approach to protecting the environment in its first two years than the environmental public interest community would have preferred. Distracted by political controversies over how to respond to demands that environmental laws be significantly pared back, Clinton's EPA managers promulgated watered-down versions of certain new regulations—making some of them so ambiguous, complex, or overbroad as to be all but unenforceable. Those managers confused some members of the Agency's enforcement staff by blending renewed enforcement initiatives with a new emphasis on "compliance incentive programs," "compliance assistance," and "reinvention of government," programs that seemed to some of their employees to be at odds with EPA's traditional deterrent enforcement approach. They also engaged in a structural reorganization of the Agency's headquarters office that, while bold in concept and undoubtedly well-intentioned, was implemented too slowly and chaotically to realize its maximum potential.

As we shall see, these early mishaps resulted, in the fiscal year 1995, in a dramatic decline in the traditional output numbers by which EPA enforcement success was measured. That brief decline came to an abrupt end soon thereafter, however, when the Republican Party won a majority status in the House of Representatives and the Senate—an unforeseen situation that created new sets of obstacles (together with some significant new political opportunities) for EPA's top managers.

At the outset, the selection and confirmation of managers to fill EPA's highest positions proceeded slowly. Although Clinton's choice for EPA administrator (Carol M. Browner) was announced the month after his election in 1992, other high-level Agency officials—including its deputy administrator and its assistant administrator for enforcement—were not nominated by the president until several months after his administration had taken power (and not confirmed by the Senate until May 1993). Still other EPA appointees were announced as late as July 1993—midway through the first year of Clinton's term—and not confirmed until a few weeks after that. These delays created discomforting uncertainties for EPA's professional staff, environmental organizations, and regulated firms.

Nonetheless, once they were finally selected, EPA's new set of top managers was greeted with broad approval and prompt Senate confirmation. Browner, the Agency's new administrator, was particularly well regarded by environmental organizations while remaining acceptable to regulated industries. She had previously served for two years as head of the Florida Department of Environmental Regulation. In that capacity, she had skillfully negotiated settlement of a complex, contentious lawsuit regarding cleanup of the Florida Everglades. Prior to that, Browner had been legislative director for then-Senator Al Gore (D-TN), general counsel for the Senate Committee on Environment and Natural Resources, and a legislative aide in the office of former senator Lawton Chiles (D-FL).[2] She was politically associated with Vice President Gore, and her selection as administrator was viewed as a political tribute and benefit to him.

The Clinton administration's nominee for EPA deputy administrator was Robert Sussman, an expert in toxic substances law who had been a partner in a Washington, D.C., law firm and an active participant in Democratic Party politics.[3] Sussman's tenure at the EPA proved brief, however. He left the Agency in October 1994 to assume another position within the Clinton administration.[4] Sussman's replacement as deputy administrator was Fred Hansen, director of the Oregon Department of Environmental Quality, who had previously served as a congressional aide, an executive officer in the Peace Corps, and deputy treasurer of the State of Oregon.[5]

For the position of assistant administrator for enforcement, President Clinton nominated Steven ("Steve") Herman, a veteran career attorney with the Department of Justice, who had specialized in litigating cases arising under the National Environmental Policy Act (NEPA).[6] As Herman later recalled:

> I was a career attorney at DOJ, an assistant section chief who oversaw the case that DOJ had brought on behalf of the federal government against the State of Florida to protect the Florida Everglades. I came to know Carol Browner professionally while negotiating a settlement in that case. When she was named EPA administrator by Clinton, [Browner] called and said she wanted someone for the assistant administrator for enforcement position who wouldn't be perceived as political. That's how I got the job.[7]

Upon assuming office, EPA's new leaders faced unanticipated resistance to the Agency's basic mission from some unexpected sources. As Browner put it: "In 1993 and 1994, I was fighting for the Agency's survival. The anti-regulatory movement, which had considerable support among both Republicans and Democrats, was very active in those years. . . . It really took us awhile to get up and going."[8]

Congressional demands for steps to roll back and limit the costs of environmental regulation increased. These demands in turn fueled a vigorous debate within the Clinton administration as to the positions the administration should take regarding the renewal of key federal environmental legislation. After anxious and heated internal discussion, the administration determined to proceed with proposals to renew and strengthen the Clean Water Act, Superfund, and the Safe Drinking Water Act.[9] It also proposed legislation to elevate the EPA to the status of a cabinet-level department. At the same time, however, as part of a strategy to fend off anti-regulatory legislation, the Clinton administration proposed a package of regulatory cutbacks that would have waived penalties and granted grace periods to small businesses that were making good-faith efforts to comply with environmental requirements.[10]

In the end, the administration's efforts to build a consensus among opposing interests and convince Congress to strengthen federal environmental statutes met with defeat. After what Browner later characterized as "huge, ugly fights,"[11] Congress declined to extend the regulatory reach of the Clean Water Act or the Safe Drinking Water Act. The administration's campaign to elevate EPA to cabinet level was also abandoned after the House of Representatives voted to allow debate on an anti-regulatory amendment to the EPA cabinet bill that would have required EPA to conduct cost-benefit analyses and risk assessments before issuing any new regulations.[12] Moreover, notwithstanding the emergence of a remarkable consensus among industries, environmental organizations, and other interested parties, Congress failed to reauthorize the Superfund Act, and the statute's taxing authority subsequently expired, on December 31, 1995.[13]

Beyond preoccupying EPA's new management team with fending off potential threats to the Agency's legislative agenda—and to its fundamental legal authority as well—the anti-regulatory mood of Congress in 1993 and 1994 appears to have had other significant affects on EPA (including its enforcement programs) in the early years of the Clinton period.

One such impact was an administration effort to supplement the Agency's traditional deterrent enforcement approach—a method that emphasized formal enforcement actions, penalty collection, and tracking numbers of enforcement inspections, numbers of enforcement actions initiated, etc.—with "compliance assistance" to particular regulated industries and "compliance incentive" programs designed to provide regulatory relief to firms whose alternative pollution control proposals met certain EPA criteria.[14] This change in emphasis, which EPA's political appointees often referred to as the "full tool chest" approach, was intended to expand the discretion of EPA enforcement personnel without interfering with traditional enforcement work. Regrettably, though, it gave rise to considerable confusion and misunderstanding among EPA's permanent career enforcement staff. As Bill Muszynski, a veteran administrator in EPA's Region II office, observed: "It is difficult to explain to the staff that the Agency must strike the right balance between compliance assistance and enforcement. Steve Herman had difficulty doing that, especially in the early years of the Clinton administration. He tried not to send a mixed message, but he was perceived as doing so nonetheless."[15]

Herman (and one of his closest aides, Sylvia Lowrance) subsequently maintained that aggressive EPA enforcement was emphasized clearly and consistently by the EPA's top managers during all eight years of the Clinton administration.[16] Interviews with experienced members of EPA's enforcement programs in several regional offices, however, reveal that an unambiguous, pro-enforcement emphasis was not conveyed to the Agency's key enforcement personnel in the field in 1993 and 1994.

One senior enforcement manager in EPA Region V stated: "At the very beginning of the Clinton administration, it wasn't terribly clear where they stood on enforcement. . . . There was a lot of talk about taking a collaborative approach to environmental protection."[17] Similarly, Walter Mugdan, an experienced enforcement administrator in EPA Region II, indicated:

> I would not consider the first two years of the Clinton administration as standing out with respect to enforcement activity. . . . On the contrary, in those years I believe there was a decreased emphasis on what might be called the "hard path" and an increased emphasis on the "soft path." It was during this time that compliance assistance — the "soft path" — was established as a priority. Many states had become critical of EPA, asserting that the agency was too focused on counting penalties and the number of enforcement cases. In the first two years of the Clinton administration, EPA's leadership seemed to accept some of that criticism, and sent signals that EPA regions were to shift resources from hard enforcement to compliance assistance and other "soft path" approaches.[18]

Moreover, an attorney in EPA Region IX expressed the view that "there was no strong environmental philosophy espoused in the early Clinton administration's enforcement activities. Vice President Gore had his pet projects and ideas. But even then the idea was to avoid confrontation and get to the point where you can still survive. It was a defensive posture. There was not much in the way of an overall enforcement initiative at all."[19]

One of the more contentious controversies between EPA's career enforcement staff and the Clinton administration's political appointees during the first two years of the Clinton era appears to have arisen in the Agency's San Francisco regional office. As an EPA enforcement official who worked in the Region IX Office of Regional Counsel during much of the Clinton administration remembered those disputes:

> During the Clinton period, the politicos weren't really communicating their message very well. There was a lot of management nonsense, like

reinvention, but there was no clear direction. This was especially true towards the beginning of the Clinton years. The senior [enforcement] staff didn't really know what the politicos wanted. It was a fiasco.[20]

The same interviewee added the perspective that Clinton's political appointees were "not the most enforcement-oriented people." Instead, they were "very into the political resolution of problems and 'collaborative' ways of getting things done. That was a big change from the middle years of the Bush I administration, [when] the whole operation seemed much more professional."[21]

In contrast, Felicia Marcus, the regional administrator in Region IX throughout the Clinton era, recalled this disagreement in this way:

> Our view in the administration was: let's find those environmental violators who are really bad, really obvious and describable in terms of harm to the environment and public health, and the enforcement staff should go after those. But there is a big mass of people who are also confused by our complicated EPA regulations, or who say they are committed to environmental results and can do better than our regulations if we can cut through some of the paperwork burden. Let's do something more sophisticated by announcing [that] we are going to enforce, . . . go after the intelligible targets [and] send a clear message . . . but let's also find the companies we can collaborate with and collaborate with them, so we can better isolate the truly bad guys and maximize our net environmental gain by using different strategies with different actors.
>
> This culture change was confusing for the [regional enforcement] staff. It felt for many of us that many EPA staff had never really been managed to the degree that our administration was stepping in to do. They had been allowed to be cowboys, for want of a better word. [They] liked going after the bad guys and keeping the world relatively simple. "We" were good and "they" were bad. That is sometimes true but it is rarely that simple. . . . We [the administration staff] were trying to get people to be a little less judgmental and a little more strategic and creative, and that was hard for some people.
>
> Our administration came in, Democrats, all very environmental, and we underestimated what we had to do. I think the staff people thought we would come in and they would just get to enforce even more. Instead, it was sort of like Nixon going to China, we came in and we wanted to do reinvention. . . . Some people heard the "reinvention" part and heard "instead of enforcement" which was not at all what we meant. We meant

a combination of strong enforcement and new incentives to do more environmental protection. We eventually did the course correction when we realized how we were being misheard.[22]

EPA's compliance assistance and compliance incentive programs (such as Project XL, the Small Business Compliance Policy, the Common Sense Initiative, Compliance Auditing, and the Self-Audit Program) may well have created good will among some of the many entities regulated by the Agency. Nonetheless, as former Region V Regional Counsel Gail Ginsberg put it:

> These programs sometimes siphoned off resources from enforcement, especially where regional program managers did not believe in enforcement. As a result, the [regional] technical staff who remained devoted to enforcement [in those programs] were not the shining stars of the staff, i.e., not the most capable people. Also, when technical people [in EPA regional offices] left enforcement they were replaced by very inexperienced staff that did not know how to do enforcement.[23]

In addition to that, from the perspective of another manager familiar with EPA enforcement efforts, compliance assistance and incentive programs

> made it more difficult to do enforcement, because where you are trying to reach collaborative solutions with people they sometimes have the impression that they have some kind of a pass from enforcement and that, if we bring an enforcement action against them, we are somehow . . . betraying them. . . . There was a need for some clear policy direction that just because we were working together did not mean that we were not going to enforce.[24]

Another unfortunate EPA response to congressional anti-regulatory pressure in the early Clinton years (and thereafter, in some instances) was the promulgation of new sets of Agency regulations that contained a number of difficult-to-enforce requirements. As a former assistant regional counsel in EPA Region IX aptly observed, "excessive flexibility within EPA's regulations make it very difficult to establish compliance. This was especially true in the underground storage tank area, and it is also true as to some maximum achievable control technology (MACT) clean air standards. . . . In the long term this will lead to environmental problems and pressure for more rigid regulations."[25] Similarly, another EPA enforcement official observed that

> EPA has written many rules [the way that it has] . . . because of a desire to move quickly, to not offend the people fighting over what the rules should say, or to obfuscate in order to get the rules through the regulatory and OMB approval process. However, that all comes home to roost when the Agency tries to write a permit or take an enforcement action. The enforcement program bears a lot of the weight for that lack of clarity and it hurts the [enforcement] program's reputation. [The enforcement staff] is seen as unreasonably stretching the law when the problem is really the vagueness—or overbroadness—of the regulations themselves.[26]

One early regulatory controversy in the Clinton administration— with important enforcement implications—concerned the continuous emission monitoring requirements for stationary sources of air pollution, called for by the 1990 Clean Air Act amendments. EPA proposed an effective set of regulations in that area but subsequently pared them back. As Bruce Buckheit, a senior Agency enforcement manager, later viewed it: "The 1990 amendments were written to have better self-monitoring. There we won the battle in the legislation but we lost the battle in the implementation. We do not have better self-monitoring today, by and large."[27] Another EPA employee who works primarily on Clean Air Act enforcement issues, substantially agreed: "In the Clinton administration there was a pervasive 'let's make a deal' atmosphere. This was probably most true in air [policy matters]. Enhanced monitoring was greatly watered down in the Clinton administration. Industry won more than it should have in that debate."[28]

Non-enforceability problems also arose with respect to EPA's MACT standards, which the Agency was required to establish to control the emission of toxic air pollutants. Significant portions of those regulations were drafted, at the invitation of EPA's Office of Air Quality Planning and Standards, by the very industries that were later subject to them.[29] In interviews, EPA enforcement personnel were highly critical of certain sections of those regulations including (but not limited to) the MACT requirements that apply to wood-coating and degreasing operations, and to bulk gasoline terminals.[30] Bruce Buckheit conceded that EPA's MACT enforcement was "spotty, scattered and not coordinated," and observed that "there are an enormous number of [MACT] standards coming out. Who can know them all? We try to put some organization on it but it is very difficult."[31] Steve Rothblatt, formerly the director of the Air and Radiation Division in EPA Region V held a similar view. In an interview, he exclaimed: "There is . . . so much complexity in how to manage this [set of MACT regulations] that it is just mind-boggling!"[32]

One of the most significant management initiatives undertaken by the Clinton administration in its first two years in office was a large-scale reorganization of EPA's headquarters in order to create a new, expanded Office of Enforcement and Compliance Assurance (OECA). Touting this restructuring as "a major accomplishment" of his tenure in office, Steve Herman, EPA's former assistant administrator for enforcement and compliance assurance, explained some of the rationale for the changes his office engineered:

> The reorganization consolidated headquarters enforcement personnel in one office. It also led to some reorganizations in the regions. The reorganization at headquarters allowed us to use resources more efficiently. Having both attorneys and technical people in one office allowed us to focus on big, difficult issues and cases. It gave the office independence in terms of looking at and addressing enforcement problems. . . . Once it was done it really worked.[33]

Herman's deputy assistant administrator, Sylvia Lowrance, had a similar opinion of the benefits of the 1993–1994 headquarters reorganization. She stated:

> It was a wonderful concept because there was a single assistant administrator–decision maker, not a series of fiefdoms, as long as the administrator backed the assistant administrator up (which Carol Browner routinely did). The reorganization was an attempt to go back to square one and set up an entire framework for compliance. It was massive. It created synergies between and among enforcement people from different media working together for the first time.[34]

Following a relatively lengthy review by a thirty-five-member EPA task force, headed by Associate Deputy Administrator Michael P. Vandenbergh, Carol Browner expanded the headquarters Office of Enforcement into a new office that housed both EPA headquarters enforcement lawyers and headquarters enforcement technical personnel who had previously been situated in media-specific program offices.

The newly formed OECA incorporated several previously existing entities as well, such as an Office of Criminal Enforcement, the Office of Federal Activities, and the National Enforcement Investigations Center. It also included a new Office of Site Remediation, with jurisdiction over Superfund matters; and it became the institutional home of two entirely new organizational units: the Office of Regulatory Enforcement (ORE) and the Office of Compliance (OC).

ORE was given the lead role in supporting enforcement case development, and it was organized along media-specific lines. ORE thus contained separate divisions devoted to enforcement of the Clean Air Act, the Clean Water Act, RCRA, etc., along with a new Multi-Media Enforcement Division. In contrast, the OC was given the leading role in enforcement planning, data management, inspection targeting, compliance monitoring and compliance assistance, and it was organized by regulated sectors (such as manufacturing, energy and transportation, and chemical, municipal, and commercial services). The OC also contained separate divisions for environmental planning, targeting, data analysis, agriculture, and ecosystems.[35]

After deliberation, Administrator Browner decided not to require EPA's regional offices to create separate regional enforcement divisions that paralleled the structure of the new OECA. Instead she allowed the regional offices discretion to fashion their own new enforcement structures. The regions, however, were subject to a minimum requirement: each region that did not reestablish an enforcement division was required to appoint a single enforcement coordinator who reported directly to the deputy regional administrator, and to create an identifiable, separate enforcement unit within each regional program division.[36]

Without question, EPA's reorganization of 1993–1994 did succeed in accomplishing some of the laudable, ambitious goals of its designers. Thus the Clinton administration's restructuring efforts successfully eliminated some redundancy and waste within the Office of Enforcement. The reorganization allowed for some helpful cross-media and interdisciplinary contact that had not previously been a feature of EPA's enforcement culture. Additionally, the mere fact that it was taking place sent a signal to at least some EPA headquarters and regional managers that enforcement was indeed an administration priority.[37]

At the same time however, in both its design and its implementation, the Agency's massive reorganization of the early 1990s was flawed and incomplete. As one of the reorganization's principal architects later reflected: "I can't look back at the reorganization that I was a part of and say that it was an unqualified success. I think we probably took some wrong turns in some places."[38] In fact, EPA enforcement officials who had designed, observed, or been professionally affected by the reorganization did subsequently identify a number of specific wrong turns in the way it was conceived and carried out.

One such imperfection concerned the organization's disruptive affect on ongoing enforcement work. As one knowledgeable EPA enforcement official candidly stated: "Planning the reorganization took a little over one year. It took an additional year to put it in place. We lost some momentum in enforcement during that time period."[39]

In particular, the reorganization appears to have had a negative (although temporary) impact on the Agency's previously established efforts in the areas of compliance monitoring, state-federal relationships, and the integration of enforcement strategies.[40] Ann Lassiter, then an EPA headquarters enforcement supervisor, viewed it this way:

> In the reorganization, the compliance assessment and analysis function of EPA headquarters simply got lost. . . . OECA lost control of some of headquarters' tools for looking at enforcement program trends and overall performance at the regional office level. A fair amount of the resources associated with the compliance assessment and analysis function were lost in the transfer to the new organization; and people in headquarters who had been performing that work were suddenly asked to carry out the mostly new function of compliance assistance.[41]

Beyond this, the reorganization gave rise to new institutional jealousies and rivalries within EPA headquarters. According to Eric Schaeffer, OECA's first director of the Office of Regulatory Enforcement:

> When the headquarters program offices lost [their enforcement components] in the reorganization, it became a lot easier for the programs to take potshots at enforcement. They no longer had internal people who lobbied for balance in execution in the regulations. They also lost an important link to the regions, and they became further involved in inside-the-Beltway policy questions, and more removed from what was going on in the field.[42]

Understandably, the post-reorganization program offices had not been happy about ceding their enforcement components to a new, very powerful OECA. In some cases, this resentment soon evolved into an increased antipathy to enforcement work itself, which some of the now-reduced program offices viewed as very much "a legalistic obstacle" to the collaborative approaches they were pursuing.[43] As will be seen further in the next chapter, this friction grew more intense and troublesome after the Clinton administration left office.

In addition, significant antipathy developed between the new Office of Regulatory Enforcement (ORE) and the Office of Compliance (OC). Some of this rivalry concerned the distribution of scarce OECA resources since the creation of ORE and OC had split up OECA's resources in such a way that "neither office really was left with enough to get a lot of things done."[44] Other aspects of this intra-OECA dispute involved questions of professional prerogative (since ORE contained more attorneys and the OC tended to be dominated by non-lawyers) and "turf issues" regarding which office was to handle what enforcement function(s).[45]

The EPA reorganization of 1993–1994 was a chaotic and highly uncertain process for many EPA enforcement employees, especially for those (mostly technically trained) staff members who ended up situated in the OC. Some insight into their disorienting experiences may be gleaned from the recollections of one EPA employee, initially a program analyst in EPA's headquarters Office of Air Quality Planning and Standards, who began his career at EPA in September 1992 just a few months before the reorganization was planned:

> In the spring of 1993 EPA announced the reorganization and I didn't quite know what that meant for me. I was then still new at the Agency, and trying to learn about the Clean Air Act and what my job was.
>
> Reorganization work groups were started and then, some time later, a reorganization plan [for EPA headquarters] was ultimately put in place. Then they had competitions to select the new OECA office directors, then the division directors, then the branch chiefs. At that point, I thought that someone would put together position descriptions [for staff-level] jobs and start having people compete for those jobs, or else be assigned to them. That was not done.
>
> So they said to the staff in OE [Office of Enforcement] and the program offices who were in the reorganization mix, "This is your chance to go wherever you want to." We on the staff were given the opportunity

to select three job choices and they would try to place us in one of them. But of course, how can you choose to go work someplace if you don't know what the job is?

The people who formulated the reorganization didn't appear to know what many of our existing jobs were and they never really bothered to ask. I thought to myself "this is a recipe for chaos."

Anyway, some staff people were beginning to be told where they would or could move to in the restructured OECA so I went to my deputy division director and asked him, "Where is my job going?" He said, "I have no idea." I also called several newly appointed branch chiefs and asked them what work their branches would be doing. They too said, "Heck, I don't know."[46]

Beyond its unplanned, chaotic quality—especially as perceived by the Agency's headquarters technical enforcement staff—the reorganization has also been criticized on the basis that, in the drawn-out interoffice negotiations that had preceded it, OECA came away with too few (and sometimes the wrong) resources. As one experienced federal enforcement manager saw it,

OECA got taken to the cleaners on resources during the reorganization. We really missed out on getting some key people in. The program offices did not cough up all that they should have.[47]

Finally, with the benefit of hindsight, the reorganization has been criticized by some of its own principal proponents for not creating sufficient changes in the structure of EPA's regional offices. As Steve Herman now sees it:

If I had to do [the reorganization] over again I would try to ensure a bit more uniformity across the regions. I'm now not sure that the geographical differences that exist among the regions drives the need for different organizational structures at the regional level. I would also try to build in more direct accountability from the regions to headquarters in terms of enforcement. We did have that in some regions and we didn't have that in other regions.[48]

In sum, the EPA reorganization of 1993–1994 was a mixed success. On the positive side, it boldly restored some of the historical size and prestige of the Agency's headquarters enforcement component; it also set the stage for some important enforcement successes in the balance of the Clinton era. Nonetheless, the Agency's reorganization resulted in a temporary loss of enforcement momentum, a decline in the morale of some components of the enforcement staff, the creation of an avoidable set of intra-institutional rivalries, a smaller resource base for enforcement work than was later found to be needed, and an inconsistent set of regional organizational structures which allowed some regional managers a degree of autonomy in enforcement matters that was denied to their counterparts in other EPA regions.

Overall, the Clinton administration's first two years in office were a period of uncertainty and confusion with respect to EPA enforcement. During this time, the Agency's new top managers were still inexperienced at federal agency management. They were also still unskilled in communicating and negotiating with their enforcement staff, and in some cases they seem to have been distracted by sharply negative congressional reactions to the administration's legislative agenda.

This is not to suggest that 1993 and 1994 saw no progress in the EPA enforcement programs. In this beginning period, EPA's new management team strengthened the Agency's initial commitment to environmental justice.[49] EPA also placed long overdue emphasis on environmental protection of Native American tribal lands.[50] Moreover, in the same period, the Agency began its staunch (and ultimately successful) opposition to misguided state legislation intended to grant "amnesty" or "immunity from prosecution" to environmental law violators who conducted environmental self-audits and then reported their firm's violations to state environmental authorities.[51]

These achievements and successes notwithstanding, the first two years of the Clinton era in EPA enforcement remain, on balance, an undistinguished time. As we shall see, though, 1993–1994 was the precursor of a very different sort of period in American political history, an era when issues of EPA enforcement were located at the epicenter of a bitter, highly publicized, partisan budgetary dispute, whose resolution had important consequences for all involved in it. Moreover, as we shall see further, the initial two years of the Clinton period stand in sharp contrast to the innovations, initiatives, and solid achievements in EPA enforcement that ultimately characterized Clinton's second term in office.

Meanwhile, the results of the election of 1994 came as a shock to many observers. For the first time since the early 1950s, the Republican Party won majority control of both the House of Representatives and the Senate. Led by Representative (and Speaker of the House) Newt Gingrich

(R-GA), a fiery partisan with very conservative views, who had angrily criticized "abuses of power" by the Democratic House leadership before and during the 1994 campaign, the Republican victory became known as the "Gingrich Revolution." Its "manifesto" was a slim volume of proposed reforms, the Contract with America,[52] some of whose provisions seemed likely to all but dismantle the then-existing federal environmental laws and the enforcement of those laws by EPA.

Specifically, the Contract proposed a new "Job Creation and Wage Enhancement Act" that would have granted individuals being inspected or investigated by a federal agency the right to remain silent, refuse a warrantless search, be warned that statements they made might be used against them, have an attorney or an accountant present (or both), be present at the time of the agency inspection or investigation, and receive reimbursement for "unreasonable damages." The proposed act would also have authorized individuals to bring lawsuits against any federal agency that had threatened them with "a prohibited regulatory practice," which was defined as "an inconsistent application of any law, rule or regulation causing mismanagement of agency resources by any agency or employee of the agency."[53] The Contract with America also contained proposals—quickly introduced as legislative bills after the 104th Congress convened—that would have required elaborate risk assessment and cost-benefit analyses prior to the promulgation of any new agency regulations, imposed a "regulatory budget" which would have imposed a specific ceiling on the cost of complying with all federal regulatory requirements, and mandated additional requirements regarding regulatory flexibility, regulatory impact analysis, and compensation of owners of private property that was subject to regulation.[54]

EPA's leadership responded swiftly to these radical legislative proposals, which began to be passed by various House committees—and then by the entire House of Representatives—in the winter of 1995.[55] Administrator Carol Browner declared that the Republican legislative initiative undermined every single environmental and public health standard in the country.[56] She further stated that "every person in this administration" was "greatly alarmed" by the GOP proposals,[57] saying that "this legislation is not reform, it is a full frontal assault on protecting public health and the environment."[58] Browner also declared:

> There is a very hostile tone that has been set, and I am fearful it will endure. Congress [has] acted in haste, did not involve the people on whose behalf they serve and did not do their business in the open. It doesn't

serve anyone well [for Congress] not to work with the agencies of the executive branch, which has the ultimate responsibility for implementing
the laws. . . . There is no doubt that we need reform. Unfortunately, they
weren't willing to do the hard work with us and the American people to
do an intelligent system of change.[59]

Environmental organizations, working cooperatively with the Clinton
administration, mounted a concerted lobbying effort to defeat the Republican reforms. Those proposals, in turn, received the active backing
of a broad coalition of business interests.

Ultimately, in July 1995, the anti-regulatory measures that had passed
the House were defeated in the Senate, when the Republicans were unable
to overcome a Democratic filibuster against them. At that point, however,
the Republican congressional leadership shifted tactics. Following Newt
Gingrich's declaration that "when you have revolutions you never give
up; you keep looking for pressure points to break through,"[60] House Republicans began to look to the federal budget as the principal means of
accomplishing their anti-regulatory goals.[61]

In the final week of July 1995, the House of Representatives considered legislation that would cut approximately one-third, or $2.4 billion,
from EPA's overall budget (including a $431 million cut from the Super-
fund Program), and that would target a 50 percent cut in funding for
the Agency's enforcement work.[62] The bill, which President Clinton
promptly threatened to veto,[63] included some seventeen specific riders
intended to curtail EPA's enforcement authority and limit its regulatory
powers, along with provisions that would force Congress to reauthorize
the Clean Air Act, the Clean Water Act, and the Safe Drinking Water Act
in order for the implementation of those statutes to receive funding.[64]
After initially rejecting the measure,[65] the full House reversed itself and
passed the bill on a vote of 228 to 193.[66] President Clinton responded by
labeling the bill a "polluter's protection act," and once again threatening
to veto it.[67]

The House-passed EPA spending bill then moved to the Senate. There
the Committee on Appropriations (followed soon afterward by the full
Senate) voted to cut approximately $1 billion from what had been the
EPA's 1995 fiscal-year budget—an immense cut, but one that was nonetheless somewhat more modest than the EPA budget reductions and restrictions that had passed the House.

This development was followed by a series of House-Senate conference committee meetings in which House negotiators agreed to remove,

or soften, the most intensely disputed "rider provisions" of the legislation that the House had originally adopted and to cut EPA's budget only to the extent that the Senate bill had called for.

The compromise spending bill (which would still have cut the Agency's overall budget by 14 percent and EPA's enforcement budget by 21 percent from the prior year) remained unacceptable to the Clinton administration. President Clinton formally vetoed the bill along with certain other proposed appropriation measures, in mid-November 1995. That decisive action by the president led to an immediate, disruptive, and extensively publicized, six-day partial shutdown of the federal government, including the EPA and numerous other federal agencies and departments.[68]

This shutdown—the first of two that would be caused by this dispute—was resolved by a stopgap agreement to finance EPA and other agencies at a reduced level, on a temporary basis, until mid-December. In the meanwhile, President Clinton agreed to meet directly with the Republican congressional leadership—including House Speaker Gingrich and Senate Majority Leader Bob Dole—to work out a compromise spending package.[69]

These high-level negotiations soon stalled, however.[70] The House and Senate responded to that stalemate by passing a new set of spending bills almost identical to the bills that President Clinton had previously vetoed with respect to the levels of spending they permitted, and which also added back a number of the anti-regulatory riders that House negotiators had previously agreed to abandon in conference committee sessions.[71] President Clinton vetoed these bills as well, and the budgetary impasse continued.[72]

In the meanwhile, on December 15, the temporary spending authority of a number of executive branch agencies and departments, including EPA, expired. As a result, 280,000 federal workers, including nearly all EPA employees, were classified as "non-essential" and placed on "furlough status." Their forced layoffs (for which the employees did ultimately receive full back pay) lasted for some twenty-seven days. Virtually all EPA operations were suspended during this period—including ongoing work at approximately five hundred Superfund sites—and the EPA administrator publicly warned that if the Republican budget cuts went into effect, three thousand to five thousand EPA employees would lose their jobs on a permanent basis, beginning in May 1996.[73]

Finally, after returning from a holiday recess, Congress voted on January 5, 1996, to approve three bills that reopened closed federal programs to various degrees and returned many federal workers to their jobs. President Clinton quickly signed that legislation. With the federal government (including EPA) open and operating once again, negotiations between Congress and the White House over the federal budget were renewed.[74]

Following the January 5 vote, Rep. John R. Kasich (R-Ohio), chairman of the House Budget Committee, publicly declared, "[W]e're not anywhere near raising a white flag."[75] Soon afterward, however, events were to prove that statement false. During their holiday visits to their districts, a number of representatives found many of their constituents angry over the continuing government shutdown, and also tending to blame congressional Republicans more than the Clinton administration for the continuing impasse. These impressions dovetailed with the results of several public opinion polls, commissioned by Republican politicians, which found broad public disdain for the anti-environmental positions of the Republican leadership.[76] In addition, early in February 1996, Ron Wyden, a Democrat, won an upset victory in a special election to replace Bob Packwood, U.S. senator from Oregon. Exit polls from that election indicated that the efforts of congressional Republicans to undermine EPA had played a crucial role in Wyden's victory.[77]

In response to those clear public signals, Republicans in the House and Senate, with the support of their allies in regulated industries,[78] gradually began to back away from further confrontations on environmental issues. On March 6, 1996, faced with the potential defection of a bloc of Republican representatives, House Republican leaders postponed debate on a conservative bill to roll back government regulations, and they promised to work on less-sweeping versions of the legislation.[79] Two days later they entered into an agreement with the administration to extend the government's borrowing authority for two more weeks, thus averting a third unpopular government closure.[80]

Finally, in the last week of April 1996, after continued, contentious negotiations, Congress and the administration reached an agreement on a $160-billion spending bill for fiscal 1996. This bill eliminated riders that would have impaired EPA's enforcement and regulatory activities and restored funding for the Agency (including its enforcement programs) at a level of $6.6 billion, only slightly below the amount that EPA had spent in the previous fiscal year.[81]

Although it ended with little immediate change in the EPA's resource levels, the lengthy and often bitter partisan struggle over fiscal policy in late 1995 and early 1996 did have very significant impacts—both in the short-term and in the longer run—on the EPA and its enforcement work. The lengthy dispute, with its two employee furloughs and months of uncertainty, led to a precipitous (if short-lived) decline in the morale of the Agency's career staff. The controversy also created a "chilling effect" on EPA enforcement work.[82] As Ann Lassiter later recalled:

> People got scared that their reputation among Congress was that they were heavy handed and beat up on the little guys. This created a tough environment for [EPA] enforcement to be aggressive. The Agency's re-action was to be cautious, not to do anything that would get it negative publicity.[83]

In addition, the EPA employee furloughs in the winter of 1995–1996 set back the Agency's internal timetable for conducting inspections of regu-lated facilities, and some EPA regional offices, unsure what their budgets would ultimately be, held back resources from inspections and other rou-tine enforcement-related tasks during the entire budget dispute, in favor of what they perceived as higher-priority projects. These steps delayed EPA's enforcement process for the rest of 1996. They contributed to a significant drop in the Agency's enforcement output levels (number of administrative enforcement actions taken, number of civil case referrals to the Department of Justice, amounts of civil penalties collected, etc.) for fiscal year 1996.[84]

Over the longer term, the budget impasse of 1995–1996 resulted in a substantial change in the political dynamics in Washington, at least with respect to environmental policies. The Republicans' spring 1996 retreat on environmental issues proved relatively lasting, at least on a publicly visible level. Throughout the rest of the Clinton presidency, in fact, the Republican Party attempted to reposition itself in the public mind as champions of the environment.[85] Their disagreements with the Clinton administration over environmental issues were greatly downplayed, even during the tumultuous period when President Clinton was impeached in the House of Representatives and partisan bickering in Washington, in general, was acrimonious and intensive. As Carol Browner later as-sessed it:

> In some ways, the Gingrich Congress was the best thing that ever hap-pened to the EPA. We really drew a line in the sand with them over certain issues. For years after that, the Agency was relatively free of Congressional directives and interference. We came out of it much stronger.[86]

EPA's budget—including its allotment for enforcement—did (as will be seen) experience some significant decreases during the remainder of the Clinton years. Nevertheless, none of those monetary decreases were as dramatic or as devastating as the EPA budget cuts that had been proposed by the leaders of the 104th Congress.

Beyond this, the policies and preferences of EPA's top managers took on a more distinctive form and shape in the aftermath of the budget impasse. With regard to enforcement, as Walter Mugdan later recalled:

> [F]rom then on, the signals from OECA changed. The message to the regions now was: Wait a minute, you misinterpreted us in the past. We never wanted less enforcement. We wanted more and better targeted enforcement. Yes, we want you to do compliance assistance; but we also want you to follow the "hard path" by taking actions and collecting penalties. We even expect you to overfile if a state enters into a clearly inappropriate settlement.[87]

As we shall explore, with that unambiguous direction from headquarters, and the threat of elimination by a hostile Congress no longer present, in many regions, at least, EPA enforcement embarked on a period of notable success and accomplishment during President Clinton's second term in office.[88]

One potential measure of the successfulness of a presidential administration's enforcement efforts at a federal administrative agency or department is the impact that administration has on the sensitive set of intra-governmental relationships that are an important aspect of federal enforcement work. These working relationships are often affected by past events—some of which may predate a given administration's term in office. Moreover, these relationships are sometimes entirely outside federal officials' control. Nonetheless (at least within the limits just noted), the positions, attitudes, and actions of an agency's political appointees do, at least sometimes, have a significant impact on both the agency's internal and its external government relationships respecting enforcement.

With respect to the working relationship of EPA's headquarters and EPA's regional offices in the Clinton years, little consensus emerged among those whom I interviewed. A clear plurality—but not a majority—of the people I spoke with expressed partial or full satisfaction with the way that relationship had functioned during the Clinton era.[89] This appears to have been particularly the case in the Superfund Program, where differences that arose tended to be ironed out in frequent headquarters-regional conferences at the staff and mid-management levels.[90]

Other people I interviewed perceived some improvement in headquarters-regional relationships, in the enforcement area, during Clinton's second term in office.[91] Those individuals differed, however, as to how and why those improvements occurred. Thus, some participants felt that headquarters had upgraded its working relationship the most with regions that participated in large-scale, sector-based enforcement initiatives.[92] Another senior EPA enforcement official, on the other hand, noted Clinton second-term improvements in the extent of headquarters-regional cooperation mainly in regional offices that had chosen to re-structure their organizations in order to re-create regional enforcement divisions that reported directly to OECA.[93]

Still other members of EPA and DOJ's enforcement staff emphasized the inherent variability of the relationship between EPA headquarters and the Agency's regional offices. Of that group, some interviewees described the relationship as "cyclical" within each region.[94] Others noted high levels of variability based upon the environmental medium in which particular issues arose[95] and differing professional styles and personalities of managers and staff members.[96]

Another subset of individuals with whom I spoke was more negative in its assessment of the relationship between headquarters and regional office enforcement personnel during the Clinton era. Some regional office enforcement officials, for example, complained that the level of knowledge, experience, and expertise of the headquarters enforcement staff had declined over this time.[97] This perceived decline seems consistent with the view that the headquarters staff had become "overseers and second guessers" of regional decisions in particular cases, as opposed to providers of valuable information as to what other regions were doing regarding similar problems, what national policies were being developed by OECA, and what the trends were likely to be with regard to EPA's budget.[98]

Some I interviewed noted that, as was always traditionally true at EPA, conflicts between headquarters and regional offices in the enforcement area often centered on whether considerations of national consistency outweighed the need of the regions for flexibility in resolving problems and settling priorities consistent with unique regional or local circumstances.[99] Similarly, other EPA officials noted tensions in particular subject areas—such as with regard to pesticide enforcement cases, asbestos matters, lead in drinking water, and the levels of pollution control to be placed on SO_2 and NOx emissions in industry-wide settlement agreements—areas in which regional and national priorities differed.[100]

Many of the individuals I spoke with were wholly or partially pleased with the quality and professionalism of the interaction between EPA's enforcement attorneys and engineers in the Clinton years.[101] Others indicated that relationships had improved over the course of the Clinton administration,[102] particularly after the Agency reorganization of 1993–1994.[103] In contrast, though, another subset of EPA enforcement officials viewed the attorney-scientist relationship as continuing to be mostly strained and troubled,[104] or at least highly variable in this period.[105] Some attributed the Agency interdisciplinary tensions they had identified to personality differences among particular sets of individuals[106] and the varied approaches of EPA regional managers[107] during the 1990s. Other interviewees noted that, until relatively late in the Clinton administration, EPA headquarters enforcement attorneys worked for higher pay than EPA headquarters enforcement engineers. This unfair disparity in compensation was evidently a source of some interdisciplinary tension and discontent during much of the Clinton era.[108]

Although it had fluctuations, and it included several periods of relative calm, the relationship between EPA enforcement officials and their counterparts in a number of state environmental departments and agencies was frequently stormy and contentious during the Clinton administration. A number of the EPA and DOJ enforcement officials whom I interviewed noted a great deal of variation—by state, by program, and by EPA region—in the tenor of EPA's dealings with the states.[109] Many federal enforcement staff members and managers also expressed the view that EPA-state relations were often more cooperative at the career staff level than at upper management levels, where political and ideological factors tend to play a greater role.[110]

EPA and DOJ did make an active effort to "reach out to the states" in the enforcement area.[111] As a result, EPA and the states (usually acting through the offices of their attorneys general) acted as co-plaintiffs in a number of federal civil enforcement matters,[112] and EPA and DOJ established cooperative relationships as well with state and local law enforcement officials with regard to some criminal enforcement cases.[113] Moreover, immediately following EPA's reorganization, the Agency's enforcement oversight of the states declined,[114] and the Agency created a new, more flexible policy framework, the National Environmental Performance Partnership System (NEPPS), to govern a number of aspects of federal-state relations.[115]

Notwithstanding NEPPS, however, after the middle of the 1990s EPA tried to convince the states to continue following critical aspects of its traditional deterrence-based enforcement approach, as set forth in the Agency's 1986 Revised Policy Framework (RPF) for state-EPA enforcement agreements. As Clifford Rechtschaffen and David Markell have perceptively observed in their fine book, *Reinventing Environmental Enforcement and the State/Federal Relationship*,[116] this inconsistent federal approach had the unfortunate effect of sending "mixed signals" to the states as to what EPA truly expected of them. It resulted in increased state-level frustration with Agency oversight of state enforcement work. As one EPA regional enforcement coordinator described it, "NEPPS raised the expectations of some states that EPA would leave them alone. When that didn't happen, it raised their hackles."[117]

Some of EPA's initial policy changes, which the states generally favored, were lobbied for or supported by the Environmental Council of States (ECOS), an organization composed of state environmental commissioners that was formed in 1993 to increase the influence and autonomy of state officials in environmental policy making.[118] From the outset, ECOS expressed dissatisfaction with what it viewed as inflexible EPA oversight, burdensome reporting requirements, and a paucity of state input in EPA policy decisions. With regard to enforcement, a number of its members favored greater reliance on compliance assistance, the enactment of environmental immunity and privilege laws, and a reduced emphasis on traditional inspections, formal enforcement actions, and penalties.[119]

As the Clinton administration progressed, state-federal enforcement relationships gradually became more strained. EPA began to increase its pressure on the states to make use of a more traditional deterrent enforcement approach.[120] This policy shift—which came in the aftermath of the administration's protracted budgetary struggle with Congress in 1995 and 1996—gave rise to angry protests from state officials, particularly during Clinton's second term in office.[121] As Gail Ginsberg described it, "ECOS developed a bash-EPA orientation. They would invite people like Steve [Herman] and Sylvia [Lowrance] and other high-ranking EPA officials to come to their meetings, and then they would just attempt to humiliate them."[122]

Although it had multiple causes, a good deal of the animosity between EPA and state officials in the Clinton years seems to have been inspired by partisan rivalry. As Mike Stahl later pointed out, during much of the Clinton period "thirty-seven or so governors were Republican, and EPA was run by Democrats. That fact alone led to friction."[123]

Whatever its precise genesis however, many of the disputes between EPA and state environmental enforcement personnel in the Clinton era focused on a limited set of policy questions. One of these issues was a controversy over state privilege and immunity statutes. In the 1980s, in response to more aggressive environmental enforcement by both government agencies and private citizens, a number of companies had begun to conduct voluntary audits in order to make an independent, systematic review of their facilities' compliance with environmental requirements. Some of those firms subsequently lobbied both Congress and the states for audit privilege and immunity laws.[124] Although these companies were unsuccessful in gaining the passage of favorable federal legislation, they did convince nearly half of the states to pass some version of an audit privilege or immunity statute.[125]

Throughout the Clinton administration, EPA and the Justice Department staunchly and consistently opposed these state laws on the basis that they severely undercut state enforcement efforts. The Agency threatened to revoke previously issued delegations, and withhold delegation of new authority for federally delegated environmental programs until the states effectively repealed their audit and privilege statutes.[126] In the end, nearly all states that had enacted such laws did later modify or narrow them to EPA's satisfaction.[127] Nonetheless, the battling that took place over this issue left a bitter taste in the mouths of some state environmental officials.

Another key point of dispute between EPA and the states concerned EPA's occasional practice of "overfiling," i.e., initiating a federal enforcement action after the completion of a state enforcement action for the same environmental violations. Such actions, which usually reflected EPA's strong dissatisfaction with a state's failure to assess sufficient penalties to redress the violations in question, have tended to provoke bitter protests from state enforcement officials. Ultimately, the overfiling issue was addressed by the federal courts.

In 1999, in *Harmon Industries, Inc. v. Browner*, the U.S. Court of Appeals for the Eighth Circuit invalidated an overfiled EPA administrative enforcement order that had assessed penalties under RCRA against a firm that had previously entered into a consent decree with the state of Missouri covering the same violations.[128] This surprising decision, which has subsequently been squarely rejected by several other federal courts,[129] resulted in an especially "cautious approach" to overfiling by EPA and DOJ during the final years of the Clinton era. Regrettably, that self-imposed federal caution took away some of EPA's negotiating leverage, both with individual violators and with recalcitrant states, because it undercut the perceived probability that EPA might overfile in any given case.[130]

In stark contrast with EPA's frequently troubled enforcement relationship with the states during the Clinton period, the Agency's working relationship with the Department of Justice during the same era was generally harmonious. Some twenty-two of the officials I spoke with described the EPA-DOJ relationship as being "excellent," "great," "respectful," "good," "cooperative," "harmonious," or "collegial."[131] A far smaller number of interviewees took the view that the Clinton era EPA-DOJ relationship varied depending on the individuals involved[132] or made note of occasional contention between the organizations over questions of policy.[133]

With respect to the kinds of issues that arose when the relationship did experience some frictions, a significant number of EPA and DOJ employees whom I spoke with referred to an ever-increasing shortage of DOJ attorneys to work on EPA enforcement cases.[134] As George Czerniak, an experienced enforcement manager in EPA's Region V's program, put it:

> DOJ has limited resources for [enforcement] cases. They can get consumed by very large cases. Cases you refer to them may not get filed for a couple of years. Then, when they do get filed, the cases may not proceed as quickly as you want them to.[135]

Other common points of tension arose from the attitudes and perceptions of EPA and DOJ staff attorneys. As one EPA regional enforcement attorney saw it:

> DOJ attorneys sometimes viewed themselves as superior to EPA attorneys, and as in charge of [enforcement] cases, despite their relative lack of experience. Also, DOJ often treated EPA with skepticism, as bean counters who go after smaller cases and ignore larger ones. [Additionally] DOJ sometimes rushed cases to settlement, despite EPA's wishes.[136]

Moreover, as EPA Region II manager Bill Muszynski observed:

> There were tensions as a result of DOJ concerns about taking weak cases and establishing bad national precedents. That view conflicted with EPA's desire to be more assertive [in enforcement].[137]

These occasional rivalries and tensions, however, should not obscure the extent to which EPA and DOJ's enforcement staff typically worked together effectively and harmoniously during the Clinton administration. Substantial credit for that beneficial—and far from inevitable—situation must go to Assistant Administrator Steve Herman and Assistant Attorney General Lois Schiffer. The smooth and respectful working relationship that those two political appointees established with one another set a healthy, positive tone for the rest of their respective organizations.[138] As Steve Herman recollected:

> DOJ was always brought in at the beginning when EPA was developing a policy, and Justice did the same thing with their policies that affected EPA. Lois Schiffer and I talked an awful lot. If a problem came up, we didn't let it get out of hand. God knows, we didn't always agree. But it was always handled in a professional way, with no backbiting, and always with the best interests of both agencies in mind. There was an awful lot of constructive collaboration present, which really paid off.[139]

Lois Schiffer's observations were to the same effect:

> I had hired Steve Herman at DOJ back in the 1970s. We were friends. That really helped because it meant that if our staffs were at loggerheads on a particular issue we would work it out together. . . . We set an example for working things out between the agencies that our staffs observed and followed.[140]

In contrast to its largely effective dealings with "main Justice," EPA's enforcement relationship with the U.S. Attorneys' offices in the Clinton years was played out on a much smaller stage. According to a number of the EPA and DOJ people I spoke with, U.S. Attorneys' offices are usually far more interested in handling environmental criminal prosecutions than they are in initiating civil enforcement actions.[141] Their collective role in environmental enforcement in the 1990s was thus relatively minor.

The interest of U.S. Attorneys in environmental matters appears to have varied considerably from office to office.[142] Thus, in a few (mostly large) cities around the United States, U.S. Attorneys did voluntarily become involved in important EPA enforcement cases during the Clinton era.[143] For the most part, however, as noted above, those relatively autonomous political appointees chose not to involve themselves in redressing environmental violations during that period.

As we have previously seen, the lengthy budgetary dispute between the 104th Congress and EPA had significant short-term and long-term impacts on the Agency's enforcement efforts during the Clinton administration. Congressional hostility to environmental regulation was also influential in other ways. From 1995 on, the fundamental message of Congress to EPA altered dramatically. As David Nielsen put it:

> Expectations changed. In the late 1980s Congress's oversight focused on [the adequacy of] EPA's implementation of regulatory requirements. [During the mid-1990s] the focus on the Hill was on things like: Are you being too harsh on small businesses? Are you imposing penalties that are too great?[144]

As noted above, the Clinton administration's long battle with Congress in 1995–1996 culminated in what appeared to be a victory for the opponents of drastic budget cuts for EPA and its enforcement programs. Nonetheless, using techniques that were far less visible to the public, from the mid-1990s forward Congress made modest (but cumulatively significant) annual cuts in the money available for environmental enforcement at EPA and DOJ.

In significant part, this was accomplished by what some EPA employees refer to as "Congress's cost-of-living allowance (COLA) trick." Congress mandated that all federal agencies and departments provide their employees with cost-of-living salary increases. At the same time, Congress did not appropriate any funds to pay for these required payroll increases. Federal agencies and departments (including EPA) were thus forced to economize on other items that were included in their supposedly "approved" and "funded" budgets in order to comply with congressional dictates.

Federal agencies and departments chose to cope with this situation—which continued into the Bush II administration—in several ways. Some froze staff hiring, and saved money by diminishing the size of their staffs by attrition. Others left staff positions (for which funds were appropriated) vacant for extended periods—a strategy that tended to present the false impression that the agency or department had a larger work force than it actually did.

The most widely used response to the "COLA trick," however, was for agencies to increase their salary pools by diverting funds from their "extramural budgets," which—in EPA's case—are used to contract the services of needed expert witnesses and to pay for other crucially important enforcement litigation expenses. This approach (which began in the Clinton years but continued long after the Clinton administration left office) led to long-term imbalances. In particular, a number of EPA's regional offices suffered to a very significant extent from the ever-growing resource crunch that it created.

In addition to open budget cuts and the reduction of EPA enforcement funding through the "COLA trick" Congress also interfered with the Agency's enforcement work in the latter part of the Clinton administration by earmarking enforcement funds for particular, narrow purposes. It also sometimes included language in committee reports ordering that the Agency not engage in certain types of enforcement activities, e.g., settlements under the Comprehensive Environmental Response, Compensation, and Liability Act (CERCLA) involving the removal of sediment deposits.[145]

EPA's bickering with the Congress clearly affected the outlook of the Agency's enforcement employees throughout the Clinton years. As one former DOJ official put it, "after the GOP took over the House, EPA felt tremendously under siege—the whole Agency. They felt their funding was going to be cut and that lots of other things would happen."[146] Some EPA employees had a sense of "looking over their shoulders" throughout the Clinton administration, and of having to be careful not to have any of their cases become a "poster child" for anti-regulatory forces on Capitol Hill.[147] As Steve Herman expressed it, "[W]e had to do our work very, very well and not make stupid mistakes that would serve to help the people who wanted to undercut enforcement. . . . The Agency was certainly a target for people who did not like it."[148]

Finally, with respect to EPA's relationship with the White House during the Clinton administration, a majority of the enforcement officials I spoke with indicated that, as far as they were aware, the president and his staff consciously avoided any direct involvement in ongoing Agency enforcement matters.[149] As Steve Herman observed: "The White House generally stayed out of enforcement. They appreciated that environmental enforcement was a law enforcement function. They tried to avoid even the appearance of manipulation."[150]

Notwithstanding its self-imposed lack of direct involvement in individual enforcement cases, however, the Clinton White House was still perceived as generally supportive of the Agency's enforcement work by a number of EPA and DOJ enforcement personnel.[151] In part, this perception stemmed from the Clinton administration's firm defense of the Agency's enforcement budget in its clashes with Congress. It may have also been a result of the fact that, on the rare occasions when Carol Browner became involved in controversies with other federal agencies and departments over proposed EPA regulations, President Clinton consistently supported the positions that Browner had taken.[152]

EPA's relationship with the White House Office of Management and Budget (OMB), however, contrasted sharply with the cordiality of its ties with the rest of the White House. OMB was sharply critical of some aspects of EPA management, and it often pressed the Agency to find new ways in which to economize. As Carol Browner bluntly observed:

> OMB was a pain in the ass, no two ways about it, and you know, in the end, [it was] not a helpful one. It could have been helpful but it was not. [OMB Director] Sally Katzen tried, to her credit, to be constructive. However, she was stuck with the work product of the OMB's small staff, who just put the same junk out there all the time—the same stuff that those people had been grinding out for years. Sally Katzen tried hard to help us think creatively, but she didn't really have the backup.[153]

As noted above, in the months that followed the Clinton administration's showdown with the 104th Congress in 1996 over the federal budget, EPA enjoyed a period of relative freedom from congressional threats and interference. Additionally, the Agency's reorganization was by then completed, and its top managers communicated to the regional offices— unambiguously and with enthusiasm—their support for vigorous enforcement of environmental enforcement. These convergent conditions created fertile ground for the rapid growth of EPA enforcement and for the implementation of some innovative enforcement approaches that yielded excellent results. As Walter Mugdan thoughtfully observed: "The latter four to five years of the Clinton administration hold their own against any comparable period in the Agency's enforcement history."[154]

Perhaps the most significant new enforcement approach of this era was the vastly increased use of "targeted national enforcement initiatives." At the direction of OECA, EPA regional offices began to deemphasize single-facility, single-medium enforcement cases. Instead, the Agency devoted many more of its enforcement resources to company-wide or industrial sector-wide efforts to compel compliance and extract penalties. During the late 1990s EPA and DOJ proceeded with quite a few of these large-scale initiatives.

Under the leadership of Eric Schaeffer and Bruce Buckheit, and with

DOJ's full and active support, the Agency developed and brought comprehensive cases against violators in the petroleum refining, wood products, mini-mill steel, diesel engine, coal-fired electric utility, and farming industries, as well as against universities and large municipalities found to have violated EPA's requirements as to combined sewer overflows. These cases were typically preceded by intensive EPA investigations and analyses, a key purpose of which was targeting companies and industries whose exceptionally poor environmental compliance records made the initiation of large-scale cases against them an efficient use of federal enforcement resources.[155] EPA also made an effort to bring its larger enforcement cases in populous areas, where people were more likely to be affected by pollution.[156]

Targeted national enforcement cases were often managed by OECA staff attorneys and (after referral to the Justice Department) by DOJ lawyers. EPA regional office enforcement personnel were offered an opportunity to participate in those cases, and many in the regions did so. The cases were frequently settled by consent decrees that mandated very substantial cutbacks in emissions, along with payment of substantial civil penalties by the defendants.[157]

The largest targeted sector-wide initiative of the Clinton era involved the electric utility industry. In the late 1990s, EPA's targeting efforts focused on which industrial sectors were "the dirtiest," along with which sectors were growing the most rapidly. As Bruce Buckheit stated:

> Coal consumption [in the United States] had increased greatly since the Clean Air Act Amendments were passed. Yet there had been virtually no new power plants built. So the question arose: where is all this additional coal burning happening? EPA's investigation of that sector found approximately a 70 percent rate of noncompliance with new source review (NSR) requirements. In 1999 [following referrals from EPA] the Justice Department filed lawsuits against twelve power companies representing approximately 40 percent of the megawattage in the country. [At EPA] we also continued to investigate another 40 percent of the megawattage.[158]

Regrettably, as described in more detail in the next chapter, EPA's continued investigation of electric utility noncompliance with NSR regulations was long-delayed in the Bush II administration for essentially political reasons.[159] Thus, the full potential of this particular, high-priority, resource-intensive EPA enforcement initiative took a very long while to be realized as a means of forcing the abatement of millions of tons of the utility industry's air pollutants, and significantly improving public health.

Part of the reason for the dramatic success of many of EPA's targeted enforcement initiatives in Clinton's second term was the fact that, from the mid-1990s forward, the Agency developed greatly improved methods of targeting for potential large-scale national enforcement cases. Those included the use of enhanced computerized databases, such as IDEA/ECHO.[160] The implementation of these improvements (which one EPA participant described as "a very resource-intensive process"),[161] together with increased EPA use of other databases (such as Public Utility Commission and Federal Energy Regulatory Commission records of utility capital projects) greatly enhanced the Agency's ability to do enforcement targeting that was far more accurate, swift, and effective.[162]

In addition, the effectiveness of EPA's targeted enforcement initiatives as deterrents to all other violations was further enhanced by EPA's practice of publicizing its own enforcement objectives and achievements. During Clinton's second term, Eric Schaeffer, Mike Stahl, and their staffs routinely described EPA's new enforcement agenda (including its ongoing and planned initiatives) in a regularly published, widely subscribed to OECA publication titled *Enforcement Alert*.[163] Carol Browner and Janet Reno also made it a frequent practice to appear together at press conferences, in order to publicize the filing or settlement of large federal environmental cases.[164] Beyond this, as Eric Schaeffer described:

> [W]e also wrote letters to some companies (refineries, [telecommunications] firms, metal finishers, municipalities, airlines) flagging compliance problems and inviting them to disclose and correct in exchange for a significant penalty reduction. We almost always got a good response to these initiatives. These were most effective where the compliance cost was fairly low (e.g., where it involved reporting instead of big capital spending), but it saved the Agency a lot of resources relative to the results we obtained.[165]

Another significant EPA enforcement achievement of the late Clinton administration was what one perceptive observer described as "a relatively dramatic increase in the criminal enforcement program."[166] In the early 1990s, at the direction of Congress, as expressed in the Pollution Prosecution Act of 1990, EPA expanded its permanent criminal investigation staff from approximately sixty-five to nearly two hundred investigators.[167] The

Agency then established a number of criminal investigation "field offices" around the United States. This change "placed the criminal investigators much closer to the places they had to investigate, and dramatically increased their capabilities."[168] It also put the investigators in closer touch with local U.S. Attorneys' offices, who began playing more of a role in environmental criminal prosecutions.[169]

As a result of these developments, together with considerable management attention to criminal enforcement on the DOJ side by Assistant Attorney General Lois Schiffer and a growing sophistication about environmental crime among federal district court judges, the federal environmental criminal enforcement effort "revved up into high gear" in the late 1990s.[170] EPA and DOJ brought many more criminal cases than they had done in the past. Moreover, upon the conviction of criminal defendants, those cases resulted in more stringent prison terms than had been given previously.[171]

With respect to Superfund, beginning in 1995 and continuing into President Clinton's second term, the administration's emphasis shifted from the passage of "consensus legislation" that would have reformed the program to administrative reforms that the Agency could implement unilaterally to make the Superfund Program (in Carol Browner's words) "faster, fairer, and more efficient."[172] These reforms included such measures as an increased emphasis on the completion of construction at Superfund sites, expanding the use of orphan shares and de minimus settlements, establishing *de micromis* contributor policies, targeting a wider range of PRPs, streamlining oversight costs, increasing community participation in site decisions, promoting CERCLA settlements more effectively, establishing new measures of program success, and addressing the special problems of lending institutions, municipalities, and legitimate recyclers.[173] Taken together, this reform package "defused" much of the criticism of the Superfund Program and "got rid of a lot of the irritants that were creating part of the call for new legislation."[174] It also—at least to a modest extent—appears to have promoted better functioning of the CERCLA Program at the Agency.

Another useful enforcement innovation in the late 1990s was the EPA's increased willingness, during that time, to forego some amount of civil penalties in particular enforcement cases in exchange for Supplemental Environmental Projects (SEPs), i.e., environmentally beneficial activities by defendants that do not profit the defendants in any way and that provide sound environmental results.[175] Although the significance of SEPs is difficult to gauge, a number of EPA (and DOJ) enforcement professionals appear to agree with Gail Ginsberg's judgment that SEPs have resulted in "some worthwhile community-oriented projects and some good environmental results."[176]

The EPA's administrative enforcement program also took some steps forward in the late 1990s. EPA added a contingent of new administrative law judges (ALJs) to this program in the mid-nineties, a welcome change which greatly speeded up administrative enforcement under FIFRA, RCRA, and the Clean Air Act.[177] Following that, the Agency began to handle many more routine enforcement matters administratively—including National Emissions Standards for Hazardous Air Pollutants (NESHAP) enforcement in asbestos demolition or renovation cases and Clean Air Act automobile emission tampering cases—rather than referring them to DOJ for civil litigation as had been done in the past.[178]

EPA also continued to devote significant resources to multimedia enforcement cases. These cases were resisted by some of the Agency's career enforcement staff, in both the regional program offices and headquarters.[179] Nonetheless, multimedia cases were supported by other career enforcement staffers, and also by a number of senior enforcement managers in OECA and the regions, as representing an effective use of scarce Agency enforcement resources to achieve favorable environmental results.

Finally, EPA's enforcement programs seem to have benefited, at least incrementally, from the Agency's adoption of additional measures of the successfulness of environmental enforcement work. After a lengthy, intensive evaluation of various potential enforcement metrics by a task force headed by Deputy Assistant Administrator Mike Stahl, the Agency began to supplement its reliance on enforcement "outputs" (e.g., number of inspections, penalties, etc.) by attempting to measure the actual environmental impacts of its individual enforcement cases on a regular basis. This approach may well have had the advantage of explaining the value of enforcement efforts "in layperson's terms."[180] Its adoption may also have goaded the Agency into taking bolder, industry-wide enforcement cases because of their potentially greater environmental impacts.[181]

At the same time, however, the quantification of the environmental results of cases is an inherently "inexact science,"[182] and it certainly has no applicability to programs whose main focus is to prevent pollution.[183] Thus, Sylvia Lowrance may well have been correct when she stated, "I'm not sure that this effort can be taken much further without an enormous investment in new data collection—well beyond EPA's financial means."[184]

Overall then, as described above, the second term of the Clinton administration was a time of considerable progress and innovation in EPA enforcement. It is worth noting, however, that this period was something less than a golden era in the Agency's enforcement history. Some of the problems that began in the early days of the Clinton period continued into its final four or five years. These included the lingering sense on the part of some career staff members that they still needed to look over their shoulders for the possibility of congressional interference with EPA enforcement work,[185] the slow but steady erosion in the enforcement resources of EPA and the DOJ as a result of Congress's "COLA trick,"[186] the absence of adequate funding for certain aspects of the Superfund Program due to expiration of the Superfund tax,[187] and the EPA's continuing poor enforcement relationship with a number of state environmental agencies.[188]

In the late 1990s, EPA also suffered from a series of misguided attempts to impose various inconsistent and largely irrelevant managerial approaches on the Agency's career staff. As one thoughtful, experienced Agency enforcement manager recalled:

> Every three to four years, EPA seemed to change its overall management philosophy. This required a lot of training of the managers and it got in the way of the work. It was time-consuming and completely process-oriented. This problem seemed to build to a crescendo until the end of the Clinton administration. It was a boon to high-priced consultants. Yet [the management approaches they espoused] seemed totally unrelated to governmental regulatory programs.[189]

Of the various management schemes imposed upon EPA during the Clinton years, the least beneficial appears to have been a government-wide requirement—created by Vice President Al Gore's Reinvention of Government Program—that required every manager in the Agency to supervise no fewer than eleven employees. This mandate, known to EPA employees as "the 1 to 11 ratio," may well have made good sense in other federal agencies and departments as a means of combating the "thickening of hierarchy" that plagues a number of governmental entities. Nonetheless, as implemented, it had an unfortunate, negative impact on EPA enforcement personnel, particularly in some of the Agency's regional offices. As one enforcement official viewed it:

> As a result [of the 1 to 11 ratio requirement] Region V had to take forty-five to fifty people out of management and back into senior staff posi-

tions. No matter how you try to do that you are going to end up with unhappy people. . . . [The ratio requirement contributed to] a climate of distrust and discontent within the region.[190]

Similarly, from a headquarters perspective, Mike Stahl was especially critical of the impact of the 1 to 11 ratio:

This had an impact on the reorganization. It torqued the structure of the [new] organization. It also required that some existing supervisors be placed in non-supervising jobs after they switched from program offices to OECA. Many of them were very bitter about that. This caused morale problems for two to three years after the reorganization [was completed].[191]

As I was told by one former EPA attorney who has a fondness for the writing of Charles Dickens: "EPA enforcement in the Clinton administration was neither the best of times nor the worst of times."[192] In fact, the period from January 1993 to January 2001 was an era of sharp contrasts, bitter partisan conflicts and, toward its end, some bold innovations and significant strides for the Agency's enforcement efforts. The Clinton administration's first two years in office were clearly that administration's least distinguished period with respect to EPA enforcement work. However laudable their motives may have been during that time, the Agency's top leaders were widely seen as sending mixed messages as to the importance of an assertive enforcement effort. They were also immersed in unproductive political wrangling with a Congress that, while controlled by Democrats, was substantially anti-regulatory in philosophy. Moreover, in that period, EPA's enforcement program was in the throes of an Agency-wide reorganization that was, on balance, only a partial success in streamlining and bolstering EPA's enforcement efforts.

In late 1994 and 1995, the Agency experienced a major confrontation between the administration and the Gingrich Congress over the size of the budget for a number of federal agencies and departments, prominently including EPA. This protracted partisan struggle led to a victory for the Clinton administration that allowed EPA some measure of autonomy and breathing room for the remainder of the Clinton era. Nonetheless, among some of the Agency's professional staff it also left a legacy of continuing anxiety and resentment. Moreover, through a low-visibility scheme known as the "COLA trick," EPA's opponents in Congress were able to continue to gradually erode EPA's extramural budget for enforcement, one of the Agency's key budget accounts for enforcement work.

Finally, however, during President Clinton's second term in office, EPA enforcement blossomed. Thanks to a more clear set of signals from EPA's political appointees, a gradual settling in by all concerned to a recently reorganized enforcement structure, and the relatively smooth working relationship between EPA and the DOJ on enforcement matters, EPA and the Justice Department were able to launch a number of "targeted enforcement initiatives" against multi-facility companies—and entire industrial sectors—that yielded impressive results. Moreover, notwithstanding rocky relationships with ECOS and a number of individual states—along with some self-imposed distractions and dislocations caused by counterproductive managerial initiatives—EPA's enforcement leaders fashioned a number of innovations (from SEPs to CERCLA administrative reforms) that moved EPA's enforcement programs forward to new levels of achievement.

Clearly, the Clinton administration's EPA enforcement efforts were uneven and even problematic at times. Nonetheless, particularly toward the end of its tenure, that administration gave responsible, stable leadership to an innovative, assertive, and well-coordinated federal environmental enforcement program.

Suspicions, Schisms, and Partial Revival: EPA Enforcement during the Bush II Administration

Although it is scarcely unique to them, the permanent career staff at EPA who are tasked with enforcing the nation's environmental laws have an exquisite sensitivity to signs and signals from their politically appointed leaders that relate to the work they do. These employees often have well-developed, informal channels of communication with one another, and (particularly at the beginnings of new presidential administrations) they engage in frequent and earnest discussions among themselves regarding the actions, leanings, quirks, and tendencies of the presidential appointees whose policies and decisions will importantly affect the direction and pace of their work.

In part for this reason, the ways in which these politically appointed officials present themselves and their policy preferences to their career staffs is of immense practical importance. As David A. Ullrich, a highly experienced and well-respected former EPA regional manager, explained it:

> Because enforcement has always been and will always be controversial and contentious, it is very critical that the people working on it have entirely clear signals that enforcement is important, that compliance with environmental laws is important, and that the people who do the work will be supported. Those signals have to come from the top. They have to come from the administrator and from the assistant administrator for enforcement and compliance assurance [OECA].[1]

Regrettably for all concerned, the first contacts between EPA's career enforcement staff and the Agency's new top managers in the administration of President George W. Bush (the Bush II administration) did not go well. Instead, many such staff members quickly came to view those early meetings and actions as the harbinger of an era in which federal enforcement of environmental laws would be given short shrift. Many EPA enforcement staff members assumed that the states would be given a far more prominent role in enforcement than the federal government would be permitted to play, and that the Agency, in general, would drastically cut back on its commitment to regulate and enforce actively, in the public interest.

The first perceived sign of what the new set of political appointees at the EPA would do regarding enforcement occurred only a few days into the tenure of Christine Todd Whitman as EPA's administrator. Whitman, a former governor of New Jersey who had actively supported and campaigned for George W. Bush in the general election of 2000, had never previously managed a regulatory agency. At the time Whitman assumed office at EPA, her environmental policy views were largely unknown to her career staff, and her positions on enforcement issues were similarly an enigma. At least some staff members, however, viewed her as at least moderately progressive. It thus came as a shock to some that, without consulting with or notifying in advance any members of her enforcement staff, Whitman publicly announced that the president's first budget for EPA would ask Congress to set aside $25 million from the OECA budget and use it for grants to individual states to help fund their enforcement programs.

That proposal provoked an immediate outcry from environmental organizations and their allies among the Democratic minority on Capitol Hill. As then–EPA Deputy Administrator Linda Fisher later remembered it, "nobody really liked [the state grant proposal] other than the states, and the states didn't even fight for it that much."[2] Concerned about the potential harm that the fund transfer arrangement would have on the ongoing efforts of OECA, these administration critics, after eliciting an analysis from the General Accounting Office (GAO) which found the proposal deeply flawed, moved swiftly and successfully to defeat it in the Senate Appropriations Committee. One year later, a scaled-down Bush II administration proposal to convert $15 million in OECA funds into federal enforcement grants to the states, also went down to defeat in congressional committees.[3]

Notwithstanding congressional rejection of these administration moves, some of the EPA career enforcement staff viewed these proposed state enforcement grant proposals as particularly worrisome. Not only had the new administrator tendered a proposal that would have cut significantly into OECA's already resource-starved work in several areas, she had done so, the staff noted, without any prior discussions with them. The staff thus began to have concerns that the new administration might be anti-enforcement in its orientation—and also unwilling to accept their own input on important issues.

Those perceptions were strengthened soon thereafter by the Bush II administration's unsuccessful attempts to gain congressional approval for Donald Schregardus, the former head of the Ohio EPA, who was the administration's first nominee to be assistant administrator for enforcement and compliance assurance. Schregardus had little direct experience in environmental enforcement. His nomination, which was made late in June 2001—once again without any advance consultation with the Agency's career staff—almost immediately engendered sharp opposition from both Ohio-based and national environmental organizations.

Schregardus did not help his own faltering cause when he submitted written answers to questions posed by Democrats on the Senate's Committee on Environment and Public Works, responses that some members of that committee viewed as "incomplete, evasive and implausible."[4] In the end, however, Schregardus's confirmation chances were irrevocably damaged by the release of a report prepared in EPA's Midwest regional office that was sharply critical of the Ohio EPA's enforcement record during the eight-year period in which Schregardus had headed that agency.[5]

At EPA headquarters, and in some regional offices, the Agency's career staff viewed the entire Schregardus nomination and confirmation battle with deep anxiety. Career staff members had not been consulted on an important decision affecting enforcement, and only the actions of Congress, rather than the preferences of the new administration, seemed to have protected the integrity of EPA's enforcement program.

As time went by, the EPA staff also began to note what they perceived as other signs of trouble. They observed, for example, that in her public statements and speeches, Administrator Whitman repeatedly declined to single out enforcement of applicable laws as a high Agency priority. Instead, Whitman often referred to enforcement in the context of a litany of EPA activities—including regulatory standard-setting, compliance assistance, and research—as examples of what the Agency did. Enforcement was almost never specifically identified by her as an important and worthwhile EPA task.

In addition, in at least some EPA offices, Bush II administration political appointees continued to leave experienced EPA career staff members out of decision loops, or even to seek from the staff pertinent information that would have been highly useful to them. As Gail Ginsberg, the former EPA Region V regional counsel observed:

> This administration showed no respect for the knowledge base that existed among EPA career staff employees and managers. People at the career level were not only cut out but decisions were made that were stupid, avoidable, and politically disadvantageous to the administration. People were not consulted who had the institutional knowledge to at least help them know when sensitive issues might arise.[6]

Other senior staff members observed early administration reluctance to enforce in certain circumstances. Sylvia Lowrance, for example, indicated:

> The [Bush II] administration would typically say "Oh, I want you to enforce, but can you please check in with us before you do any major new cases," e.g., concentrated animal feeding operations (CAFOs). That was taken by the staff as a directive not to enforce. . . . Whitman also sent her political staffers out to check on particular cases. That also chilled enforcement.[7]

Beyond the enforcement realm, EPA's staff was well aware of other highly publicized early Bush II administration decisions that affected EPA's enforcement work and its reputation for independence and scientific integrity. The first of those determinations, announced in March 2001, was an ill-advised decision not to finalize a standard proposed by EPA at the end of the Clinton administration as to the allowable concentration of toxic arsenic in drinking water.[8] That major regulatory shift was met with a loud and sustained outcry from scientists and environmental organizations. It proved to be a significant political embarrassment to the administration, and a lasting stain on its environmental reputation.

Even more damaging than the arsenic fiasco, however, was the Bush II administration's controversial announcement, in March 2001, that the United States would not ratify the Kyoto Protocol with regard to carbon dioxide pollution.[9] This international agreement, which George W. Bush had unambiguously endorsed during his campaign for the presidency in 2000, would have required significant cuts in CO_2 emissions to the atmosphere from power plants and other sources. Within the administration,

Christine Whitman had vigorously advocated continued adherence to the Kyoto Protocol, and her position on the issue had been widely known. The sudden decision by the White House to abandon the Protocol was thus viewed, both outside of the EPA and among its permanent staff, as a public slap in the face to the EPA's administrator, as well as a clear sign that the Agency was anything but its own boss on important, contentious issues of environmental policy.

The work of the Agency's senior career staff was also affected, beginning in November 2001, by an Agency-wide plan, devised by then–EPA Deputy Administrator Linda Fisher, to rotate members of EPA's Senior Executive Service (SES)—its highest-ranking career staff members—from program office to program office in headquarters, and among top management positions in the program divisions at EPA regional offices. As Fisher subsequently explained the plan's rationale:

> We had situations where people had been in their jobs for over ten years. We had people who wanted other [career] opportunities but did not know how to create them. The main idea was to keep people fresh. Very few people do their job well if they have done it for ten years. We all get stale. Secondly, the Agency has more and more been looking at issues from a multimedia point of view. But a lot of senior EPA managers have not had jobs in their careers outside of one program. There was a lot of interesting work going on in different programs. It was really an opportunity to strengthen career managers and get them prepared to lead the Agency in a more holistic way. Also, it gave new managers coming up an opportunity to work for someone new.[10]

To implement this new personnel rotation plan, the EPA administrator and her deputy administrator asked each member of the SES to fill out and return a survey regarding long-term career goals and ambitions, and to identify several other SES positions within the Agency that the executive would like to be considered for. These surveys were followed up by individual interviews with SES members conducted by Linda Fisher and her staff, to further elicit SES job preferences and plans.

Over the course of twelve years, approximately seventy people (roughly one-fourth of the SES staff) did rotate to new positions within EPA under this rotation plan. Most of those job changes occurred at the headquarters level; EPA regional office personnel were affected less significantly.

Unfortunately, however, this SES position rotation came at a time of growing suspicion among EPA's career staff as to the motives of the Agency's political appointees and other Bush II administration officials. Not surprisingly, among some staff members the move raised caveats and concerns. As EPA SES member Mike Walker stated, "[T]he idea for many of the skeptics was that this [rotation] was a chance to make [SES] people more vulnerable. You could be removed. There might now be some retaliation [against dissenters]."[11] Similarly, Gail Ginsberg noted that "there was a lot of angst among the SES corps, because they didn't even know where they would be a week from now, and even more angst at the [line] staff level, not knowing whom their boss was going to be."[12] At the same time, however, other SES members either welcomed the rotation pledge or viewed it as a mixed blessing.[13]

In the end, the EPA may have benefited modestly from the rotation of some of its senior career executives. Certainly, the appropriateness and utility of a round of forced high-level staff changes for a governmental agency like EPA is a question as to which reasonable people may differ. Moreover, from her demeanor during our interview, I am fully convinced of the sincerity of Linda Fisher's statement that "the rotation was not politically motivated. I felt that it needed to happen, that it was good for the Agency and good for the career folks."[14]

Nonetheless, particularly coming when it did, the SES rotation initiated in November 2001 would undoubtedly have benefited if its aims and potential benefits had been more clearly articulated at the time—beyond the circulation of a memorandum—both to those who were directly affected by it and to those who were not. Regrettably, that explanation was not provided effectively. Thus, in the event, the SES rotation proved to be yet another dry stick tossed on the glowing embers of discontent and fear that were quietly smoldering among EPA's permanent enforcement staff.

The policy change which EPA's staff viewed as the clearest and most deleterious signal of Bush II administration antipathy to EPA enforcement, however, occurred in a different context. It stemmed from a decision, apparently made in mid-2001 within the White House, over the express objections of EPA Administrator Whitman, to "reform" EPA's Clean Air Act new source review (NSR) regulations.[15] This obtuse, entirely avoidable error weakened the equitable basis of EPA and the DOJ for pursuing already-initiated lawsuits against electric utility companies found in violation of NSR requirements. It slowed and then brought to a temporary but damaging standstill the vast, time-consuming, labor-intensive investigations that a number of EPA regional offices had pursued with regard to suspected NSR violations at aging generating stations. Moreover, it complicated the work of DOJ attorneys, harmed the reputation of EPA's enforcement efforts, demoralized a significant segment of EPA's enforcement staff, and cast a pall of gloom and disaffection over almost all of the Agency's ongoing enforcement work, for many months.

The NSR reform debacle had its roots in a comprehensive set of 1977 amendments to the Clean Air Act.[16] At that time, codifying a compromise among politically opposed lobbyists, Congress accepted the notion that electric utility companies should not be required to improve air pollution problems at their oldest power plants all at once. Instead, it was deemed best to have the industry gradually improve its air pollution problems by replacing the plants with new facilities, equipped with the best available pollution control technology, as the old facilities became obsolete. The amendments also required that if existing plants were "modified" through a physical change that resulted in increased pollutant emissions, those facilities too were to be subject to the strict standards imposed under new source review. These standards generally necessitated the installation, at electric generating stations, of sulfur dioxide scrubbers, electrostatic precipitators, and other very effective, although in some cases relatively expensive, air pollution control technology.

From the late 1970s through the early 1990s, with only a few exceptions, EPA did little to enforce NSR requirements against electric utilities.[17] Focusing on other priorities, the Agency's regional offices typically deferred to state governmental findings that virtually no aging power plants were being modified in a way that would subject them to NSR requirements.

In the mid-1990s, however, EPA's regulatory and enforcement passivity with respect to aging power plants and NSR standards evaporated. An important catalyst for that change was the appointment of Bruce Buckheit—an energetic and experienced DOJ attorney who had also previously worked on auto safety issues with the Department of Transportation—to direct the Air Enforcement Division of the Office of Regulatory Enforcement in OECA. As Bob Kaplan (one of Buckheit's former colleagues at the Justice Department and now himself an enforcement official in EPA) told me:

> To a large extent, this [power plant] initiative was leadership- and personality-driven. To do something big takes a lot of energy and personal investment, and it takes someone who can really do the stuff. Bruce Buckheit is someone who can. He is a person who accomplishes things.[18]

Together with his staff, Buckheit became aware that since the 1977 Clean Air Act amendments had been passed, coal consumption across the United States had increased significantly. At the same time though, virtually no new power plants had been commissioned and almost no utility companies had applied for or received governmental permits to operate modified facilities under NSR standards. "Thus," Buckheit later indicated, "the question that arose was where was all this additional coal-burning happening?"[19]

With the full support of Eric Schaeffer, then the head of the Office of Regulatory Enforcement, as well as Steve Herman, at that time EPA's assistant administrator for enforcement and compliance assurance, Buckheit launched a massive investigation of the electric utility industry that involved numerous EPA enforcement personnel in headquarters and in several regional offices. This investigation rather stunningly revealed that approximately 70 percent of coal-fired generating stations across the United States were in violation of NSR standards.[20] The violations it uncovered ranged from failures by utility officials to complete Clean Air Act permit applications properly to instances in which power plants had not sought modification determinations from appropriate authorities on the pretext that they were merely engaged in "routine maintenance activities" while actually engaging in very large and costly equipment replacement projects that increased their plant capacity and emission levels.[21]

On the basis of these findings, in 1999 EPA referred to the Justice Department nine lawsuits against large electric utility companies whose plants generated approximately 40 percent of the megawattage created in the United States.[22] It also continued its investigation of electric utility companies, with a view toward filing subsequent lawsuits against power plants generating yet another 40 percent of U.S. electricity megawattage.[23]

The potential environmental implications of those civil enforcement cases, which DOJ filed in 1999, were immense. As one current EPA headquarters enforcement official indicated:

> There is no bigger air pollution problem than utility pollution. It is an order of magnitude bigger than the second-biggest problem (refineries), which is in turn an order of magnitude bigger than anything else.[24]

The potentially vast environmental gains of these enforcement lawsuits were significantly delayed, however. Viewing EPA's enforcement suits as overregulation, as well as a potentially expensive problem for them, significant parts of the electricity industry devised a massive political lobbying strategy to derail the suits and avoid liability. The utilities contended that EPA's NSR regulations subjected them to harsh penalties for "light bulb changing." Their first step was to turn to Congress and request that a rider be attached to the appropriations bill which would fund EPA, allowing electric utility companies to perform "routine maintenance" while the EPA's lawsuits were pending. That effort was unsuccessful.[25]

At that point however, segments of the utility industry took a different tack. They began to contribute heavily to the presidential campaign of George W. Bush, in the hope that, if elected, a Bush II administration would be more sympathetic to measures that would eliminate the industry's regulatory exposure under NSR. In fact, a number of utility lawyers and lobbyists earned the label of executive "Pioneers" in Bush's campaign by personally raising more than $100,000 in campaign contributions. These included executives from electric companies (such as First Energy, Reliant Resources, MidAmerican Energy, and the Southern Company) that were already in litigation with the government regarding NSR regulations, or else under active investigation by EPA's enforcement staff.[26] Their contributions to Bush's 2000 election campaign were the largest sum donated to it by any single industry.

After Bush was sworn in as president, the utility industry did indeed find helpful, influential supporters within his administration. Their new inside allies included appointed officials at the Department of Energy (DOE) and the White House Council on Environmental Quality (CEQ). The industry found a steadfast friend in Vice President Richard ("Dick") Cheney who, when he was president and chief executive officer in the Halliburton Company, had been a member of a National Petroleum Council Committee on Refining that had sharply criticized new source review and the lawsuits EPA had brought against oil refiners.[27] In addition, the industry had a good friend in Jeffrey ("Jeff") Holmstead, an attorney who had worked with the law firm of Latham and Watkins that had represented electric utilities and sympathized with their perspective. Holmstead, who had served in the Office of the White House Counsel during the Bush I administration, served as a consultant at EPA from March through July of 2001. He was confirmed as the Agency's assistant administrator for air and radiation in August 2001.[28]

Jeff Holmstead entered EPA with strongly held views regarding the Clean Air Act, based on his past experiences with that statute. He told me in an interview that "in some ways [the Act] has been very successful, but what happens, at every stage, is that they keep adding things without figuring out how it will all fit together.[29] Holmstead had a particularly negative view of the Act's NSR provisions that, as he saw them, "did more harm than good in terms of discouraging companies from doing good." In Holmstead's words, "I was convinced that in order to have a fair, predictable regulatory program that functioned, we really ought to reform the way that NSR worked."[30]

Only nine days after assuming office, Bush created a task force headed by Vice President Cheney, the National Energy Policy Development Group, which was given responsibility for crafting a new national energy policy. According to the best available information, this task force received considerable advice and information from utility industry sources, and relatively little input from any other sources. Its recommendations, released in May 2001, called for changes and rollbacks in a number of aspects of U.S. energy and environmental laws, along with a formal review of both EPA's NSR rules and the legal basis for the DOJ's already-filed lawsuits.[31]

Soon thereafter, President Bush ordered the EPA to conduct a three-month public review of its NSR rules, and he directed the Justice Department to review the adequacy and appropriateness of its previously filed NSR cases. The latter review was conducted by the Office of Legal Policy (OLP), a previously obscure office within DOJ best known for its role in screening judicial candidates. OLP closely scrutinized the Justice Department's files in each of the ongoing NSR power plant cases. According to one former DOJ lawyer, this extraordinary review raised concerns among the Justice Department attorneys litigating the power plant NSR cases, because they feared that anything detrimental that the OLP found would have undermined the ongoing cases, both in court and on Capitol Hill.[32] In the end, however, the OLP issued an opinion that was largely limited to constitutional issues, and reasonably favorable to the positions taken by DOJ's utility NSR case litigators.

Within the EPA, however, events developed quite differently. During the pendency of the ninety-day NSR rule review, Holmstead and his staff, with active input from the Department of Energy and other utility industry sympathizers within the executive branch, began the task of rewriting EPA's NSR rules. A key focus of their efforts was the regulatory definition of "routine maintenance," i.e., the amount of money a utility company would be permitted to spend annually to upgrade a power plant without "modifying" the facility, and thus triggering the NSR requirements. OECA, through its then–Acting Assistant Administrator Sylvia Lowrance, recommended that companies be allowed to spend annually up to 0.75 percent of a generating unit's replacement cost without becoming subject to NSR requirements.[33] In August 2003, however, when the Agency's final NSR revisions were at last announced, EPA's new regulations included an "equipment replacement rule" that permitted electricity manufacturers to spend as much as 20 percent of generating unit replacement costs on plant upgrades each year before NSR standards could be applied.[34] In effect, although the framework of new source review was retained, the new rules established a threshold so extraordinarily high as to make it almost inconceivable that NSR standards would ever apply to generating stations in particular cases.

As J. P. Suarez, EPA's assistant administrator for enforcement and compliance during parts of 2002 and 2003, perceived it:

> It became clear to me, fairly early on, that the NSR reform was focused solely on power plants. It also became clear to me during my tenure at EPA that the goal of NSR reform was to prevent any enforcement case from going forward. Some people thought the [NSR power plant enforcement initiative] should never have been brought. The reform was really designed to thwart our ability to do it.[35]

Suarez, who (along with Administrator Whitman) had opposed the reform proposal in private debates within the administration, called the 20 percent rule that was finally adopted "overdone," and he stated that the "reason for reform was oversold." Suarez indicated that, while some form of NSR reform might have been beneficial, "because we were so inflamed and overheated about the reform, we ended up with a reform package that doesn't pass the laugh test."[36]

The protracted struggle within the Bush II administration over NSR enforcement "reform" (and its regulatory outcome) did not escape the notice of the administration's critics among environmental groups and some state officials, along with their allies on Capitol Hill. In fact, beginning in 2002, a number of prominent state attorneys general, senators, representatives, and environmental organizations expressed serious substantive and procedural concerns with the way EPA was going about reconsidering its NSR regulations, concerns that were ultimately ignored by the administration.[37]

Meanwhile, the Justice Department continued to pursue the NSR lawsuits it had filed against power plants, and to attempt settling those cases on terms favorable to the government. Those negotiations soon faltered, however. Utility company defendants began to anticipate that the suits pending against them would be eviscerated by EPA changes in the NSR rules.[38] As Bruce Buckheit remembered the situation, "we were 80 percent of the way done, with seven or eight companies, and one by one they backed away."[39]

EPA's investigations of additional NSR violations also continued during 2001 and 2002. The pace and scale of those investigations began to diminish however, amid staff uncertainty and concern over the future direction of the NSR power plant enforcement initiative.

The impact of EPA's approach to NSR reform on the Agency's enforcement program was profound and long-lasting. A number of high-ranking Agency officials, including Eric Schaeffer, Rich Biondi, and Bruce Buckheit, as well as Christine Whitman herself, all resigned or retired from the government within a relatively short period. Some, like Schaeffer and Biondi, publicly announced that their departure was in protest against the new direction the Agency was taking with regard to NSR.[40] Others, such as Administrator Whitman, gave more personal reasons for leaving their posts.[41] J. P. Suarez, the assistant administrator for enforcement and compliance, who was to resign from the EPA himself early in 2004, regretfully informed members of his staff in November 2003, that the Agency would very likely not further pursue NSR investigations against utility companies that were not directly related to already-filed NSR enforcement cases.[42]

Soon thereafter, in late December 2003, the U.S. Court of Appeals for the D.C. Circuit breathed some new life into the federal government's all-but-defunct power plant enforcement initiative. Ruling in a lawsuit initiated by a group of state governments in challenge to EPA's NSR reforms, the court issued an order staying EPA's implementation of the equipment replacement rule that was at the heart of the promulgated reforms.[43] In response, EPA's then-Administrator Michael Leavitt announced that the Agency's policy of abandoning its investigation of NSR violations at electric generating stations would be reversed.[44]

The NSR controversy was far from resolved at that stage, however.[45] In October 2005, in an undated memorandum sent out to all EPA regional administrators and state environmental commissioners, the Agency's deputy administrator, Marcus Peacock, wrote:

> [I]t is time to update the agency's coal-fired NSR enforcement strategy. I have asked EPA's Office of Enforcement and Compliance Assurance (OECA) to . . . refocus its resources on other areas that will likely produce significant environmental benefits. EPA should continue to pursue existing filed utility cases and those matters in ongoing negotiations. In

deciding which additional cases to pursue, it is appropriate to focus on those that would violate our NSR reform rules and our latest NSR utility proposal, which the Agency is releasing today."[46]

This memorandum, which one EPA enforcement manager described as "our biggest stumbling block,"[47] effectively stalled the development of new NSR cases against electric utilities for several years. It also weakened the hand of EPA and Justice Department attorneys, who were still attempting to negotiate settlement of cases that had already been filed against electric utilities. As one regional office participant in those negotiations remembered:

> This [Peacock memo] had a chilling effect. We treaded more lightly than we would have if we had had more confidence in the underpinnings of our rules. . . . We were consistently backtracking, figuring out what our position was. The defense bar is well organized. They exchange information. They sometimes knew before we did what was going on. . . . It was very difficult.[48]

EPA's new NSR regulation was challenged in court by a coalition of environmentalists and approximately a dozen state governments. After an intense struggle, these challengers won a major victory in the D.C. Circuit, in March 2006, when that court ruled that EPA's equipment replacement rule violated the plain language of the Clean Air Act.[49] Writing for a unanimous three-judge panel, Circuit Judge Judith Rogers indicated that the statute's wording clearly required that NSR requirements be applied to "*any* type of physical change" to an industrial plant that increases emissions. She opined that "[o]nly in a Humpty Dumpty world would Congress be required to use superfluous words while an agency could ignore an expansive word that Congress did use."[50] This important decision buoyed EPA's continuing NSR enforcement actions against utilities and dealt a crucial blow to the efforts of EPA's Office of Air and Radiation, and its allies in industry and within the Bush II administration, to "reform" the NSR rules.

EPA's NSR enforcement initiative against utilities was also considerably bolstered in 2007 by a unanimous decision of the U.S. Supreme Court in *Environmental Defense v. Duke Energy Corporation*.[51] In that case, the Justice Department had filed a civil enforcement action against Duke Energy after the company had replaced tube assemblies in a number of its power plant boilers in order to extend the life of the units and allow them to run longer each day, increasing pollutant emissions in the process. In court, Duke Energy argued that EPA was required to define the "baseline" against which its emissions increases were to be measured in terms of kilograms per hour of pollutant discharges, rather than focusing on the actual average of the company's pollutant emissions for the prior two years. The utility prevailed on that theory in the trial court and the U.S. Circuit Court of Appeals for the Fourth Circuit. The U.S. Supreme Court disagreed however. Ruling in favor of the government, the court upheld the interpretation of the Clean Air Act that had, from the beginning, been the legal underpinning of EPA's NSR enforcement initiative.

Ultimately, after years of delay, fierce intra-Agency and intra-administration struggle, and an enormous investment of resources at both EPA and the Department of Justice,[52] EPA's NSR enforcement initiative against electric utilities yielded rather dramatic results. In 2008, the government settled pending civil cases against a number of large coal-burning utilities in the Midwest. The largest settlement, with American Electric Power Company, resulted in commitments to abate more than 800,000 tons of air pollutants (including sulfur dioxide, nitrogen dioxide, and particulate matter) at a cost of approximately $4.2 billion. Moreover, the company agreed to spend $60 million on environmental improvement projects and to pay $15.5 million in civil penalties.[53] Other settlements—with such large utility companies as Ohio Edison, Illinois Power, and Southern Indiana Gas and Electric—also yielded immense pollutant reductions, high penalties, and commitments to perform very substantial amounts of environmental mitigation.

These impressive case settlements, which are a source of considerable pride and satisfaction to those government employees who participated in them, reflect favorably on the persistence and dedication of the enforcement attorneys, engineers, and managers at EPA and the Department of Justice, whose indefatigable efforts yielded huge benefits to public health and environmental quality. They also reflect well on the role of courts, as the impartial interpreters of important legislation. However, as I will discuss further below, it seems clear that the internal governmental bickering that pervaded the development of these large, complex enforcement actions delayed and complicated their resolution to an extraordinary (and needless) extent, while greatly exacerbating tensions among EPA's offices at the same time. The prolonged controversy provides a cogent illustration of the disruption and inefficiency that can result when indirect, yet potent, political interference affects inherently nonpolitical, professional enforcement of environmental laws.

Beyond the drastic changes that it fashioned in the area of NSR enforcement, and its early manifestations of antipathy to—or disinterest in—EPA enforcement activities, the Bush II administration's initial handling of EPA enforcement matters had a number of other unfortunate distinguishing characteristics. One of those was secretiveness in the development of enforcement policies. In the words of one well-respected regional office career manager whom I interviewed in 2003:

> Nearly all of the political appointees in the Bush [II] administration play things very close to the vest. They are now open in terms of getting information [from their staffs] that will help them make decisions. But then when it comes time for them to make those decisions they will retire to their own chambers.[54]

A perception—both outside of and within EPA—that the Bush II administration had "politicized" EPA enforcement took firm hold, particularly in 2002 and early 2003. In addition to the NSR reform controversy, that view was reinforced by two long-standing controversies, also internal to EPA, with regard to enforcement-related policy questions.

The first question involved an air pollution problem with significant public health implications: concentrated animal feeding operations (CAFOs). These operations emit vast quantities of harmful air pollutants. As the late Steve Rothblatt, director of EPA Region V's Air and Radiation Division told me: "[T]he amount of pollutants [CAFOs] give off—both PM-25 and ammonia—is mind-boggling; and the ammonia contributes to fine particulate formation, too. It is very bad."[55] In the early days of the Bush II administration, OECA, then under the acting leadership of Sylvia Lowrance, was told that no Clean Air Act enforcement actions regarding CAFOs were to be taken without the advance approval of the headquarters Office of Air and Radiation (OAR), headed by Jeff Holmstead. Convinced that approval of such cases would never be forthcoming, the head of the Office of Regulatory Enforcement at that time, Eric Schaeffer, decided not to seek CAFO enforcement cases from regional offices or to refer any such matters to DOJ.[56] As Bruce Buckheit saw it:

> Regarding CAFOs, the politics have slowed us down. It has been a battle within EPA, and with the Department of Agriculture, to mount an effective enforcement program there. Again, we started getting some momentum and we were stopped.[57]

The next phase of EPA's contentious in-house struggle with respect to CAFO enforcement was described quite candidly by J. P. Suarez in an interview:

> OECA had been working with industry for six months on an agreement whereby the industry would sign up and pay a modest penalty and then EPA would gather data for eighteen months about air emissions from CAFOs—mostly from chickens and hogs. We worked with the industry and we pounded out a deal. The industry agreed with us that more data was needed [to set more specific emissions limits] because a National Academy of Sciences report has told us that we had inadequate data.
>
> We told the Air Office that we were doing all this. We wanted their buy-in. We coordinated with them.
>
> We finally got to the point, in our negotiations with the industry, where we were literally on the doorstep, ready to go within a week, when the Air Office contacted us and told us they were drafting a regulation that would treat all CAFO air emissions as "fugitive" and [thus] take them outside the realm of regulatory control. To say that something like that brings you to a grinding halt is an understatement. We scrambled back to the head of the Air Office who told us, "I don't understand that. That's not the direction I've given." Then we went back to our negotiations with the industry only to find, three weeks later, that the Air Office had in fact decided, and had started to communicate with people that they were going to treat [CAFO emissions] as fugitive emissions. It was unbelievable and it was frustrating![58]

The best available evidence suggests that Suarez's account was accurate and that his frustrations were justifiable. In 2003, the National Academy of Sciences (NAS) issued a report evaluating the scientific basis for estimating the emissions to the atmosphere of pollutants from CAFOs.[59] This report found that the "emission factors" that the Agency had developed to estimate the air emissions from individual CAFOs could not be supported because the "model farm construct" that EPA had used to develop its emission factor had inadequately characterized feeding operations. As a result of this NAS report, in the words of a well-informed EPA enforcement manager: "It was a rocky road. We became really worried about our authority to bring new cases and, given the NAS study, about our ability to prevail."[60]

In light of this, EPA decided not to bring additional CAFO Clean Air

Act enforcement actions. Instead, it entered into lengthy negotiations with various components of the feedlot industry that ultimately resulted in a controversial administrative order (known as the "AFO/CAFO"). Under the terms of this agreement, a large number of agricultural concerns promised to cooperate with EPA in the design and implementation of a study of a representative number of farms with the aim of developing a scientifically supportable emissions factor for CAFOs. In return, EPA promised the companies that consented and signed the order a covenant not to bring any enforcement actions while the study was being performed unless the farm owners in question refused to pay a share of the costs of the research, denied the researchers access to their property, or refused to accept the emission factor that resulted from the study. Pursuant to this agreement, EPA Clean Air Act enforcement against CAFOs halted for the remainder of the Bush II administration. The emission factor study called for in the AFO/CAFO was ultimately designed and carried out over a multiyear period. As of this writing, its results are pending.

Another intra-Agency controversy that arose regarding an enforcement-related policy during the Bush II period concerned a draft guidance document for permit users, prepared by EPA's Office of Water at the urging of representatives of sewage treatment operators. That guidance document would have permitted sewage treatment plants to blend fully treated sewage with rainwater and partially treated sewage during periods of heavy rainfall. OECA objected to the proposal on the basis that it would not be enforceable against companies that blended sewage in a way that ran afoul of the proposed guidance, and that the only way that dischargers could have complied with NPDES permit limitations, consistent with the guidance, would have required the use of such limited amounts of chlorine that health threatening pathogens would be discharged through untreated sewage treatment plant outfalls.[61]

From the perspective of EPA's career enforcement staff, these developments were still further evidence that EPA's enforcement work, which had mostly been managed to that point on a professional, nonpartisan basis, was now far more politicized. As one EPA regional official put it in 2003: "There is now a greater sense, among the staff, that there is greater political scrutiny of our cases."[62] Moreover, for at least some of the Agency's enforcement managers, that perception led to a more constrained, circumspect approach to potential enforcement cases. To quote Tom Bramscher, then a water enforcement manager in EPA Region V, whom I also interviewed in 2003:

There is now always attention, that we did not have in the past, to "What are the political ramifications [of our cases]?" It is always an internal issue. We always ask ourselves: "Where can we expect conflicts to arise from specific cases, and why?"[63]

Taken together these various developments had powerful, negative effects on the morale of a number of members of EPA's career enforcement staff. Thus, when I interviewed EPA enforcement employees during the first term of the Bush II presidency, I received such comments as: "We are hunkered down. There has been a chilling effect. There is a pervasive concern that if you pick up the ball and run with it you are going to get hammered by Washington."[64] "People are nervous," Cheryl Wasserman said. "They are trying to keep a low profile. They don't have that fire in the belly."[65] According to Mike Walker, "We've been treading water and marking time. There's a lot of nervousness."[66] "The situation is very depressing," said Tom Mintz,[67] while another staffer said, "If I were writing a book on EPA enforcement right now I might title it *Bleak House.* I just try to push out of my mind all of the changes I see happening right now. . . . The situation is dire."[68]

Beyond these difficulties, certain components of EPA's enforcement program faced some unique, specific obstacles during the first years of the Bush II era. For example, late in 2003, in the area of wetlands enforcement, a knowledgeable, experienced EPA enforcement official confided that "wetlands enforcement in general is in a mess."[69] That individual explained that the problem stemmed from *Solid Waste Agency of Northern Cook County (SWANCC) v. U.S. Army Corps of Engineers,*[70] a U.S. Supreme Court decision, handed down in 2001, that had interpreted the Clean Water Act as not conferring federal authority over "an abandoned sand and gravel pit in Northern Illinois which provided habitat for migrating birds." The court's opinion left in doubt the precise extent of federal jurisdiction to regulate the dredging and filling of wetlands. In its aftermath, the DOJ objected to the filing of any civil enforcement cases referred to it by EPA that had facts at all similar to those in *SWANCC.*[71] The Justice Department also declined to bring cases that sought the restoration of relatively small tracts of damaged wetlands. At the same time, however, EPA was also limited in its authority to obtain wetlands restoration by means of administrative orders. The Agency was thus stymied in key facets of its regional wetlands enforcement initiatives.

These difficulties were magnified in 2006 when the U.S. Supreme

Court decided another wetlands case, *Rapanos v. United States*.[72] The *Rapanos* decision set aside the U.S. Army Corps of Engineers interpretation of the jurisdictional limits of the federal government's authority to regulate wetlands. In an unusual 4-1-4 split, Justice Anthony Kennedy (who concurred in the court's result but rejected its reasoning) fashioned a legal test under which the government's wetlands jurisdiction depended upon the existence of a "significant nexus" between the wetlands in question and waterways that are traditionally navigable. Kennedy's legal test—which most (but not all) observers took to be the prevailing Supreme Court doctrine—created immense practical problems for EPA's enforcement program. In effect, the new rule required EPA's inspectors to "walk the watershed" of each wetland where they suspected that unpermitted dredging and filling might be taking place simply in order to determine whether the Agency had the legal authority to bring an enforcement action. As a result of this difficulty, and the strain it placed on EPA's limited enforcement resources, the Agency's wetlands enforcement efforts ground to a halt for the remainder of the Bush II administration.

With respect to criminal enforcement, at the end of 2001 and in the first half of 2002, the EPA's efforts were set back considerably by a large-scale diversion of EPA criminal investigators to non-environmental matters. In the aftermath of the September 11, 2001, terrorist attacks on New York City and Washington, D.C., many of those investigators were reassigned to focus on the adequacy of security for public water supplies, chemical manufacturing facilities, pipelines, and the like. Other agents were diverted to "security details" which provided personal security for Administrator Christine Whitman. Beyond this, a number of FBI agents, who would previously have been available to accompany EPA criminal investigators on witness interviews, and to testify in court with regard to the results of such interviews, were also ordered to spend all of their work time on national security matters.

Those personnel shifts had major consequences for federal environmental criminal enforcement. As I was told by an attorney familiar with EPA's criminal enforcement program who requested anonymity, "that [diversion of investigators] . . . had a big impact. It has not been easy to integrate that role with the Agency's traditional environmental responsibilities."[73]

Toward the end of his tenure, OECA Assistant Administrator Suarez initiated a review and ultimately a restructuring of EPA's criminal enforcement program. These actions appear to have had some beneficial effect after Suarez left the Agency. During the second term of George W. Bush, the program brought a significant number of indictments, and developed a small, but successful system to help train assistant U.S. Attorneys in environmental criminal enforcement. It also established improved coordination with the civil enforcement side of EPA's enforcement program.[74]

The EPA's Superfund Program faced continuing financial shortfalls, and other systemic problems, during the Bush II administration. Notwithstanding some sporadic, unsuccessful efforts in Congress (which that administration declined to support) to revive the tax on petroleum and chemical feedstocks that had been the source of Superfund trust monies until that tax expired late in 1995,[75] the Superfund Program was drastically underfunded. This circumstance had several consequences. First, EPA put more effort into Superfund enforcement, particularly in the area of "cost recovery" cases against PRPs, than it had done previously. Second, with the encouragement of some state environmental agencies, EPA became very reluctant to list new hazardous waste sites on the National Priorities List.[76] Finally, the Agency put more emphasis on short-term removal actions at disposal sites than on long-term remedial actions, an approach which tended to "piecemeal" hazardous waste site cleanups, in the view of some at the Agency.[77]

Not surprisingly, particularly during the first few years of the Bush II administration, the trends, events, and obstacles described above had the cumulative impact of decreasing the "outputs" of civil enforcement referred to the DOJ, Superfund site cleanup completions, and other traditionally employed measures of enforcement success. Despite their widespread use by critics of EPA enforcement, those statistics standing alone do not provide a complete and accurate picture of the Agency's enforcement effectiveness. Nonetheless, as noted previously, these numbers may sometimes present a crude measurement of how active EPA's enforcement personnel have been in a particular period. For that reason, it seems significant that the number of cases that EPA referred to the DOJ in 2002 for civil judicial enforcement fell by 20 percent from earlier much higher levels, from 203 to 158.[78] In fiscal year 2002, the federal government received $51 million in civil enforcement case settlements, a decline by half compared to the average of civil settlement funds received in the preceding three fiscal years.[79] Criminal enforcement penalties declined from $122 million in fiscal year 2000 to $62.2 million in fiscal year 2002. During that same period, the number of annual facility inspections conducted by EPA plummeted from 20,417 to 17,668.[80] Moreover, the rate of Superfund cleanups fell from an average of eighty-seven per year during the Clinton administration to forty-seven in fiscal year 2002.[81]

Notwithstanding the significant shortcomings in EPA enforcement, there were also some modest EPA enforcement successes during George W. Bush's first term in office. Most of those successes occurred during the fourteen-month period (from August 2002 to January 2004) in which the Agency's enforcement program was led by J. P. Suarez, some of whose views and perceptions I have recounted above. After the Senate's September 17, 2001, rejection of Donald Schregardus as the Bush II administration's choice to be EPA assistant administrator for enforcement and compliance assurance,[82] the administration engaged in a relatively lengthy search for a second nominee to fill the position. Suarez, whose selection by the president was announced on February 26, 2002, was strongly supported by EPA Administrator Christine Whitman. He was then thirty-seven years old. He had served as an assistant U.S. Attorney in New Jersey from 1992 to 1998, as counsel for Whitman for criminal justice matters when she was the governor of New Jersey, and for three years as the director of the New Jersey Division of Gaming Enforcement.[83] His nomination was approved by the Senate in August 2002, after having been temporarily blocked by California Senator Barbara Boxer in a protest against EPA's refusal to provide her with documents she had requested concerning the Superfund Program.[84]

Personable, dynamic, passionate, and a quick study, J. P. Suarez quickly won the approval of both those he reported to at EPA and the career staff who worked for him. Thus, Linda Fisher, EPA's deputy administrator during Suarez's tenure, told me: "J. P. came in and he kind of energized the place."[85] Along similar lines, Bob Tolpa, a member of Suarez's headquarters staff, stated: "J. P. Suarez was very energetic, very personable, and worked well with the staff. You wanted to do good work with him. He had charisma and a good environmental heart. He was a firm manager who was not afraid to take on the big issues."[86]

Under Suarez's leadership, EPA's enforcement program made several modest, but not insignificant, strides forward. OECA rededicated itself to gathering more (and more accurate) data on industrial and municipal compliance with environmental requirements, on the environmental outcomes of enforcement actions, and on the environmental impacts of EPA's compliance assistance efforts. The same office also pressed for the creation of an Enforcement Compliance History Online (ECHO) database that would make environmental compliance information regarding EPA-regulated facilities available on the Internet. After some resistance by industry,[87] and delay at the White House pending a review of whether the proposed website would provide information of potential benefit to terrorists, this database was ultimately launched as a publicly accessible pilot in November 2002 and (following a public comment period) converted to a fully operational public website in August 2003.[88]

Perhaps the most publicized of Suarez's actions was the so-called "Smart Enforcement Initiative," developed by the assistant administrator and his staff during "a little retreat, including all of the [OECA] office managers, in which we really focused on how to make the enforcement program go to the next level."[89] Although the results of that thinking process were not entirely original,[90] they were nonetheless sensible, reasonable, and largely noncontroversial.

As Suarez later explained, this policy initiative

> forced people in EPA enforcement to ask themselves, "Is this the most significant case we should be working on?" And also, as a corollary to that, "Is this really a federal enforcement case?" We don't have limitless resources for enforcement at EPA, and thus we should only be doing those cases that are the most significant because, for example, they are trans-boundary cases, they are significantly complex, they have significant [environmental] impacts, or we are uniquely situated to make sure that nobody gains an unfair competitive advantage by complying in one state but not another. We should not be doing work that is merely a duplication of what a state could be doing."[91]

In a more formal sense, the "Smart Enforcement" policy asserted five "key areas of focus" for EPA enforcement officials: 1) addressing significant environmental, public health, and compliance problems, 2) using data to make strategic decisions for better utilization of resources, 3) using the most appropriate tool to achieve the best outcome, 4) assessing the effectiveness of program activities, and 5) communicating effectively the environmental, public health, and compliance outcomes of the Agency's enforcement activities.[92]

Notwithstanding these modest EPA enforcement gains during late 2002–2003, however, the good intentions and focused efforts of Assistant Administrator Suarez and his personal staff met with numerous obstacles—and very determined resistance—from within the EPA itself. As we've seen, in the intra-administration disagreement over NSR reform, Suarez—a firm supporter of maintaining the regulatory status quo and continuing to pursue vigorously the EPA's NSR enforcement initiative as to fossil-fuel-fired power plants—did not prevail.[93] Beyond this, Suarez and his staff were embroiled in a number of other internal controversies in which they made determined but unsuccessful efforts to alter proposals for Agency guidance documents or policy changes that would seriously complicate, if not thwart completely, EPA's enforcement of environmental requirements. Suarez later described these intense policy debates as "an unforgiving assault by the program offices on the enforcement program."[94] He stated:

> Except for [the office of] research and development, I cannot point to one single media program that looked on us as a team player to be called upon to help, but rather as an obstacle to be gotten around or to be ignored, and hopefully avoided at all costs. Every single one of the media programs in EPA resents the existence of enforcement. . . . It was confounding to me that we would reach out to our fellow program offices, we would tell them what we were going to do, we would get their "buy-in" and "communication," only to find that they had gone out and tried to undermine what we were doing.
>
> It makes our job [at OECA] very difficult when at the end of the day we are asked to enforce a regulation where we have never been asked before . . . whether it is even enforceable. It becomes a real impediment when we are asked to sign off on a regulation that is not protective on its face, that is not enforceable by us or [by] the states. [When we refuse, however, OECA] is then viewed as a roadblock to good regulation.[95]

J. P. Suarez's position in internal EPA negotiations was further undermined when, on May 21, 2003, his principal supporter within the Bush II administration, EPA Administrator Christine Todd Whitman, resigned from her post. Whitman cited personal reasons—particularly the hardships caused by a commuter marriage—as the principal factor in her decision to leave the Agency.[96] It seems very likely that those hardships were at least part of what motivated her departure. Whether other factors were also involved in that decision, including the EPA administrator's reported isolation and powerlessness within the Bush II administration, is a question on which this account can shed no light.[97] Without doubt, however, Whitman's departure did deprive Assistant Administrator Suarez of a key EPA ally at a time when his office was participating in a number of sensitive discussions as to policy matters with major implications for the Agency's enforcement efforts.

In reflecting on the reasons for his own resignation from office, in January 2004, Suarez confided that his time of service in EPA was "a long, long fourteen months, a very long fourteen months."[98] He candidly indicated:

> I got tired of going at it on every front, internal and external. . . . You know, you find the daggers are drawn at every turn. It becomes very difficult when you feel that the people who are your colleagues do not believe in you or your mission, the people on the outside do not believe in you or your mission, and you are a little island out there trying to do the right thing. You start to question: what on earth am I doing here?[99]

The resignations of Christine Whitman and J. P. Suarez initiated another period of anxiety and concern, among members of EPA's career enforcement staff and others, as to the identity of those top officials' successors and the positions those appointees might take regarding Agency enforcement questions. That apprehension was compounded when EPA Deputy Administrator Linda Fisher—who had been rumored to be a candidate to replace Whitman, and whose professionalism and managerial ability were highly regarded by many on the Agency's enforcement staff—announced that she, too, would be leaving her post at EPA.

After a search in which a number of candidates were considered,[100] the Bush II administration nominated the Republican governor of Utah, Michael Leavitt, to be EPA's new administrator in August 2003. Leavitt's confirmation by the Senate was temporarily delayed when five Democratic senators placed "holds" blocking a Senate vote on his nomination pending resolution of their particular concerns or submission by the administration of certain specific information.[101] In the end, however, after partisan debate, Leavitt's nomination was confirmed by the full Senate, on October 28, 2003, by a vote of 88–8.[102]

Anxious to avoid similar delays, debates, and public controversies concerning its EPA appointees in an election year, the Bush II administration took a decidedly different approach to replacing J. P. Suarez as assistant administrator for enforcement and compliance assistance. Rather than nominate a permanent replacement for Suarez, whose selection would require Senate confirmation, the administration instead chose to appoint Tom Skinner, EPA Region V's regional administrator, to serve as the enforcement assistant administrator on an "acting" basis, beginning in April 2004.

Skinner, who had deliberately taken a "hands off approach" to enforcement case development while heading Region V,[103] attempted no new major initiatives or "signature programs" during his term as acting assistant administrator. As one high-ranking career civil servant remembered Skinner's tenure:

> I actually like Tom very much and I enjoyed him a lot, but I have the impression that Tom took his role in OECA kind of as a broadening experience for himself and maybe one to prepare him for something bigger.
> I always thought of Tom as approaching things with a short-term time horizon. He stayed very much within the case [management] part of the job and didn't do a lot with the data or other parts of the organization.[104]

Skinner, who subsequently denied that he had aspired to become EPA's administrator,[105] "managed to keep the power plant cases alive" in the words of an EPA enforcement manager.[106] Nonetheless, the temporary nature of his position left a number of OECA employees frequently wondering who would succeed him, and what that individual's attitude toward enforcement would be.

EPA enforcement during the second term of the Bush II administration was a period of continued and deepening conflict between EPA's enforcement personnel and the staff and leadership of several of the program offices. It was also a time of surprising successes in certain areas, together with notable decline and a loss of enforcement momentum in other respects.

Mike Leavitt's tenure as EPA administrator proved to be brief. He resigned from that post in January 2005 and moved on to become the administration's secretary of health and human services. Tom Skinner left his acting assistant administrator position and resumed his job as regional administrator in Region V for a short period before leaving the Agency to practice law with a private firm in Chicago. To replace Leavitt, President Bush appointed Steve Johnson, a longtime career EPA civil servant with no independent political base. The president's choice to lead EPA's enforcement office in his second term was Granta ("Grant") Nakayama, a partner with the Washington, D.C., law firm of Kirkland and Ellis, who had previously served under Admiral Hyman Rickover as an engineer in the U.S. Navy's nuclear submarine program.

Steve Johnson's term as EPA administrator was steeped in controversy. The visible representative of an administration that had already raised the ire of environmental advocates and congressional critics of EPA, Johnson was seen by his adversaries as a "hatchet man" who was prepared to do the bidding of regulated industries and anti-environmental elements within the Bush administration. His denial of a waiver to the State of California that would have allowed it to reduce the emission of greenhouse gases from automobiles met with fervent opposition from environmentalists and their congressional allies. So too did Johnson's failure to respond to a U.S. Supreme Court directive that he determine whether greenhouse gases cause or contribute to climate change,[107] as did his decision to close certain EPA libraries both in headquarters and in several regional offices which had been used extensively by EPA staff members—including enforcement staff members—in their daily work.[108] Johnson also clashed with politically influential unions representing the Agency's employees, who (for an extended period) viewed him as unwilling to negotiate with them in good faith.[109]

Notwithstanding these controversies, and despite the low regard in which he was held by a number of members of EPA's enforcement staff,[110] Johnson, like his predecessors in the Bush II administration, declined to reorganize the Office of Enforcement and Compliance Assistance.[111] Moreover, there appear to have been no instances in which Administrator Johnson attempted to interfere politically with any specific enforcement action. To the contrary, Grant Nakayama, who directed the Agency's enforcement office during almost all of Johnson's tenure as administrator, later stated that "Steve Johnson never asked me to do a single thing on any case. He said 'enforce the law, that's what I'm going to tell you to do.' He always said, 'you've got to do what you think is right, Grant.' I'm eternally grateful to him."[112] Nonetheless, Johnson's hands-off approach to enforcement controversies within his Agency, together with his active support for numerous voluntary programs that detracted from the EPA's enforcement efforts, contributed significantly—in ways explored below—to deep interoffice divisions at the Agency that slowed and greatly complicated EPA's enforcement work.

In the summer of 2005, Grant Nakayama arrived at EPA very shortly after Hurricane Katrina had devastated New Orleans and much of the Gulf Coast. The administration's maladroit handling of that disaster, along with tensions within the Bush II administration that followed the storm, had created significant pressure on EPA from some parts of the administration to suspend its enforcement of environmental laws in the areas affected by flooding. Nakayama flatly refused to do so, however. He insisted that considerations of public health mandated that the Agency continue to pursue environmental violations in communities damaged by the storm. Nakayama's strong stance prevailed within the administration and was noted by EPA's enforcement staff, which formed a very positive first impression of their new leader's dedication, decisiveness, and work habits. As one EPA headquarters attorney remembered it, the new assistant administrator's handling of the challenges caused by the hurricane "gave us a sense of whether this new guy had enforcement in his blood or would just say 'do whatever you want.' What he did set the tone for what Grant wanted to do and where he was going to take us."[113]

Following this auspicious beginning, Nakayama quickly earned lasting respect and admiration from many on his staff. Patterning his managerial approach after that of Admiral Rickover—his former boss and mentor—Nakayama challenged his staff to identify programmatic problems and concerns and bring them to his attention. He also established a modified open-door policy, which became known as "Fridays at Five," where all EPA employees who wished to do so could talk with him about any issue they wanted to bring to his attention beginning at 5:00 p.m. on Friday afternoons.[114] A number of members of his staff did take Nakayama up on this invitation, and the Agency's enforcement program—as well as the morale of at least some EPA employees, particularly in EPA headquarters—benefited as a result.[115]

Nakayama made a concerted effort to develop a positive working relationship with the Agency's regional administrators, and to be supportive of regional enforcement programs. He traveled to each region at least once or twice a year to discuss enforcement matters, always making it a point to speak directly with that region's administrator regarding the positive value of enforcement as a means of protecting the environment. A charming and persuasive individual with a polite and friendly manner, Nakayama met regularly with every regional administrator appointed during his tenure in office, very soon after they took office.[116] These meetings, in which he also touted the environmental benefits of vigorous enforcement, built some effective working partnerships that strengthened EPA's enforcement work[117] and provided Nakayama with very valuable regional support when OECA later objected to proposed Agency rules on the basis that they were unenforceable or that they would undercut ongoing enforcement cases.[118]

Under Nakayama's shrewd and strong leadership, certain aspects of EPA's enforcement work enjoyed a partial revival. The Agency continued to devote resources in the pursuit of "global settlements" in cases with the greatest potential for protecting human health and the environment. It put greater emphasis on explaining enforcement success in terms of pounds of pollutants reduced—and medical costs avoided—as a result of enforcement actions.[119] Moreover, beyond its long-delayed but nonetheless striking successes in its NSR cases against electric utilities, which yielded meaningful public health benefits, EPA's enforcement program negotiated important environmentally beneficial settlement agreements with oil refineries, acid plants, cement plants, and large homebuilders.[120] OECA and the Justice Department reached enforcement agreements requiring abatement of environmental violations at certain federal facilities, as well as agreements reducing "wet weather discharges" from both municipal combined sewer systems (CSOs), and sanitary sewers (SSOs).[121] Nakayama also oversaw a change in the Agency's self-audit policy that created a substantial incentive for companies that purchase facilities with environmental problems to bring those facilities into compliance with environmental requirements.[122] Moreover, he established a "tips and concerns" link for citizen complaints on the EPA website that led to the development of some successful enforcement cases, as well as an electronic "most wanted list" that resulted in the capture of some fugitive environmental criminals.[123]

Notwithstanding these successes and improvements, however—and despite Grant Nakayama's diligent, well-motivated efforts to upgrade EPA's enforcement work—the Agency's enforcement efforts in the Bush II second term remained troubled in important respects. The problems that plagued EPA enforcement during this period emanated from all three branches of the federal government. Although they did not negate or overshadow all of EPA's enforcement achievements in the second term of Bush II, when viewed together these obstacles and shortcomings present a less sanguine picture of that period in EPA's enforcement work than some participants and observers might wish.

As described above, the internal EPA debates regarding NSR enforcement and proposals for "NSR reform" were intense, time-consuming, and at times acrimonious. Following Jeff Holmstead's return to private practice, he was succeeded by his top assistant, William ("Bill") Wehrum, who served as EPA's acting assistant administrator for air and radiation from August 2005 to June 2007. Wehrum had been an engineer in the chemical industry for seven years before going to law school. He then practiced law privately for eight years for the law firms of Swidler & Berlin and Latham & Watkins. At the latter, Wehrum had worked closely with Holmstead, who offered him a job at EPA when Holmstead became an assistant administrator, and Holmstead supported Wehrum to be his successor at the Agency.[124] Wehrum's negative views of parts of the Clean

Air Act and of NSR enforcement closely resembled those of Holmstead. Thus, for example, Wehrum was sharply critical of the reorganization of the Agency that had taken place in the early 1990s:

> This [organizational arrangement] creates a disconnect between the people who know the rules best and people who interpret and enforce the rules. . . . At the end of the day, the guys in enforcement are not the guys who are the sector experts. They are not the people who rolled around in the data to develop what the standards are. They are not the people who sat through the interminable meetings to decide how to structure these very complicated regulations. They are just guys who parachute in at the end of the process and look at the regulation and decide what it means.[125]

Wehrum also opined that the NSR regulations "create incentives for regulated entities to do silly things from a productivity and efficiency standpoint," and he defended the NSR reforms he had championed as "an attempt to orient the program with [appropriate] incentives," and to make the NSR regulations "smarter and more efficient."[126]

With the exception of J. P. Suarez, the Bush II administration's political appointees who were involved in the internal disputes regarding NSR enforcement were reluctant to discuss them in greater detail, or to be openly critical of other participants with whom they had disagreed. Grant Nakayama, for example, simply indicated that "there were strong policy differences between the offices," and he remarked that those disputes had been "natural," since "where you stand depends on where you sit."[127] Nonetheless, as Jeff Holmstead observed, EPA's interoffice disputes generated "a lot of tension" and "it was fairly out in the open."[128] In fact, the NSR dispute was a well-publicized, closely watched, protracted internal battle that attracted the attention and involvement of Congress, the Department of Justice, other executive departments, environmental organizations, and some states. It had an immense effect on the Agency's enforcement. As one longtime EPA regional enforcement official recalled:

> There was just a huge gulf between the enforcement program and the rest of the Agency, and in particular the [headquarters] Office of Air and Radiation. There was absolute outright antagonism between those two offices. I had never experienced anything of that nature. It certainly made it harder for us to do our jobs. . . . We had to divert lots of energy into fighting internal battles, energy we could have used for doing something for the environment. It was kind of lost energy.[129]

The schism that developed between EPA's enforcement and air offices was not unique. In the Bush II administration, the Agency's enforcement office also came into conflict with EPA's Office of Water on several issues. As Ben Grumbles, EPA's assistant administrator for water told me (with some irritation in his voice), there was "a lot of friction" between the enforcement and water offices:

> In a growing number of instances in the second term of the [George W.] Bush administration, the enforcement office made environmental policy by establishing criteria and guidelines and standards, in the context of an enforcement action that would become, in essence, a driving rule or policy. . . . The enforcement office really began to own much of that arena. . . . Within the Agency, some of the heads of the waste, water, and air offices felt as though there was some encroachment, where the enforcers were expanding their role in permit decisions and regulatory policy making.[130]

EPA's enforcement program was involved in a significant number of interoffice disputes in this period. One such conflict involved an EPA rule proposed by EPA's Office of Environmental Information (OEI) with regard to "cross-media reporting, monitoring, and record-keeping" (CROMERR). This proposed rule was strenuously objected to by OECA's Office of Criminal Enforcement, Forensics, and Training (OCEFT) on the basis that it would eliminate the paper signatures of corporate officials that had previously been required on reports to the government in favor of electronic reporting, and in the process eliminate requirements with regard to the authentication of monitoring data that OCEFT reasonably saw as essential for criminal prosecutions for the false reporting of pollutant data on emissions and discharge. One EPA attorney recalled that OCEFT's discussions with OEI over this issue were exceptionally lengthy and bitter. The attorney stated: "For years we were fighting with them over this. We strove mightily to get every inch in negotiating that rule."[131] In the end, OEI acceded to OCEFT's request that the CROMERR rule be modified to protect the enforcement process. However, the protracted and immensely contentious negotiation that led to that result left some lingering resentments among the EPA career staff members who participated in it.

Another controversy that developed in the Bush II administration had to do with Performance Track, a voluntary program favored by Steve Johnson and other high-ranking Agency officials. Performance Track was begun in 2000, at the end of the Clinton administration. Its stated objective was relatively uncontroversial: "To recognize and encourage top environmental performers, those who go beyond compliance with regulatory requirements to attain levels of environmental performance and management that benefit people, communities, and the environment."[132] Membership in the Performance Track program was initially limited to companies and facilities that had a sustained record of compliance (as determined through an initial "screening" process), an ongoing environmental management system, and a commitment to make future improvements to their environmental performance.

Under the Bush II administration the Performance Track program, which was administered by EPA's Office of Policy, Economics and Innovation (OPEI), grew rapidly, both in terms of the number of its members—more than 470 in March 2007—and with regard to the prominence the program was given by top Bush II administration political appointees in EPA.[133] Under Johnson's leadership, the Agency significantly increased the personnel resources it devoted to Performance Track. EPA offered numerous rewards to the program's corporate members, whom it referred to as its "preferred customers." Those rewards included positive publicity for member companies, access to the administrator and other top EPA officials that was not given to other companies or to any representatives of environmental organizations or members of the general public, access to a members-only website, marketing materials (such as flags and posters), advance notification in cases of forthcoming EPA rule making, and other regulatory incentives.[134] Performance Track members also received low priority for EPA inspections. EPA regional personnel who wished to inspect a Performance Track member facility were required to obtain the prior approval of EPA headquarters, and to demonstrate a "reason to believe that a compliance problem existed."[135]

While not opposed to its goals, EPA's enforcement program very firmly objected to the way that Performance Track was implemented by OPEI. They believed that OPEI's managers did an inadequate job of assuring that program members were meeting the environmental improvement commitments that they had made. OECA maintained that the low inspection priorities given to program participants had created an unfortunate incentive for some of them to shirk their environmental responsibilities and fall out of compliance. The enforcement office also contended that positive publicity and other valuable rewards were being given to some firms that had poor overall compliance records, and that scarce EPA resources were being spent on this and other cooperative Agency partnerships with industry that could and should have been put to more productive use in protecting health and the environment.

The conflict between OECA and OPEI over Performance Track reached a head in 2006, when OPEI proposed that Monsanto Company be given an award by EPA's administrator for its overall corporate environmental performance. Monsanto was being prosecuted at that time by the Department of Justice under the Foreign Corrupt Practices Act for having allegedly bribed an Indonesian environmental official, and the Justice Department, together with OCEA, strongly objected to the proposed award. OECA also objected to an OPEI proposal to admit U.S. Steel's Clairton Works to the Performance Track program on the ground that Clairton Works had a poor record of environmental compliance. Performance Track's managers vigorously opposed these objections, and the controversy between these two EPA offices became emotionally charged and highly acrimonious. As one EPA enforcement official remembered,

> It was very bitter. To the Performance Track people, anything their members told them was true, and anything told to them by anyone else was an attack or a lie. That was the atmosphere that developed. Any challenge to the Performance Track program was met forcefully, sometimes with very personal attacks.[136]

For their part, OPEI's Performance Track personnel resented what they perceived as officious intermeddling by OECA. In Deputy Administrator Marcus Peacock's words, "there was a perception [in OPEI] that at every turn the enforcement office would undermine the policy office."[137]

In the end, OPEI withdrew its proposal to award Monsanto's environmental performance and it did not admit U.S. Steel's Clairton Works to the Performance Track program. In March 2006, EPA's independent Office of Inspector General investigated the performance of a sampling of Performance Track members and issued a report that sharply criticized the program. The Inspector General's report found that

> Performance Track did not have clear plans that connected activities with its goals, and did not have performance measures that show[ed] if it achieve[d] anticipated results. The program tied an EPA goal to member commitments, but did not meet the goal because members did not make sufficient progress toward their commitments. The implementation challenges detracted from EPA's anticipated results (only 2 of 30 sampled Performance Track members met all of their environmental improve-

ment commitments). . . . [T]he presence of underperforming facilities in this leadership program reduces the integrity and value of the brand.[138]

In fact, in May 2009, several months after George W. Bush left the presidency, a new EPA administrator terminated the Performance Track program, and the controversy regarding it between OECA and OPEI came to an end. Among EPA's career staff, however, the ill feelings created by those controversies lingered.

Certainly intra-Agency disputes involving EPA's enforcement office were nothing new in the Agency's history. What seems striking about the internal enforcement controversies that arose within EPA during the eight years of the Bush II administration, however, is their remarkable bitterness and intensity, and the extraordinary public openness that characterized some of them. This pattern appears to have resulted from several circumstances. One factor was the strong personalities of some of the competing assistant administrators who were involved. Grant Nakayama, Jeff Holmstead, J. P. Suarez, and Bill Wehrum, for example, were skillful, intelligent, strong-willed individuals who were strongly committed to the positions that they took. These men enlisted passionate allies, within and outside of EPA, and they advocated forcefully for the positions they espoused. Another factor was some preexisting antipathy among the EPA career staff in the various Agency offices which were involved in the disputes, some of which had its roots in the 1993 reorganization of EPA's headquarters described in the preceding chapter. With few exceptions, during the Bush II administration these EPA career employees liked and were loyal to the political appointees who headed the offices in which they worked. The attitudes and dispositions of office leaders shaped and reinforced the policy positions taken by their staff members, and the views of career staff members in turn reinforced the leaders' own fervor for the positions they favored. Finally, throughout this period, EPA's top leadership seems to have done very little to mediate and quietly resolve the interoffice conflicts that arose. EPA's administrators and deputy administrators during the Bush II administration made few attempts to pacify the internal strife that had arisen. Steve Johnson and Marcus Peacock, for example, relied excessively on EPA's assistant administrators to work out most disputes. In performing his work, Peacock actually did arbitrate a number of intra-Agency policy disagreements that concerned enforcement. Nonetheless, he seems to have rarely—if ever—taken it upon himself to get to the roots of ongoing clashes and to encourage interoffice teamwork. With regard to the bitter OPEI-OECA controversy regarding

Performance Track, Peacock candidly stated: "I was never able to come to grips with that. . . . It was too shadowy, too difficult to try to get people together to resolve the issue."[139] His passivity in that and other disputed matters, despite bitter internal Agency dissension, appears to have contributed indirectly (yet significantly) to the length and intensity of EPA's widely noted interoffice squabbles.

The need for OECA's assistant administrator and staff to invest considerable time and effort pursuing intra-Agency disputes was scarcely the only problem that plagued EPA's enforcement efforts in the Bush II period. EPA's enforcement program was also undercut by a trend that had begun in the second term of the Clinton administration: resource and budget constraints in a period of ostensibly flat EPA budgets.

Many people I spoke with in 2003 and 2004 at the Agency echoed the view of one experienced EPA official that "enforcement resources has been an issue almost constantly in the 1990s and the 2000s. There are a lot of budget constraints at the present time, especially in the area of compliance monitoring inspections. Payroll has [also] been an area where there has been growth, and that has put pressure on other aspects of the account. There is much less money available than previously."[140] These resource shortages continued through the balance of the Bush II presidency.

Some EPA regional office enforcement efforts suffered to a very significant extent in the Agency's resource crunch. Thus, for example, beginning in the mid-1990s, EPA Region V lost approximately 10 percent from its budgetary allocations for regulatory enforcement programs.[141] As a result, that region's Office of Regional Counsel was forced to cut its workforce (mostly by attrition) to a notable extent. The number of enforcement attorneys in that office declined from a peak of 116 to under 100 in late fiscal year 2002.[142] Region V and other EPA regions also sustained deep cuts in their important enforcement extramural budgets, the funds used to contract the services of expert witnesses and for other crucially important expenses in support of litigation. In Region V, the regional budget decreased from $1.46 million in fiscal year 1996 to $746,000 in the 2004. Moreover, because Congress ordered EPA to use some of those extramural budget funds only for specifically designated purposes (e.g., for lead paint inspections and enforcement on tribal lands), Region V had only $438,500 in extramural discretionary funds available to it in Fiscal Year 2002, a paltry sum relative to the region's urgent need for those monies.[143]

At the root of most of these persistent budgetary problems was Congress's "COLA trick," described in the preceding chapter, as a result of which EPA and other federal agencies and departments were forced to economize on other budgeted items in order to comply with Congressional mandates that they provide cost-of-living raises to their employees.

As it had done in the Clinton years, EPA responded to the financial constraints created by this budgetary scheme by diverting funds from its already tight extramural budgets. This understandable response had its long-term difficulties, however. In 2004, not long after he resigned as the head of OECA, J. P. Suarez remarked:

> We [in OECA] do not have enough extramural dollars. I actually think it is at a crisis stage. The last budget I worked on, EPA [enforcement] was going to be in a position where we had people and not enough dollars to support them. We did not have money for travel, for technical support, for investigations, for depositions, [or] for experts. . . . I can tell you that there is going to be a major collapse if that is not rectified in terms of our ability to get work done.[144]

Five years later, another well-positioned EPA headquarters enforcement manager indicated that these sorts of resource shortfalls had continued:

> Could we do more with additional resources? Absolutely yes! We need more people. Enforcement work, by its nature, is not something you can farm out to a contractor. It is core government work. . . . To identify problems and address those problems you have identified, you need bodies.[145]

Other present and former EPA enforcement officials whom I spoke with in 2009 identified some specific aspects of EPA's enforcement work as having been especially affected by resource constraints during the Bush II administration's second term. Those included the Superfund Program,[146] the data management work of OECA's Office of Compliance,[147] the criminal enforcement program,[148] compliance assistance,[149] and enforcement of the Resource Conservation and Recovery Act (RCRA).[150]

Notably, the same kinds of resource limitations that were harmful to EPA's enforcement effort also raised problems for EPA's counterparts at the Department of Justice. The situation came to a head in the spring of 2003, when the Justice Department was forced to postpone the filing of a large number of EPA civil enforcement case referrals until the end of the fiscal year.[151] The resulting delays caused understandable frustrations among EPA's enforcement staff, and temporary strains in the Agency's working relationship with the DOJ. As former DOJ manager David Buente perceptively noted in 2004, funding for the DOJ's and EPA's enforcement work was then basically equal to 1994 levels. However, over the preceding decade there had been slow but steady inflation and also an increase in the number of entities that had to be regulated. Thus, Buente declared, "you have to wonder whether, in the long range, the available resource base [for federal environmental enforcement] will be even remotely adequate to the task."[152]

The deterrent aspect of EPA's enforcement work was also undermined in the Bush II years by the Agency's failure to publicize its enforcement successes as fully as it might have done. Under prior administrations, EPA's enforcement program regularly issued press releases when the Agency took enforcement actions. In some regional offices, including Region V, press releases were routinely issued regarding enforcement actions ranging from the issuance of notices of violation to the filing and settling of enforcement lawsuits. In 2005 however, Region V stopped issuing such releases, as did some other EPA regional offices.[153] Not all regions followed suit,[154] and EPA did continue to issue an annual "Accomplishments Report" touting the Agency's enforcement achievements. Nonetheless, in the aggregate, the amount of publicity given to EPA enforcement achievements declined a good deal in the Bush II years, and the extent of some of its more significant achievements were sometimes understated. As Catherine McCabe observed in the aftermath of the Agency's very significant settlements in NSR enforcement cases against large electric utility companies, "we were quietly proud with each other, but we weren't exactly allowed to celebrate here very much."[155] EPA's reluctance to publicize fully its own enforcement achievements contributed to a widespread but inaccurate perception that the Agency had entirely abandoned its enforcement efforts, a notion that was reinforced by some negative newspaper coverage of the EPA's record.[156]

Finally, despite the helpful leadership of Grant Nakayama and the EPA's important successes in 2008 in NSR utility enforcement cases, low morale continued through George W. Bush's second term among significant segments of EPA's career staff. As one thoughtful regional enforcement manager later described it:

> The enforcement community [including enforcement people at EPA, the Justice Department and some state environmental agencies] was really its own island. If you were in enforcement you could feel, down to the

secretary level, a kind of under-appreciation. . . . You just knew that the work you did was not valued. The only support you got was within the enforcement community. The mental oppression I felt during this period was worse than during the Gorsuch era.[157]

Others interviewed after the Bush II administration was out of office shared this assessment. Mike Walker said, "I saw many examples of morale problems throughout the eight years [of the Bush II administration]. There was fear of retaliation if you said the wrong thing."[158] Other former staffers concurred, citing "significant morale problems"[159] and saying that "people were most frustrated."[160]

The web of institutional intra-governmental relationships that have a crucial effect on EPA's enforcement work continued throughout the eight years of George W. Bush's presidency, and within EPA's enforcement programs many of the patterns that had prevailed during the Clinton administration continued to prevail. A number of the EPA employees whom I interviewed expressed satisfaction with the working relationship in enforcement matters between EPA headquarters and regional personnel.[161] In fact, to some within the Agency, the sense of being under siege by anti-enforcement elements within and outside of EPA during the Bush II period brought enforcement people in the regions and headquarters closer together. In one senior enforcement manager's view,

> These were some of the best years in headquarters-regional relations, primarily because everybody felt they needed to stick together or perish separately. So there was a greater sense of collegiality.[162]

On the other hand, however, some EPA enforcement professionals who served during the same years did note some frictions and tensions between EPA headquarters and regional enforcement staffs.[163] Within some regions, for example, complaints were voiced regarding the "hierarchical" and "bureaucratic" culture of OECA, delays in settlement negotiations resulting from requirements that the regions obtain headquarters approval or concurrence, the relative inexperience of some headquarters staff members, and the absence of communication between some headquarters offices.

Mimi Newton, an attorney in EPA Region IX, took the position that regional attorneys were frequently not provided with needed information as to whom they should speak with within EPA headquarters regarding particular questions of enforcement policy.[164] She also opined that headquarters did an inadequate job of making certain that the Agency's regional offices responded, in a consistent fashion, to large information requests submitted under the Freedom of Information Act (FOIA).[165] Moreover, Bill Muszynski, a former deputy regional administrator in EPA Region II, noted some ongoing tensions between the national case priorities of OECA and the more narrowly focused, locally oriented priorities of EPA's regional offices, especially (but not exclusively) with regard to the enforcement of requirements regarding asbestos in demolition and renovation, violations of pesticide application standards, and enforcement of requirements as to lead in drinking water.[166]

From the comments of regional EPA attorneys who are most familiar with the Superfund Program, it appears that regional-headquarters relationships in that program continued to be close and cooperative during the Bush II era.[167] The major exception to that was evidently with respect to the occasionally contentious issue of regional office autonomy and independence in settlement negotiations with PRPs.[168]

The headquarters enforcement managers I met with were mostly satisfied with the nature of their interactions with regional office enforcement personnel. However, they seemed to feel that regional-headquarters relations were a "mixed bag." One former headquarters manager felt the relationship had "improved" relative to the early to mid-1990s,[169] and most would probably agree with David Nielsen's statement that the relationship of headquarters with regional enforcement people is "cyclical." "These things go up and down," Nielsen stated. "In some regions the relationship with headquarters is good. In others the relationship is more problematic. It depends on personalities and the problems that come up."[170] Many would also agree with the observation of Adam Kushner, however, that the headquarters-regional relationship benefited during the second Bush II term from the institution of a personnel rotation policy under which regional and headquarters experts in particular substantive areas of enforcement were put on enforcement teams in other regions where their expertise could be made use of on a temporary basis.[171]

Many EPA enforcement managers and staff members were of the view that the interrelationship of EPA enforcement attorneys and EPA scientists and engineers varied widely from individual to individual, and from enforcement team to enforcement team during the Bush II period. They also agreed that those relationships were substantially unaffected by the actions and approaches of the administration's political appointees.[172] Both within the regional offices and in OECA, a clear majority of those whom I interviewed felt that (with occasional exceptions) the Agency's enforcement staff worked effectively across disciplinary lines. Many credited that success to the positive motivation and maturity of the staff members involved, as well as sound guidance provided to the staff by the EPA enforcement program's first-line supervisors.[173]

As in prior administrations, during the Bush II years EPA's relationships with state environmental officials varied immensely from state to state (and sometimes from environmental medium to environmental medium within particular states). Some EPA officials perceived at least a marginal improvement in these relationships, as compared with the 1990s. Others observed that EPA-state enforcement relationships were most fruitful and cooperative at the staff level, as opposed to the relationship that existed at higher levels of the respective governmental entities, where discussions tended to be higher profile, more "ideological," and more divisive than those which occurred at the career staff level.[174]

One complicating factor in EPA-state enforcement relations was the budget shortfalls experienced by many state agencies, especially toward the end of the Bush II administration when economic conditions in the United States declined overall. A number of the EPA enforcement professionals whom I interviewed made note of that problem.[175] However, none of them mentioned any change in the EPA's relationship with state enforcement personnel, as distinct from the negative impact that economically forced budget cuts had on state environmental enforcement capability and morale.

With regard to EPA's interactions with Department of Justice during the Bush II administration, many EPA and Justice Department lawyers and managers opined that the solid foundation of cooperation and mutual respect that had been established between the two institutions over the 1990s remained intact. John Cruden, a key Justice Department manager, went so far as to state in 2009, "We are probably at a high point right now in our relations with the regions and EPA headquarters. Although there are occasional bumps on the road, I have a profound respect for the men and women of EPA."[176]

EPA and Justice Department enforcement managers met on a regular basis during this time to discuss the status of every filed and potential enforcement case. Each civil enforcement case referred by EPA to the Justice Department was reviewed and "triaged" by the latter, with the top priority afforded to "health impact cases," and cases in which there was concern that a defendant was about to file a petition for bankruptcy. This procedure appears to have helped eliminate or avoid some interdepartmental tensions and rivalries. Another helpful factor was the con-

certed effort made by Assistant Attorney General Tom Sansonetti to cooperate with EPA. Nonetheless, some tensions and problems between
EPA and Department of Justice did remain.

From EPA's perspective, resource shortages among the Justice Department's staff sometimes unduly delayed the filing of civil enforcement
cases that the Agency referred to the DOJ. That gave rise to frustration
on the part of some of EPA's enforcement staff.[177] In addition, certain
EPA regional attorneys perceived that some Justice Department lawyers viewed themselves as "superior" to EPA lawyers, notwithstanding
the relative lack of experience of some of those same Justice Department
attorneys in environmental enforcement matters. In a similar vein, J. P.
Suarez told me:

> [The] Department of Justice has good attorneys. However, some of them
> overanalyze everything. My biggest frustration with them [was] that they
> second-guessed EPA's policies on cases. It is not the Justice Department's
> job to tell us we should get better environmental results in cases. They
> sometimes [saw] themselves as superior to EPA and that it [was] appro-
> priate for them to question EPA's substantive policy judgment.[178]

In contrast with the "main" Justice Department, the offices of the U.S.
Attorneys appear to have played only a very minor role in EPA civil judicial enforcement matters. Where they were involved in such cases, however, the quality of their work earned the praise of several of the EPA
employees I interviewed.[179] U.S. Attorneys often have a relatively greater
role in prosecuting criminal cases developed by the EPA's criminal investigators and criminal enforcement attorneys. In that context, their level
of interest and their willingness to invest staff resources in pursuing such
cases evidently varied greatly from office to office during the Bush II
period.

With regard to the EPA's relationship with Congress, quite a few of
the officials I spoke with made a point of noting the extent to which congressional oversight of the Agency's enforcement work declined during
this period, particularly when compared to the very active (and effective)
oversight that Congress undertook in the 1980s and early 1990s. Many
enforcement officials at EPA and the Justice Department would clearly
agree with the opinions of one experienced attorney (who not to be identified): "Candidly, from the 1990s on, I don't think Congress has done a
particularly good job in its oversight of either EPA or the Department of
Justice. The public has not been well served by that." Another senior EPA

enforcement official, Catherine McCabe, was even more negative in her 2009 assessment of Congress's role in EPA enforcement:

> Congress has not been able to do anything functional that is pro-environmental in a long time and that is a sad state of affairs. . . . There are a lot of hearings [on Capitol Hill] and there is a lot of puffing and a lot of racing around calling each other names. We [at EPA] get to be the pawns in the middle because enforcement is explosive. The Agency gets pushed one way and then the other depending on who is in power. It is quite exhausting for the Agency frankly because it requires a lot of head-quarters attention.[180]

Aside from occasional congressional oversight hearings and generalized requests for information, the main contact that EPA enforcers appear to have had with Congress during the Bush II period was responding to requests for information submitted by individual senators and representatives regarding particular enforcement care. These so-called congressionals are viewed as "just a fact of life" by the EPA enforcement staff members who are assigned to respond to them. Typically, however, they have little impact on the progress of the cases they concern.

The collective influence of Congress on federal enforcement of environmental laws is not limited to its oversight activities and its requests for information, however. The federal legislative branch is the architect—and, potentially, the modifier—of the fundamental environmental legislation that EPA and the Justice Department are charged with enforcing. Moreover, Congress has ultimate control over the size and direction of the Agency's (and the Justice Department's) budget. With regard to the last of those functions, the record of Congress during the Bush II administration was decidedly mixed.

On the one hand, Congress tended to rebuff attempts by the Bush administration for decreases in EPA's budgetary allotments, including cuts in the monies the Agency would use for its enforcement work. On the other hand, however, as we have seen, the congressional "COLA trick" once again had the result of reducing the environmental enforcement budgets of EPA while presenting a misleading appearance of budgetary stability. The congressional practice of "earmarking" certain EPA funds for particular types of enforcement and compliance work (compliance assistance, for example) also limited the discretion of Agency officials to spend EPA's very limited enforcement funds where they were the most needed.

The relationships between EPA's enforcement programs and federal agencies and departments (other than the Department of Justice and U.S. Attorneys and their staffs) generally tended to be short-lived, case-specific, and highly varied in the Bush II years. The government officials I interviewed mentioned that they had collectively worked with numerous federal agencies and departments in the course of their enforcement work. These institutions included the Customs Service, the Department of Energy, the Department of Defense, the Drug Enforcement Agency, the Department of Agriculture, the Army Corps of Engineers, the Bureau of Indian Affairs, the Fish and Wildlife Service, the National Oceanic and Atmospheric Administration, the Department of Housing and Urban Development, the Federal Bureau of Investigation, the National Park Service, the Securities and Exchange Commission, the Coast Guard, the Occupational Safety and Health Administration, the Department of Veterans Affairs, and the federal trustees of natural resources. Some of these entities provided EPA with expert assistance in developing its enforcement cases; other agencies sought EPA's help with environmental pollution problems. Some federal institutions opposed EPA's positions in intra-administration policy discussions, and still other federal departments were the targets of EPA enforcement investigations or actions.

For the most part, those EPA officials I spoke with indicated that their contacts with the other federal institutions they mentioned were too relatively temporary in nature to provide a basis for characterization. One of the few exceptions to that was with respect to the Army Corps of Engineers, which, together with EPA, is responsible for administering the wetlands protection program established under the Clean Water Act. In that regard, a difference of opinion emerged among those I spoke with. Some interviewees discussed EPA's working relationship with the Army Corps of Engineers in terms of persistent conflict.[181] Others viewed EPA's interactions with the Army Corps in a more positive light.[182]

Another federal entity with which EPA had very frequent contact—albeit in an adversarial context—was the Department of Defense (DOD). One protracted conflict between the Agency and the DOD—which was never fully resolved during the Bush II administration—concerned which of those two federal entities' budgets would be used to fund oversight costs at Superfund sites.[183] Another contentious issue was whether EPA had the legal authority to issue unilateral administrative enforcement orders to military facilities that were in violation of federal environmental laws. On that question, the Defense Department sought the opinion of the Justice Department's Office of Legal Counsel, which, in December 2008—to the great satisfaction of Grant Nakayama and his staff—indicated that EPA did indeed have such order-issuing authority.[184] In this period, EPA and the DOD also locked horns over whether the Agency should exempt the armed forces from the requirements of the Clean Air Act and the Ocean Dumping Act when military personnel fired weapons into the navigable waters of the United States during training exercises. That dispute—in which OECA and EPA's Office of Water were perhaps atypically unified in their opposition to an exemption—remained unresolved when the Bush II administration left office.[185]

Finally, with regard to the White House, the consensus among those I met with is that, following a tradition established in previous presidential administrations, there was virtually no attempt by the Bush II administration to interfere directly in the enforcement of specific, individual environmental cases. In sharp contrast however, the Bush II White House appears to have had a far greater involvement than its predecessor administrations in the establishment of EPA policies that affected significant numbers of enforcement matters. As discussed previously, the White House apparently played a critical role in the attempted anti-enforcement reform of EPA's Clean Air Act NSR regulations as they affected electric generating stations.[186] Moreover, several of the EPA enforcement staff members whom I interviewed had a clear impression that the White House, including particularly its Office of Management and Budget (OMB) and the Council on Environmental Quality (CEQ), were involved, quietly but nonetheless quite directly, in the development of other enforcement-related Agency policies.[187]

What may be gleaned from this summary of the Agency's recent institutional relationships in enforcement about the Bush II administration's role in, and impact upon, EPA enforcement? On balance, the answer appears to be less than one might expect.

While, in the words of Bruce Buckheit, "To my knowledge, the [Bush II] White House has not called over and killed [enforcement] cases, at least not directly,"[188] as noted above, the bulk of the available evidence suggests that the White House did involve itself—quietly but directly, and to an unprecedented extent—in decision making involving EPA policies that had major implications for EPA's environmental enforcement work. This major exception aside, however, the Bush II administration's preferences and activities seem to have had no more than a minimal impact on EPA's ongoing institutional enforcement relationships. The Agency's headquarters–regional office and attorney–technical staff interactions remained substantially unchanged from what they were under the Clinton administration. The same may be said with respect to the EPA's working relationships in the enforcement realm with the Department of Justice, U.S. Attorneys, and other federal agencies and departments. Finally, although the Congress played less of a role overall with respect to EPA enforcement questions during the Bush II administration than had been the case in prior years, that fact seems to have been more a result of decisions made in the legislative branch than a function of anything that the Bush II administration did or did not attempt.

In sum, the eight years of the presidency of George W. Bush were a contradictory period for EPA's enforcement program. Particularly during Bush II's second term, the Agency had some meaningful enforcement successes. Nonetheless, during much of the Bush II presidency EPA's enforcers faced a host of obstacles—from resource restrictions to confusing court opinions to fierce and sustained conflicts with other Agency offices—that consumed much of their scarce time and energy. The fact that the Agency's beleaguered enforcement program was able to score any victories during this period is a testament to the fortitude and dedication to duty of a number of members of EPA's career enforcement staff and their counterparts in the Department of Justice. The passionate work of J. P. Suarez and the steady and capable leadership of the Bush II administration's last assistant administrator for enforcement, Grant Nakayama, also merit praise. Nevertheless, one can't help but wonder how many more successes the Agency's enforcement program might have achieved—for human health and the environment—if it had been fully funded and staffed, openly supported by the Bush II White House and administration officials, and freed of ideologically motivated political constraints. We can only guess, with some measure of sorrow and disappointment, at what might have been.

Lessons Learned: Some Observations on Congressional Oversight, Organizational Structure, Management Approaches, and Career Staff Trends

What are the larger lessons of EPA's enforcement history? What does the Agency's past performance in this critical aspect of its responsibilities contribute to our broader understanding of regulatory enforcement in general? What has been the impact of congressional oversight of EPA enforcement? How has Agency enforcement been affected by changes in organizational structure and the managerial styles of political appointees? And what has been the role of the EPA's career enforcement staff?

In the past few years, the writings of American scholars have reflected a modest but growing interest in both congressional oversight of federal agency activities and the general nature of the enforcement process in regulatory bureaucracies. In addition, a handful of academics, writing from differing perspectives and on varying themes, have assessed EPA's performance of its statutory mandates and broader societal responsibilities.[1]

The study of regulatory enforcement—as an aspect of agency behavior—was given new impetus in 1984 by the publication of *Enforcing Regulation*, a collection of essays edited by Keith Hawkins and John M. Thomas.[2] In their introduction to this provocative volume, the editors make a distinction between two vastly different approaches to regulatory enforcement by governmental agencies: the "compliance system" and the "deterrence system." In a compliance system, they write, the primary concern of agency personnel is with satisfying the broad aspirations of applicable regulatory statutes by preventing violations and remedying underlying problems. Enforcement officials rely heavily, if not exclusively, on "privately practiced, low-visibility bargaining and bluffing." Formal legalistic enforcement tools are resorted to with extreme reluctance in a compliance system. Instead, emphasis is placed on the development and maintenance of an amicable social relationship between regulatory personnel and regulated entities—a relationship presumed beneficial for the discovery of future problems and the effective detection of violators. A deterrence system of regulatory enforcement, in contrast, is much more an arm's-length process whose essential purpose is to detect offenses and punish violators. The enforcement style is generally "accusatory and adversarial," and formal legal processes are routinely relied upon for the resolution of enforcement disputes. In a deterrence system, the major preoccupation of agency officials is with punishing wrongdoers, both as a means of doing justice in individual cases and as a way of deterring future violations of regulatory standards.[3]

This formulation raises an empirical question: should the enforcement process that prevails at EPA be seen as a compliance system or a deterrence system? The better view seems to be that the Agency's enforcement activities as they have developed over time constitute a deterrence system of regulatory enforcement. With the brief exception of the Gorsuch era of the early 1980s, both the EPA's written enforcement policies and its actual practices have consistently emphasized the initiation of *formal* enforcement actions against violators of federal environmental standards. Those formal actions have ranged from notices of violation and administrative orders to civil judicial actions and, more recently, criminal prosecutions.

The formal, legalistic nature of EPA's enforcement efforts is reflected in the Agency's system for measuring and publicizing enforcement success. It is also evident in the EPA's sizeable legal staff, the high volume of cases it regularly refers to the Justice Department for civil action or criminal prosecution, the monetary value of the civil and administrative penalties it has assessed against violators, and the large body of enforcement policies, guidance documents, and studies it has issued that require or urge the use of formal enforcement methods.

One clear example of the Agency's preference for a formal approach to enforcement can be found in an RCRA implementation study that it prepared. In discussing the compliance and enforcement aspects of the implementation of RCRA, the study included a sort of declaration of principles that comes very close to defining a deterrence system: "An effective enforcement program must detect violations, compel their correction, ensure that compliance is achieved in a timely manner, and deter other violations. The RCRA enforcement program will obtain substantial voluntary compliance only if the regulated community perceives that there is a greater risk and cost in violating a requirement than in complying with it."[4]

It should be acknowledged that these formal measures, practices, and policies do not represent every aspect of EPA's enforcement approach. For various reasons the written policies and guidance documents drafted at the Agency's headquarters have not always been followed by enforcement officials in regional offices or state agencies. This is particularly true with respect to state officials, some of whom have traditionally favored informal enforcement activities and resisted the imposition of monetary penalties on environmental violators.[5] The commitment of at least some EPA inspectors to a formal legalistic approach to enforcement has also been questioned by some Agency attorneys.[6]

Notwithstanding these circumstances, however, it seems most accurate to describe EPA's enforcement practices as constituting, in the main, a deterrence system. Though the Agency's enforcement approach may lack uniformity, its legalistic nature is historically rooted and deeply ingrained.

Another pertinent set of inquiries concerns a different topic: the effects of congressional oversight on EPA's enforcement performance. To what extent have congressional investigations of EPA activities had an impact on the Agency's policies and practices? Steven Shimberg, former minority staff director and chief counsel of the Senate Committee on Environment and Public Works, contends that congressional influence on EPA has been minimal:

> With respect to the hundreds or thousands of relatively minor decisions confronting EPA, congressional oversight, or the mere threat of oversight, can be used to alter behavior and change decisions. With respect to the major policy decisions, however—decisions that shape federal environmental policy—traditional forms of congressional oversight have little effect. Behavior may be altered but rarely are decisions altered solely as a result of congressional oversight. When a major policy question is working its way through the system (first within EPA and then within the executive branch as a whole) the voices heard from Congress in the name of "oversight" are treated just like those from any other interest group.[7]

This observation stands in stark contrast to the conclusion reached by Joel D. Aberbach in his analysis of the politics of congressional oversight.

After examining the relationship between congressional investigators and executive branch officials in some detail, Aberbach concludes that

[c]ongressional oversight has a significant effect on agency behavior. . . . Congress plays an active role both in writing the laws that establish the skeleton and muscle and in setting the budgets that give the lifeblood to administrative agencies. When Congress shows an interest, agencies ignore it at their peril.[8]

Who is correct? Do congressional investigations affect agency policy decisions significantly or marginally? While not dispositive of the question, aspects of the record of congressional oversight of EPA enforcement activities suggest that both Aberbach and Shimberg are partially correct. In a number of instances, important EPA decisions regarding the approach the Agency should take in carrying out its enforcement responsibilities have been shaped more or less directly by congressional oversight and concern. On the other hand, during some time periods, Congress has done little to influence the direction of EPA's enforcement policies.

One good example of the potential impact of congressional oversight, which we considered in Chapter Five, is the Agency's renewed emphasis on enforcement (both generally and in the Superfund context specifically) in the period that followed Anne Gorsuch's departure as EPA administrator in 1983. Having forced Gorsuch's resignation, Congress continued to press the EPA for improvements in its enforcement programs. The Agency's attempt to intensify its enforcement efforts, to emphasize civil penalties based on the economic benefits attained by violators through noncompliance, and to elevate the importance of enforcement in the CERCLA Program can all be traced to congressional influence.

Similarly, EPA's 1985 decision to launch a loss of interim status (LOIS) initiative—to enforce various requirements of RCRA against land disposal facilities—was a result of intensive pressure on the Agency for stronger action in this area by the Dingell Committee. Additionally, the "enforcement first" approach to EPA's administration of CERCLA, adopted by William Reilly in the Ninety Day Study of 1989, was part of an attempt by the Agency's then-new leaders to satisfy persistent congressional critics by taking a new direction in that closely watched field.

Beyond these direct effects on EPA enforcement policies, congressional oversight has also sometimes influenced EPA decision making indirectly in other critical respects. Thus, for example, the sustained insistence of Congress on active and vigorous enforcement activity has encouraged the Agency to emphasize the volume of its formal enforcement actions (including its annual count of civil judicial referrals, administrative orders, criminal prosecutions, civil penalties, etc.) in measuring and evaluating its enforcement successes. Congressional interest has motivated EPA officials to expand the scope of EPA's criminal enforcement work, and congressional inquiries have periodically placed demands on the time and energy of the Agency's top managers, as well as its professional enforcement staff.

In the 1990s, the prevailing congressional attitude toward EPA enforcement shifted dramatically. Faced with anti-regulatory pressure from Capitol Hill, EPA's leadership reacted initially by modifying its enforcement program in ways that partially blunted the program's vigor and aggressiveness. That "softer" approach changed in 1995 however, when the Clinton administration openly and successfully challenged a more radical attempt by a Republican Congress to undermine almost all of the EPA's activities. Bold executive branch resistance, combined with overreaching by the Agency's congressional opponents, opened the door to a six-year period of active and largely effective enforcement unfettered by congressional pressures.

Finally, as I have noted, congressional interest in EPA's enforcement activities waned considerably in the 2000s. Although there were some notable exceptions—including congressional hearings into Bush II administration attempts to scuttle Clean Air Act new source review (NSR) enforcement through a strategy of regulatory changes and certain other enforcement failings—most EPA enforcement employees viewed the Bush II years as a period of congressional quiescence and a gradual decline in the Agency's enforcement effectiveness.

The more active periods of congressional attention to EPA enforcement give rise to a normative question: was what Congress did during these times helpful? Taking congressional oversight of the Agency's enforcement programs as a whole, has it contributed to a more effective and credible effort in this area or, as some have contended, was it one important cause of a generalized regulatory failure?

One thoughtful, productive scholar, Richard Lazarus, has been largely negative in his assessment of congressional oversight of EPA. He believes that the consistently adversarial tone of Congress has unduly harmed the Agency's reputation, chilled innovative decision making, placed excessive demands on EPA resources, skewed the Agency's priorities, and damaged the morale and self-esteem of its employees.[9]

Lazarus's analysis conflicts with the conclusion of Joel Aberbach. Though his work does not concentrate on EPA specifically, Aberbach is far more optimistic than Lazarus concerning the impacts of congressional oversight. He defends the overall performance of the federal legislature in these terms: "It seems fair to say that oversight addresses problems and checks, or even corrects, many errors affecting at least the more organized and articulate members of the polity. As a result, congressional oversight probably improves policy at the margins."[10] The history of EPA's relationship with Capitol Hill in the enforcement area seems largely supportive of Aberbach's conclusion. While some of Lazarus's criticism of congressional oversight of EPA is undoubtedly well taken, a careful review of the performance of Congress in overseeing the Agency's enforcement efforts—particularly during the 1970s and 1980s—reveals more success than failure. Although not free of mistakes, during these years Congress mainly pushed EPA's enforcement policies in directions that improved their efficacy and benefited the public at large.

At the outset, it is important to note that much of Lazarus's thesis is premised on the notion that EPA's history has been characterized by what he refers to as "a destructive pattern of regulatory failure." As Lazarus sees it, the competing efforts of the OMB, on the one hand, and EPA's congressional critics, on the other, combined with frequent judicial rejection of important EPA regulations have given rise to a "pathological cycle" in which "agency distrust has begotten failure, breeding further distrust and further failure." This seems an overstatement. While EPA's situation has been regularly enveloped in conflict, in part for the very reasons that Lazarus describes, his assessment of the Agency's overall efficacy seems unduly gloomy and overdrawn.

Other observers have taken a different position. In a thoughtful evaluation of the Agency's work, for example, Steven A. Cohen opined:

> The U.S. Environmental Protection Agency has made a significant positive contribution to the protection of environmental quality in the United States. . . . My argument is simply that, given its mission and resources, and the political bureaucratic arena in which it operates, the EPA's performance can be termed a success, albeit a qualified one.[11]

To the same effect is the writing of Dean E. Mann, who stated respecting the Agency's work, "That environmentally protective policies were adopted and implemented with modest effectiveness is obvious."[12]

Moreover, even the GAO, whose persistent criticisms of EPA's work I have earlier noted, has expressed a more favorable view of the Agency's achievements than has Lazarus. In a detailed and lucid analysis of EPA's management of environmental programs, the GAO stated: "EPA has accomplished much to protect human health and the environment since its creation in 1970. It has put in place a comprehensive regulatory structure and has made notable progress in identifying and combating many of the major causes of pollution."[13]

When one turns to EPA's overall enforcement record, Lazarus's undiluted negativism seems all the more misplaced. Although significantly flawed in a number of respects, the Agency's enforcement programs have also enjoyed some notable successes. As Kevin Gaynor observed: "In fact, [EPA's] civil enforcement of many environmental programs is arguably quite good and may be the best kept secret."[14] Over time, the Agency has gradually increased both the volume of its enforcement casework and the total amount of the penalties it has assessed against environmental violators. Additionally, EPA's criminal enforcement program, which has also expanded, has had a significant impact on the behavior of regulated corporate officers. In the words of one private environmental attorney: "The fact that there is a serious threat of criminal enforcement out there for serious violations has certainly gotten people's attention in the private sector. It has had a vast impact.[15] Other private lawyers and consultants in the environmental field have expressed a similar view.[16]

In his examination of congressional scrutiny of EPA, Lazarus takes the position that the actions of Congress have "chilled decision making and innovation within the EPA" and denied the Agency needed flexibility to respond to "the uncertain contours of environmental problems."[17] Whatever validity this conclusion may have with respect to the EPA's rulemaking activities, it seems of little relevance in the enforcement arena. EPA's management and staff have devised some innovative approaches in several areas of the Agency's enforcement work, as illustrated by EPA's multimedia enforcement efforts and its thematic enforcement initiatives. In addition, as described earlier, EPA's RCRA loss of interim status enforcement initiative and its "Superfund enforcement first" policy were bold changes in EPA practices that were stimulated, rather than inhibited, by congressional interest. Moreover, with the exception of the 1992–1993 period, congressional anti-regulatory pressures appear to have stimulated innovation and efficiency in the Agency's enforcement efforts.

Equally difficult to credit is Lazarus's claim that congressional oversight has made unreasonable demands on EPA resources that have "significantly reduced" the Agency's capabilities.[18] Though several of the present and former Agency enforcement officials I spoke with did identify this as a problem,[19] the overwhelming majority of the individuals whom I interviewed in that category did not mention this concern. Indeed, a number of those who talked with me saw positive value in congressional oversight of EPA, especially during the Gorsuch period.[20]

In noting this, however, I do not wish to suggest that the resource demands placed on EPA by congressional investigations are either minimal or unimportant. Nor do I contend that the congressional method of overseeing the Agency is efficient and non-duplicative. EPA's budget is not presently designed to take account of the Agency's work in responding to congressional oversight, a fact that contributes to a chronic underestimation of EPA's workload. This situation should be remedied. Furthermore, as Lazarus persuasively demonstrates, EPA is potentially subject to intense and adversarial oversight from an immense number of committees and subcommittees with overlapping concerns and, at times, conflicting agendas. Given this, Lazarus's suggestions that Congress reduce the number of committees and subcommittees with jurisdiction over the Agency and that it take steps to improve oversight coordination among existing committees seem well worth considering.[21]

Another objection that Lazarus raises regarding congressional oversight of EPA relates to EPA's policy priorities. He contends that extensive congressional investigations "skew" EPA's agenda as it responds to the multiple requests and complaints of individual committee and subcommittee chairs with oversight leverage.[22] At least as it relates to EPA's enforcement policies, this concern seems exaggerated. In responding to Lazarus, Steven Shimberg aptly noted: "While oversight does affect EPA's priorities, this is not necessarily a bad thing. EPA must be responsive to public concerns. If the Agency cannot garner public support for its priorities, those priorities *should* be 'skewed' by Congressional oversight."[23]

Shimberg's point is borne out by the experience of congressional oversight of EPA in enforcement matters. Although Congress has indeed had considerable influence, both directly and indirectly, over the shape and thrust of the Agency's enforcement programs, that influence has, for the most part, been constructive. Administrative agency autonomy is, in many instances, efficient and worthwhile. However, it should not be seen as an end in itself. To the extent that EPA's congressional overseers have succeeded in guiding the Agency in the direction of improved effectiveness and societal benefit, it seems inappropriate to condemn their efforts.

Finally, Lazarus identifies two additional difficulties with congressional scrutiny of EPA: it damages EPA's reputation among the public at large and it harms the self-esteem of Agency professionals. Of those two concerns, the first seems far more valid than the second. Lazarus believes that "the intensity and negative quality of Congressional oversight of EPA has done much to create and perpetuate the view that EPA is incompetent, negligent and even corrupt." He argues that this negative public image, which has been mostly unjustified in his opinion, has eroded judicial and public confidence in the Agency's decisions and undermined EPA's ability to implement federal statutes.[24]

Lazarus's point has some merit. As the EPA enforcement oversight experience reveals, congressional investigations of EPA's work have been almost unrelievedly critical in both tone and substance. In many respects this is quite understandable. From its initial investigations of EPA and Justice Department implementation of the Clean Air and Refuse Acts in the early 1970s, through its first examinations of EPA's lackluster response to uncontrolled hazardous waste dumping, its confrontations with Anne Gorsuch and her colleagues, its inquiries into the inadequacies of EPA's enforcement of RCRA, and its investigations of Superfund administration in the late 1980s and early 1990s, congressional critiques of the Agency's activities have often been based on genuine and serious problems. A number of these problems were later corrected by executive branch officials in ways that significantly improved the quality of governmental administration.

That achievement notwithstanding, congressional oversight in its cumulative impact indeed may have excessively diminished EPA's overall public reputation. As noted previously, a number of objective observers—from well-regarded scholars to the GAO—have found much to praise in the Agency's overall performance. Most oversight hearings and reports on EPA do not reflect this. If public confidence and respect are prerequisites for enhanced EPA effectiveness, then the Agency's congressional critics should tailor their rhetoric accordingly.

Regrettably, such an approach creates problems. When congressional investigators find fundamental flaws in an administrative agency's practices and policies, it is entirely appropriate for them to bring those shortcomings to public attention. Attempts to present a full portrait of the agency's overall performance may, in the event, mute the investigators' message and thus diminish the likelihood of their success in coaxing needed reforms. Moreover, as several scholars have noted, oversight proceedings which present and dramatize only the negative aspects of agency performance often have obvious political advantages for their sponsors, advantages that many elected officials will be loath to abandon.[25]

Despite this, it seems reasonable to urge members of Congress and their staffs to be aware of the unintended as well as the contemplated consequences of their oversight of administrative agencies. When the activities of EPA and other agencies merit praise, congressional overseers should give it openly.[26] Rather than undercutting its efforts, such candor would, in the long view, only serve to reinforce the credibility of Congress. It would also provide the public with a balanced and undistorted picture of how some of its most important governmental institutions are performing.

With respect to the impact of congressional oversight on the self-esteem of EPA employees, however, Lazarus appears to miss the mark. He writes: "Another victim of oversight has been Agency morale, since the barrage of [congressional] criticism has inevitably affected employee self-esteem. . . . This has made it more difficult for EPA to recruit the most qualified Agency personnel and may also be a cause of high Agency turnover."[27] Among the numerous present and former EPA enforcement officials I interviewed, *not one* shared this perception.

To be sure, some EPA employees were highly critical of congressional oversight of the Agency. For example, one former EPA headquarters official told me that "the number of oversight hearings, in toto, was excessive."[28] Another Agency employee referred to congressional oversight committee staff members as "arrogant, snobbish and very tough to deal with" and stated: "[At] times, their job was to grandstand and make political hay out of what they could and annoy working stiffs like myself."[29]

The majority of EPA officials I interviewed, however, were generally, although not uniformly, positive in their view of congressional investigations of the Agency's enforcement work.[30] Most significantly, none of the officials I spoke with identified congressional criticism as a significant source of diminished Agency morale, a barrier to effective personnel recruitment, or a contributing cause of generalized turnover among EPA's professional staff. In view of this arguably subjective but nonetheless telling evidence, that facet of Lazarus's argument seems misinformed. At the same time, my interviews with EPA personnel only partially support Steven Shimberg's claim, in response to Lazarus, that more often than not EPA's staff feels "betrayed from within." Although that may have been true during the relatively brief Gorsuch period, and (in certain respects) much of the Bush II administration, it was not the case much of the time.

Congressional oversight of EPA enforcement raises one final question: to what extent have other aspects of the work of Congress, including the decentralized nature of the lawmaking process and the manner in which

Congress allocates resources to EPA, affected the efficacy of the Agency's administration of federal environmental statutes? Lazarus has addressed this question as well.

As Lazarus sees it, the oversight responsibilities of congressional committees and subcommittees are divided in such a way that each committee and subcommittee tends to examine environmental problems through its own "narrow jurisdictional lens." The result of this "excessive fragmentation," in Lazarus's opinion, is "different laws and even different provisions of the same laws working at cross purposes."[31] In some respects, this observation is certainly correct. There are, indeed, a number of ways in which federal environmental statutes are duplicative and conflicting.[32] Moreover, overlapping demands from congressional investigators can, at least sometimes, strain the scarce resources of EPA's management and staff.

At the same time, the *enforcement* provisions of the legislation implemented by the Agency have not, in general, posed a serious barrier to EPA's work. As Jeffrey G. Miller concluded in his thorough discussion of EPA's statutory enforcement authorities and their interpretation in the courts: "While the [EPA's] enforcement tools . . . could be sharpened and augmented in some respects, EPA generally has sufficient enforcement authority to mount credible and effective enforcement programs, if it has the will to do so."[33]

With respect to the resources made available to EPA by Congress, Lazarus concluded: "Increases in EPA's budget have lagged far behind increases in the agency's statutory responsibilities."[34] In this regard, his discussion is entirely accurate and is fully confirmed by EPA's enforcement programs.

Budgetary shortfalls have long characterized EPA's situation. As early as 1980, John Quarles, a former deputy administrator of EPA, observed: "In the nine years of EPA's existence, its manpower has roughly doubled while its program responsibilities have been multiplied by a factor of twenty. . . . Today, it cannot perform its workload."[35] Inadequate as it may have been in 1980, this situation clearly worsened during the 1980s. In an analysis presented to the Senate Committee on Environment and Public Works in March 1991, Richard L. Hembra, then the director of environmental protection issues of the GAO's Resources, Community, and Economic Development Division, testified that for over a decade EPA's budget had been "essentially capped" despite a considerable growth in its responsibilities. In Hembra's words:

In constant (1982) dollars, EPA's operating budget, which covers all its programs except for the Superfund cleanup program and construction grants for sewage treatment plants, went from $1.7 billion in 1979 down to $1.0 billion in 1983 and rose back up to $1.7 billion again in 1991.

Yet during this same period, EPA's responsibilities grew enormously. The 1984 amendments to the Resource Conservation and Recovery Act, for example, known as the Hazardous and Solid Waste Amendments, significantly broadened EPA's responsibilities for regulating the generation, treatment, storage and disposal of hazardous waste. The amendments also directed EPA to issue regulations for underground storage tanks. In 1986, the Safe Drinking Water Act was amended, requiring EPA to regulate 83 specific drinking water contaminants. In the same year, the Asbestos Hazardous Emergency Response Act was passed, requiring EPA to set standards for responding to the presence of asbestos in school buildings, and to study the problems of asbestos in other public buildings. The 1980's also saw significant new responsibilities for the EPA under amendments to the Clean Water Act, the Federal Insecticide, Fungicide and Rodenticide Act, and Superfund legislation (in Title III, the Emergency Planning and Community-Right-to-Know Act).[36]

EPA's budgetary woes in enforcement continued through the 1990s and early years of the new millennium. As noted in Chapters Seven and Eight, Congress mandated staff salary increases during most of this period while increasing the Agency's budget, a disingenuous approach—the so-called "COLA trick"—that caused little-noticed cuts in important enforcement programs.

These financial shortfalls, combined with a persistent paucity of resources at the Environmental Enforcement Section of the Department of Justice, have caused significant problems for EPA's enforcement efforts. In recent years, the most acute problems have surfaced in the areas of criminal enforcement, RCRA enforcement, and Superfund enforcement. Nonetheless, the entire enforcement program has been unable to keep pace with overall economic growth that has spawned new pollution sources that require monitoring and enforcement attention. Moreover, budget limitations have stymied EPA's efforts to upgrade its data management systems, a key facet of its high-priority, targeted initiative programs.

Beyond this, chronic budgetary problems have made it more difficult for EPA to handle information requests under the Freedom of Information Act, to maintain accurate records of enforcement activities, to influence state enforcement appropriately, and to identify PRPs in Superfund cases.[37] These difficulties are also an important cause of what is widely perceived to be inadequate clerical and secretarial support for the Agency's enforcement staff, a situation that often leads to inefficient use of the scarce time of professional enforcement personnel.[38]

Why has EPA been persistently underfunded? Part of the answer lies in the opaque and intensely competitive process by which Congress allocates monies to all federal agencies and departments. After protracted, complex, and contentious discussions within EPA and the executive branch as a whole, the president usually presents a budget request to Congress in January or February of each year.[39] That request includes proposals for EPA as well as for all other components of the federal government. Following this, the Budget Committees of both houses of Congress pass budget resolutions that contain advisory recommendations with respect to different budget functions, as well as binding limits on domestic discretionary spending. The House and Senate Appropriations Committees then allocate domestic discretionary funds among thirteen subcommittees, each of which has jurisdiction over particular federal agencies or departments. At that point, each subcommittee becomes responsible for preparing a bill that divides its particular allocation among the various agencies that fall within its jurisdiction. At this stage, the subcommittee chairs frequently give priority to the preferences of members of their subcommittee, as well as members of the Appropriations Committee as a whole. The views of representatives of interest groups are also considered, and there are continuing discussions among subcommittee staff members and representatives of the agencies and departments whose budget requests are being considered.[40]

In EPA's situation, most critical decisions with respect to the Agency's funding are made by the House and Senate Appropriations Committees' subcommittees on veterans' affairs, independent agencies, and transportation, housing, and urban development. These panels have remarkably broad and diverse budgetary responsibilities. In addition to EPA, their jurisdiction includes, among some twenty-four other agencies and entities, the Consumer Products Safety Commission, the National Science Foundation, the Department of Veterans Affairs, the Department of Housing and Urban Development, and the Selective Service System. The competition among those various agencies and departments for the limited allocations available to the same subcommittee is remarkably intensive.

While EPA does have supporters among individual members of Congress, as well as lobbyists representing a coalition of interests that range from state and local governments to national environmental organizations, the Agency is chronically disadvantaged in this process by several factors. First of all, in the tangle of powerful agencies and interests that regularly vie for HUD, VA, and Independent Agencies Subcommittee funding, EPA's needs are easily overlooked. Despite its size and relative importance to the environmental and economic life of the nation, EPA is perennially cast in the role of small fish in an extraordinarily big subcommittee pond.

Second, unlike several of its more formidable competitors — such as the Department of Veterans Affairs and the National Aeronautics and Space Administration — EPA does not have a single, unified, and well-organized constituency in support of its budget requests. Instead, members of Congress with an interest in EPA issues range from strong supporters of environmental protection to bitter opponents of specific Agency programs or activities. This hampers EPA in its efforts to compete with agencies and departments whose work does not engender controversy.[41]

Third, in the House of Representatives there is no single committee whose responsibility it is to authorize substantive legislation for EPA to administer. Instead, as we have observed, EPA is overseen by a multiplicity of standing committees with varying and sometimes directly competing interests. This situation denies the Agency a unified institutional base of support within the House itself in the rough and tumble of budgetary competition.[42]

Another unfortunate outcome of this diffuse situation, as well as of the overall budgetary stringency that began in the late 1980s, has been a tendency for individual members of Congress to lobby for appropriations that are both narrow in scope and clearly identified in budget legislation. This procedure, known as "earmarking," has increased in recent years with respect to EPA's budget. Several typical examples of this practice can be found in the bill reported by the Subcommittee on HUD, VA, and Independent Agencies of the Senate Appropriations Committee for fiscal year 1992. With regard to EPA abatement, control, and compliance, this bill included appropriations of "$1,000,000 for the Lake Onondago management conference" and $500,000 for lake-water-quality activities by the State of New Jersey, including such activities at Lake Hopatcong, Swartswood Lake, Musconetgong Lake, and other lakes the state might deem appropriate.[43]

How might the congressional appropriation process be reformed to allow EPA a greater chance of receiving the budgetary allocation it needs to function effectively? Several changes would be helpful. First, the jurisdictions of the various subcommittees of the House and Senate Appropriations Committees could be restructured to create a separate subcommittee for environmental protection. While this subcommittee would still need to compete with other appropriations subcommittees with respect to the relative size of its pot of money, such a rearrangement would minimize, at least at the subcommittee level, the need for EPA to compete against a large number of agencies and departments that enjoy united and potent political backing. Second, the committee structure in the House of Representatives could be modified to create a single committee with the exclusive authority to authorize legislation pertaining to pollution control. This would create a core of support and sympathy for adequate EPA funding. It would also decrease the burden that widely decentralized oversight places on EPA resources. Finally, committee memberships in both the House and the Senate could be altered so that there is an overlap between the members of committees who draft the statutes EPA must implement (and oversee its performance) and the committee members who have control over the Agency's budget. This reform, too, would make it more likely that Appropriations subcommittee members would be familiar with the Agency's needs and supportive of its budgetary requests.

Even if all of these changes were accomplished, however, EPA would still face formidable barriers to obtaining all the funding it needs. Since the mid-1980s, Congress has operated in an atmosphere of extreme budgetary restraint as it has grappled with the problem of an ever-expanding federal deficit. This difficulty paints a grim backdrop against which the budgetary dramas of the next several years must be played out.

Nonetheless, in considering future funding levels for EPA, one can hope that Congress will take account of the true dimensions of the Agency's expanded workload, the urgency of its budgetary needs, and the larger cost to society if federal environmental legislation is not implemented effectively. If Congress fails to do this, it seems certain that many of our environmental laws, so proudly heralded at the time of their enactment, will be administered haltingly—and inadequately enforced.

As noted in Chapters Four and Seven, the organizational structure of EPA's enforcement program experienced wrenching changes in 1981 and 1993–1994. Administrator Anne Gorsuch abolished the Agency's Office of Enforcement and placed EPA's enforcement engineers and attorneys in separate offices, both in headquarters and the Agency's regional offices. In an attempt to remedy the perceived harm which that change caused, Administrator Carol Browner reestablished a headquarters enforcement office that included both legal and technical components but allowed regional offices the discretion to fashion their own organizational arrangements for enforcement work. These changes have had important consequences.

In the face of challenges from other components of the Agency during the Bush II administration, EPA's unified headquarters enforcement structure proved an effective bulwark against strong pressure to thwart the Agency's enforcement work—particularly its complex and environmentally important new source review initiative against coal-fired power plants. The determined effort made by EPA's Office of Air and Radiation (OAR) to undermine that program would doubtless have succeeded if the EPA's air enforcement engineers and scientists had been housed in OAR, rather than the Agency's enforcement office.

At the same time, however, the relocation of enforcement technical people from headquarters program offices to a unified OECA left a residue of bitterness in the offices that were required to give up some of their personnel. It also left enforcement without a voice in headquarters program offices, whose remaining staff members often had little sense of the value or importance of EPA's enforcement function. This fact left the Agency more prone to the sort of interoffice staff rifts and rivalries that characterized much of the Bush II period.

There may be no easy solution to the unintended problems that resulted from the enforcement reorganization of the 1990s, a change that in retrospect seems, on balance, justified and worthwhile. Nonetheless, some innovations in workforce management—and additional structural adjustments at the regional office level—may well prove constructive. One approach that seems worth trying would be for EPA to systematically rotate some portion of its personnel, so that OECA staff members are temporarily detailed to program offices while program office personnel are placed in an enforcement office setting. Such an arrangement—which would have to be done carefully, to avoid disrupting ongoing projects— might give program office staff a greater appreciation of the demands and rigors of enforcement work. It might also expose enforcement staffers to the intricacies and difficulties of drafting regulations amidst cross-pressures from regulated entities and environmental organizations.

Another needed change is a realignment of personnel in those EPA regions where enforcement attorneys and engineers are housed in separate regional offices and divisions. This restructuring—which was contemplated but never completed during the Clinton administration—will end the rivalry among headquarters offices for influence at the regional level. It will also end the confusion engendered by the Agency's multiplicity of regional enforcement arrangements. Undoubtedly and unfortunately, regional reorganizations may cause some temporary slowdowns in enforcement casework, and (regrettably) it may also limit the opportunities for career advancement of some attorneys in large offices of regional counsel. Nonetheless, such a realignment will prevent future regional program division directors and regional administrators from withdrawing resources from enforcement work by "reassigning" enforcement engineers to other tasks in the event that enforcement is once again besieged by its opponents in a future administration. Reassignments of that sort can clearly impair regional enforcement effectiveness by draining the enforcement effort of badly needed resources.

This account of EPA's enforcement history has made clear that certain political appointees play a critical role in the Agency's enforcement work. The most important of those appointees are EPA's administrator and deputy administrator, the assistant administrator for enforcement and compliance assurance, and the Agency's regional administrators. Each of the officials faces unique challenges, and each has the potential to make an important contribution to EPA's enforcement success.

Beyond keeping the Agency in the good graces of Congress, the White House, and interested segments of the general public, EPA's administrator and deputy administrator can bolster enforcement work in two distinct ways. First, they can negotiate with steadfastness and skill for additional resources for the Agency in general and OECA in particular. Second, they can actively communicate, both outside of EPA and to the Agency's hard-pressed enforcement staff, that they fully support a vigorous enforcement posture. William Ruckelshaus did this with some success, in both of his terms as administrator, as did deputy administrators Hank Habicht, Alvin Alm, and Barbara Blum during their respective terms in office. In contrast, as we have seen, the absence of supportive signals from Administrator Christie Todd Whitman, combined with some apparently unintended miscommunication at the outset of her term, had a negative effect on enforcement staff morale and program effectiveness. So too did the passivity of Administrator Steven Johnson and Deputy Administrator Marcus Peacock in the face of bitter (and public) interoffice disputation.

The EPA's assistant administrator for enforcement and compliance assurance must carry out an exceedingly challenging set of tasks. As the most visible representative of the Agency's enforcement program, he or she must "carry the flag" for the enforcement cause at meetings with state officials, the Justice Department and other federal entities, the White House, other appointed EPA officials, representatives of regulated companies, and others. The assistant administrator must also cultivate favorable working relationships with key members of Congress and their staffs, and also communicate effectively with members of the Agency's own career enforcement staff.

On balance, EPA has been quite fortunate with regard to the individuals who have led its enforcement efforts. Just as Steven Herman effectively defended EPA enforcement against external attacks from Capitol Hill, Grant Nakayama ably fended off internal efforts to undercut the Agency's enforcement effectiveness. Along with Nakayama, John Quarles and J. P. Suarez each did a skillful job of encouraging the productivity and earning the respect of EPA's career staff; and, with support from others within the Bush I administration, Jim Strock was an innovative manager who displayed great skill in dealing with a skeptical Congress at a difficult time. The outstanding work of these individuals—and others—helped to build (and, in some cases, to salvage) a credible enforcement program at the Agency.

EPA's regional administrators are also in a position to have an important impact on the Agency's enforcement work. As I have noted, by tradition those officials are selected with the consent of the leadership of the state environmental protection agencies in particular regions. As a result, a number of regional administrators have made efforts to curry favor with state officials—some of whom view enforcement activities with disfavor. Thus, those regional administrators have shown little enthusiasm for regional enforcement work, sometimes setting an anti-enforcement tone that has diluted enforcement effectiveness within their regions. At the same time, however, other appointed regional administrators—such as Valdas Adamkus in Region V and Wayne Nastri in Region IX—were staunch supporters of their regional enforcement programs. As those individuals and others have shown, the politicized manner in which EPA's top regional officials are vetted does not guarantee that regional administrators will support state efforts to dilute enforcement effectiveness.

Nonetheless, to the extent that Congress can muster the political will to do so, the selection of EPA regional administrators from the ranks of senior career civil servants seems a more workable arrangement. Such an approach, which prevails in other federal agencies and departments, will add more stability and predictability to a number of regional programs, including but not limited to enforcement. It will also take away the (sometimes misused) leverage that some state officials enjoy in the setting of EPA regional office enforcement policies and priorities.

Beyond being lucky with many of the individuals who have been appointed to EPA positions that affect enforcement work, overall the Agency has also had good fortune with respect to the quality and dedication of its professional enforcement staff. For the most part, members of that staff have proven dedicated, resourceful, capable, and well focused. Over time the staff has collectively gained in experience, know-how, and maturity, and from time to time it has provided both momentum and stability in the midst of changes at the political appointee level.

Despite this—and notwithstanding notable improvements in employee working conditions from the bleak days of the 1970s—certain problems among the enforcement staff have persisted. As noted above, staff morale has fluctuated dramatically over time, from relatively hopeful and upbeat times during significant periods of the 1970s and much of the Bush I and Clinton eras to decidedly negative during the Gorsuch era and much of the Bush II administration. For reasons divorced from logic, enforcement attorneys and engineers are subject to pay scales that are unfairly weighted in favor of attorneys. Moreover, as we have seen, pervasive resource shortages have continuously overtaxed EPA enforcement employees, many of whom have had to log numerous hours of unpaid overtime to complete their demanding work assignments. Despite what appears to be genuine recent progress, relations with the Department of Justice have sometimes been fractious and, like other federal agencies over the next decade, EPA faces the prospect of the retirement of large numbers of experienced enforcement staff members from the baby boom generation, along with the on-the-job knowledge and institutional memory that those individuals possess—a problem considered further in Chapter Ten.

Many of these staff-level problems will not be easily solved. Nonetheless, the Agency's managers would certainly do well to work with the federal Office of Personnel Management to equalize pay scales for differently trained enforcement professionals, to step up their recruitment of well-qualified younger staff members, to expand opportunities for career advancement, and to devote time and effort to training new generations of enforcement professionals. All of these measures are essential if staff-level weaknesses are to be shored up and the most successful and effective aspects of EPA's enforcement programs are to be preserved and perpetuated.

Did Industry Capture EPA Enforcement? Captive Agency Theory and Its (Partial) Applicability

EPA's varied enforcement experiences raise a further question that deserves systematic attention: has the Agency enforcement program been "captured" by the entities that EPA monitors and regulates? This chapter examines the extent to which the captive agency theory, first articulated in 1955 by Princeton University professor Marver Bernstein in his influential book, *Regulating Business by Independent Commission*,[1] applies to EPA's enforcement work. After summarizing Bernstein's theories of administrative regulations as a paradigm of captive agency theory, and describing the legislative reforms of the 1970s and 1980s that attempted to take account of the insights and criticisms of captive agency theorists in reshaping key facets of U.S. administrative law, I will critically evaluate Bernstein's captive agency theory in light of the key trends, developments, and events in EPA regulation and enforcement.

The basic notion of the captive agency theory of administrative agencies is that such agencies have a tendency to move so far in the direction of accommodating the interests of the entities they are charged with regulating that ultimately these agencies may be fairly considered a "captive" of those regulated firms.[2] Captive agency theory typically views regulators as subject to unique pressures and influences that invariably push their actions and their decisions on policy questions in a direction favored by regulated firms. Among other things, the theory posits, captive agencies tend to be unduly inefficient, passive, and ponderous, failing to enforce their own regulatory requirements with needed vigor and enthusiasm.[3]

This chapter assays the extent to which the captive agency theory first formulated by Bernstein continues to have viability as an explanation of the behavior of federal regulatory agencies in the twenty-first century in general and EPA in particular. It asks whether the theory is still valid and if so how and to what extent.

EPA and its enforcement work seem an apt subject of study in this context for several reasons. First, in a number of respects, the regulatory legislation under which EPA operates was fashioned by Congress with certain lessons from captive agency theorists in mind. The Agency's authorizing statutes (the Clean Air Act, the Clean Water Act, the Resource Conservation and Recovery Act, etc.) tend to be lengthier, more detailed, and more directive of specific agency actions than the legislation that authorized the independent commissions (such as the Interstate Commerce Commission, the Securities and Exchange Commission, and the Civil Aeronautics Board) that Marver Bernstein studied in the early 1950s. EPA's authorizing statutes also include provisions for judicial review, and for lawsuits by private citizens to enforce Agency standards and requirements, and they give EPA power to regulate a broad range of industries, rather than only one or a small number of industries (as had been common prior to the 1970s). If EPA is a captive agency notwithstanding these legislative reforms, one may well conclude that captive agency theorists were far more effective at diagnosing administrative maladies than they were at prescribing cures for them.

EPA *enforcement* work is also highlighted because other scholars have concluded that administrative agency enforcement efforts are especially vulnerable to capture by regulated activities.[4] Enforcement takes place at low visibility. It lacks the regularity and transparency of agency rule making, and it often calls for close interactions between government regulators and individual companies. If agency capture can be found anywhere, it therefore seems likely to be manifested in the enforcement context.

In the middle years of the 1950s, Marver Bernstein set out to evaluate critically the role of independent regulatory commissions.[5] Focusing on seven such federal agencies,[6] *Regulating Business By Independent Commission*, a slim, concise volume, also had two other objectives: to develop a more realistic concept of governmental regulation than that which supported the commission form and to appraise the independent commission as an agent of governmental regulation at the national level.[7]

Bernstein's book began with a two-chapter overview of the intellectual development of the regulatory movement.[8] From the efforts of the agrarian, post–Civil War Granger movement to establish state commissions that regulated railroad practices in rates and competition, Bernstein traced the evolution of U.S. regulatory reform through the Progressive

Era (1906–1917), the decade of the Great Depression, and World War II and its aftermath. He noted that progressive reformers of the early twentieth century were urban, middle-class citizens who believed in purifying government of fraud and corruption by tinkering with the machinery of government, making government more efficient by using sound business management methods, and allocating responsibility to independent, nonpolitical regulatory commissions that made decisions based upon expert knowledge and impartial judgment. In the 1930s, the imperatives of economic recovery turned the regulatory spotlight away from the independent commission and toward new emergency relief agencies and expanded programs administered by older federal departments such as Agriculture and Interior. Nonetheless, throughout the New Deal period, the public remained interested in independent commissions like the SEC, which were widely viewed as a potential antidote to the stock market scandals of the late 1920s and (to many in Congress) as a bulwark against presidential domination of government. During World War II, as Bernstein describes, the demands of mobilization for war and defense dramatized economic programs and policies outside the scope of the independent commissions, and thereafter the government emphasized promotion of maximum employment, production, and purchasing power in a free-market economy—an effort that still involved and implicated independent regulatory commissions at the time that Bernstein wrote his major work.

Bernstein viewed regulatory reformers, particularly those of the Progressive Era, as simplistic and naive. From his standpoint, "a middle class tradition of genteel reform has resulted in reliance on simple panaceas to achieve far reaching changes."[9] Regulatory reformers "lacked staying power and the ability to maintain the interest of the public in their programs."[10] Moreover, they were "unable to understand the nature of the major problem the commissions had to face—tendencies in Congress to undermine the independence of the commissions."[11]

In particular, Bernstein took issue with the Progressive Era reformers' central belief that administrative regulation requires a high degree of expertness, a mastery of technical detail, and a neutral institutional environment that is entirely free from partisan political considerations. As Bernstein saw it, the expertise of governmental administrators does not give them any special competence to formulate regulatory policy, especially where the problems that face agencies are complex and the scope of agency discretion is great.[12] Expertness does not improve the ability of agencies to plan their activities or to relate to public needs and desires. Instead, Bernstein wrote, it promotes "myopia" in interpreting the public welfare[13] and creates "a special kind of class system which views public policy through blinders."[14] Similarly, agency independence "does not insure judge-like wisdom, balance and insight."[15] Instead, according to Bernstein, it stands in the way of needed coordination of government policy, and leads to bureaucratic lethargy, lack of imagination, inefficient management, isolation, and insularity.[16]

The reformers' misguided premises led, in turn, to the enactment of inadequate regulatory legislation. In Bernstein's words:

> Regulation often deals with matters about which there is no settled national policy and no stable communal consensus. A regulatory statute more likely than not represents a vaguely worded compromise of conflicting attitudes in Congress as well as the country. It is accepted as a basis for commencing regulation but does not furnish a workable set of goals and policies. . . . No agency finds a regulatory recipe or formula ready-made for its use.[17]

In this legally guideless, unstructured setting, regulatory agencies are subject to persistent challenge and antagonism. Their search for the public interest in regulatory matters "must be carried on against formidable obstacles."[18] They are frequently at the center of a rivalry between Congress and the president to have more influence over their policy making.[19] Moreover, especially in their early years, regulatory agencies are subject to intense pressures from the well-organized interests they regulate.

In a concerted attempt to influence the regulatory process, these individuals and companies often initiate litigation with respect to the legal scope of the agency's regulatory powers and the meaning of its legislative mandates.[20] Bernstein suggested that regulated groups publicly criticize the agency as biased against them and unduly zealous. Those regulated may also resort to "subterfuge, distortion and concealment," and they may "simulate a campaign of propaganda to make the environment of the regulatory agency as hostile as possible."[21]

At the core of Bernstein's concept of the "captive agency" is his discussion of the "life cycle" of regulatory agencies. As Bernstein saw it, the useful lives of these governmental institutions may be divided into four phases: gestation, youth, maturity, and old age. During the gestation phase, public pressure on Congress to produce regulatory legislation gradually mounts. Despite vigorous resistance from opposition groups, the passage of such legislation is finally achieved. However, as

noted above, the statute that is finally enacted is often an ambiguous compromise that fails to provide clear directions to the regulatory agency it
establishes.[22]

In its youthful stage, following passage of pertinent regulatory legislation, the agency is endowed with "an aggressive, crusading spirit."[23] It
tends to take a broad view of its mission, and it may develop daring and
inventiveness in resolving regulatory problems.[24]

Gradually, however, the circumstances of the agency change. Until the
courts have outlined the legal scope of the agency's regulatory powers,
litigation forms the framework for much of the regulatory process. In
addition, open public support for regulation fades away. The agency be-
gins to operate in a technical climate that defies public comprehension.
Congress is reluctant to champion public control of business activities
without strong, active public support, and public supporters of regulation,
tired after their long struggle to pass regulatory legislation, mistakenly
tend to regard administration as automatically following legislation.[25]

In this environment, according to Bernstein, the regulatory agency
enters a period of "maturity" or "devitalization." It relies more and more
upon settled procedures, its goals become routine and accepted, and it
slowly becomes primarily concerned with the health of the industry it
is charged with regulating. Unable to count on either public or congressional support for firm regulation, the agency grants regulated parties
numerous opportunities to challenge its positions and to persuade it that
contemplated action is unfair or incorrect. Agency passivity grows until
it borders on apathy, and there is an ever-increasing desire to avoid conflicts and enjoy good relationships with regulated groups.[26]

At the close of its maturity phase, the regulatory agency enters a period
of "old age" in which it completes its "surrender" to the groups it is nominally regulating. As Bernstein described it:

> Politically isolated, lacking a firm basis in public support, lethargic
> in attitude and approach, unsupported in its demands for more staff
> and money, the commission finally becomes a captive of the regu-
> lated groups. During old age, the working agreement that a commission
> reaches with regulated interests becomes so fixed that the agency has no
> creative force left to mobilize against the regulated groups. Its primary
> mission is the maintenance of the status quo in the regulated industry,
> and its own position as recognized protector of the industry. . . . In their
> declining days, commissions can be described as retrogressive, lethargic,

sluggish and insensitive to their wider political and social setting. They are incapable of securing progressive revision of regulatory policies and fall further behind in their work.[27]

In Bernstein's opinion, the length of each life cycle phase varies from one regulatory agency to another, and some agencies may skip an entire period as they evolve.[28] However, in his view, the best antidote to agency capture is a strong and continuing internal sense of agency mission,[29] combined with astute agency leadership actively engaged in seeking political support from the president, Congress and the public at large.[30] Thus, for Bernstein,

> the area of [regulatory agency] freedom from the standards of private parties depends heavily on the prestige and competence of the regulatory officials, the prevailing political temper of the times, the capacity of the agency to find support in the presidency and Congress, the vitality of public opinion in favor of regulation and the [political] strength of the private parties themselves.[31]

The eighth chapter of *Regulating Business by Independent Commission* contains Marver Bernstein's thoughts with respect to regulatory enforcement. Bernstein envisioned enforcement as a vital component of regulatory work. He observed that "[o]ne of the crucial tests of the effectiveness of a regulatory commission is its capacity to obtain the compliance of persons subject to regulation and to enforce its regulations against violators."[32] Moreover, Bernstein observed that:

> [t]he attitude of a commission towards its enforcement responsibilities affects its entire regulatory program. Unless it demonstrates a capacity to enforce its regulations, they will be honored more in the breach than in the observance. Those (regulated firms) who discover that violations go undetected and unpunished will have little respect for the commission and will violate regulations with impunity if it is to their financial or commercial advantage.[33]

The more passive a regulatory agency is, the less likely it is to organize effective compliance and enforcement activities. Conversely, the absence of vigorous enforcement typically reflects an agency's lack of active regulation in the public interest.[34]

Bernstein saw eight elements as being crucial to the establishment and maintenance of effective regulatory enforcement. First and foremost, the regulatory agency must have broad public support for the goals of the regulation and the agency's general regulatory policies.[35] Second, the agency's regulations themselves must be drafted so as to be understandable to all regulated parties,[36] and they must be enforceable in the sense that violations can be readily detected and proven by the agency's staff.[37] Third, the inspection and enforcement work of an agency should be implemented by a separate, designated unit of the agency that has no other program responsibilities.[38] Fourth, when participating in litigation involving or affecting enforcement, a regulatory agency must have access to a judiciary "sympathetic to the broad purpose and goals of the statute and regulations that have been violated."[39] Fifth, where regulating enforcement is undertaken, the level of sanctions and penalties assessed should be commensurate with the type of violation that is the basis for the enforcement action.[40] Sixth, effective enforcement requires the close cooperation of investigators, attorneys, and other personnel trained in different disciplines.[41] Seventh, Bernstein recommended that regulatory agencies issue explanatory materials describing their regulations and explaining how they might be complied with, in order to promote regulatory compliance.[42] Finally, Bernstein suggested that government agencies take advantage of the importance of government as a source of credit, as a source of supply, and/or as a consumer, to help create additional incentives for regulated parties to comply with applicable standards.[43]

These enforcement and compliance elements are not present in most regulatory agencies, according to Bernstein. Thus, he concluded his observations on regulatory enforcement with the pejorative comment that

> [e]nforcement activities of the regulatory commissions tend to be weak, poorly staffed and inadequately supported. They are marked by overall inadequacy and reluctance to experiment with new enforcement techniques. Incentives to induce compliance are rarely articulated, and deliberate planning of compliance programs is conspicuously absent.[44]

Although well received by other scholars of regulation, it took some time for Marver Bernstein's work to result in changes in government policies. Gradually, however, the findings and suggestions of Bernstein (and captive agency theorists like him) proved immensely influential with respect to the ways in which regulation by administrative agencies was authorized by Congress, implemented by the agencies themselves, and reviewed by federal courts. Particularly in the late 1960s and early 1970s, in response to the criticisms that Bernstein and his colleagues initiated, Congress enacted a series of new regulatory statutes that were longer, more detailed, and more specifically directive toward regulatory agencies than had been true in the past. For the first time, these statutes encouraged citizen participation in agency decision making, direct citizen involvement in regulatory enforcement, and greater openness and accountability in the work of administrative agencies. Additionally, the federal courts began to scrutinize more carefully the administrative procedures adopted by agency administrators, together with the reasoning those administrators relied on to support their regulatory decisions.

One type of regulatory legislation enacted in response to the captive agency theory of Bernstein and his fellow theorists has been termed the "coercive model" of regulatory delegation. In a perceptive article,[45] professors Sidney Shapiro and Robert Glicksman describe the coercive model in these terms:

> Congress mandates agency regulation by removing an agency's discretion to regulate, but permits the agency to choose the appropriate model of regulation. . . . This model typically forces the agency to regulate by mandating some kind of agency action—such as listing chemicals as hazardous or issuing regulations applicable to industrial polluters—before a set deadline. The substantive delegation, however, is couched in general terms.[46]

Shapiro and Glicksman also posit a "ministerial model" of congressional control. Under the latter approach, Congress includes in a regulatory statute both a set of detailed regulatory criteria that the administrative agency is required to follow in establishing regulations and a binding set of deadlines by which it must act.[47]

In their analysis of federal pollution control legislation, Shapiro and Glicksman aptly note that not all statutory prescriptions to EPA fit squarely into the models of control of regulatory agencies that their work describes.[48] Nonetheless, many sets of amendments to EPA-authorizing statutes enacted in the late 1970s and 1980s clearly exemplify coercive control legislation that attempts to accelerate the pace of regulation (and facilitate legislative oversight) by forcing the EPA to make particular regulatory decisions within a specified time.[49] Other environmental regulatory statutes supplement mandatory deadlines with specific regulatory criteria that bind EPA in its rule making.[50] Both species of this legislation are responsive to the concerns of Bernstein and others that regulatory legislation not endow agencies with unfettered discretion to regulate as they see fit.

Beyond this, as mentioned above, much of the federal environmental regulatory legislation enacted since the late 1960s reflects captive agency theory in another significant respect: it includes specific provisions intended to open up the regulatory process to participation by members of the public at large. One example of such a provision is the statutory authorization of private petitions for initiation of rule making proceedings and other agency actions. Typically, such petition sections allow for judicial review of all agency decisions that deny citizen petitions.[51]

Other common provisions of federal environmental statutes permit private citizens to initiate lawsuits to enforce certain requirements imposed in other portions of the same legislation. The "citizen suit provisions" generally authorize individuals to act as "private attorneys general" by instituting civil enforcement in federal district court against any person who is violating an applicable substantive requirement of the statute (or an EPA regulation promulgated thereunder). Additionally, they entitle citizens to bring civil actions to compel the EPA administrator to carry out nondiscretionary requirements of the statute.[52]

The influence of captive agency theory on regulatory policy was not limited to the regulatory enactments of Congress, however. As Thomas Merrill perceived:

> [C]apture theory also suggests that aggressive judicial oversight and control of agencies is needed in order to counteract the distortions of the administrative process introduced by interest group capture and other pathologies. Specifically, by forcing agencies to adopt an administrative process that is more open, and to give greater consideration to underrepresented viewpoints in that process, courts may be able to counteract the distortions emphasized by the theory.[53]

The judicial responses to the concerns embodied in the writing of Bernstein and other proponents of the captive agency theory were effectively catalogued—and then criticized—in an important law review article by Richard Stewart, "The Reformation of American Administrative Law."[54] Stewart observed that judicial skepticism regarding the efficacy and fairness of administrative agency regulation had led the courts to abandon a more restrained traditional model of judicial review in favor of what he termed a "fundamental transformation" of American administrative law.[55] As Stewart saw it, that transformation, which took place in the late 1960s and early 1970s, had three significant aspects. First, the courts substantially eliminated the doctrine of standing to sue as a barrier to challenging agency action in court.[56] Second, the courts granted individuals broad permission to intervene in proceedings pending before regulatory agencies.[57] Finally, in reviewing regulatory agency decisions, federal judges imposed on administrators a duty to consider, fully and adequately, the views of all participating interests in decisions regarding agency rules and policies.[58]

How accurately does the captive agency theory enunciated by Marver Bernstein describe the circumstances of EPA's enforcement programs? Did the governmental responses to that theory, described above, succeed in resolving the problems that Bernstein identified?

In a 1991 law review essay,[59] Howard Latin stated:

> I have found little evidence that EPA and other agencies are "captured" by regulated interests as a result of bribes or career opportunities for bureaucrats who adopt pro-industry practices. More subtle influences, however, often do condition the behavior of administrators in favor of regulated interests. . . . Industry representatives appear regularly in Agency proceedings and can usually afford to offer detailed comments and criticisms on possible Agency decisions, while environmental groups intervene on an intermittent basis and the unorganized public seldom participates at all. This routine asymmetry will increase Agency responsiveness to industry criticism. No matter how sincere and public spirited officials are when appointed, a process of negative feedbacks will produce shifts toward the positions espoused by regulated parties.[60]

Latin concluded that, to the extent that agency capture does take place, it is a result of eight "laws" of administrative behavior that he sets forth in his article.[61]

Mark Seidenfeld reached conclusions substantially similar to those of Latin. As Seidenfeld saw it:

> Although evidence suggests that traditional capture mechanisms are not a pervasive problem today, that does not mean that domination is not a potential threat or that particular interest groups no longer exert undue influence on agency decisionmaking.[62]

Seidenfeld noted that firms in regulated industries and interest groups with strong central staffs continue to occupy "a favored position" in regulatory and political structures, a position that grants them "an advantage in influencing Agency decisions."[63] Such industries and groups have the incentive and means to monitor what EPA does on a day-to-day basis. They also have information that the Agency requires to do its job.[64]

Dan Esty expressed agreement with Howard Latin's point with respect to asymmetries of political involvement between regulated industrial interests and environmentally concerned citizens. Esty adroitly observed:

> [T]he complexity and opacity of many environmental issues and the public's difficulty in perceiving its own interest make the risk of special interest manipulation much more severe in the environmental realm than in other fields of regulation or government activity. Simply put, the average citizen knows if he or she is getting adequate roads or schools and even has a sense of whether the government regulation of banks seems appropriate. In many environmental circumstances, however, no comparable basis for judging the adequacy of outcomes exists. . . . In this nontransparent world, the threats of special interest manipulation and public choice failures are very real and also very large.[65]

Matthew Zinn wrote that environmental regulation is "not immune from capture,"[66] and that "the risks of capture of environmental regulation in general are mixed."[67] At the same time, however, Zinn found that environmental enforcement "appears uniquely susceptible to influence by regulated entities."[68] He explained:

> An agency's choices about monitoring, whether or not to bring an enforcement action, and the type of enforcement action to bring, lack the regularity and transparency of rulemaking. Much more so than policy development, enforcement activity is insulated from the close scrutiny of pro-regulatory interests, of Congress, and of the general public. It also calls for closer interaction between regulators and individual firms. This confluence of obscurity and familiarity allows agencies and regulated firms to move closer together.[69]

Finally, citing the work of others, Clifford Rechtschaffen noted both the general dangers of special interest ascendancy in environmental law and the susceptibility of environmental regulatory enforcement personnel to special interest influence.[70] Rechtschaffen rejected a proposal by Shapiro and Glicksman that administrative agencies use their enforcement discretion to adjust general regulatory commitments in specific circumstances in order to accommodate unique or anomalous situations. In doing so, he pointed out that "providing regulators with additional enforcement discretion could exacerbate the already-existing tendency toward special interest influence or domination."[71]

In the remainder of this section of this chapter, I will examine how Bernstein's notions of agency capture have or have not been borne out in the EPA's enforcement record. Before that, however, some words of caution and qualification seem in order. First, while instructive and (I hope) provocative, this chapter's assessment of the captive agency approach through the lens of EPA enforcement may not present a complete and definitive test of the descriptive and predictive value of that theoretical approach. EPA is, after all, only one of many federal regulatory agencies. This chapter does not attempt to evaluate the regulatory work of any other federal agencies, nor does it consider state or local regulatory activity in any comprehensive or systematic way. The conclusions I will reach are thus limited to that extent and more research on this area, focusing on other agencies than EPA, will surely be beneficial.

Second, in emphasizing EPA enforcement, I consider the regulatory policymaking activities of EPA only at the margins. While I have no basis for criticizing Bernstein's assertion that "the lack of a vigorous [enforcement and] compliance program probably reflects the lack of vigorous regulation in the public interest,"[72] the data on which my assessment of his work will be based will not be extensive enough to either prove or negate that observation.

Third, in *Industry Influence in Federal Regulatory Agencies*, Paul J. Quirk aptly wrote that "[j]udging the validity of [accusations of capture] can become quite complex and uncertain. [A]n allegation of industry influence usually rests on an (often unstated) assumption about what the agency would have done in the absence of industry influence—an assumption that tends to derive from what the critic thinks should have been done."[73] In this analysis, I have made an effort to separate my own personal preferences about the past direction of the EPA's implementation of environmental legislation from objective observations regarding what the Agency has actually done—and how its actions do or do not coincide with Marver Bernstein's captive agency notions (along with other aspects of his writings). Nonetheless, Quirk's overall point is well taken. To the extent that my analysis simply reflects my own policy biases, my own conclusions may be fairly questioned.

Finally, one further caveat: Bernstein obviously could not predict the future nor could he have been expected to. In particular, Bernstein cannot be faulted for failing to anticipate the extraordinary success of his own work in influencing Congress and the federal courts. Nor can he be justly criticized for not predicting the future existence of agencies like the EPA, which regulate the practices of a very broad range of U.S. industries (as well as many municipalities and, at times, all members of the public). Moreover, Bernstein can scarcely have prognosticated the myriad profound changes in American society—and political culture—that have occurred since *Regulating Business by Independent Commission* appeared in 1955. In reviewing his work of fifty years ago, I have attempted to keep those precepts in mind.

That being said, let us move to Bernstein's capture theory, beginning with his pronouncement that regulatory agencies must operate in a constant atmosphere of antagonism and challenge. Does EPA's enforcement experience support that finding? The answer is an emphatic yes. As we have noted, the enforcement process is indeed highly demanding and contentious. EPA's conduct of enforcement has certainly been subject to vigorous criticism from a variety of quarters. In the late 1970s, for example, EPA's new policy of "file first, negotiate later" led to a marked increase in industry resentment of the Agency. EPA's managers and staff were publicly criticized at that time—and subsequently—as antibusiness zealots and ineffective bureaucrats.[74] EPA's enforcement work was also subject to periodic, harsh criticism from Capitol Hill,[75] state officials,[76] and (in intra-governmental internal disputes) from the Department of Justice, the Department of Energy, and other agencies and departments. Moreover, EPA has experienced repeated budgetary shortfalls that have detracted from the effectiveness of its enforcement efforts.

Bernstein wrote that, particularly in the early stages of an agency's implementation of regulatory legislation, regulated parties often resort to litigation to gain favorable judicial interpretations of the statutes themselves. This has certainly been true in the EPA's case. In many instances, regulated industries or trade associations have taken advantage of the pre-enforcement review provisions included in most federal environmental legislation to file lawsuits challenging the stringency or affordability of regulations promulgated by the EPA. In addition to giving EPA's industrial critics the prospect of having to comply with requirements that they find more acceptable, these suits also benefit their proponents by delaying the enforceability of the regulatory standards being challenged until judicial review of them has been completed.

Bernstein mentioned that industrial opponents of regulation might resort to subterfuge and propaganda in order to gain public support for their political positions. This has been true with regard to the EPA as well. Beginning with the "jobs versus environment" controversy that emerged in the Ford and Carter administrations, various regulated industries have engaged in overdrawn, orchestrated media campaigns to convince the public that EPA and its fellow regulatory agencies were obtuse, dictatorial, unreasonable, and a drag on national economic prosperity.

Notably, public issue advertising by U.S. industries is anything but a new phenomenon. As political science professor Tom Konda wrote in 1993, in a letter to the editor of the *New York Times* regarding a *Times* article on television campaign ads against the early Clinton administration health-care plan:

> The idea that only "rarely" and on a few issues has industry used advertising to sway public opinion on policy issues is dead wrong. Issue advertising is not new. It was not new 10 years ago, when the nuclear power industry initiated a $30 million television ad campaign as part of its lobbying efforts. Only 20 years ago . . . Russell Train, EPA director, attacked "a well organized campaign . . . to propagandize the public into believing that our environmental concerns have been overstated."
>
> Issue advertising was not even new in 1950, when the American Medical Association fought President Harry Truman's health care plan with advertising in 10,000 newspapers, 30 national magazines and 1,000 radio stations. Or in 1936, when "The Ford Sunday Evening Hour" of orchestral music devoted its commercial time to "talks" excoriating New Deal policies such as Social Security. Or even when President Woodrow Wilson complained that the "newspapers are being filled with advertisements calculated to mislead the judgment not only of public men, but also the public opinion of the country itself."
>
> Eighty years ago, when Senator Charles Thomas denounced the sugar lobby's advertising during a tariff battle, issue advertising was new. Since then, business has repeatedly turned to advertising to sell its policy views to the public.[77]

Despite its lack of originality, however, inaccurate industry advertisements castigating government regulation in general (and EPA implementation of environmental laws in particular) are certainly an unfortunate fact of life for EPA and its public supporters.

Marver Bernstein also posited a "life cycle" for regulatory agencies in which they pass through four distinct stages—gestation, youth, maturity, and old age—while becoming ever-increasingly dominated by the industries they have been asked to regulate. How close of a fit is there between this key aspect of Bernstein's theory and EPA's regulatory enforcement experience? Here the evidence appears ambiguous. As to most of the environmental legislation that EPA became responsible for implementing, the Agency did indeed pass through a "gestation period" in the early 1970s as Congress debated and ultimately enacted the Clean Air Act, Clean Water Act, Federal Insecticide, Fungicide and Rodenticide Act, and a number of other environmental regulatory statutes. Moreover, EPA seems to have experienced the "youthful phase" that Bernstein wrote of at least twice in its enforcement history. In its first two years of existence, EPA took vigorous steps to enforce then-existing environmental laws against various Fortune 500 corporations under the Refuse Act and other federal laws. Acting out of a strong sense of mission, the young Agency enjoyed strong public support for its work in that period. Similarly, EPA's pre-Superfund hazardous waste enforcement under 7003 of the Resource Conservation and Recovery Act, as carried out by the Agency's short-lived Hazardous Waste Enforcement Task Force,[78] also exemplified the sort of idealistic, highly motivated regulatory programs that, according to Bernstein, typify regulatory agencies in their early days. However, since that time, how far the EPA has moved into what Bernstein described as "maturity," and whether or to what extent it has been captivated by industry groups in an "old age" phase, are more difficult questions.

Undoubtedly, in Bernstein's terms, the Agency is no longer youthful. Since the early 1970s, EPA has relied more and more on settled procedures (in its enforcement activities and elsewhere). Moreover, its goals also seem to have become more routine and accepted. It is much more questionable, however, whether EPA has consistently manifested the "passivity that borders on apathy" which Bernstein referred to as "the most marked development" in a mature regulatory entity.[79] And only occasionally and temporarily has EPA manifested the complete debility that Bernstein considers characteristic of a captive agency that has reached "old age." A more accurate conclusion appears to be that EPA is an agency that has only partially matured, and is still vulnerable to further decline and industry captivity.

Over the years of its existence, EPA enforcement work has, at the very least, bordered on captivity at several points. For example, during the tenure of Anne Gorsuch as EPA administrator, in the opening years of the Reagan administration, the Agency narrowly survived an attempt by its own political leaders to dismantle the Agency's enforcement programs. In the face of determined congressional opposition, that misguided attempt at agency capture failed. Had it succeeded, however, that anti-regulatory initiative would have gone far in the direction of rendering EPA the toothless, ineffectual bureaucracy that Bernstein's theoretical "maturity" and "old age" phases so vividly describe.

Industrial capture of EPA might also have occurred if in 1992, during the late Bush I administration, the vice president's Council on Competitiveness had made more headway in forcing the Agency to relax environmental requirements, or if the Clinton administration, in 1993, had tilted further than it did in the direction of regulatory reform and compliance assistance as a substitute for an assertive, deterrent enforcement program.

In 1995, after a bitter political struggle, the EPA succeeded in defeating an effort by the newly elected, anti-regulatory "Gingrich Congress" to slash drastically the Agency's budget for enforcement and other important functions. Had those budget cuts become effective, they would undoubtedly have disabled the EPA's ability to regulate industry effectively. In addition, during the Bush II administration, a political decision to use regulatory interpretations to undermine EPA's massive, ongoing enforcement initiative against the electric utility industry appears to have brought about at least a partial capture of the Agency's enforcement work, by a politically influential industry that successfully gained support for its anti-regulatory positions from key political figures within the EPA and other parts of the executive branch.

These examples of near and partial EPA capture notwithstanding, however, throughout most of its history the Agency does appear to have maintained at least a measure of independence and a reasonably progressive outlook on the appropriate role of environmental regulation and regulatory enforcement. Additionally, EPA has displayed little of the extreme passivity—and entrenched resistance to change and innovation—that Bernstein described as exemplifying regulatory agency maturity and old age.

In the enforcement area, the Agency's record contains several examples of innovation and a willingness to walk along fresh paths to encourage regulatory compliance. These include EPA's adoption of a multimedia enforcement approach, the "enforcement in the 1990s" reforms championed by then–Assistant Administrator Jim Strock, and the EPA enforcement innovations of the Clinton period (including targeted national enforcement initiatives, letters to regulated companies inviting voluntary corrections of known violations, and publicizing enforcement objectives).

Overall, then, the key trends and events in EPA's enforcement history do appear to support the conclusions of Matthew Zinn, Clifford Rechtschaffen, Mark Seidenfeld, and Daniel Esty that EPA is not immune from regulatory capture, and that its enforcement program is uniquely susceptible to influence by regulated parties. The Agency does indeed work in an atmosphere of antagonism and challenge, and most of the criticism it encounters comes from regulated entities and their allies in Congress and the executive branch—opponents much better situated than the EPA and its political allies to use public advertising, sometimes in disingenuous ways, to influence public opinion in their favor.

As we have seen, at several points in the Agency's history, the viability of EPA's enforcement work has been greatly threatened by its industry critics. Moreover, with regard to new source review of power plants, some of those regulated parties did succeed in halting a high-priority, resource-intensive EPA enforcement initiative during the Bush II administration. Nonetheless, despite those notable near misses and the partial capture, EPA's enforcement programs thus far appear to have avoided complete capture at the hands of the very industries whose governmental impacts the Agency regulates. Whether that pattern will continue remains an open question.

If EPA has not followed key aspects of the captive agency model spelled out by Bernstein, it seems fair to inquire why not? Why (at least thus far in its history) has the EPA not become a consistently and completely dysfunctional, reactionary captive of the industries it has been charged with regulating? The happy coincidence of several independent factors seems to supply at least a tentative answer.

First, EPA was fortunate to enjoy strong political support from the president at a time—during the challenge of the Gingrich Congress to the Agency's integrity—that such support was desperately needed. Conversely, when EPA's enforcement work was obstructed by an administration with strong anti-regulatory preferences early in the Reagan administration, the Agency had the good luck to be defended skillfully and resolutely by influential, politically sophisticated leaders in Congress.

Second, throughout its history, EPA has maintained at least some support from organized, politically active environmental groups. Those public interest groups did not exist when Marver Bernstein first posited the captive agency theory in the mid-1950s. Notwithstanding the political "asymmetries" that Esty, Latin, and Seidenfeld aptly noted, the work of these groups appears to have succeeded, at least in part, in helping the EPA avoid the complete political isolation—i.e., the absence of a base of regular political support—that Bernstein described with respect to the small, regulatory commissions which preceded EPA's existence.

Third, throughout its history, EPA has been blessed with a highly motivated, dedicated, mission-oriented professional staff. Although the permanent staff's collective preferences were not always heeded, the Agency's staff clearly did serve at times as an anchor of stability in a sea of political turmoil.

Fourth, at least for the most part, EPA's appointed leadership has been neither as uninspiring nor as mediocre as the regulatory commissioners whom Bernstein criticized, nor have those leaders been as politically naive and uninvolved. Concededly, the EPA has had its share of weak (and even destructive) leadership—particularly during the early Reagan administration. Nonetheless, the Agency has also been fortunate to have been led for lengthy periods by such able administrators as Bill Ruckelshaus, Russell Train, Douglas Costle, Bill Reilly, and Carol Browner. All of those top EPA leaders were savvy, decent, and institutionally loyal individuals. They understood the U.S. political system and were able to find and maintain political support for EPA, both in the executive and legislative branches and among the public at large, when that support was critical to the Agency's autonomy and integrity.

Finally, EPA's failure to follow the pessimistic pattern described by Bernstein and other capture theorists must be credited, in no small measure, to the success of Bernstein's own scholarly work. As we have seen, in the 1960s and 1970s, captive agency theory was widely respected in both Congress and the federal courts. As a result, in fashioning environmental statutes, Congress was highly receptive to the recommendations of captive theorists that agencies like the EPA have a single administrative head and that it have numerous industries as its regulatory "clients." Congress also saw to it that the Agency's decision making did not result primarily from a sterile process of administrative adjudication, and that environmental regulatory legislation did not grant EPA the unlimited discretion to set and alter its own regulatory agenda. In EPA's case, these congressional decisions—all traceable to the writings of Marver Bernstein and other captive agency theorists—have played no small part in preventing the traditional forms of regulatory agency captive by industry that those theorists so passionately decried.

If EPA has not—at least not yet—been a captive agency (at least in the way that Bernstein defined that term) to what extent do Bernstein's notions, preferences, and predilections as to regulatory enforcement itself jibe with the realities of the Agency's stormy, uneven enforcement history? In fact, as this brief overview will illustrate, with few exceptions

Bernstein's observations on regulatory enforcement have proven to be sensible and remarkably prescient.

As I have noted, Bernstein viewed it as essential that regulatory agencies have broad public support for their goals and policies. For the most part, EPA has enjoyed such support. As mentioned above, a number of its administrators have skillfully garnered public sympathy for the Agency's efforts, including its enforcement programs. At critical times, the Agency has also received key assistance from allies in Congress, the executive branch, and environmental organizations.

Bernstein also stressed the importance of the comprehensibility and enforceability of regulatory requirements. His point was well taken and widely acknowledged. Nonetheless, in that regard, EPA's record appears mixed. For example, the first set of Clean Air Act state implementation plans (SIPs), drafted by the states and hastily approved by the Agency, were very general in nature and lacking in meaningful reference to the kinds of industrial facilities they ostensibly controlled. As a result, once the early SIPs became enforceable, EPA was forced to devote a good deal of time and effort to determining how to apply these requirements to specific pollution sources. Non-enforceability problems have also arisen under the maximum achievable control technology (MACT) standards established by EPA to control the emission of toxic air pollutants. In the enforcement process, those regulations have proven opaque, enormously complex, and immensely difficult to administer.

Bernstein soundly recommended that the enforcement work of regulatory agencies be implemented by a separate, designated agency unit. EPA's record in this area has been uneven. In 1981, EPA Administrator Anne Gorsuch abolished such a separate unit in EPA headquarters (the Office of Enforcement) and divided its legal and technical personnel into separate organizational units. Although the Agency's enforcement efforts underwent a formal reorganization in 1990, those changes failed to overcome the continuing fragmentation of EPA enforcement authority. Only in 1993 and 1994 did the EPA again reorganize its headquarters to create a new, expanded Office of Enforcement and Compliance Assurance (OECA). That massive change once again brought the Agency's enforcement attorneys and technical staff at headquarters into the same headquarters organizational unit—a beneficial shift in the long term.

Bernstein noted the importance for regulatory agency enforcement of having access to a generally sympathetic judiciary. In that respect, EPA has been fortunate. Together with the Department of Justice—which represents the Agency in the federal courts—EPA has compiled a reasonably successful record in its judicial enforcement cases. EPA's (and the DOJ's) most striking and notable achievement, perhaps, came in the early 1980s when the federal government won a series of key cases under the Superfund statute that established the principle of strict, joint, and several liability, and various other doctrines that gave the government considerable authority to enforce the statute against potentially responsible parties (PRPs) at hazardous waste sites.

Bernstein sensibly recommended that the level of sanctions and penalties assessed be commensurate with regulatory violations being redressed. At least in its formal enforcement policy pronouncements, EPA has attempted to do precisely that. The Agency's RCRA penalty policy, for example, attempts to distinguish among more serious and less serious violations, and to assess penalties against violators that are appropriate to their offenses.

Bernstein suggested that regulatory enforcement be characterized by cooperation between attorneys and technically trained personnel. Although it is difficult to draw definite conclusions regarding EPA's performance in this area, the best evidence seems to be that the Agency has done reasonably well in that respect. Interdisciplinary disputes among the staff have arisen on occasion. Nonetheless, for the most part since the 1970s, EPA's enforcement attorneys and technical staff appear to have worked together efficiently and harmoniously toward shared goals.

Bernstein also recommended that government agencies promote regulatory compliance by issuing explanatory materials describing their regulations and appropriate ways of complying with them. EPA has done relatively little in this regard, with one notable exception. Beginning in the Clinton administration, EPA did make a conscious, sustained effort to provide "compliance assistance" to regulated industries. While likely beneficial, however, this compliance assistance program had the initial, unwanted result of creating confusion and misunderstanding among the EPA's permanent career enforcement staff as to whether traditional Agency enforcement approaches were still in favor with EPA's top managers.

Finally, Bernstein urged that government agencies promote regulatory compliance by taking advantage of the importance of the federal government as a creditor, supplier, and consumer. Congress accepted this notion by including provisions in the Clean Water Act and Clean Air Act that prohibit criminal violators of those statutes from doing business with the government unless and until those parties have brought their offending facilities into compliance with applicable regulatory standards.[80] EPA has dutifully implemented those provisions. They have proven effective in enforcement cases, however, only as to the relatively small minority of environmental polluters who do most or all of their business with federal agencies and departments.

In sum, Marver Bernstein's *Regulating Business by Independent Commission* presented an informed, thoughtful, and vigorous critique of business regulation in the United States at the time it was written. His volume gave impetus to a highly influential movement to alter the ways in which regulatory agencies are legally authorized and politically controlled. This chapter has shown that, despite the passage of more than half a century, many of Bernstein's notions regarding regulation of business and the enforcement of regulatory requirements still ring true.

Ironically, what I have just asserted seems to be *least* true regarding the part of Bernstein's work for which he is best known: his ideas regarding the life cycle of administrative agencies. My review of highlights from the EPA's enforcement history has suggested that for the most part EPA has only partially matured (to use Bernstein's term), and that the Agency has successfully managed to avoid the complete domination by regulated industry that Bernstein posited. In part, this salutary situation may be a result of the success of Bernstein, other captive agency theorists, and their political allies, in convincing Congress to reform regulatory legislation in ways that they favored.

Nonetheless, EPA's record also has a bleaker side. It suggests that EPA's enforcement work has been nearly captured by industry several times and that it was partially captured on one occasion. The political mechanisms by which this industrial domination occurred—through policy initiatives of two presidents and a Congress highly sympathetic to industries regulated by the EPA—were different from those that Bernstein predicted. Nonetheless, the record makes clear that in some political settings EPA—and its enforcement program—is distressingly vulnerable to the industry capture that Bernstein's writing described and protested against. Indeed, the Agency's enforcement efficacy and integrity seem anything but assured. In view of the immense practical significance of EPA enforcement as a means of redressing and preventing environmental lawlessness and pollution, their protection must remain a continuing priority for concerned citizens, environmental organizations, Congress, and the general public.

CHAPTER II

EPA Enforcement in the Context of Federal Civil Service Decline

EPA is only one of a plethora of federal agencies and departments that collectively employ millions of people and a large (and apparently indeterminate) number of contractors. In 2008, in an important book-length contribution to the literature of public administration, *A Government Ill-Executed: The Decline of the Federal Service and How to Reverse It*,[1] Paul C. Light carefully examined and documented an overall decline in the quality of the federal civil service and the manner in which it implements federal laws. In Light's view, "[t]he federal service is suffering the greatest crisis since it was founded in the first moments of the Republic. At best, it is running out of energy at what seems to be an accelerating rate. At worst, it is already unable to faithfully execute the laws."[2]

For the most part, Light adopts a normative framework suggested by the writings of Alexander Hamilton in *The Federalist Papers*. Hamilton believed that an energetic federal service was necessary to the faithful execution of the laws, and he contended that seven characteristics were central to such an energetic service:

1. Missions that matter for the public benefit;
2. Clarity of command among the chief executive and other officers of government;
3. Civil servants with merit and expertise, drawn from the highest ranks of society;
4. A commitment, up and down the hierarchy of government, to execute the laws with vigor and expedition;
5. Excellent training for civil servants;
6. Steadiness in administration; and
7. Safety and accountability through transparency of results.

For most of his book, Light introduces empirical evidence, derived from surveys regarding the opinions and experiences of government employees and the public at large, to assess the institutional performance of contemporary federal agencies as measured against the seven Hamiltonian notions mentioned above. Light notes that some agencies, and some programs within agencies, have been relatively successful in maintaining a high level of efficiency and effectiveness. Nonetheless, his overall assessment of the performance of the federal career civil service—and current prospects for it—is relatively bleak:

> As the federal government's agenda has expanded over the decades, Hamilton's energetic federal service eventually became the victim of his own vision. Its mission is far broader than its capability; its chains of command are complex and confused; its process of filling the senior offices of government has become a source of embarrassment and delay; its workforce is drawn more by pay, benefits and security than the chance to make a difference; its future employees would not know how to find a federal job even if they wanted one; its reform agenda has become a destination for fads; and execution of the laws now involves a large and mostly hidden work force that cannot be held accountable for results."[3]

In his final chapter, Light offers recommendations for building an energetic federal service. He suggests that Congress and the president need to make hard decisions about which of the federal government's missions it can sustain, and reduce the distance between the top and bottom of federal organizations. He also recommends that the president and Congress create an appointments process that makes it easier to attract talented Americans to government service, provide enough organizational resources to allow federal agencies to achieve their goals, concentrate on a handful of workable management reforms, and create more flexible careers and a clearer purpose for government employees.

To what extent does EPA's enforcement program, as we have examined it, fit into Light's model of civil service decline? At the outset, it must be observed that, in a number of respects, EPA's enforcement program appears to be among the least dysfunctional parts of the federal service. Its employees are generally dedicated and highly motivated, they have a clear sense of the importance of their mission, they are professionally capable, and, for the most part, their work is ably supervised by competent, hardworking managers. These virtues notwithstanding, however, EPA's enforcement program does indeed suffer from a number of the maladies that Light identified in his more general overview of trends in the federal service. Although some of his critique appears inapposite, on balance the EPA enforcement program's tendencies and attributes tend to lend credence to Light's findings with respect to federal service decline, and to underscore the validity of his recommendations for governmental reform.

In discussing Hamilton's notion that the federal service has public beneficial missions that matter, Light observes that, particularly during the 1960s and early 1970s, Congress created a large number of federal missions. Even though the number of new laws requiring government implementation has slowed since that time, "there has not been any significant decline in the number of federal missions."[4] Moreover, for most of the past three decades presidents have urged that the federal government "do more with less," and Congress has gone along in a number of respects. As a result, in Light's words, "the federal government has emerged with fewer resources, but an ever-expanding agenda."[5]

Without question, this aspect of Light's analysis describes the circumstances of EPA's enforcement programs. As noted previously at several points, throughout much of EPA's history the Agency's enforcement resources have either remained constant or been cut back. At the same time, the demands on the EPA enforcement program have grown rapidly. Congress has passed new environmental laws that have placed new challenges before EPA's staff, and economic expansion has spawned a large number of new sources of pollution that EPA is charged with regulating. Although, by design, much environmental enforcement in the United States is done at the state level, state resources for environmental enforcement have also contracted considerably in recent years, and EPA cannot delegate to states enforcement work that it can no longer do itself. As a result, as we have seen, EPA's enforcement resource base remains woefully inadequate, and still more work demands may be imposed by proposed federal legislation to curb greenhouse gas emissions, demands that may well put EPA's beleaguered enforcement staff under even greater strain if they come without the addition of new resources.

In his chapter "Clarity of Command," Light decries the "thickening" of the federal hierarchy, at all rungs of the organizational ladder, by the addition of "more layers of leaders and more leaders per layer."[6] As Light sees it:

The thickening of government has a host of unsavory consequences for an energetic federal service. It clearly dilutes accountability, but also increases the distance between the top and bottom of government and shrouds the federal hierarchy in a dense thicket of reporting relationships. It distorts information, weakens the unity of command that presidents seek, and creates enormous frustration in guiding the federal bureaucracy."[7]

EPA's enforcement program has not been immune to the trend towards thickening that Light describes. In EPA Region V, for example, line enforcement attorneys and engineers must report to a cohort of managers that includes section chiefs, branch chiefs, division directors, the deputy regional administrator, and the regional administrator. Their work is also subject to review by other sets of managers at both EPA headquarters and the Department of Justice. Lower-level enforcement staff professionals in EPA's headquarters must report to similar, although somewhat more attenuated, layers of managerial hierarchy.

Despite this arrangement, however, at least thus far EPA's enforcement work has displayed relatively little of the distortion of information, weakening of unity, and managerial frustration that Light refers to. Although the Agency's management structure is less than ideal, EPA's enforcement staff and managers appear to have adapted effectively to the Agency's multilayered and complex organizational structure. Generally, effective leadership at the political appointee and mid-management levels, combined with a strong sense of mission among the staff and considerable (even if intermittent) congressional oversight, has resulted in a reasonably effective system for sharing information with regard to ongoing enforcement matters. Moreover, despite periodic rivalries between the Agency's regional and headquarters components, and between some of its enforcement attorneys and engineers, EPA's enforcement program has been able to achieve a unity of purpose that seems—in view of the numerous challenges it has faced—quite impressive.

Light is also critical of the current process for nominating and confirming presidential appointees. He describes a "centralization" of the presidential appointments process that in his opinion places undue emphasis on "political and ideological loyalty as a primary marker of a candidate's qualifications for office."[8] Light describes a highly involved vetting process, in which potential presidential appointees are subject to numerous checks and counterchecks that unreasonably delay appointments and which may well drive talented leaders away from government service.

EPA's enforcement program has certainly suffered from appointment delays. As we have seen, those slowdowns were especially problematic in the Reagan and Clinton administrations, and overall they were unhelpful to the effective management of the Agency's enforcement efforts. EPA has been quite fortunate, however, in that many of its assistant administrators for enforcement have been non-ideological and professional in their managerial approaches—with the exception during early Reagan administration. As noted in Chapter Eight, even in the difficult period of the Bush II administration, EPA's top enforcement leadership supported a vigorous, deterrent enforcement approach and provided a buffer between the Agency's career enforcement staff and anti-regulatory, anti-enforcement elements within EPA and elsewhere in the executive branch.

Paul Light's treatment of the "vigor and expedition" of the federal workforce is also downbeat and pessimistic. Although he concedes that "[t]here are numerous examples of highly motivated federal employees who come to work each day for the chance to make a difference,"[9] Light writes:

> Nevertheless, the federal service as a whole appears to be at the edge of losing the vigor and expedition to execute. Too many federal employees come to work for the pay, benefits, and security, not the chance to make a difference on missions that matter; too many report that their coworkers are closed to new ideas and that their organizations are unwilling to encourage risks; too many say that they do not have the resources to do their jobs well; too many believe their organizations fail at helping people; and too many do not trust their own organizations to do the right thing.[10]

As we have seen, on the whole, EPA's enforcement employees tend to be highly motivated and idealistic. For that reason, a number of Light's observations may not apply in the EPA enforcement context. Nonetheless, other concerns that Light expressed with regard to institutional vigor and expedition do have relevance to EPA's enforcement program. As adverted to at several points, EPA's resource base is simply inadequate, and the Agency's enforcement staff and managers I interviewed were certainly well aware of that fact. Moreover, although my research was not specifically directed at eliciting the perceptions of EPA's enforcement employees with regard to the overall efficacy of the Agency's enforcement work, the comments I received did make quite clear that—particularly during certain periods in EPA's history—those enforcement employees lacked confidence in the boldness and effectiveness of their organization.

Light's study of the federal service noted that the aging of the federal

workforce is likely to result in a flurry of retirements over the next decade. He cites research that concludes that 60 percent of the federal government's white-collar workforce and 90 percent of the Senior Executive
Service will be eligible to retire by 2016.[11] Light also cautions that the
federal government is poorly configured to handle the changing supply
of potential recruits. In a telling survey of college seniors, Light found
that the government is often out-competed by nonprofit organizations
in its quest for the "best and brightest." He blamed the government's
public reputation for poor performance, its lack of consistent advertising
of meaningful work, the slowness and complexity of its hiring process,
and the negative attitudes of federal employees themselves, for the federal government having become a "destination of last resort" for talented,
young, public-service-minded Americans.[12]

Without a doubt, EPA in general, including its enforcement program,
faces the problems of the imminent retirement of its more experienced
employees.[13] How well the Agency will respond to this challenge remains an open question. EPA's enforcement program has an advantage
over other federal agencies and departments in that its current workforce
is generally invested in their Agency's mission and EPA's enforcement
program may perhaps have a better public reputation than that of other
agencies. Additionally, overall economic conditions may have changed
sufficiently since Light surveyed college seniors that entirely motivated
graduating students may now be more attracted to the security and higher
pay of government service than was true a few years ago. Nonetheless,
it remains to be seen whether EPA's managers will make the concerted
effort to sharpen the Agency's recruiting techniques, and provide sufficient opportunities for on-the-job training and career advancement for
EPA staff members, that will be needed to attract a talented crop of new-
comers to replace the Agency's graying workforce.

Light's chapter "Steadiness in Administration" tracks the sometimes
conflicting trends in government reform that have been fashionable since
World War II. He identifies four reform philosophies. Two of them,
which he labels "scientific management" and "liberation management,"
reflect a generally trusting view of the federal service and its capability to
execute the laws. The other two approaches, "the war on waste" and "the
watchful eye," take a more distrustful attitude toward the federal service
and are concerned about the perceived tendencies of federal agencies to
overspend or cover up mistakes.[14] Light notes that 50 percent of the federal employees he surveyed said that the reforms they had encountered
had made their jobs somewhat or much more difficult.[15]

Instead of the numerous, inconsistent governmental management "fads" that have prevailed in recent decades, Light looks to the views of two founding fathers for a more lasting and effective solution:

> The answer perhaps is to take the best of Hamilton and Jefferson, and leave the war on waste behind. Use Hamilton's scientific management sparingly to improve performance measurement so that pay and other resources can be tied to actual impacts; Jefferson's watchful eye sparingly to make sure that government is exposed to the scrutiny needed for honest evaluation; and a mix of Hamilton and Jefferson to liberate the federal government from Hamilton's execution in detail and tight chains of command, and temper Jefferson's attacks on fraud, waste, and abuse.[16]

EPA has clearly been affected by three of the four reform philosophies that Light refers to. Many of the statutes the Agency is charged with implementing were premised on a "watchful eye" approach, as was much of the congressional oversight that was directed toward EPA during the Reagan and Bush I years. A "war on waste" ethos motivated the strong congressional opposition to EPA enforcement that arose during parts of the Clinton administration along with the budgetary constraints that have consistently limited the scope and effectiveness of EPA's enforcement work, and notions of scientific management have been relied upon to bolster various structuring and restructuring of the Agency's organizational arrangements. Although EPA's enforcement has persisted throughout these tides of reform, it is at best unclear that the Agency has benefited from all of them. Moreover, under different sets of top managers, EPA's enforcement program has had to adjust to a shifting array of management philosophies, including management by objective, zero-based budgeting, total quality management, and other managerial innovations. Given the staff time and energy required to respond to these varied approaches, Light's call for a stable approach to reform, abandonment of the war on waste, and for a moderate philosophy with regard to accountability and chains of command, seems entirely sensible in the context of EPA enforcement.

Finally, Light advocates "safety" in the executive branch, which "flows in large part from the ability to oversee those who actually deliver the goods and services for the government."[17] He views with alarm what he refers to as "today's vast collection of mostly hidden contractors, grantees, and other partners of government" whose proliferation, in his view, "vitiates the transparency that provides accountability."[18] He calls for tight performance terms in contracts and grants, increased competition in the selection of contractors, improved oversight of contractors and grantees, and transparent financial statements.

Although contracting plays a role in EPA's enforcement program, most enforcement work there is performed by full-time government employees. Nonetheless, the Agency's enforcement program does make use of contractors in a variety of ways, from retaining expert witnesses to testify in enforcement litigation to performing important tasks at Superfund sites. Light's recommendations undoubtedly provide a sound guide for EPA to follow in all of its enforcement contracting work.

In sum, a number of the disquieting trends in the performance of the federal work force that Paul Light identifies may be perceived in EPA's enforcement programs. While EPA enforcement does not suffer from all of the shortcomings that Light describes, as we have observed, it does share some of the weaknesses of EPA's sibling agencies. As a result, the Agency's enforcement program faces numerous obstacles and challenges, and the efficacy of its collective efforts—in the medium and long term—remains far from certain.

Persons Interviewed

Note: All of the persons listed below presented their personal views during the interviews referred to in this Appendix. In none of the interviews conducted with employees of the U.S. Environmental Protection Agency did any of those employees purport to represent the Agency in the interview or indicate that they were providing the official, formal positions of the Agency.

INTERVIEWEE	DATE(S) AND PLACE(S) OF INTERVIEW
Valdas Adamkus	May 3, 1988, Chicago
Thomas Adams	March 18, 1991, Washington, DC
Anne Allen	April 19, 1981, Washington, DC
David Andrews	March 28, 1986, Washington, DC
Carrie Apostolou	May 28, 1992, Washington, DC
Anne Asbell	May 6, 1986, Atlanta
Julie Becker	April 18, 1991, Washington, DC
Michelle Benson	June 24, 2003, and October 13, 2009, San Francisco
Charles Bering	July 28, 1984, Boston
Kirby Biggs	July 9, 1984, Washington, DC
Frank Biros	April 17, 1991, Washington, DC
Jane Bloom	May 27, 1992, New York
Joan B. Boilen	May 5, 1986, Atlanta
Phil Boxell	October 12, 1984, Boston
Joe Boyle	March 4, 2004, and April 29, 2009, Chicago
Tom Bramscher	March 3, 2004, Chicago
Michael Brown	March 21, 1986, Washington, DC
Carol Browner	May 17, 2004, Washington, DC
Gerald Bryan	July 25, 1986, Washington, DC
Dale Bryson	September 8, 2009, Chicago
Bruce Buckheit	June 18, 2003, Dulles Airport, Virginia

INTERVIEWEE	DATE(S) AND PLACE(S) OF INTERVIEW
David Buente	April 4, 1986, and March 22, 1991, Washington, DC
Jim Bunting	March 27, 1986, Washington, DC
Michelle Burkett	May 29, 1992, Washington, DC
Jonathan Cannon	March 19, 1991, Washington, DC
Keith Casto	May 6, 1986, Atlanta
Maria Cintron	April 19, 1991, Washington, DC
Stephanie Clough	May 28, 1992, Washington, DC
Eric Cohen	March 2, 2004, and April 29, 2009, Chicago
Bill Constantelos	May 1, 1986, Chicago
Douglas Costle	July 25, 1984, Washington, DC
John Cruden	April 1, 2004, and May 22, 2009, Washington, DC
Phil Cummings	March 22, 1991, Washington, DC
George Czerniak	March 2, 2004, and May 1, 2009, Chicago
Michael Deland	July 28, 1984, Boston
Charlie de Saillan	March 4, 1991, Washington, DC
Bill Drayton	May 28, 1992, Washington, DC
Rick Duffy	April 17, 1991, Washington, DC
Barbara Elkus	April 1, 1986, Washington, DC
Richard Emory	May 8, 2009, Davie, Florida
Doug Farnsworth	July 25, 1984, Washington, DC
Margie Fehrenbach	July 25, 1986, Washington, DC
Linda Fisher	April 14, 2004, Washington, DC
Ben Fisherow	April 2, 2004, Washington, DC
Dick Frandsen	March 28, 1986, and March 5, 1991, Washington, DC
Bert Frey	April 22, 1991, Washington, DC
Scott Fulton	April 18, 1991, Washington, DC
Tom Gallagher	April 18, 1986, and March 15, 1991, Denver
Kevin Gaynor	March 4, 1991, Washington, DC
Bruce Gelber	April 14, 2004, and May 22, 2009, Washington, DC
Gail Ginsberg	March, 8, 2004, Ridgeway, Wisconsin
Anne Gorsuch	March 19, 1986, Washington, DC
Don Gray	March 20, 1991, Washington, DC
John Gregory	June 16, 2003, and April 16, 2009, Washington, DC
Joel Gross	May 19 and 22, 2009, Washington, DC
Louise Gross	October 5, 2009, Chicago
Ben Grumbles	December 29, 2009, Phoenix
Lloyd Guerci	April 28, 1986, and March 8, 1991, Washington, DC
George Harlow	May 5, 1986, Atlanta
Arthur Haubenstock	June 27, 2004, San Francisco
George Hayes	June 27, 2003, San Francisco
Bill Hedeman	March 27, 1986, Washington, DC

INTERVIEWEE	DATE(S) AND PLACE(S) OF INTERVIEW
Richard Hembra	April 22, 1986, Washington, DC
Steve Herman	June 17, 2003, Boston
Jeff Holmstead	September 24, 2009, Washington, DC
Art Horowitz	June 2, 2003, and May 19, 2009, Washington, DC
Tinka Hyde	March 10, 2004, Geneva, Illinois
John Johnson	May 5, 1986, Atlanta
Kathleen Johnson	June 23, 2003, and October 6, 2009, San Francisco
Gary Jonesi	May 18, 2009, Washington, DC
Bob Kaplan	June 17, 2003, Washington, DC, and October 9, 2009, Chicago
David Kee	June 19, 1984, Chicago
Peter Kelly	June 29, 1984, Chicago
Mike Kilpatrick	April 1, 1986, Washington, DC
Alan Kirk	July 9, 1984, Washington, DC
Edward Kurent	March 30, 1986, Washington, DC
Adam Kushner	April 15, 2009, Washington, DC
Lawrence Kyte	May 2, 1986, and April 22, 1991, Washington, DC
Ann Lassiter	April 2, 2004, Alexandria, Virginia
Stan Legro	July 9, 1984, Washington, DC
Steve Leifer	March 6, 1981, Washington, DC
Jonathan Libber	September 22, 2009, Washington, DC
Sylvia Lowrance	June 18, 2003, Bethesda, Maryland
Gene Lucero	April 28, 1984, Washington, DC
Lisa Lund	September 25, 2009, Washington, DC
Ann Lyons	June 25, 2003, San Francisco
John Lyons	June 24, 2003, San Francisco
Doug MacMillan	April 4, 1986, Washington, DC
Felicia Marcus	June 23, 2003, San Francisco
Nancy Marvel	June 24, 2003, and Dec. 18, 2009, San Francisco
Richard Mays	March 20, 1986, Washington, DC
Catherine McCabe	December 1, 2009, Washington, DC
Jim McDonald	June 26, 1984, San Diego
Jeff Miller	March 21, 1986, Washington, DC
Lamar Miller	April 14, 1986, Gainesville, Florida
Bill Miner	May 3, 1986, Washington, DC
Tom Mintz	June 26, 2003, San Francisco
Jim Moorman	April 1, 1986, Washington, DC
Walter Mugdan	March 30, 2004, New York
Bill Muno	July 31, 1986, April 23, 1991, and March 2, 2004, Chicago
Bill Muszynski	May 18, 2004, Philadelphia
Grant Nakayama	May 18, 2009, Washington, DC
Rett Nelson	April 22, 1991, March 3, 2004, and April 28, 2009, Chicago

INTERVIEWEE	DATE(S) AND PLACE(S) OF INTERVIEW
Mimi Newton	June 27, 2003, and October 12, 2009, San Francisco
Norm Niedergang	April 22, 1991, Chicago
David Nielsen	June 16, 2003, Washington, DC
Sheldon Novick	March 7, 1986, Washington, DC
Ann Nutt	June 25, 2003, San Francisco
Erik Olson	March 30, 1991, Washington, DC
Chuck Orzihoskie	September 8, 2009, Chicago
Marcus Peacock	September 24, 2009, Washington, DC
Jimmie Powell	March 22, 1991, Washington, DC
James Prange	April 18, 1946, Denver
Courtney Price	March 26, 1986, Washington, DC
Martha Prothro	July 9, 1984, Washington, DC
Mark Raabe	March 28, 1986, Washington, DC
Steve Ramsey	May 2, 1986, Chicago
Joyce Rechtschaffen	March 7, 1991, Washington, DC
Ed Reich	July 9, 1984, and March 7, 1991, Washington, DC
Mark Reiter	March 22, 1991, Washington, DC
Tony Roisman	March 31, 1986, Washington, DC
Steve Rothblatt	June 25, 1986, Chicago
John Rothman	June 25, 2003, San Francisco
Jay Sargent	May 6, 1986, Atlanta
Amy Schaeffer	April 29, 1986, Washington, DC
Eric Schaeffer	April 13, 2004, Washington, DC
Lois Schiffer	April 14, 2004, Washington, DC
Jane Schulteis	April 30, 1986, Chicago
Dave Schultz	April 30, 2009, Chicago
Tom Skinner	September 10, 2009, Chicago
Al Smith	May 6, 1986, Atlanta
Art Smith	June 29, 1984, Chicago
Bruce Smith	April 21, 1986, Philadelphia
Mike Smith	August 1, 1984, and April 22, 1991, Chicago
Rich Smith	March 18, 1986, Washington, DC
Walker Smith	April 13, 2004, Washington, DC
Jane Souzon	July 28, 1984, Washington, DC
Mike Stahl	March 31, 2004, and December 2, 2009, Washington, DC
Elaine Stanley	March 19, 1991, Washington, DC
Jud Starr	April 3, 1986, Washington, DC
Rena Steinzor	March 31, 1986, Washington, DC
Allyn Stern	June 24, 2003, San Francisco
Fred Stiehl	March 19, 1986, Washington, DC
Jack Stonebraker	May 6, 1986, Atlanta

INTERVIEWEE	DATE(S) AND PLACE(S) OF INTERVIEW
Ann Strickland	March 17, 1986, and December 29, 2009, Washington, DC
Jim Strock	March 22, 2008, Miami
J. P. Suarez	May 21, 2004, Bentonville, Arkansas
Bill Sullivan	April 29, 1986, Washington, DC
David Swack	April 1, 2004, Washington, DC
Anne Swofford	August 1, 1984, Chicago
Dave Taliaferro	March 3, 2004, and April 30, 2009, Chicago
Bob Tolpa	March 31, 2004, Washington, DC
Dave Ullrich	June 28, 1984, and March 5, 2004, Chicago
Tom Voltaggio	April 21, 1986, Philadelphia
Mike Walker	March 29, 2004, and April 16, 2009, Washington, DC
Jacqueline Warren	May 27, 1992, New York
John Warren	March 29, 2004, Washington, DC
Cheryl Wasserman	March 21, 1991, June 16, 2003, and April 14, 2009, Washington, DC
Bill Wehrum	December 17, 2009, Washington, DC
Dick Wilson	July 26, 1984, Washington, DC
Neil Wise	April 21, 1983, Washington, DC
Noël Wise	June 26, 2003, San Francisco
Deborah Woitte	March 18, 1991, Washington, DC
Doug Wolf	March 5, 1991, Washington, DC
Allan Zabel	June 25, 2003, and October 5, 2009, San Francisco

Government Service Job Titles of Individuals Interviewed by Author

This list indicates all government job titles of persons interviewed for this book, up to the day of the author's last interview with those individuals. Some people interviewed held additional government positions subsequent to the time of their interview that are not reflected in this list. A number of the interviewees held more than one position prior to being interviewed. Additionally, in some instances, more than one person interviewed had the same job title(s) as one or more other interviewees. All of the individuals I interviewed spoke in their personal capacities only and not in any official capacity. The views that they expressed did not reflect the positions of the U.S. Environmental Protection Agency, the U.S. Department of Justice, or any other entity or institution. Asterisks in the list indicate positions outside the Environmental Protection Agency.

Acting Assistant Administrator for Air and Radiation
Acting Assistant Administrator for Enforcement
Acting Assistant Administrator for Enforcement and Compliance Assurance
Acting Assistant Administrator for Solid Waste and Emergency Response
Acting Assistant Administrator for Water
Acting Assistant Attorney General for Environment and Natural Resources,
    U.S. Department of Justice*
Acting Chief, Hazardous Law Branch, Office of Regional Counsel, EPA
    Region IV
Acting Chief, Special Projects and Policy Branch
Acting Deputy Assistant Administrator for Hazardous Waste Enforcement
Acting Deputy Division Director, Office of Waste Program Enforcement
Acting Director, Enforcement Division, EPA Region III
Acting Director, Hazardous Waste Enforcement Division
Acting Director, Legal Division, Office of Hazardous Waste Enforcement
Acting Director, Office of Legal Enforcement Policy
Acting Director, Office of Waste Programs Enforcement
Acting Legal Director, Criminal Enforcement Program
Acting Regional Counsel, EPA Region V

Administrative Officer, Office of Solid Waste and Emergency Response
Administrator, U.S. Environmental Protection Agency
Assistant Administrator for Air and Radiation
Assistant Administrator for Enforcement
Assistant Administrator for Enforcement and Compliance Assurance
Assistant Administrator for Enforcement and Compliance Monitoring
Assistant Administrator for Planning and Management
Assistant Administrator for Water
Assistant Attorney General, Lands and Natural Resources Division, U.S.
   Department of Justice*
Assistant Chief, Environmental Enforcement Section, U.S. Department of
   Justice*
Assistant Chief, Hazardous Waste Section, U.S. Department of Justice*
Assistant Chief, Pollution Control Section, U.S. Department of Justice*
Assistant Regional Counsel, Office of Regional Counsel, EPA Region V
Assistant Regional Counsel, EPA Region IX
Assistant to the Assistant Administrator for Solid Waste and Emergency
   Response
Associate Branch Chief, Office of Regional Counsel, EPA Region V
Associate Director of Policy Analysis, Office of Federal Activities
Associate Division Director, Office of Superfund, Waste Management Division,
   EPA Region V
Associate Division Director, Waste Management Division, EPA Region V
Associate Enforcement, EPA Region V
Associate Enforcement Counsel for Waste
Associate Enforcement Counsel for Waste Enforcement
Associate General Counsel for Waste Enforcement
Associate Regional Counsel, Office of Regional Counsel, EPA Region V
Associate Regional Counsel, EPA Region IV
Associate Regional Counsel and Senior Attorney, RCRA and Superfund
   Enforcement Program, EPA Region V
Attorney, International Enforcement Compliance Division
Attorney, National Projects Branch, Office of Enforcement and Compliance
   Monitoring
Attorney, Office of General Counsel
Attorney, Office of Regional Counsel, EPA Region I
Attorney, Solid Waste and Emergency Response Branch, Office of Regional
   Counsel, EPA Region V
Attorney/Advisor, Office of Enforcement
Attorney and General Counsel, Senate Committee on Environment and Public
   Works
Branch Chief and Deputy Division Director, Air Management Division, EPA
   Region V
Branch Chief, Office of Enforcement and Compliance Monitoring
Budget Officer, Hazardous Waste Enforcement Task Force
Budget Officer, Office of Emergency and Remedial Response

Chemical Engineer, RCRA Enforcement Program, Office of Enforcement
Chief, Air and Hazardous Waste Enforcement Branch, EPA Region III
Chief, Air and Toxics Branch, Office of Regional Counsel, EPA Region V
Chief, Air Branch, Office of Regional Counsel, EPA Region V
Chief, Air Compliance Section, Enforcement Division, EPA Region V
Chief, Air Enforcement and Compliance Branch, EPA Region V
Chief, Air Enforcement Branch, Enforcement Division, EPA Region V
Chief, Air Enforcement Proceedings Branch
Chief, Air Legal Section, Enforcement Division, EPA Region V
Chief, Air, Water, Toxics and General Law Branch, Office of Regional Counsel,
    EPA Region V
Chief, Compliance Branch, Office of Waste Programs Enforcement
Chief, Compliance Evaluation Branch, Office of Enforcement
Chief, Compliance, Policy and Planning Branch, Office of Enforcement and
    Compliance Monitoring
Chief, Compliance Section, Office of Waste Programs Enforcement
Chief, Cost Recovery Branch, CERCLA Enforcement Division, Office of Solid
    Waste and Emergency Response
Chief, Emergency and Remedial Response Branch, Waste Management
    Division, EPA Region IV
Chief, Enforcement Branch, Enforcement Division, EPA Region I
Chief, Environmental Enforcement Section, Environment and Natural
    Resources Division, U.S. Department of Justice*
Chief, Guidance Development Branch, Office of Legal Enforcement Policy
Chief, Hazardous Waste Branch, Office of Regional Counsel, EPA Region IV
Chief, Hazardous Waste Enforcement Branch, EPA Region III
Chief, Hazardous Waste Enforcement Branch, EPA Region V
Chief, Hazardous Waste Section, Lands and Natural Resources Division, U.S.
    Department of Justice*
Chief, Legal Branch, Division of Stationary Source Enforcement
Chief, Legal Review Section, Enforcement Division, EPA Region I
Chief, Legislative and Policy Analysis Branch, Office of Planning and
    Management
Chief, Litigation Branch, Office of Waste Programs Enforcement
Chief, Multi-Media Branch I, Office of Regional Counsel, EPA Region V
Chief, Multi-Media Branch II, Office of Regional Counsel, EPA Region V
Chief, National Projects Branch, Hazardous Waste Enforcement Division
Chief, Pollution Control Section, U.S. Department of Justice*
Chief, Program Integration Branch, Program Evaluation Division
Chief, RCRA Branch, Office of Enforcement and Compliance Monitoring
Chief, RCRA Enforcement Section, Waste Management Division, EPA
    Region V
Chief, Remedial Response Branch, Waste Management Division, EPA Region V
Chief, Superfund Branch, EPA Region III
Chief, Superfund Branch, Hazardous Waste Enforcement Division
Chief, Technical Section, Air Enforcement Branch, EPA Region V

Chief, Technical Support Branch, Office of Waste Programs Enforcement
Chief, Technical Support Group for Hazardous Waste Enforcement, EPA
  Region III
Chief, Waste Compliance Section, Enforcement Division, EPA Region V
Chief, Water Quality Branch, Water Division, EPA Region V
Chief Attorney, Hazardous Waste Enforcement Task Force
Chief Counsel and Staff Director, Subcommittee on Oversight and
  Investigation, House Committee on Energy and Commerce*
Chief Investigator, Subcommittee on Environment, Energy and Natural
  Resources, House Committee on Government Operations*
Chief of Criminal Investigations, Criminal Enforcement Program, National
  Enforcement Investigations Center
Combustion Process National Oracle, Air Enforcement and Compliance
  Assurance Branch, EPA Region V
Counsel, House Committee on Energy and Commerce*
Counsel to the Assistant Administrator for Air and Radiation
Deputy Administrator, U.S. Environmental Protection Agency
Deputy Assistant Administrator for Civil Enforcement
Deputy Assistant Administrator, Office of Solid Waste and Emergency
  Response
Deputy Assistant Administrator for Water
Deputy Assistant Attorney General, Environment and Natural Resources
  Division, U.S. Department of Justice*
Deputy Assistant Enforcement Counsel for Waste
Deputy Chief, Emergency and Remedial Response Branch, EPA Region IV
Deputy Chief, Enforcement Division, EPA Region V
Deputy Chief, Environmental Enforcement Section, U.S. Department of
  Justice*
Deputy Director, Office of Compliance
Deputy Director, Office of Emergency and Remedial Response
Deputy Director, Office of Waste Programs Enforcement
Deputy Director, Office of Water Standards and Regulations
Deputy Director, Waste Management Division, EPA Region IV
Deputy Director, Water Division, EPA Region IV
Deputy Director, Water Division, EPA Region V
Deputy General Counsel and Acting Enforcement Counsel
Deputy General Counsel for Litigation and Regional Operations
Deputy Regional Administrator, EPA Region V
Deputy Regional Counsel, EPA Region V
Deputy Regional Counsel and Enforcement Coordinator, EPA Region V
Director, Air and Hazardous Materials Division, EPA Region V
Director, Air Enforcement Division, Office of Enforcement and Compliance
  Assurance
Director, Air Management Division, EPA Region V
Director, CERCLA Enforcement Division, Office of Solid Waste and
  Emergency Response
Director, Division of Stationary Source Enforcement

Director, Enforcement Division, EPA Region V
Director, Enforcement Division, EPA Region VII
Director, Environmental Crimes Unit, Lands and Natural Resources Division,
     U.S. Department of Justice*
Director, Environmental Protection Issues, Resources, Community and
     Economic Development Division, U.S. General Accounting Office*
Director, Hazardous Waste Division, EPA Region V
Director, Hazardous Waste Enforcement Task Force
Director, National Enforcement Investigation Center
Director, Noise and Radiation Enforcement Division
Director, Office of Civil Enforcement
Director, Office of Compliance
Director, Office of Compliance Analysis and Program Operations
Director, Office of Superfund
Director, Permits Division, Office of Water
Director, RCRA Enforcement Division, Office of Waste Programs Enforcement
Director, Stationary Source Compliance Division
Director, Water Division, EPA Region V
Director, Water Enforcement Division, Office of Enforcement
Director of Mobile Source Enforcement
Director of Public Affairs, EPA Region IX
Director of Waste Programs Enforcement
Enforcement Counsel
Enforcement Counsel and Deputy Associate Administrator for Enforcement
Environmental Counsel to Senator Joseph Lieberman*
Environmental Engineer, Enforcement Division, EPA Region V
Environmental Protection Specialist, Office of Solid Waste and Emergency
     Response
Environmental Protection Specialist, RCRA Enforcement Program
Environmental Scientist and Compliance Enforcement Manager, Land and
     Chemicals Branch, Waste, Pesticides, and Toxics Division, EPA Region V
Interim Supervisor, Office of Regional Counsel, EPA Region V
Legal Advisor for Nationally Managed Cases, Hazardous Waste Enforcement
     Task Force
Legal Counsel and Special Assistant for Policy to the Deputy Administrator
Principal Deputy Assistant Administrator, Office of Enforcement and
     Compliance Assurance
Professional Staff Member, Senate Appropriations Committee, Subcommittee
     on HUD, VA and Independent Agencies*
Professional Staff Member, Senate Committee on Environment and Public
     Works*
Professional Staff Member and Investigator, House Committee on Government
     Operations*
Program Analyst, Office of Compliance
Program Analyst, Office of Permit Programs
Program Assistant, Hazardous Waste Enforcement Task Force
RCRA Program Attorney, State of North Carolina*

Regional Administrator, EPA Region I
Regional Administrator, EPA Region V
Regional Coordinator, Hazardous Waste Enforcement Task Force
Regional Counsel, EPA Region III
Regional Counsel, EPA Region IV
Regional Counsel, EPA Region V
Regional Counsel, EPA Region IX
Regional Liaison Specialist, Office of Waste Programs Enforcement
Remedial Project Manager, Superfund Branch, Waste Management Division,
    EPA Region V
Section Chief, Solid Waste and Emergency Response Branch, Office of
    Regional Counsel, EPA Region V
Senior Attorney, Enforcement Division, EPA Region V
Senior Attorney, Environmental Enforcement Section, U.S. Department of
    Justice*
Senior Attorney, EPA Region IV
Senior Attorney, Office of Regional Counsel, EPA Region V
Senior Attorney/Advisor, Special Litigation Process Division, Office of
    Enforcement and Compliance Assurance
Senior Counsel for Homeland Security, Office of Criminal Enforcement,
    Forensics, and Training
Senior Counsel for Strategic Litigation, Office of Civil Enforcement, Office of
    Enforcement and Compliance Assurance
Senior Enforcement Counsel, Office of Enforcement
Senior Enforcement Counsel, Office of Enforcement and Compliance
    Assurance
Senior Policy Coordinator, Office of Waste Programs Enforcement
Special Agent, Office of Criminal Investigations, EPA Region X
Special Assistant for Policy and Planning
Special Assistant to the Assistant Administrator for Enforcement
Special Assistant to the Assistant Administrator for Enforcement and
    Compliance Monitoring
Special Assistant to the Deputy Assistant Administrator for Enforcement
Special Assistant to the Enforcement Counsel
Special Assistant to the General Counsel
Special Assistant to the Regional Administrator, EPA Region III
Special Litigator for Hazardous Waste, U.S. Department of Justice*
Staff Assistant, Subcommittee on HUD, VA and Independent Agencies, House
    Appropriations Committee
Staff Attorney, Division of Stationary Source Enforcement
Staff Attorney, Enforcement Division, EPA Region IV
Staff Attorney, Hazardous Law Branch, Office of Regional Counsel, EPA
    Region IV
Staff Attorney, Hazardous Waste Enforcement Task Force
Staff Attorney, Office of Criminal Enforcement, Forensics, and Training
Staff Attorney, Office of Enforcement and Compliance Monitoring
Staff Attorney, Office of Pesticide and Toxic Substances Enforcement

Staff Attorney, Office of Regional Counsel, EPA Region IV
Staff Counsel, House Subcommittee on Commerce, Transportation, and
    Tourism*
Staff Director, Subcommittee on Environment and Natural Resources, House
    Committee on Government Affairs*
Staff Director, Subcommittee on Intergovernmental Relations, Senate
    Committee on Government Affairs*
Staff Engineer, Hazardous Waste Enforcement Task Force
Staff Engineer, NPDES Permit Program, EPA Region V
Staff Engineer, Office of Waste Programs Enforcement
Staff Engineer, Technical Section, Air Enforcement Branch, EPA Region V
Supervisor, Legal Section, Enforcement Division, RCRA and Superfund
    Enforcement Program, EPA Region V
Supervisor, Superfund Branch, Waste Management Division, EPA Region V
Supervisory Attorney, Office of Regional Counsel, EPA Region IX
Supervisory Attorney, Office of Waste Programs Enforcement
Supervisory Attorney, Steel Enforcement Task Force
Technical Director and Deputy Director, Hazardous Waste Enforcement Task
    Force
Trial Attorney, Environmental Crimes Section, U.S. Department of Justice*
Trial Attorney, Environmental Enforcement Section, U.S. Department of
    Justice*
Unit Chief, Enforcement Division, EPA Region V
Unit Chief, Water and Hazardous Materials Enforcement Branch, EPA
    Region V
Vice Counsel, Subcommittee on Oversight and Investigation, House
    Committee on Energy and Commerce*

Standard Interview Questionnaire in Interviews Prior to 2003

I. Preliminary Questions of a General Nature
   A. What position (or positions) did you hold which involved EPA enforcement work?
   B. As you look back on each of the periods in the history of EPA's enforcement program in which you were personally involved (or were aware of), what do you consider the most significant events, developments, and trends?
   C. As to those same periods, what do you view as the most important achievements in EPA enforcement programs and the most significant problems which arose in those programs?
II. Questions Regarding the Management and Working Environment of EPA Enforcement Programs
   A. Please comment upon the following aspects of EPA enforcement programs:
      1. The adequacy of EPA's resources.
      2. The capability of EPA's professional staff.
      3. The quality and extent of supervision given to EPA's professional staff.
      4. The adequacy of the training given to EPA's professional staff.
      5. The physical conditions under which EPA's professional staff works (architecture, noise level, etc.).
      6. The adequacy of the clerical and secretarial support given EPA's professional staff.
      7. The adequacy of the agency's system for keeping records of enforcement activities.
      8. The opportunities for promotion and career development given to EPA's professional staff.
      9. The salary level of EPA's professional staff.
III. Questions Regarding Institutional Relationships in EPA Enforcement Work
   A. How would you characterize the following sets of institutional interrelationships among EPA enforcement personnel?

     1. EPA regional enforcement people and EPA headquarters enforcement people.

     2. EPA enforcement attorneys and EPA enforcement technical people.

  B. How would you describe the institutional interrelationships between EPA enforcement people and the following other government entities?

     1. State environmental protection agency personnel.

     2. Department of Justice attorneys and managers.

     3. U.S. Attorneys and their professional staffs.

     4. Congress.

     5. Other federal agencies and departments.

     6. The White House.

IV. Question Regarding the Elements of an Effective Enforcement Program

  A. What elements do you feel are necessary for the creation of an effective and appropriate EPA enforcement program?

Standard Interview Questions Asked in All Interviews Beginning in 2003

I. Preliminary Questions of a General Nature
   A. What position (or positions) did you hold which involved EPA enforcement work?
   B. As you look back on the EPA enforcement program(s) in which you were personally involved (or were aware of), what do you consider the most significant events, developments, and trends?
   C. As to that same period, what do you view as the most important achievements in EPA enforcement programs and the most significant problems which arose in those programs?
II. Questions Regarding Institutional Relationships in EPA Enforcement Work
   A. How would you characterize the following sets of institutional interrelationships among EPA enforcement personnel?
      1. EPA regional enforcement people and EPA headquarters enforcement people.
      2. EPA enforcement attorneys and EPA enforcement technical people.
   B. How would you describe the institutional interrelationships between EPA enforcement people and the following other government entities?
      1. State environmental protection agency personnel.
      2. Department of Justice attorneys and managers.
      3. U.S. Attorneys and their professional staffs.
      4. Congress.
      5. Other federal agencies and departments.
      6. The White House.

Notes

Chapter One

1. The most significant of these are the Clean Air Act, 42 U.S.C. § 7401 et seq.; the Federal Water Pollution Control Act, 33 U.S.C. § 1251 et seq.; the Resource Conservation and Recovery Act, 42 U.S.C. § 6901 et seq.; the Comprehensive Environmental Response Compensation and Liability Act, 42 U.S.C. § 9602 et seq.; the Toxic Substances Control Act, 15 U.S.C. § 2601 et seq.; the Federal Insecticide, Fungicide and Rodenticide Act, 7 U.S.C. § 136 et seq.; the Safe Drinking Water Act, 40 U.S.C. § 300(f) et seq.; the Marine Protection, Research and Sanctuaries Act, 33 U.S.C. § 1401 et seq.; and the Emergency Planning and Community Right-to-Know Act, 42 U.S.C. § 11001 et seq.

2. The internal government debates that preceded EPA's establishment by executive order in 1970 have been chronicled in John Quarles, *Cleaning up America: An Insider's View of the Environmental Protection Agency* (New York: Houghton Mifflin, 1976), 14–36.

3. In 1990 a survey conducted by the *New York Times* found that approximately three out of four people polled felt that protecting the environment was so important that continuing improvements needed to be made regardless of cost. Cited in U.S. General Accounting Office, *Observations on the Environmental Protection Agency's Budget Request for Fiscal Year 1992*, statement of Richard L. Hembra, director, Environmental Protection Issues, Resources, Community and Economic Development Division, before the Senate Committee on Environment and Public Works, GAO/T-RCED-91-14 (1991), 1–2.

4. Foreword, in Christopher H. Schroeder and Richard J. Lazarus, eds., "Assessing the Environmental Protection Agency after Twenty Years: Law, Politics and Economics," *Duke Journal of Law and Contemporary Problems* 54 (Fall 1991): 1.

5. Cheryl E. Wasserman, "An Overview of Compliance and Enforcement in the United States: Philosophies, Strategies and Management Tools," in U.S. Environmental Protection Agency and Netherlands Ministry of Housing, Physical Planning and Environment, *International Enforcement Workshop Proceedings* (Utrecht, Netherlands, May 8–10, 1990), 38.

6. U.S. General Accounting Office, *Alternative Enforcement Organizations for EPA*, GAO/RCED-92-107 (April 1992), 21.

7. Peter C. Yeager, *The Limits of Law: The Public Regulation of Private Pollution* (Cambridge: Cambridge University Press, 1990).

8. Colin S. Diver, "A Theory of Regulatory Enforcement," *Public Policy* 28 (1980): 297.

9. Senate Committee on Environment and Public Works, statement of Senator Joseph I. Lieberman, *Oversight of the Environmental Protection Agency's Enforcement Program: Hearings before the Subcommittee on Toxic Substances, Environmental Oversight, Research and Development*, 101st Cong., 1st sess., Senate Hearing 101-503, November 15, 1989, 2.

10. See Appendix A for a list of the persons interviewed. The positions held by people I interviewed that involve or relate to EPA enforcement work are indicated in Appendix B.

Chapter Two

1. Interview with Douglas Farnsworth. Farnsworth's contributions to EPA's early enforcement efforts were both innovative and noteworthy. In the late 1970s he received a gold medal, the Agency's highest award, for his extraordinary achievement as a supervisor with EPA's steel task force in negotiating "company-wide" consent decrees that called for very significant commitments to air pollution control by much of the steel industry. Douglas Farnsworth's tragic death in January 1986 was a major loss to the entire community of individuals who have a continuing interest in the Agency's work.

2. See, for example, Marver H. Bernstein, *Regulating Business by Independent Commission* (Princeton: Princeton University Press, 1955), 75–76.

3. Latham, "The Group Basis of Politics: Notes for a 'Theory,'" *American Political Science Review* 46 (1952): 391.

4. Marc K. Landy, Marc J. Roberts, and Stephen R. Thomas, *The Environmental Protection Agency: Asking the Wrong Questions* (Oxford: Oxford University Press, 1990), 204.

5. Bernstein, *Regulating Business*, 224.

6. Colin S. Diver, "A Theory of Regulatory Enforcement," *Public Policy* 28 (1980): 280.

7. Cheryl E. Wasserman, "An Overview of Compliance and Enforcement in the United States: Philosophies, Strategies and Management Tools," in U.S. Environmental Protection Agency and Netherlands Ministry of Housing, Physical Planning and Environment, *International Enforcement Workshop Proceedings* (Utrecht, Netherlands, May 8–10, 1990), 16, 17–18, 40.

8. With respect to most violations of the Clean Air Act, the EPA is required to commence its enforcement activities with such a notice. See Clean Air Act, § 113(a)(1), 42 U.S.C. § 7413(a)(1).

9. See Dale S. Bryson, "Practical Applications of an Enforcement Management System," in U.S. Environmental Protection Agency and Netherlands Min-

istry of Housing, Physical Planning and Environment, *International Enforcement Workshop Proceedings* (Utrecht, Netherlands, May 8–10, 1990), 114.

10. Diver, "A Theory of Regulatory Enforcement," 287.

11. Bernstein, *Regulating Business*, 226.

12. This appears to be a persistent problem with respect to the enforcement of the Resource Conservation and Recovery Act (RCRA). In particular, as an EPA report openly admits, the Agency's RCRA recycling regulations (40 CFR 261.2[e] and 261.6) and the miscellaneous exclusions discussed throughout 40 CFR 262.1 have proven "extremely difficult to understand and enforce due to their complexity." U.S. Environmental Protection Agency, *The Nation's Hazardous Waste Management Program at a Crossroads: The RCRA Implementation Study*, EPA/530-SW-90-069 (July 1990), 38.

13. Peter C. Yeager, *The Limits of Law: The Public Regulation of Private Pollution* (Cambridge: Cambridge University Press, 1990), 251.

14. In some instances, the DOJ has delegated responsibility for EPA enforcement matters to local U.S. Attorneys and their staffs. For a cogent description of the role played by the DOJ and U.S. Attorneys' offices in regulatory enforcement, see Bernstein, *Regulating Business*, 240–242.

15. Landy, Roberts, and Thomas, *The Environmental Protection Agency*, 204–205.

16. Presentation of Vicki Masterman, attorney, Jones, Day, Reavis and Pogue, at ALI-ABA-ELI Course of Study on Environmental Law, Washington, D.C., February 15, 1992.

17. See Landy, Roberts, and Thomas, *The Environmental Protection Agency*, 205.

18. Presentation of Vicki Masterman.

19. Interview with Joel Gross.

20. This comment was made by an enforcement supervisor in EPA Region V in the spring of 1977 during internal discussions to decide the Agency's negotiating strategy in a major case.

21. Bryson and Ullrich, "Legal and Technical Cooperation for Effective Environmental Enforcement," in U.S. Environmental Protection Agency and Netherlands Ministry of Housing, Physical Planning and Environment, *International Enforcement Workshop Proceedings* (Utrecht, Netherlands, May 8–10, 1990), 145.

22. Interview with David Buente.

23. In the brief overview that follows, I am intellectually indebted to the thorough summaries found in Lawrence E. Starfield, "The 1990 Contingency Plan: More Detail and More Structure but Still a Balancing Act," *Environmental Law Reporter* 20 (1990): 10222; and Environmental Law Institute, *Toward a More Effective Superfund Enforcement Program*, vol. 2, appendix 3 (Washington, D.C., March 1989).

24. See CERCLA § 105, 42 U.S.C. § 9605.

25. See CERCLA § 104, 42 U.S.C. § 9604.

26. See CERCLA § 111, 42 U.S.C. § 9611.

27. See CERCLA § 107, 42 U.S.C. § 9607. Liability under this provision has

been generally held to be strict, joint, and several. The defenses available to PRPs are narrowly limited to acts of God, acts of war, and acts of third parties with whom the PRP did *not* contract regarding the hazardous wastes.

28. See CERCLA § 106, 42 U.S.C. § 9606.

29. See CERCLA § 107, 42 U.S.C. § 9607.

30. See CERCLA § 106, 42 U.S.C. § 9606.

31. In many instances, EPA will agree to permit PRPs to conduct necessary remedial measures at the site themselves at their own expense. From the perspective of PRPs, one major goal of negotiating with EPA is to arrive at the least costly cleanup program that is mutually agreeable.

32. If EPA and the PRPs have so agreed, this work can be carried out directly by PRPs with EPA oversight.

Chapter Three

1. In fact, the Ash Council's staff had originally proposed a new cabinet-level Department of Natural Resources and the Environment to include the Department of the Interior as well as important components of the Departments of Commerce, Agriculture, and Health, Education and Welfare, the U.S. Army Corps of Engineers, and the Atomic Energy Commission. Though this plan was seriously considered, it was dropped after Walter Hickel, then secretary of the interior, fell from favor in the Nixon administration as a result of his well-publicized letter to the president sharply criticizing the attitudes of the White House toward young people protesting the Vietnam War. For a lively account of the birth of EPA, see John Quarles, *Cleaning up America: An Insider's View of the Environmental Protection Agency* (New York: Houghton Mifflin, 1976), 14–36.

2. U.S. Environmental Protection Agency, *The First Two Years: A Review of EPA's Enforcement Program* 2 (1970).

3. Ibid., 89. Armco Steel, Dupont, ITT, and Florida Power and Light Company were among EPA's enforcement targets during this time.

4. Ibid., 3.

5. Interview with James O. McDonald.

6. Interview with Richard Wilson.

7. Interviews with David Kee, Gerald Bryan, Thomas Gallagher, and James O. McDonald.

8. See generally Grad, "Intergovernmental Aspects of Environmental Controls," in Frank P. Grad, George W. Rathjens, and Albert J. Rosenthal, *Environmental Control: Priorities, Policies and the Law* (New York: Columbia University Press, 1971), 47, 117–129, for a discussion of problems faced by state and local enforcement authorities during this period.

9. Interview with Thomas Gallagher.

10. See House Committee on Government Operations, *Mercury Pollution and Enforcement of the Refuse Act of 1899: Hearings before the Subcommittee on Conservation and Natural Resources*, 92nd Cong., 1st and 2nd sess., 1971 and 1972, 1134–1228, 1281–1363; Senate Committee on Public Works, *Implementation of the Clean*

Air Acts Amendment of 1970, Part 1; Hearings before the Subcommittee on Air and Water Pollution, 92nd Cong., 2nd sess., 1972, 224–228, 236, 243; Joel D. Auerbach, *Keeping a Watchful Eye: The Politics of Congressional Oversight* (Washington, D.C.: Brookings Institution, 1990), 19; Congressional Record, 1973, 119: 41127–41129.

11. 33 U.S.C. § 1251(1).

12. 33 U.S.C. §§ 1401–1445.

13. 7 U.S.C. §§ 135–136.

14. U.S. Environmental Protection Agency, *EPA Enforcement: Two Years of Progress* (1975), iv.

15. Interviews with Edward Reich and James O. McDonald.

16. Interview with David Kee.

17. As of January 1, 1975, a total of nineteen states had secured EPA approval to operate their own NPDES permit program. U.S. Environmental Protection Agency, *EPA Enforcement*, 37.

18. This phrase was mentioned by both Edward Reich and James O. McDonald in interviews.

19. 42 U.S.C. § 7414.

20. Interviews with Richard Wilson and Edward Reich.

21. It should be noted that the SIPs in question did not specifically require the particular pollution control technology that gave rise to this controversy. The thrust of the Clean Air Act is that sources of air pollution must meet performance standards, rather than standards that require the application of specified technology. As a practical matter, however, many of the first sets of SIP standards for electric utilities, steel mills, and other industries could not be complied with by those sources unless expensive and relatively untried pollution controls were employed.

22. Interviews with Richard Wilson and James O. McDonald. I do not mean to suggest that during this period EPA's enforcement efforts were solely focused on stationary sources. Another development in this period was the initiation of enforcement efforts aimed at stemming air pollution from automobiles and other mobile sources.

23. Interview with James O. McDonald. Steve Rothblatt's remarks in an interview were to the same effect.

24. From January 1971 to March 1977 pollution control requirements were significant factors in decisions to close 107 U.S. plants, affecting 20,318 employees. In contrast, 677,900 people were employed directly for pollution abatement in calendar year 1974. U.S. Council on Environmental Quality, *Environmental Quality—1977: The Eighth Annual Report of the Council on Environmental Quality*, 332. It should also be noted that many so-called environmental plant closures were strongly associated with other causes as well.

25. U.S. Environmental Protection Agency, *EPA Enforcement*, 5, 37.

26. Interviews with Peter Kelly and James O. McDonald.

27. Interview with Thomas Gallagher.

28. James L. Regens and Robert W. Rycroft, "Funding for Environmental Protection: Comparing Congressional and Executive Influences," *Social Science Journal* 26 (1989): 295.

29. Interviews with Thomas Gallagher, James O. McDonald, William Muno, and Marjorie Fehrenbach.

30. In fact, this Agency policy closely paralleled the noncompliance penalty approach authorized by the 1977 amendments to the Clean Air Act. Under § 120 of the act, EPA for the first time was permitted to assess civil penalties for certain violations of the act based upon the economic savings attained by the owners and operators of non-complying sources (42 U.S.C. § 7420). No explicit parallel authority exists under the Federal Water Pollution Control Act or other federal environmental legislation.

31. Interviews with William Muno and James O. McDonald.

32. Interviews with Thomas Gallagher and James O. McDonald.

33. Interviews with Arthur Smith and David Ullrich.

34. Interview with James Moorman.

35. Interviews with James O. McDonald, David Ullrich, Jane Schulteis, Thomas Gallagher, and Peter Kelly.

36. Interview with Thomas Gallagher.

37. Ibid.

38. Judson W. Starr, "Turbulent Times at Justice and EPA: The Origins of Environmental Criminal Prosecutions and the Work that Remains," *George Washington Law Review* 59 (April 1991): 902–904. Moorman later reiterated that position in testimony before a U.S. Senate subcommittee. See Senate Committee on Environment and Public Works, *Enforcement of Environmental Regulations: Hearings before the Subcommittee on Environmental Pollution*, 96th Cong., 1st sess., 1979, 339.

39. Starr, "Turbulent Times at Justice and EPA," 904.

40. Barbara Blum, deputy administrator, EPA memorandum to regional administrators, director, National Enforcement Investigations Center, and acting assistant administrator for enforcement, January 5, 1991.

41. Starr, "Turbulent Times at Justice and EPA," 905–908.

42. House Committee on Public Works and Transportation, 97th Cong., 2nd sess., 1982, H. Rept. 97-968, 4–5.

43. Interview with Jeffrey Miller; telephone interview with Thomas Jorling.

44. Telephone interview with Thomas Jorling.

45. Interview with Lamar Miller.

46. U.S. Environmental Protection Agency, *Hazardous Waste Enforcement Activities: Chronology of Important Events* (1979), 2.

47. Interview with James Moorman.

48. In fact, the Superfund legislation Congress enacted was not the only funding available for the cleanup of chemical contamination. Under the authority of the Federal Water Pollution Control Act, 33 U.S.C. § 1321, EPA developed a response program to deal with the spills of oil and hazardous materials to surface waters. The Agency also utilized a $20-million contingency fund to remedy chemical spill emergencies resulting from tanker truck accidents, train wrecks, and other sources. Interviews with Jack Stonebraker and Al J. Smith.

49. Barbara Blum, memorandum to regional administrators, "Managing EPA's Response to Inactive Hazardous Waste Sites," March 28, 1979.

50. Telephone interview with Barbara Blum; interview with James Moorman.

51. Barbara Blum, memorandum to assistant administrators, "Agencywide Hazardous Waste Site Enforcement and Response System," June 2, 1979.

52. Interviews with David Andrews, Jeffrey Miller, Douglas MacMillan, and Edward Kurent.

53. Interviews with Lamar Miller, Jeffrey Miller, Edward Kurent, and Douglas MacMillan.

54. Interview with Lamar Miller.

55. Interview with Jane Schulteis.

56. Interview with Douglas MacMillan.

57. Ibid.

58. Ibid.

59. The data developed by this subcommittee came to be known as the Eckhardt List after Congressman Bob Eckhardt (D-TX), the subcommittee's chairman. House Committee on Interstate and Foreign Commerce, *Waste Disposal Site Survey*, 96th Cong., 1st sess., 1979, Committee Print, 33.

60. Interviews with Lamar Miller, Marjorie Fehrenbach, and Douglas MacMillan.

61. Interviews with Jeffrey Miller, Edward Kurent, Douglas MacMillan, Richard Smith, Frederick Stiehl, Richard Mays, Marjorie Fehrenbach, and Lamar Miller. This experience was not limited to headquarters personnel. It was also shared by some regional enforcement officials. Interviews with Thomas Voltaggio and Jane Schulteis.

62. Interview with James Bunting. Interestingly, this high level of morale was maintained despite extremely poor working conditions for the task force staff. These descriptions are instructively and amusingly portrayed in a 1980 EPA memorandum from Douglas MacMillan to Gerald Bryan titled "Doom and Destruction."

63. Interviews with Douglas MacMillan, Jeffrey Miller, Lamar Miller, Frederick Stiehl, and Ann Strickland.

64. Interviews with James Bunting, Ann Strickland, Lloyd Guerci, Douglas MacMillan, Lamar Miller, and Frederick Stiehl; Steven Cohen and Marc Tipermas, "Superfund: Preimplementation Planning and Bureaucratic Politics," in James P. Lester and Ann O'M. Bowman, *The Politics of Hazardous Waste Management* (Durham, N.C.: Duke University Press, 1983), 43.

65. Interview with Edward Kurent.

66. Interviews with Neil Wise, Lawrence Kyte, and Frederick Stiehl.

67. Interview with Michael Kilpatrick.

68. 42 U.S.C. §§ 6934, 6973(b).

69. Interview with Douglas MacMillan.

70. This is not to suggest that an optimistic perspective was universally shared by *all* former members of the HWETF (which was formally renamed the Office of Hazardous Waste Enforcement in the late autumn of 1980). Notations in a diary I kept from November 5, 1980, the day after President Reagan's election, until March 10, 1981, shortly before I left government service, reveal that several rumors of deep cuts in EPA's work force began to circulate among the enforcement staff almost immediately following the election. The identity of the new administrator was a topic of intensely prolonged, guarded, and pessimistic specu-

lation among EPA enforcement staffers. Many of the enforcement staff members at the Agency were in what I perceived at the time to be a subdued, somber, philosophical mood.

71. Interview with Anthony Roisman.

Chapter Four

1. Inasmuch as she went by that name for most of her term, I shall refer to EPA's fourth administrator as Anne M. Gorsuch, Anne Gorsuch, or Gorsuch. In fact, close to the end of her tenure, on February 20, 1983, EPA's administrator married Robert Burford and took his last name.

2. Subcommittee on Oversight and Investigations, House Committee on Energy and Commerce, *Report of the President's Claim of Executive Privilege over EPA Documents, Abuses in the Superfund Program, and Other Matters*, 98th Cong., 2nd sess., 1984, notes 15, 16.

3. Interview with William Hedeman. For further evidence to the same effect, see Jonathan Lash, *A Season of Spoils: The Reagan Administration's Attack on the Environment* (New York: Pantheon, 1984), 10.

4. Interview with William Sullivan.

5. Interview with William Hedeman.

6. Interview with Anne Gorsuch.

7. Interview with William Sullivan.

8. Interview with Sheldon Novick.

9. "Decentralizing of Regulatory Programs Seen," *Washington Post*, March 13, 1981.

10. Interview with Valdas Adamkus. An incident recounted by William Sullivan also provides an indication of Gorsuch's personal attitude toward enforcement. Sullivan summarized a plan that he and his staff had devised for a special enforcement initiative with respect to plants that were discharging pollutants in the Niagara River Basin. He then described his attempt to brief Gorsuch regarding that proposal in these words: "I went in and made the presentation and Anne loved the part that concluded that the Niagara River Basin was not terribly dirty. . . . When we got to the enforcement section she said, 'Sullivan, you're getting too enforcement-minded' and walked out. So we had a program and no authority to go ahead with the key piece, which I think would have made it work." Interview with William Sullivan.

11. Interview with Edward Kurent. Several other present or former EPA officials share these impressions regarding the attitudes of the Agency's top leadership at the outset of their terms. The following individuals also made comments regarding this matter: Jay Sargent ("The attitude from headquarters, at least initially, was plug up the pipeline and stop those enforcement cases"); Richard Mays ("One perceived, over a period of months, that enforcement was something that was not in favor"); Ann Strickland ("There was no longer support for enforcement from the top. At best there was silence. At worst there was an effort to stop the cases and to prevent further cases in the area"); Michael Kilpatrick ("(T]here

was a very clear attitude that enforcement was part of a program that should only speak when spoken to. I mean there was a real attitude that enforcement was a dirty word"); David Ullrich ("There was a perception in the regional offices that the administration had attempted to emasculate the enforcement program"); and Richard Wilson ("It was relatively clear for a while that they were seriously considering disbanding enforcement"). See also Marc K. Landy, Marc J. Roberts, and Stephen R. Thomas, *The Environmental Protection Agency: Asking the Wrong Questions* (Oxford: Oxford University Press, 1990), 245–246, who suggest that, at the outset, the Reagan administration intentionally pursued a low-visibility strategy to deregulate environmental protection quickly that included the appointment of loyalists to key EPA posts, budget restrictions, and internal EPA reorganizations.

12. Anne Burford, *Are You Tough Enough?* (New York: McGraw-Hill, 1986), 101.

13. Interview with Frederick Stiehl. Similar comments were also made by the following interviewees: Lawrence Kyte, Steve Rothblatt, Douglas MacMillan, Arthur Smith, and Richard Wilson.

14. Interview with William Sullivan.

15. Interview with David Ullrich.

16. Interview with Lawrence Kyte. EPA's strong preference for negotiation and "jawboning" as a means of encouraging voluntary compliance was also noted in interviews with John Skinner, William Sullivan, and David Ullrich. Valdas Adamkus recalled that he interpreted this policy as a direction to "negotiate until you are blue in the face." Interview with Valdas Adamkus.

17. Interview with Valdas Adamkus.

18. Interviews with John Skinner and David Ullrich. See also William Sullivan, memorandum to EPA regional administrators, "Enforcement Policies and Procedures," February 26, 1982.

19. Anne M. Gorsuch, memorandum, "Agency Re-organization," June 12, 1981. For Gorsuch's defense of her reasons for making this change, see Burford, *Are You Tough Enough?*, 57.

20. Subcommittee on Oversight and Investigations, House Committee on Energy and Commerce, *Hazardous Waste Enforcement*, 97th Cong., 2nd sess., 1982, Committee Print, 33.

21. Ibid.

22. For example, Douglas MacMillan, the former HWETF director, drafted a series of memorandums during late 1981 in which he outlined "serious programmatic problems" that might arise if various proposed reorganization schemes were implemented. See Douglas MacMillan, memorandum to William A. Sullivan, "Phase II Re-organization," June 25, 1981; Douglas MacMillan, memorandum to William Sullivan and Christopher Capper, "Resources for Technical Support for Superfund Program," September 17, 1981; and Douglas MacMillan, memorandum to Christopher Capper, "Location of Enforcement-Support Resources," November 17, 1981.

23. President Reagan, "Memorandum for the Heads of Executive Departments and Agencies," January 20, 1981.

24. Landy, Roberts, and Thomas, *The Environmental Protection Agency*, 250.

25. James L. Regens and Robert W. Rycroft, "Funding for Environmental Protection: Comparing Congressional and Executive Influences," *Social Science Journal* 26 (1989), 298.

26. Interview with Richard Wilson. Similar comments were made by Martha Prothro.

27. Interviews with Kirby Biggs, William Muno, and Keith Casto.

28. Staff turnover during the Gorsuch years was mentioned as a significant problem by several present or former EPA enforcement officials I interviewed, including Jane Schulteis, Keith Casto, John Skinner, and Richard Mays. One interviewee also stated that the attrition rate would have been higher, particularly among EPA's enforcement attorneys, if the job market for attorneys had not been unusually slow during the 1982 and 1983 recession. Interview with Keith Casto. Agencywide, between the beginning of 1981 and the end of 1982, more than four thousand employees—close to 40 percent of EPA's workforce—resigned from government service. Landy, Roberts, and Thomas, *The Environmental Protection Agency*, 250.

29. Interviews with Douglas MacMillan, Richard Smith, and Keith Casto.

30. Interview with Richard Mays. The same views were expressed in interviews with Jane Souzon and Michael Brown.

31. Interview with Richard Mays. Douglas MacMillan had the impression that it had been Sullivan's intention "to put a politically loyal EPA attorney in each operating unit with the function of reporting deviant behavior back to the central committee." Interview with Douglas MacMillan.

32. Interview with Thomas Gallagher. Similar views were expressed in interviews with William Hedeman, Ann Strickland, and Keith Casto. In discussing Broccoletti's work, William Sullivan stated, "Broccoletti never had a light touch [with the staff]. I think he went out of the way to offend them." Interview with William Sullivan. Anne Gorsuch stated in an interview with me that she would "not know [Broccoletti] if he walked in the door. Generally speaking, I don't manage below my management." Interview with Anne Gorsuch. In contrast, however, in her memoir of her tenure as EPA administrator, Gorsuch wrote: "I knew my agency cold, down to the smallest local levels." Burford, *Are You Tough Enough?*, 76.

33. Interviews with James Bunting, Keith Casto, Ann Strickland, and Frederick Stiehl; telephone interviews with James Dragna and Charles Hungerford.

34. Telephone interview with Peter Broccoletti.

35. Interview with James Bunting.

36. Interview with William Hedeman.

37. Interviews with James Bunting and Douglas MacMillan; Subcommittee on Oversight and Investigations, House Committee on Energy and Commerce, *Hazardous Waste Enforcement*, 97th Cong., 2nd sess., 1982, Committee Print, 36–37.

38. Interviews with Gene Lucero and Anthony Roisman.

39. Interview with Frederick Stiehl.

40. Interviews with Keith Casto and James Bunting.

41. Interview with Douglas MacMillan.

42. Interview with Ann Strickland. Similar views were stated during my interviews with Keith Casto, James Bunting, and Douglas Farnsworth.

43. Interview with Michael Kilpatrick.

44. Interview with Barbara Elkus.

45. Interview with William Hedeman. In Anne Gorsuch (Burford)'s memoirs, Hedeman was quoted to a similar effect: "[T]here was a lack of cohesiveness unlike anything I had ever seen in government, and, essentially, a trial period in which each individual was attempting to establish their own notoriety and their own recognition within the Agency, perhaps at the expense of their peers." Burford, *Are You Tough Enough?*, ix.

46. Interview with William Hedeman.

47. Interview with Anne Gorsuch.

48. Interview with Michael Brown.

49. Interviews with Joan Boilen, John Johnson, and Jane Schulteis.

50. Interview with William Hedeman.

51. Interviews with Barbara Elkus, William Hedeman, Michael Kilpatrick, and Gene Lucero.

52. "A Conversation with Superfund Chief Bill Hedeman," *Environmental Forum* 2 (August 1983): 7.

53. Interview with Keith Casto.

54. Ibid.

55. See *Federal Register* 47 (1982): 214–215.

56. Christopher J. Capper, acting assistant administrator for solid waste and emergency response, memorandum to regional administrators, January 19, 1982; Rita M. Lavelle, assistant administrator for solid waste and emergency response, memorandum to regional administrators, January 28, 1983.

57. Interviews with Joan Boilen, Keith Casto, William Constantelos, William Hedeman, Gene Lucero, Steve Rothblatt, and Neil Wise. See memorandum from enforcement counsel to regional administrators, "Enforcement Policies and Procedures," February 26, 1982, 3, 7; Robert M. Perry, associate administrator for legal and enforcement counsel and general counsel, memorandum to associate administrator for policy and resource management, assistant administrator, regional administrators and office directors, "General Operating Procedures for the Civil Enforcement Program," July 6, 1982.

58. Interview with Michael Brown.

59. Interview with Gene Lucero.

60. Interviews with Kirby Biggs, Gene Lucero, William Constantelos, and John Skinner.

61. Subcommittee on Oversight and Investigations, House Committee on Energy and Commerce, *Hazardous Waste Enforcement*, 30.

62. Interview with William Sullivan. Similar comments were made in my interviews with Jane Schulteis, Michael Smith, Al Smith, and Fred Stiehl.

63. Interviews with Mel Hohman, Steve Rothblatt, David Kee, and Keith Casto.

64. Interviews with Frederick Stiehl, Richard Mays, Ann Strickland, Richard Smith, Michael Smith, David Ullrich, Neil Wise, Douglas MacMillan, Lamar Miller, and Jane Schulteis.

65. Interviews with Lawrence Kyte, Peter Kelly, and Jane Schulteis.

66. Interviews with Joan Boilen, James Bunting, Keith Casto, Barbara Elkus, John Skinner, Michael Smith, Anne Swofford, Jane Souzon, and Neil Wise; Burford, *Are You Tough Enough?*, 125.

67. Interview with William Muno.

68. Interview with Martha Prothro.

69. Interview with Richard Smith.

70. John Jones and Jack Smith [pseudonyms], "Critics of EPA Are Right," *New York Times*, September 1, 1982, 23. This article is an anonymously written employee criticism of EPA enforcement in a public forum.

71. Interview with Steve Rothblatt.

72. Ibid.

73. Interviews with Jeffrey Miller, Edward Kurent, Michael Brown, James Bunting, and Keith Casto.

74. Interview with Barbara Elkus.

75. Interview with Gene Lucero.

76. Interviews with Jane Schulteis, Richard Mays, and Gene Lucero.

77. Interview with Richard Frandsen. Similar information was also supplied to the legal staff of the Senate Environment and Public Works Committee, some of it on an anonymous basis. Telephone interview with Kathy Cudlipp.

78. Interview with Richard Frandsen.

79. Garry Trudeau, *Doonesbury*, January 25, 1982. The Ted Simpson cartoons also prompted attempts at humor by the Agency's staff, which noted their publication with considerable interest.

80. Russell E. Train, "The Destruction of EPA," *Washington Post*, February 2, 1982, A15.

81. See Philip Shabecoff, "EPA Wants to Allow Burial of Barrels of Liquid Wastes," *New York Times*, March 18, 1982, A1; *Federal Register* 47 (1982): 8307 (proposed February 25, 1982).

82. See Philip Shabecoff, "U.S. Reversing Stand on Burial of Toxic Liquids," *New York Times*, March 18, 1982, A1; *Federal Register* 47 (1982): 10,059 (correction March 6, 1982).

83. As Sullivan later recalled: "At one point I testified seven times in five days. I was being offered up for cannon fodder." Interview with William Sullivan. In addition to appearing before the Dingell Committee, Sullivan also was called to testify at hearings of the Senate Environment and Public Works Committee, as well as other congressional panels. Interview with Kathy Cudlipp.

84. Subcommittee on Oversight and Investigations, House Committee on Energy and Commerce, *Hazardous Waste Enforcement*.

85. Interviews with Keith Casto and Frederick Stiehl.

86. Interview with Edward Kurent.

87. Interview with Gene Lucero.

88. Interviews with Neil Wise and Lawrence Kyte.

89. Interview with Lloyd Guerci. Similar comments were made during my interview with Steven Ramsey. In fact, on September 30, 1982, the last day of fiscal year 1982, EPA referred eight Superfund enforcement cases to the DOJ. The Superfund referrals on this day were nearly *three times* the total number of Superfund actions EPA had referred to the DOJ over the previous fifteen months. Sub-

committee on Oversight and Investigations, House Committee on Energy and Commerce, *Hazardous Waste Enforcement*, 30.

90. Starr, "Turbulent Times at Justice and EPA," 910.

91. Congressmen John Dingell and James Florio, letter to Anne M. Gorsuch, June 15, 1982.

92. Interviews with Jane Souzon, Edward Kurent, Joan Boilen, and Michael Kilpatrick.

93. Congressmen John Dingell and James Florio, letter to Anne M. Gorsuch, August 31, 1982.

94. Subcommittee on Investigations and Oversight, House Committee on Public Works and Transportation, *Hazardous Waste Contamination of Water Resources /Access to EPA Superfund Records*, 97th Cong., 2nd sess., 1982, Committee Print.

95. House Judiciary Committee, *Investigation of the Role of the Department of Justice in the Withholding of Environmental Protection Agency Documents from Congress in 1982–83*, 99th Cong., 1st sess., 1985, H. Rept. 435, pt. 1, vol. 1, 10.

96. Subcommittee on Investigations and Oversight, House Committee on Public Works and Transportation, *Hazardous Waste* Contamination, 7–8.

97. House Committee on Public Works and Transportation, *Relating to the Contempt Citation of Anne M. (Gorsuch) Burford*, 98th Cong., 1st sess., 1983, H. Rept. 323, 8–9.

98. Subcommittee on Oversight and Investigations, House Committee on Energy and Commerce, *Report on the President's Claim of Executive Privilege over EPA Documents Abuses in the Superfund Program and Other Matters*, 1984, Committee Print, 1, 20.

99. Ibid., 21.

100. House, *Relating to the Contempt Citation*, 10.

101. The extent of press interest is illustrated by the fact that from September 1982 through March 1983 at least 156 articles regarding EPA appeared in the *New York Times* and that from February 1983 through March 1983 the *Washington Post* published 131 such articles.

102. Interview with Thomas Gallagher. Similar views were expressed by Michael Brown.

103. Interviews with Douglas Farnsworth, Thomas Gallagher, Amy Schaffer, Joan Boilen, Michael Kilpatrick, Edward Kurent, Richard Smith, and Neil Wise.

104. Interview with Mark Raabe.

105. Interviews with Barbara Elkus and Amy Schaffer.

106. House, *Relating to the Contempt Citation*, 11–12; see *United States v. House of Representatives of the United States*, 556 F. Supp. 150, 153 (D.D.C. 1983).

107. Subcommittee on Oversight and Investigations, House Committee on Energy and Commerce, *Report on the President's Claim of Executive Privilege*, 23–24.

108. House, *Relating to the Contempt Citation*, 114. Approximately one month earlier, the DOJ and Congressman Levitas signed a memorandum of understanding which reflected a partial settlement of the dispute.

109. With respect to the circumstances of her departure, see Burford, *Are You Tough Enough?*, 6.

110. Subcommittee on Oversight and Investigations, House Committee on

Energy and Commerce, *Report on the President's Claim of Executive Privilege over EPA Documents Abuses in the Superfund Program and Other Matters*, 6.

111. Ibid., 262–263.

112. Ibid., 295. The Republican minority views in the Dingell Committee report are replete with similar criticisms of Gorsuch and her colleagues. See 297, 298, 309, 317–318.

113. As we have seen and will be examined further, congressional influence on EPA enforcement approaches has not, by any means, been limited to the dramatic events of the Gorsuch era.

Chapter Five

1. David Andrews, "What Would You Do If You Were Running EPA?," *Environmental Law Reporter* 18 (July 1988): 10243.

2. See EPA press release, "Ruckelshaus Takes Steps to Improve Flow of Agency Information," May 19, 1983, 1. In order to carry out this "openness policy," Ruckelshaus and his top assistants made an attempt to meet with interested parties before specifically deciding how to change the Agency's approach to Superfund and other programs. Interviews with Keith Casto and William Hedeman. Unilateral contacts with representatives of regulated industry were discontinued with the exception of a few unique situations. Interview with Courtney Price. A recusal system was also established to prevent the reality or appearance of conflicts of interest by EPA officials.

3. Interview with Barbara Elkus.

4. Interview with Keith Casto.

5. Interviews with William Hedeman, Courtney Price, and Frederick Stiehl.

6. Interviews with William Constantelos, Barbara Elkus, John Johnson, Courtney Price, Jay Sargent, Amy Schaffer, John Skinner, Al Smith, and Neil Wise.

7. Interview with Keith Casto.

8. In lieu of taking those steps, Ruckelshaus and Alm created a new headquarters Office of Enforcement and Compliance Monitoring.

9. Telephone conversation with Alvin Alm.

10. Interview with Richard Mays.

11. See "Transcript of William D. Ruckelshaus' Remarks, EPA National Compliance, and Enforcement Conference," *Environmental Forum* (April 1984): 14–15.

12. Judson W. Starr, "Turbulent Times at Justice and EPA: The Origins of Environmental Criminal Prosecutions and the Work that Remains," 59 *George Washington Law Review* 911–912 (April 1991).

13. See House Committee on Energy and Commerce, *EPA's Law Enforcement Authority, 1983: Hearings before the Subcommittee on Oversight and Investigations*, 98th Cong., 1st sess., 1983, 102.

14. Starr, "Turbulent Times at Justice and EPA," 912. In 1988 Congress formally granted full police powers to EPA criminal investigators when it passed

the Medical Waste Tracking Act of 1988, Pub. L. No. l00-588, 102 Stat. 2950, 18 U.S.C. § 3063.

15. See U.S. General Accounting Office, *Environmental Protection Agency: Protecting Human Health and the Environment through Improved Management*, GAO/ RCED-88-01 (August 1988), 161.

16. Alvin L. Alm, deputy administrator, memorandum to assistant administrators, regional administrators, et al., "Implementing the State/Federal Partnership and State/Federal Enforcement Agreements," June 26, 1984. This document was revised and expanded by the Agency in the summer of 1986. See A. James Barnes, deputy administrator, memorandum, "Revised Policy Framework for Implementing State/EPA Enforcement Agreements," August 26, 1986.

17. Policy on Civil Penalties, EPA General Enforcement Policy GM-21, February 16, 1984.

18. Interview with Michael Kilpatrick. To the same effect were interview comments by Keith Casto, Barbara Elkus, William Hedeman, Richard Mays, and Frederick Stiehl.

19. Interviews with Barbara Elkus, William Hedeman, Richard Mays, and Gene Lucero.

20. Interviews with William Hedeman and Richard Mays. Along with this preference was an acknowledgment that the Superfund trust fund would need to be renewed and expanded following its formal expiration in September 1985. Interviews with Barbara Elkus, William Hedeman, and Gene Lucero.

21. Interviews with Gene Lucero, Michael Kilpatrick, and Frederick Stiehl.

22. Interview with Mel Hohman.

23. Interviews with Steven Leifer, Scott Fulton, and Kevin Gaynor.

24. Interviews with Keith Casto, William Hedeman, and Al Smith.

25. Interview with Mel Hohman.

26. Interview with Gene Lucero.

27. In order to expedite the preparation of RI/FSs, the requirement that states furnish a 10 percent share of RI/FS costs was abandoned.

28. See "Hazardous Waste Enforcement Policy," *Federal Register* 50 (1985) 5034; Lee M. Thomas and Courtney M. Price, memorandum to regional administrators, "Participation of Potentially Responsible Parties in Development of Remedial Investigations and Feasibility Studies under CERCLA," March 20, 1984; Gene A. Lucero, memorandum to directors, waste management divisions, "Procedures for Issuing Notice Letters," October 12, 1984; Lee M. Thomas and Courtney M. Price, memorandum to regional administrators, "Guidance Memorandum on Use and Issuance of Administrative Orders Under § 106(a) of CERCLA," December 21, 1983; Courtney M. Price and Lee M. Thomas, memorandum to enforcement counsel, "Guidance on Pursuing Cost Recovery Actions under CERCLA," August 26, 1983.

29. Interviews with William Hedeman, Jack Stonebraker, and John Johnson. These planning mechanisms were referred to as the Superfund Comprehensive Accomplishment Plan (SCAP) and the Strategic Planning and Management Systems (SPMS). See Lee M. Thomas, memorandum to regional administrators, "FY 1986 Superfund Comprehensive Accomplishments Plan," December 24, 1986.

30. Interviews with John Johnson, Neil Wise, Michael Brown, Richard Mays, Sheldon Novick, and Amy Schaffer.

31. This point should not be overstated, however. During 1984 EPA headquarters did issue at least two important policy guidance memoranda. See Courtney M. Price and Lee M. Thomas, memorandum, "Final RCRA Civil Penalty Policy," May 8, 1984; and Lee M. Thomas, memorandum to regional administrators, "Enforcement Response Policy," December 21, 1984.

32. Walter Mugdan and Robert Adler, "The 1984 RCRA Amendments: Congress as a Regulatory Agency," *Columbia Journal of Environmental Law* 10 (1985): 217.

33. For a summary of the Dingell Committee's findings, see Subcommittee on Oversight and Investigation, House Committee on Energy and Commerce, *Groundwater Monitoring Survey*, 1985, Committee Print.

34. See Subcommittee on Oversight and Investigations, House Committee on Energy and Commerce, *Ground Water Monitoring*, 1985, Committee Print, 8–9.

35. "Dingell Challenges EPA Enforcement of RCRA, Oversight of the States," *Hazardous Waste Report*, May 13, 1985.

36. Interviews with Lloyd Guerci and William Muno. For an evaluation of this EPA enforcement initiative by the GAO, see U.S. General Accounting Office, *Hazardous Waste Enforcement of Certification Requirements for Land Disposal Facilities*, GAO/RCED-87-60-BR (January 1987).

37. See "Thomas Pledges Tough Enforcement Effort, New Emphasis on Bringing Criminal Actions," *BNA Environment Reporter*, February 22, 1985, 1764.

38. See U.S. General Accounting Office, *Environmental Protection Agency: Protecting Human Health and the Environment Through Improved Management*, GAO/RCED-88-101 (August 1988), 37–39.

39. "Adams Confirmed by Senate for EPA Post, Wants to 'Get Things Moving' on Superfund," *BNA Environment Reporter*, August 15, 1986, 562, 563.

40. Interview with Michael G. Smith.

41. Interview with Thomas Gallagher.

42. "Multi-Media Inspections and Enforcement Planned," *Hazardous Waste Report*, April 29, 1985, 15.

43. Interview with Thomas Gallagher.

44. U.S. Environmental Protection Agency, Office of Enforcement and Compliance Monitoring, *Summary of Enforcement Accomplishments: Fiscal Year 1985* (April 1986), 4–5.

45. U.S. Environmental Protection Agency, Office of Enforcement and Compliance Monitoring, *Summary of Enforcement Accomplishments: Fiscal Year 1986* (April 1987), 9–11.

46. Ibid., 10.

47. *Fiscal Year 1985 Enforcement Accomplishments Report*, 15.

48. *Fiscal Year 1986 Enforcement* Accomplishments Report, i.

49. U.S. Environmental Protection Agency, Office of Enforcement and Compliance Monitoring, *Summary of Enforcement Accomplishments: Fiscal Year 1987* (April 1988), i.

50. Interviews with Julie Becker, Phil Cummings, Kevin Gaynor, Cheryl Wasserman, David Buente, and Thomas Gallagher.

51. Interview with Phil Cummings.

52. Cheryl Wasserman, "Oversight of State Enforcement," in Sheldon Novick et al., *Law of Environmental Protection* (Environmental Law Institute, 1986), § 8.02, 8-119–8-120.

53. Ibid., 8-122; interview with Richard Duffy.

54. Interviews with Julie Becker, Richard Frandsen, Steven Leifer, Thomas Adams, and Edward Reich.

55. "EPA Picks 18 Issues as 'Critical Delegations' to Regions under New Superfund," *Inside EPA*, March 13, 1987, 5.

56. Thomas L. Adams Jr., assistant administrator, memorandum to regional administrators, deputy regional administrators, regional counsel, assistant administrators, associate enforcement counsel, and Office of Enforcement and Compliance Monitoring office directors, "Expansion of Direct Referral of Cases to the Department of Justice," January 14, 1988.

57. Thomas L. Adams Jr., assistant administrator, memorandum to regional administrators, "Responsibilities for Assuring Effective Civil Judicial Enforcement," February 8, 1988.

58. Thomas L. Adams Jr., assistant administrator, memorandum to regional administrators, deputy regional administrators, and regional counsel, "Criteria for Active OECM Attorney Involvement in Cases," May 2, 1988.

59. Thomas L. Adams Jr., assistant administrator, Office of Enforcement and Compliance Monitoring, and J. Winston Porter, assistant administrator, Office of Solid Waste and Emergency Response, memorandum to regional administrators, "Revision of CERCLA Civil Judicial Settlement Authorities under Delegations 14-13-B and 14-14-E," June 17, 1988.

60. Presentation of Raymond L. Ludwiszczewski, acting general counsel, U.S. Environmental Protection Agency, at ALI-ABA-ELI Course of Study on Environmental Law, Washington, D.C., February 13, 1992.

61. Interviews with Rett Nelson, Norman Niedergang, Scott Fulton, David Buente, Frank Biros, Joyce Rechtschaffen, and Jonathan Cannon.

62. Interviews with Jonathan Cannon, Richard Frandsen, Edward Reich, and Norman Niedergang.

63. Interviews with Rett Nelson and Lawrence Kyte.

64. Interviews with Rett Nelson, Lawrence Kyte, Lloyd Guerci, and Joyce Rechtschaffen.

65. Interview with Frank Biros.

66. Presentation of Raymond Ludwiszczewski.

67. Interview with David Buente.

68. "President Requests 4% Increase in Operating Costs, 45% Superfund Jump," *BNA Environment Reporter*, February 8, 1985, 1627.

69. Senate Committee on Appropriations, *Hearings on Departments of Veterans Affairs and Housing and Urban Development and Independent Agencies Appropriations for Fiscal Year 1992*, 102nd Cong., 1st sess., 1991, Senate Hearing 102-113, pt. 1, 497–507.

70. Richard Mays, "Superfund Enforcement in the Dump: What's Wrong with the Superfund Enforcement Program?," *National Environmental Enforcement Journal* (February 1989): 3, 4.

71. Interviews with Charles de Saillan, Maria Cintron, Anne Allen, Steven Leifer, Erik Olson, and Thomas Gallagher.

72. Interview with Steven Leifer. Similar views were expressed by Erik Olson.

73. Environmental Law Institute, *Toward a More Effective Superfund Enforcement Program* (Washington, D.C., March 1989), 152–153. The ELI also observed: "[I]t is frequently unclear which office has jurisdiction. There appears to be overlapping jurisdiction on some matters. Regional [EPA] personnel complain that they receive conflicting and inconsistent advice from the different [headquarters] offices. This organizational structure results in inefficiency, uncertainty and duplication. Ultimately, it reduces the accountability of each office for Superfund enforcement" (153).

74. Interviews with Deborah Woitte, Don Gray, Stephanie Clough, Steven Leifer, Mark Reiter, Phil Cummings, Joyce Rechtschaffen, and Thomas Gallagher.

75. Interviews with Lloyd Guerci, William Muno, Richard Frandsen, Rett Nelson, Deborah Woitte, Thomas Gallagher, Judson Starr, Norm Niedergang, Steven Leifer, and Frank Biros; see also U.S. Environmental Protection Agency, *The Nation's Hazardous Waste Management Program at a Crossroads*, 66–67; and U.S. General Accounting Office, *Environmental Protection Agency*, 36.

76. U.S. General Accounting Office, *Superfund: Improvements Needed in Workforce Management*, GAO/RCED-88-1 (October 1987), 4.

77. In fiscal years 1985 and 1986, the "quit rate" for Superfund employees increased from 2.9 to 7.2 percent. Several critical Superfund occupations had quit rates that were two to six times higher than the average for similar jobs in other parts of the federal government. Ibid.

78. Interview with Don Gray. Enforcement staff turnover was also identified as a problem by the following interviewees: Rett Nelson, Deborah Woitte, Richard Frandsen, Jonathan Cannon, Phil Cummings, Thomas Gallagher, Anne Allen, and Steven Leifer.

79. Telephone interview with Bill Gillespie. This was also a problem for EPA in its efforts to hire experienced law enforcement personnel as criminal investigators. FBI background checks and other safeguards frequently delayed their retention by as much as six months.

80. Interviews with Julie Becker, Erik Olson, Don Gray, Kevin Gaynor, Thomas Gallagher, Richard Frandsen, David Buente, and Deborah Woitte.

81. Alfred A. Marcus, "EPA's Organizational Structure," in Christopher H. Schroeder and Richard J. Lazarus, eds., "Assessing the Environmental Protection Agency after Twenty Years: Law, Politics and Economics," *Duke Journal of Law and Contemporary Problems* 54 (Fall 1991): 33.

82. Hearing before the Subcommittee on Toxic Substances, Environmental Oversight and Research and Development of the Senate Committee on Environment and Public Works, Oversight of the Environmental Protection Agency's Enforcement Program, 101st Cong., 1st sess., 1989, Senate Hearing 101-503; testimony of John C. Martin, inspector general, U.S. Environmental Protection Agency, 29. A number of the present and former federal officials I interviewed agreed with Martin's conclusion regarding the existence of inconsistencies among state governmental attitudes and approaches to environmental enforcement. Interviews with Rett Nelson, Lloyd Guerci, Bill Muno, Scott Fulton, Steve Leifer,

and Thomas Adams. The GAO also criticized the Agency for poor oversight of inadequate state enforcement efforts. U. S. General Accounting Office, *Hazardous Waste: Many Enforcement Actions Do Not Meet EPA Standards*, GAO/RCED-88-140 (June 1988), 2–3.

83. Interview with Rett Nelson.

84. Interview with Maria Cintron.

85. Interviews with Deborah Woitte, Steven Leifer, Thomas Gallagher, and Judson Starr; Kevin Gaynor, "Too Many Cooks," *Environmental Forum* (January/ February 1989): 9, 13.

86. See U. S. Environmental Protection Agency, Office of the Inspector General, Capping Report on the Computation, Negotiation, Mitigation and Assessment of Penalties under EPA Programs, EPA/IG/EIG 8E 9-05-0087-9100485 (September 27, 1989); and U. S. General Accounting Office, *Environmental Enforcement: Penalties May Not Recover Economic Benefits Gained by Violators*, GAO/ RCED-91-166 (June 1991).

87. American Management Systems, Inc., "Improving Information Support for EPA Compliance Monitoring and Enforcement" (Arlington, Va., April 21, 1986), 4–5.

88. Ibid. Telephone interview with Charlene Swibas.

89. Kevin Gaynor, "Too Many Cooks," *Environmental Forum* (January/February 1989): 11.

90. Environmental Law Institute, *Toward a More Effective Superfund Enforcement Program*, 157.

91. Interviews with Steven Leifer, Michael Smith, Rett Nelson, Norman Niedergang, and Lawrence Kyte.

92. Interview with Rett Nelson.

93. Interviews with Thomas Adams, Anne Allen, Julie Becker, Frank Biros, Michael Brown, James Bunting, Jonathan Cannon, Maria Cintron, Phil Cummings, Charles de Saillan, Rick Duffy, Douglas Farnsworth, Scott Fulton, Anne Gorsuch, Edward Kurent, Steven Leifer, Douglas MacMillan, Erik Olson, Joyce Rechtschaffen, Amy Schaeffer, Richard Smith, Jane Souzon, Ann Strickland, Anne Swofford, and Doug Wolf.

94. Interviews with Anne Allen, Julie Becker, Scott Fulton, Frank Biros, Charles DeSaillan, Maria Cintron, Richard Frandsen, Erik Olson, and Phil Cummings.

95. Interview with Scott Fulton.

96. Gaynor, "Too Many Cooks," 11–12.

97. Interview with Thomas Adams.

98. Interview with Frederick Stiehl.

99. Letter from Representative John D. Dingell to Lee M. Thomas, October 6, 1986.

100. Letter from EPA Administrator Lee M. Thomas to Representative John D. Dingell, December 9, 1986.

101. "A New Criminal Enforcement Branch, Policy Shop Seen in OECM Overhaul," *Inside EPA*, September 19, 1986, 8.

102. Interviews with Charles de Saillan, Steven Leifer, and Thomas Gallagher. The morale of Superfund attorneys at EPA headquarters plummeted further in

the spring and summer of 1988, when their role in Superfund cases was drastically reduced. See "EPA Gives Settlement Powers to Regions, Precludes Headquarters Concurrence," *Inside EPA*, July 1, 1988, 1, 8. Deborah Woitte, Charles de Saillan, Richard Frandsen, Thomas Gallagher, and Scott Fulton expressed similar views.

103. See *PCB Disposal: Is EPA Doing Its Job?*, hearing before a Subcommittee of the House Committee on Government Operations; no. 73-657, April 6, 1987; *Implementation of the Toxic Substances Control Act, the PCB Rule and Federal Hazardous Substance Laws: Concerning the Performance of the Environmental Protection Agency in the Matter of Texas Eastern Gas Pipeline Company*, Report from the Subcommittee on Superfund and Environmental Oversight to the Senate Committee on Environment and Public Works, 100th Cong., 2nd sess., no. 81-135, February 1988; *Laundering Waste: EPA's Efforts to Prevent Criminal Activity in PCB Disposal*, hearing before a Subcommittee of the House Committee on Government Operations, 100th Cong., 2nd sess., no. 93-980, August 19, 1988; House Committee on Government Operations, *PCB's: EPA Must Strengthen Regulations, Improve Enforcement and Prevent Criminal Activity*, 101st Cong., 1st sess., H. Rept. 101-118, June 29, 1989; *Sham Recycling*, hearing before the Subcommittee on Hazardous Wastes and Toxic Substances; Senate Committee on Environment and Public Works, 100th Cong., 2nd sess., Senate Hearing 100-663, April 13, 1988; Hearing Record, Subcommittee on Oversight and Investigations, House Committee on Energy and Commerce, *Progress of the Superfund Program*, 100th Cong., 2nd sess., no. 000-203, June 20, 1988; and Hearing Record, Subcommittee on Energy, Environment and Natural Resources, House Committee on Government Operations, *Superfund Implementation*, 100th Cong., 2nd sess., no. 88-559, April 11, 1988; *Delays and Weaknesses in EPA's Program to Ensure Proper Closure of Hazardous Waste Sites*, hearing before a Subcommittee of the House Committee on Government Operations, 100th Cong., 1st sess., no. 87-569, December 15, 1987; *Environmental Compliance by Federal Agencies*, hearing before the Subcommittee on Oversight and Investigations of the House Committee on Energy and Commerce, 100th Cong., 1st sess., no. 100-39, April 28, 1987; *Review of DOE's Compliance with Environmental Laws in Managing Its Hazardous and Mixed Radioactive-Hazardous Wastes*, hearing before a Subcommittee of the House Committee on Government Operations, 99th Cong., 2nd sess., no. 64-6890, July 11, 1986; and *Hazardous Waste Problems at Department of Defense Facilities*, hearing before a Subcommittee of the House Committee on Government Operations, 100th Cong., 2nd sess., no. 86-073, November 5, 1987.

104. See U.S. General Accounting Office, *Superfund: Interim Assessment of EPA's Enforcement Program*, GAD/RCED-89-40BR (October 1988); U.S. General Accounting Office, *Hazardous Waste: Enforcement of Certification Requirements for Land Disposal Facilities*, GAO/RCED-87-60-BR (January 1987); U.S. General Accounting Office, *Superfund: Improvements Needed in Workforce Management*, GAO/RCED-88-1 (October 1987); U.S. General Accounting Office, *Hazardous Waste Facility Inspections Are Not Thorough and Complete*, GAO/RCED-88-20 (November 1987); and U.S. General Accounting Office, *Hazardous Waste: Many Enforcement Actions Do Not Meet EPA Standards*, GAO/RCED-88-I40 (June 1988).

105. See "RCRA Compliance Suffers from Lack of Staff, Lenient Attitudes of

States, EPA Reports Say," *BNA Environment Reporter*, April 12, 1985, 2179–2180; U.S. Environmental Protection Agency, Office of the Inspector General, *Capping Report on the Computation, Negotiation, Mitigation and Assessment of Penalties under EPA Programs*, EPA/IG/EIG 8E 9-05-0087-9100485, September 27, 1989.

106. Hearing Record, Subcommittee on Energy, Environment and Natural Resources, House Committee on Government Operations, *Superfund Implementation*, 100th Cong., 2nd sess., no. 88-559, April 11, 1988, 2.

107. Hearing Record, Subcommittee on Oversight and Investigations, House Committee on Energy and Commerce, *Progress of the Superfund Program*, 100th Cong., 2nd sess., no. 100-203, June 20, 1988, 1–2.

108. *Right Train, Wrong Track: Failed Leadership in the Superfund Cleanup Program*, June 20, 1988.

109. Ibid., 1.

110. U.S. Congress, Office of Technology Assessment, *Are We Cleaning Up? 10 Superfund Case Studies*, OTA-ITE-362 (Washington, D.C.: U.S. Government Printing Office, June 1988).

111. Ibid., 1–4.

112. Phil Shabecoff, "Congress Report Faults U.S. Drive on Waste Cleanup," *New York Times*, June 18, 1988, A1.

113. "EPA Officials Defend Against Attacks in Two Reports Criticizing Superfund Cleanups," *BNA Environment Reporter*, June 24, 1988, 260.

114. "Superfund Officials Confront Critics, Call Negative Reports Unfair, Misleading," *BNA Environment Reporter*, July 29, 1988, 419–420. Kovalick also stated that EPA's definition of "performance" with respect to Superfund site remedies did not agree with OTA's. OTA calls for total destruction of all contaminants. On the other hand, Kovalick indicated, EPA believed that "permanent remedies are a spectrum of remedies that can range from total destruction, like thermal incineration, through fixation or consolidating the waste on site."

Chapter Six

1. Environmental Law Institute, *Toward a More Effective Superfund Enforcement Program*.

2. Ibid., E-1, 50–51, 54–55, 152–155, 159, 192–197.

3. Ibid., 210.

4. Senate Subcommittee on Superfund, Ocean and Water Protection, *Lautenberg-Durenberger Report on Superfund Implementation: Cleaning Up the Nation's Cleanup Program*, May 1989.

5. Ibid., 8–12.

6. Ibid., 8.

7. *Nomination of William K. Reilly*, Hearing before the Senate Committee on Environment and Public Works, 101st Cong., 1st sess., January 31, 1989, 23.

8. Hearing before the Subcommittee on Toxic Substances, Environmental Oversight, Research and Development of the Senate Committee on Environment and Public Works, *Oversight of the EPA's Enforcement Program*, 101st Cong., 1st sess., Senate Hearing 101-503, November 15, 1989, 4.

9. See U.S. Environmental Protection Agency, *A Management Review of Superfund*, Administrator's preface, June 1989.

10. "EPA Superfund Review Aims for Cease Fire with Critics, Changes Recommended," *Hazardous Waste Report*, May 22, 1989, 1.

11. Interviews with Jonathan Cannon, Joyce Rechtschaffen, Elaine Stanley, and Thomas Adams.

12. U.S. Environmental Protection Agency, *A Management Review of Superfund*, 2.

13. "Reilly Shelves Controversial Deferral Policy Until Reauthorization, to Surprise of EPA Staff," *BNA Environment Reporter*, June 23, 1989, 460.

14. In fact, Congress's response to the Ninety Day Study and Reilly's recommendations led to approximately a five-hundred-person increase in the size of the EPA staff devoted to Superfund implementation on a full-time basis. Interviews with Norm Niedergang and Jonathan Cannon.

15. Interview with Mark Reiter; Hearing before the Subcommittee on Toxic Substances, Environmental Oversight, Research and Development of the Senate Committee on Environment and Public Works, *Oversight of the EPA's Enforcement Program*, 101st Cong., 1st sess., Senate Hearing 101-503, November 15, 1989, 2.

16. "EPA Superfund Review Aims for Cease Fire," 1.

17. U.S. Environmental Protection Agency, "Strock Nominated as EPA Assistant Administrator," *Environmental News*, August 7, 1989.

18. Interview with Mark Reiter.

19. "Enforcement: Reorganization Nears Approval Despite Discontent in Regions," *Inside EPA*, April 13, 1990, 4.

20. Interview with Charles de Saillan. Similar views were expressed by William Muno.

21. James M. Strock, "EPA's Environmental Enforcement in the 1990's," *Environmental Law Reporter* 20 (August 1990): 10330.

22. Ibid., 10239.

23. Ibid.

24. F. Henry Habicht II, deputy administrator, EPA memorandum to assistant administrators, general counsel, inspector general, associate administrators, and regional administrators, "Implementation of the Administrator's Multi-Media Enforcement Goal," February 19, 1991, 1, 3–4.

25. See U.S. General Accounting Office, *EPA's Management of Cross Media Information*, GAO-IMTEC-92-14 (April 1992).

26. Strock, "EPA's Environmental Enforcement," 10331.

27. Ibid., 10327–10328, 10330, 10332.

28. James M. Strock, "Environmental Criminal Enforcement Priorities for the 1990s," 50 *George Washington Law Review* 917, 937 (April 1991).

29. U.S. Environmental Protection Agency, *Enforcement in the 1990s Project: Recommendation of the Analytical Workgroups* (October 1991), iii.

30. U.S. Environmental Protection Agency, Office of Enforcement and Compliance Monitoring, *Enforcement Accomplishments Report for Fiscal Year 1989* (February 1990), 1.

31. Ibid., 15, 16, 64. In fiscal 1989 EPA reached 218 Superfund settlements

with PRPs. The estimated total work value of these settlements exceeded $1 billion. In addition, the agency referred 153 Superfund civil judicial actions to DOJ that year. Most of those cases sought injunctive relief for hazardous waste cleanup by responsible parties, recovery of public money spent on site cleanup, or site access to perform investigations or cleanup work. Moreover, in the same time period, $34.9 million in civil penalties were assessed, including $21.3 million in civil judicial penalties and $13.6 million in administrative penalties.

32. Hearing before the Subcommittee on Toxic Substances, Environmental Oversight, Research and Development, *Oversight of the EPA's Enforcement Program*, 9.

33. "Environmental Crimes Enforcement Increases during Fiscal 1989, Justice Department Reports," *BNA Environment Reporter*, January 5, 1990, 1510.

34. "1990 Record Year for Criminal Enforcement of Environmental Violators, Justice Announces," *BNA Environment Reporter*, November 23, 1990, 1397.

35. "Lieberman Crafts Bill to Strengthen EPA's Enforcement Activities," *Inside EPA*, March 2, 1990, 6.

36. See "Corporations Face Increased Penalties under Revised RCRA Civil Enforcement Policy," *BNA Environment Reporter*, November 2, 1990, 1245.

37. Interviews with Edward Reich and Joyce Rechtschaffen.

38. Interviews with Norman Niedergang, Rett Nelson, Scott Fulton, Erik Olson, and Jimmie Powell.

39. Interview with William Frank.

40. "Enforcement Chief Vies for Major EPA Shift to Centralize Enforcement Decisions," *Inside EPA*, January 11, 1991, 1.

41. Ibid., 6.

42. See "Reilly Vetoes Enforcement Chief's Plan for Major Reorganization," *Inside EPA*, February 1, 1991, 1, 5.

43. "Enforcement Chief Expects Successor to Carry on with New Initiatives," *Inside EPA*, February 22, 1991, 12.

44. "EPA Picks New Jersey County Prosecutor for Top Enforcement Post," *Inside EPA*, June 28, 1991.

45. See U.S. General Accounting Office, *Alternative Enforcement Organizations for EPA*, GAO/RCED-92-IO7 (April 1992).

46. U.S. General Accounting Office, *EPA's Management of Cross-Media Information*, GAO/IMTEC-92-I4 (April 1992), 7–8, 12.

47. Ibid., 12.

48. Interview with Charles de Saillan.

49. Interviews with Bertram Frey and Michael G. Smith.

50. U.S. Environmental Protection Agency, *The Nation's Hazardous Waste Management Program at a Crossroads*, 60. A similar view was expressed by William Muno in an interview.

51. See U.S. General Accounting Office, *Hazardous Waste*.

52. Interviews with Mark Reiter, Jimmie Powell, Richard Frandsen, Anne Allen, Rett Nelson, Scott Fulton, Don Gray, Elaine Stanley, Joyce Rechtschaffen, Deborah Woitte, and Phil Cummings.

53. Subcommittee on Oversight and Investigations, House Committee on

Energy and Commerce, *Activities of EPA's Office of Inspector General*, June 1991, Committee Print 102-E, 2–4, 7.

54. "Reilly Considers Major Program Changes to Accelerate Site Cleanups, Define Risks," *BNA Environment Reporter*, August 30, 1991, 1187.

55. Ibid.

56. See "Study Finds Unjustified Expenditures: EPA to Standardize Limits on PRP's," *BNA Environment Reporter*, October 4, 1991, 1406.

57. "Reilly Considers Major Program Changes," 1187.

58. "Study Finds Unjustified Expenditures," 1406; "New Superfund Head, Trouble-Shooter Staff Named to Review Contracts, Speed Cleanups," *BNA Environment Reporter*, October 4, 1991, 1405.

59. "Lautenberg, Dingell Blast Superfund Studies; Reilly Focuses on Accomplishments of the Program," *BNA Environment Reporter*, October 11, 1991, 1531.

60. Ibid.

61. See U.S. General Accounting Office, *Inland Oil Spills: Stronger Regulation and Enforcement Needed to Avoid Future Incidents*, GAO/RCED-8965 (February 1989); U.S. General Accounting Office, *Water Pollution: Improved Monitoring and Enforcement Needed for Toxic Pollutants Entering Sewers*, GAO/RCED-89-101 (April 1989); U.S. General Accounting Office, *Air Pollution: Improvements Needed in Detecting and Preventing Violations*, GAO/RCED-90-155 (September 1990); and Statement of Richard L. Hembra, director, Environmental Protection Issues, Resources, Community and Economic Development Division, U.S. General Accounting Office, before the Subcommittee on Water Resources, House Committee on Public Works and Transportation, *Observations on EPA and State Enforcement under the Clean Water Act*, GAO/T-RCED-91-53 (May 1991).

62. U.S. General Accounting Office, *Environmental Enforcement: Penalties May Not Recover Economic Benefits Gained by Violators*, GAO/RCED-91-166 (June 1991).

63. Ibid., 1, 4–5. EPA officials took issue with those portions of GAO conclusions that pertained to RCRA enforcement cases. See "EPA Clash over Report Finding Fault with EPA Assessments," *Inside EPA*, June 21, 1991, 16; and U.S. General Accounting Office, *Environmental Enforcement*, 6–9.

64. Keith Schneider, "Environment Laws Are Eased by Bush as Election Nears," *New York Times*, May 20, 1992, A1; Keith Schneider, "White House Snubs U.S. Envoy's Plea to Sign Rio Treaty," *New York Times*, June 5, 1992, A1; Keith Schneider, "Industries Gaining Broad Flexibility on Air Pollution," *New York Times*, June 26, 1992, A1; and John H. Cushman, Jr., "Quayle, in Last Push for Landowners, Seeks to Relax Wetland Protections," *New York Times*, November 12, 1992, A16.

65. Interview with Michael Smith.

Chapter Seven

1. See John H. Cushman Jr., "Environmental Lobby Beats Tactical Retreat," *New York Times*, March 30, 1994, B7.

2. "Browner Portrayed as Hard-Working, Results-Oriented," *BNA Environment Reporter*, December 18, 1992, 2086.

3. "White House Nominations for Some EPA Posts Draw Varied Reactions," *Inside EPA*, March 5, 1993, 11.

4. "EPA Deputy Administrator Nominee Receives Broad Support," *Inside EPA*, September 30, 1994, 4.

5. Ibid.

6. "White House Nominations for Some EPA Posts," 12, note 10.

7. Interview with Steve Herman.

8. Interview with Carol Browner. "Environment President? Not Yet," *New York Times* editorial, February 13, 1994. ("The whole concept of environmental stewardship . . . has run head-on into a nasty sense that the cleanliness crusade has burdened the country with too much regulation and exacted too heavy a price in jobs and growth. The skeptics included many of the President's fellow Democrats.")

9. In the case of Superfund, the intra-administration deliberations were colored by a statement made by President Clinton soon after he took office that "the Superfund has been a disaster. All the money goes to the lawyers, and none of the money goes to clean up the problems that it was designed to clean up." David E. Rosenbaum, "Business Leaders Urged by Clinton to Back Tax Plan," *New York Times*, February 12, 1993, A1. In administration discussions as to what legislation to propose to "fix" Superfund, some officials proposed repealing the statute's requirement of strict joint and several liability. That approach was energetically opposed by other officials, however, led by Assistant Attorney General Lois Schiffer. Schiffer passionately and skillfully defended the law's liability scheme within the administration. Interviews with Walter Mugden and Bruce Gelber. In the end, Schiffer and her allies prevailed. The revised version of Superfund that the administration proposed left the statute's liability provisions intact. It did suggest a number of other reforms, however, including the creation of uniform national standards as to how clean a site should be, factoring future land use at a site into decision making as to how clean a site should be, increasing the influence of local citizen groups in site cleanup decisions, encouraging arbitration among responsible parties, and collecting $8 billion over ten years (most from insurance companies) to finance the Superfund. John H. Cushman Jr., "Congress Foregoes Its Bid to Hasten Cleanup of Dumps," *New York Times*, October 6, 1994, A1.

10. John H. Cushman Jr., "Proposed Changes Simplify Rules on Pollution Control," *New York Times*, March 17, 1995, A20.

11. Interview with Carol Browner.

12. "General Policy: Future of EPA Cabinet Bill Uncertain Following House Vote on Amendment Rule," *BNA Environment Reporter*, February 4, 1994, 1719; John H. Cushman Jr., "EPA Critics Get Boost in Congress," *New York Times*, February 7, 1994, A1. As Carol Browner remembered, the EPA cabinet bill "became so loaded up with anti-environmental measures that the vice president and I actually had to go to Congress and convince them to kill the administration's own bill." Interview with Carol Browner.

13. For an insightful analysis of discussions during the 103rd Congress's re-

garding Superfund, see Rena I. Steinzor, "The Reauthorization of Superfund: Can the Deal of the Century Be Saved?," 25 *Environmental Law Reporter* 10,016 (January 1995). Notably, the Superfund tax has not been reauthorized to date.

14. See Keith Schneider, "Unbending Regulations Incite Move to Alter Pollution Laws," *New York Times*, November 29, 1993, A1; John H. Cushman Jr., "EPA and Arizona Factory Agree on Innovative Regulatory Plan," *New York Times*, November 20, 1996, A18.

15. Interview with Bill Muszynski.

16. Interviews with Steve Herman and Sylvia Lowrance.

17. Interview with an EPA manager who did not wish to be identified by name.

18. Interview with Walter Mugdan.

19. Interview with an EPA regional attorney who requested anonymity in the attribution of this statement.

20. Interview with an EPA Region IX enforcement staff member who asked not to be identified.

21. Ibid.

22. Interview with Felicia Marcus.

23. Interview with Gail Ginsberg.

24. Interview with David Ullrich.

25. Interview with Arthur Haubenstock.

26. Interview with a well-informed EPA employee who asked that his or her name not be used.

27. Interview with Bruce Buckheit.

28. Interview with Allan Zabel.

29. Ibid.

30. Ibid. Another seasoned EPA enforcement attorney suggested that I compare Title 40 of the U.S. Code of Federal Regulations), part 60, subpart xx, EPA's new source performance standards for bulk gasoline terminals, with Title 40, part 63, subpart r (the MACT standards for the same type of facilities). He suggested that even though there are a number of even more egregious examples of incomprehensible MACT regulations, especially as compared with the former, it is "incredibly hard" to determine compliance with the latter. He also noted that MACT standards often contain "work practice regulations" that are labor-intensive for EPA inspectors to enforce. Interview with an EPA enforcement attorney who requested anonymity.

31. Interview with Bruce Buckheit.

32. Interview with Steve Rothblatt. Rothblatt noted that there are ninety MACT standards and that their length and complexity make them exceptionally hard to include within Title V permits and very difficult to enforce. Among the challenges for EPA that he mentioned in this area were: 1) the reluctance of personnel at regulated plants to certify compliance with so complex a set of regulations, 2) the difficulty that state personnel have in understanding the MACT regulations, 3) the problem posed for EPA regional office personnel keeping track of the adoptions (by rule making) of MACT standards by states, and 4) the technical complexity of reviewing company applications for alternative MACT standards. Ibid.

33. Interview with Steve Herman.

34. Interview with Sylvia Lowrance. *Accord* interview with Eric Schaeffer. ("It is valuable to have an independent enforcement office that is an agent for implementation of environmental laws and for having them taken seriously, that does not depend upon the program offices for inspections and so on. That was the major accomplishment of the reorganization.")

35. "Browner Splits Enforcement Office by Function and Sector," *Inside EPA*, October 15, 1993, 11, 12; "Compliance, Regulatory Offices Created under Reorganization of EPA Enforcement," *BNA Environment Reporter*, October 15, 1993, 1137.

36. "Browner Calls for Limited Reorganization of Regions," *Inside EPA*, June 24, 1994, 1, 10. Browner indicated that she had made that decision in order to allow the structure of the regional offices to reflect the unique aspects of the states. Interview with Carol Browner.

37. Interviews with Nancy Marvel and an EPA attorney and manager who declined to be identified.

38. Interview with Eric Schaeffer. *Accord*, in part, interview with Steve Herman ("The reorganization was not perfect"); Sylvia Lowrance ("A reorganization of this magnitude always has a few missteps, but that doesn't take away from its ultimate success"); and Carol Browner ("The reorganization was imperfect").

39. Interview with an EPA employee who asked not to be identified. *Accord* interviews with Bruce Gelber and Bill Muszynski.

40. Interview with Cheryl Wasserman. Wasserman pointed out that "we lost a lot of ground because the states had nowhere to connect in the new OECA." She also noted that, although the policies remained nominally in effect, OECA's management essentially abandoned the "timely and appropriate" framework as an important management construct for evaluating state and regional performances (EPA had successfully negotiated this with the states in the Bush I administration and it was still in effect in 1993). Ibid.

41. Interview with Ann Lassiter. *Accord* interview with Arthur Horowitz. ("There was a real loss of functions in the compliance area. An effort was later made to build that back. But it took quite a while.")

42. Interview with Eric Schaeffer.

43. Interview with Bob Tolpa.

44. Interview with an EPA employee who requested anonymity.

45. Interview with Eric Schaeffer. Schaeffer observed that, in hindsight, EPA's voluntary self-audit disclosure program seems a "natural fit" for the OC. If the OC had taken responsibility for that, and let the traditional compliance monitoring function go to ORE, it would have been a better arrangement since it would have given the OC a vital program role where they would have had to interact with the ORE in a positive way. Another EPA enforcement staff member felt that the reorganization had unnecessarily divided up responsibility for RCRA programs among different organizational units, and that it had needlessly de-emphasized the role of RCRA as compared with the Superfund Program. Interview with Mimi Newton.

46. Interview with Art Horowitz. In the end, Horowitz's initial job in EPA headquarters, tracking state and regional performance under EPA's Significant Violator, Timely and Appropriate Guidance, was abolished altogether. He ulti-

mately accepted a staff position in one newly formed OECA office, primarily on the basis of his initial rapport with the head of that office who had told him that she did not know what work her branch (or Horowitz individually) would do if he worked for her.

47. Interview with an EPA manager who preferred not to be identified. The same individual further explained, "[A] reorganization is seen as a hostile act against everybody else in the organization. The people who were making the final [reorganization] decisions were [thus] advised to move quickly, identify the resources [that they needed], and say, we've got those, now we're going to talk about how the responsibilities shake out. Instead, they got into protracted negotiations with the program offices about what their resources were going to be and [OECA] wound up getting less than we should have. . . . We have had a smaller base than we should have and we've been taking sustained [budget] cuts from that base over the years. I think it is starting to hurt." In interviews with Ann Lassiter and Cheryl Wasserman, both noted that responsibility for most EPA grants to states, including federal grants to do state environmental enforcement work, remained in the EPA headquarters program offices instead of being transferred to OECA. Little real effort was made to involve enforcement in the decision making, and (with the sole exception of state grants regarding pesticides) there was no reporting back to OECA on how the grant money was actually used and what it accomplished.

48. Interview with Steve Herman; *Accord* interviews with Mike Stahl, Sylvia Lowrance, Eric Schaeffer, George Hays, and Joe Boyle. Perhaps a more fundamental flaw in the regional office phase of the reorganization was that in August 1995, the administrator directed that regional restructuring be completed by September 30, 1995, several months ahead of the originally announced deadline for completion of regional reorganization. As one senior regional manager recalled: "These things take time and it takes a lot of 'tender loving care' to do it, and that just wasn't possible in that time frame. . . . We had to do [the regional reorganization] a lot more rapidly than we would otherwise would have had to, and as a result some people [in our regional office] felt they weren't treated properly." Soon afterward, employer-employee relations within EPA "took a step back," and an EPA employees' union was formed (interview with an EPA official who asked that his or her name not be revealed).

49. On its website, EPA defines "environmental justice" as "the fair treatment and meaningful involvement of all people, regardless of race, color, national origin or income with respect to the development, implementation and enforcement of environmental laws, regulations and policies." See "Environmental Justice," http://www.epa.gov/compliance/ej (accessed February 15, 2011). The Agency's environmental justice program was given an important boost when President Clinton signed Executive Order 12898, "Federal Actions to Address Environmental Justice in Minority Populations and Low-Income Populations," on February 11, 1994. This order directed all federal agencies to develop "environmental justice strategies" that would identify and address disproportionately extreme and adverse human health or environmental effects of their programs, policies, and activities on minority and low-income populations. The order also established an Interagency Working Group (IWG) that includes the heads of eleven federal agencies and departments and is chaired by the EPA administrator. The IWG

selected and helped fund fifteen environmental justice "demonstration projects" around the United States, and it has helped to coordinate interagency collaborative efforts in the environmental justice area.

50. Interview with Nancy Marvel.

51. Interviews with Gail Ginsberg and Steve Herman.

52. *Contract with America* (Times Books, 1994).

53. Ibid., 134.

54. Ibid., 24–25, 131–135.

55. See John H. Cushman Jr., "Republicans Plan Sweeping Barriers to New U.S. Rules," *New York Times*, December 25, 1994; John H. Cushman Jr., "Congressional Roundup: Backed by Business, G.O.P. Takes Steps to Overhaul Environmental Regulations," *New York Times*, February 10, 1995, A22; John H. Cushman Jr., "Congressional Republicans Take Aim at an Extensive List of Environmental Statutes," *New York Times*, February 22, 1995, A14; John H. Cushman Jr., "House Votes to Freeze Regulations as Democrats Fail to Gain Health and Safety Limitations," *New York Times*, February 25, 1995, 7; John H. Cushman Jr., "House Considers Bill to Impose Extensive Review Process on New Rules for Health and Safety," *New York Times*, February 28, 1995, A18; John H. Cushman Jr., "The 104th Congress and the Environment: House Approves Sweeping Changes on Regulations," *New York Times*, March 1, 1995, A1. In addition to proposing across-the-board regulatory reform measures, the new Republican majority in the House also worked with some conservative Democrats to propose legislation that would have made far-reaching changes in the Clean Water Act and in other specific environmental statutes. John H. Cushman Jr., "House Set to Revamp Law Cleaning Water in U.S.," *New York Times*, March 23, 1995, A22; John H. Cushman Jr., "House Votes Sweeping Changes in Clean Water Act," *New York Times*, May 17, 1995, A17.

56. Cushman, "Congressional Roundup."

57. Cushman, "Congressional Republicans Take Aim."

58. Cushman, "The 104th Congress."

59. "After 100 Days: A Legacy of Unfairness or A Bolder Direction?," *New York Times*, April 9, 1995, 157.

60. Adam Clymer, "Congressional Memo: After Bad Week, G.O.P. Looks to Budget for Help," *New York Times*, July 23, 1995.

61. Ibid.

62. Jerry Gray, "House Rebuffs Many Budget Amendments," *New York Times*, July 28, 1995, A18.

63. John H. Cushman Jr., "Clinton Threatens Veto of EPA Budget Cutbacks," *New York Times*, July 17, 1995, 1.

64. Gray, "House Rebuffs."

65. John H. Cushman Jr., "House Coalition Sets G.O.P. Back on Environment," *New York Times*, July 29, 1995, 1.

66. John H. Cushman Jr., "G.O.P. House Leaders Succeed in Advancing Limits on EPA," *New York Times*, August 1, 1995, A1.

67. Todd S. Purdham, "Clinton Lashes Out at Congress, Citing Pollution and Guns," *New York Times*, August 2, 1995, A1. Administrator Browner also remained highly critical of the House's action. In a series of speeches, she stressed the im-

portance to society of keeping the "environmental cop on the beat," and the public health significance of the legislation that the Republican leadership was seeking to curtail or repeal. Interview with Carol Browner.

68. Jerry Gray, "Negotiators on Budget Make Some Headway," *New York Times*, November 30, 1995, B14.

69. Ibid. Prior to that, at the close of the 1995 fiscal year, in September 1995, when the same set of budgetary disagreements had not been resolved, the president and leaders of the Republican-controlled Congress had agreed to keep the government open until November 13, with modestly reduced budgetary allowances to be allocated to government agencies prior to that deadline. Michael Weiss, "G.O.P. and Clinton Reach Deal to Halt Federal Shutdown," *New York Times*, September 28, 1995, A1.

70. David E. Rosenbaum, "Congressional Memo: Two Sides in Budget Talks Take the Road to Nowhere," *New York Times*, December 2, 1995, 8; David E. Rosenbaum, "Clinton Outlines Alternative Plan to Halt Deficit," *New York Times*, December 8, 1995, A1; David E. Rosenbaum, "With No Budget, Clinton and Republicans Pass the Blame," *New York Times*, December 17, 1995; Michael Wines, "High Level Talks Again Fail to End Budget Standoff," *New York Times*, December 23, 1995.

71. John H. Cushman Jr., "Senate Backs Cuts in Environmental Spending," *New York Times*, December 15, 1995, A35; John H. Cushman Jr., "Brief Clause in Bill Would Curb U.S. Power to Protect Wetlands," *New York Times*, December 12, 1995, A1.

72. Todd S. Purdham, "Two More Spending Bills Vetoed but Clinton Offers to Negotiate," *New York Times*, December 19, 1995, A1.

73. John H. Cushman Jr., "Budget Cuts Leave EPA Facing Layoffs," *New York Times*, December 24, 1995. In fact, internal EPA contingency planning for the possibility of budget cuts and employee furloughs had begun in the summer of 1995. At that time, EPA curtailed its travel budgets, laid off temporary workers, encouraged some veteran employees to take early retirements, and placed a freeze on promotions. Ibid.

74. Adam Clymer, "Congress Votes to Return 760,000 to Federal Payroll and Resume Some Services; Step Is Temporary," *New York Times*, January 6, 1996.

75. Ibid.

76. John H. Cushman Jr., "G.O.P. Backing Off from Tough Stand over Environment," *New York Times*, January 26, 1996, A1. One such pollster, Linda Di Vall, reported that "by greater than a 2-1 margin, voters have more confidence in the Democrats than the Republicans as the party they trust most to protect the environment. Most disturbing is that 55% of Republicans do not trust their party when it comes to protecting the environment, while 72% of the Democrats do trust their party." Thus, Di Vall concluded, "attacking the EPA is a non-starter." Ibid.

77. "The Environmental Counterattack," *New York Times*, February 5, 1996, A14.

78. John H. Cushman Jr., "Businesses Scaling back Plans to Defang Federal Regulations," *New York Times*, February 3, 1996.

79. John H. Cushman Jr., "House G.O.P. Chiefs Back Off Stiff Anti-Regulatory Plan," *New York Times*, March 6, 1996, A19.

80. Michael Wines, "Borrowing Authority of U.S. Is Extended Three Weeks," *New York Times*, March 8, 1996, A20.

81. Michael Wines, "The Budget Truce: The Overview: House and Senate Vote To Approve '96 Spending Bill," *New York Times*, April 26, 1996, A1; Jerry Gray, "The Budget Truce: The Details: Both Congress and Clinton Find Cause for Cheer in the Final Budget Deal," *New York Times*, April 26, 1996, A22.

82. Interview with Nancy Marvel.

83. Interview with Ann Lassiter.

84. Interview with Sylvia Lowrance. Although these disruptions contributed significantly to the FY96 EPA enforcement output declines, it seems unlikely that they were its only cause (interview with Mike Stahl). Regional office uncertainty over the importance of enforcement to EPA's top managers, combined with the temporary dislocations caused by the Agency's reorganization, also appear to have been factors leading to this temporary enforcement fall off. Interestingly, the FY96 EPA enforcement decline received relatively little public attention at the time, in large part because, from 1995 on, the Republican-dominated Congress showed no interest in conducting oversight of almost any aspect of EPA's performance. Interview with Dick Frandsen.

85. See, e.g., Richard L. Berke, "In a Reversal, G.O.P. Courts the Greens," *New York Times*, July 2, 1997, A1; Steven A. Holmes, "Republicans Trying Hard to Avoid Reprise of Past Year's Budget Battles," *New York Times*, June 17, 2000, A8. Notably, the Republicans dropped much of the harsh rhetoric that had been employed in the heat of the budget dispute, in which some of their leaders had referred to Democrats as being part of an "eco-terrorist underworld," and had analogized EPA and its enforcement staff to "the Gestapo." See James Gerstensang, "G.O.P. Clouds the Future of Environmental Protection," *Los Angeles Times*, December 25, 1995, A1; 139 Cong. Rec. S 5141 (daily ed., April 29, 1993), statement of Sen. Wallop.

The new Republican stance also made possible the passage of significant amendments to two important environmental statutes, the Safe Drinking Water Act (SDWA) and the Federal Insecticide, Fungicide and Rodenticide Act (FIFRA). With respect to the SDWA amendments, see John H. Cushman Jr., "Environment Bill's Approval Now Likely after Panel Vote," *New York Times*, June 7, 1996, A28; John H. Cushman Jr., "Bill Would Give Water Customers Pollution Notice," *New York Times*, June 23, 1996; and "Federal Water Bill Will Pay for Repairs, *New York Times*, August 1, 1996, D22. For journalistic accounts of the amendments to FIFRA, see John H. Cushman Jr., "Pesticide Measure Advances in House, Without Rancor," *New York Times*, July 18, 1996, A20; and "Food-Pesticide Overhaul Wins House Passage," *New York Times*, July 24, 1996, A18.

Prior to the end of FY95, the Republicans had also retreated from their insistence that the Superfund statute be amended to eliminate strict, joint, and several liability for responsible parties. John H. Cushman Jr., "Republicans Back Off Plan to Ease Polluters' Liability," *New York Times*, September 29, 1995, A28.

86. Interview with Carol Browner. Notably, however, the end of the budget

controversy did not coincide with the end of *all* the administration's differences with Congress over environmental enforcement issues. As the Justice Department's assistant attorney general for environment and natural resources in the Clinton administration stated:

> There were stealth attacks on both DOJ and EPA enforcement. For example, there was a [legislative] proposal to change the intent standard in environmental criminal law from general intent to specific intent. Under that, there would have had to have been proof that people knew that, by their conduct, they were violating a particular regulation. That would have been much harder to prove than merely demonstrating that they knew they were discharging to a river. There were a series of those proposals. They were hard to explain to the public, but they would have had a dramatic effect on enforcement.
>
> In addition, we began to see budgets, particularly on the criminal enforcement side, that contained 'earmarks' for specific programs. They said you should spend X amount of money on this type of case. But if you don't have this kind of case, what are you going to do? [Earmarks] cut into the budget. They disable EPA and DOJ from determining what the appropriate [enforcement] priorities are. We faced a number of those. EPA faced more, particularly in criminal enforcement. . . . They always were [supportive of enforcement] priorities that did not focus on big, corporate polluters.

Interview with Lois Schiffer.

87. Interview with Walter Mugdan. EPA's focus also returned to numbers of inspections, enforcement actions taken, etc., as key measures of enforcement success in the period that followed the budgetary turmoil (interview with Bill Muszynski).

88. Outside of the enforcement area, the weakening of Congressional opposition to environmental regulation allowed EPA's leaders to promulgate policies and regulations in Clinton's second term that were more protective of public health and the environment than had previously been possible. Thus, under the Clean Air Act, the Agency took the controversial step of creating the National Ambient Air Quality Standards for fine particulate matter and ozone. See John H. Cushman Jr., "Administration Issues Its Proposal for Tightening of Air Standards," *New York Times*, November 28, 1996, A1; John H. Cushman Jr., "Top EPA Official Not Backing Down on Air Standards," *New York Times*, June 1, 1997; Peter Passell, "Economic Scene: The Air Standards Are Set, But How Clean Is Clean Enough?," *New York Times*, July 3, 1997, D2; John H. Cushman Jr., "D'Amato Vows to Fight for EPA's Tightened Standards," *New York Times*, June 25, 1997, A13; John H. Cushman Jr., "Clinton Sharply Tightens Air Pollution Regulations Despite Concern over Costs," *New York Times*, June 26, 1997, A1; Matthew L. Wald, "Court Overturns Air Quality Rules," *New York Times*, May 15, 1999, A1; Linda Greenhouse, "Court to Hear Clean Air Test of Congressional Authority," *New York Times*, May 23, 2000, A22; and Linda Greenhouse, "Supreme Court Roundup: Justices Broaden Their Look at the Clean Air Act," *New York Times*, May 31, 2000. The Agency also approved final rules that would cut emissions from heavy-duty buses and trucks. See Matthew L. Wald, "EPA to Issue Tougher Rules

on Diesel Fuel," *New York Times*, May 17, 2000, A1; and Douglas Jehl, "New Rules to Cut Diesel Emissions," *New York Times*, December 21, 2000, A1. Additionally, it set stricter emission standards for cars and light trucks. Matthew L. Wald, "Stricter Pollution Controls Set for Cars and Light Trucks," *New York Times*, December 21, 1999, A29.

Under the Clean Water Act, EPA increased the regulation of polluted runoff from feedlots and other agricultural sources. David Stout, "To Save Waterways EPA Will Tighten Regulation of Big Farms," *New York Times*, March 5, 1998, A19. The Agency issued a new set of regulations regarding state water quality standards and total maximum daily load (TMDL) requirements. Matthew L. Wald and Steven Greenhouse, "EPA Institutes Water Regulations before a Bill Blocking Them Becomes Law," *New York Times*, July 12, 2000, A17. Moreover, EPA established tighter rules regarding the discharge of toxic materials by pulp and paper mills. John H. Cushman Jr., "EPA Seeks Cut in Paper Mill Pollution, but Not Elimination," *New York Times*, May 21, 1997, A21.

The Agency also proposed strict regulation of arsenic in tap water under the Safe Drinking Water Act. John H. Cushman Jr., "EPA Proposes New Rule to Lower Arsenic in Tap Water," *New York Times*, May 25, 2000, A20. EPA also established a policy of focusing environmental protection standards on the risks that pollutants pose to the health of children. John H. Cushman Jr., "Children's Health Is to Guide EPA," *New York Times*, September 12, 1996, A14.

89. Interviews with Allyn Stern, Allan Zabel, Bert Frye, Bob Tolpa, Rett Nelson, Walter Mugdan, Steve Herman, Sylvia Lowrance, Larry Kyte, Kathleen Johnson, and Bill Muno.

90. Interviews with Larry Kyte, Kathleen Johnson, and Bill Muno.

91. Interviews with Steve Herman, Eric Schaeffer, Mike Walker, Walter Mugdan, Sylvia Lowrance, Bruce Buckheit, and Bill Muszynski.

92. Interviews with Bruce Buckheit and Bill Muszynski.

93. Interview with Sylvia Lowrance.

94. Interviews with David Nielsen and Noël Wise.

95. Interview with Rett Nelson.

96. Interviews with Felicia Marcus and a former EPA attorney who asked not to be identified.

97. Interviews with George Czerniak, Gail Ginsberg, and Nancy Marvel. One EPA regional manager dissented from this view, observing that, in the RCRA area, EPA headquarters personnel provided helpful technical advice. Interview with Joe Boyle.

98. Interviews with Gail Ginsberg, Nancy Marvel, and a former EPA enforcement attorney who spoke on condition of anonymity.

99. Interviews with Mike Stahl, Joe Boyle, John Warren, David Buente, and one present and one former federal government environmental enforcement attorney, both of whom requested anonymity.

100. Interviews with Bill Muszynski and an EPA enforcement staff member who asked for anonymity.

101. Interviews with Nancy Marvel, Kathleen Johnson, Steve Rothblatt, Mimi Newton, David Nielsen, Bert Frey, Allyn Stern, Felicia Marcus, Bob Tolpa, George Czerniak, Michelle Benson, and Tinka Hyde.

102. Interviews with Mike Walker and Bruce Buckheit.

103. Interviews with Bill Muszynski and David Buente.

104. Interviews with George Hays and Cheryl Wasserman. Wasserman told me that the attempt made by the designers of EPA's reorganization to integrate enforcement attorneys and technical people into a single "headquarters office" led to a diminishment of stature for many of the non-attorneys, and a consequent loss of their programmatic perspectives. Interview with Cheryl Wasserman.

105. Interviews with Ann Nutt, Allan Zabel, Gail Ginsberg, Noël Wise, and John Rothman.

106. Interviews with Ann Nutt, Allan Zabel, Gail Ginsberg, John Rothman, Noël Wise, and Tinka Hyde. *Accord*, interview with Nancy Marvel. Marvel observed that, in individual cases, "the quality of the [interdisciplinary] relationship totally depends on the competence level on both sides. . . . If there is an imbalance on either side, then there is a problem."

107. Interview with Gail Ginsberg.

108. Interviews with Mike Stahl, Steve Herman, Ann Lassiter, and Eric Schaeffer. Schaeffer stated that "setting an artificial cap on technical staff pay and advancement was one of the worst personnel decisions of the Clinton era. It was grossly unfair to some of our most talented employees."

109. Interviews with Mimi Newton, Gail Ginsberg, Nancy Marvel, Bruce Gelber, David Buente, Bob Kaplan, Noël Wise, Felicia Marcus, Tinka Hyde, John Rothman, and an EPA employee who requested anonymity. One interviewee particularly emphasized the extent to which, for internal political reasons, some of the EPA regional offices "always had both hands tied behind their backs in relating to the states." Interview with George Hays.

110. Interviews with Sylvia Lowrance, Gail Ginsberg, Eric Schaeffer, Lois Schiffer, Steve Herman, Carol Browner, and an EPA enforcement official who asked for anonymity.

111. Interviews with Rett Nelson, Gail Ginsberg, and Michelle Benson.

112. Interviews with Lois Schiffer, Bob Kaplan, John Cruden, Noël Wise, and Gail Ginsberg.

113. Interview with an EPA attorney familiar with the Agency's criminal enforcement program who prefers to remain anonymous.

114. Interviews with Ann Lassiter, Joe Boyle, Tinka Hyde, and an EPA enforcement official who asked not to be identified by name.

115. See U.S. EPA, "Joint Agreement to Reform Oversight and Create a National Environmental Performance Partnership System," May 1995; http://www.epa.gov/ocir/nepps/pdf/joint_commit_create_nepps.pdf. NEPPS sought to expand the role of the states in planning their delegated program activities in the context of individual "performance partnership agreements" with EPA. It also called for reduced EPA oversight of state performance in exchange for greater state accountability for environmental results, as measured by the "outcome" of the states' work. Ibid.

Notwithstanding NEPPS, however, after the middle of the 1990s EPA tried to convince the states to continue following critical aspects of its traditional, deterrence-based enforcement approach, as set forth in the Agency's 1986 Revised Policy Framework (RPF) for state-EPA enforcement agreements. As Clifford Rechtschaffen and David Markell observed in *Reinventing Environmental Enforcement and the State/Federal Relationship* (Environmental Law Institute, 2004), this inconsistent federal approach had the unfortunate effect of sending "mixed signals" to the states as to what EPA truly expected of them. It resulted in increased state-level frustration with Agency oversight of state enforcement work. As one EPA regional enforcement coordinator described it: "NEPPS raised the expectations of some states that EPA would leave them alone. When that didn't happen, it raised their hackles." Interview with Tinka Hyde.

116. Clifford Rechtschaffen and David L. Markell, *Reinventing Environmental Enforcement and the State/Federal Relationship* (Environmental Law Institute, 2004).

117. Interview with Tinka Hyde.

118. For some interesting insights into the establishment and early history of ECOS, see "ECOS: Ten Years Putting the States on the Map," in *Ecostates: The Journal of the Environmental Council of the States*, Summer 2003.

119. In Eric Schaeffer's view, "ECOS is an organization where a handful of very ideological commissioners . . . can end up driving resolutions and passing resolutions that the rest of the commissioners never heard of or are only vaguely aware of. Their position on enforcement was: Feds, give us money and keep out!" Interview with Eric Schaeffer.

120. Interviews with John Rothman and Tinka Hyde. EPA's change of position was, in substantial part, a response to a report by the Agency's Office of Inspector General that was highly critical of the enforcement efforts of the Commonwealth of Pennsylvania and EPA Region III's lax oversight of that state's enforcement performance. Interview with Tinka Hyde.

121. Interviews with Bruce Buckheit, Bill Muszynski, and Mike Stahl. See also John H. Cushman Jr., "States Neglecting Pollution Rules, White House Says," *New York Times*, December 15, 1996.

122. Interview with Gail Ginsberg. *Accord* interview with Lois Schiffer ("ECOS, as it was at that time, was not a helpful organization. Insofar as the then-leadership of ECOS pitched it as 'the states versus EPA,' it was then quite unhelpful. At that time, ECOS drove polarization"). Steve Herman's recollections of his own contacts with ECOS were more mild and diplomatic: "Some meetings with ECOS were confrontational, others were not. At ECOS we didn't deal with day-to-day issues, we dealt with large policy issues. Thus, differences tended to be much sharper. However, we didn't run into those questions at the individual state level." Interview with Steve Herman. Similarly, Carol Browner told me, "ECOS used to drive me nuts, but overall it was a worthwhile organization that gave [state] environmental commissioners a voice with EPA." Interview with Carol Browner.

Interestingly, Browner analogized EPA's relationship with the states to "an arranged marriage." She stated, "[W]e wouldn't necessarily choose each other but we're together, and hopefully we have a shared agenda. It is a relationship that has to be worked at." Ibid.

123. Interview with Mike Stahl.

124. In general, audit privilege laws bar the use of environmental audit documents and reports as evidence in environmental enforcement litigation and allow

those papers to be withheld from public governmental disclosure. Immunity measures, in contrast, protect companies from sanctions for environmental violations if the violations are discovered in the course of an environmental audit, promptly reported to environmental authorities, and corrected within a specified time. The rationale for both kinds of laws is that they create needed incentives to conduct audits for companies that would otherwise forego systematic compliance reviews because of fear that any violations that they discover thereby will later be used against them by enforcement authorities or plaintiffs in citizen suits.

125. Rechtschaffen and Markell, *Reinventing Environmental Enforcement*, 157.

126. EPA's formal position with respect to the minimum enforcement authority that states with audit and privilege law must demonstrate to satisfy program delegation standards was set forth in U.S. EPA Memorandum from Steven A. Herman, et al. to Regional Administrators, et al., February 14, 1997.

127. Interview with Mike Walker. In 1995, EPA issued an audit policy (later revised modestly) that sought to encourage environmental auditing, without adopting a privilege and immunity approach. Under this policy, the Agency committed not to seek "gravity-based penalties" for firms that conduct audits, so long as the firm's violations are identified voluntarily, disclosed to EPA promptly, and corrected expeditiously. However, under this policy, the Agency might still decide to seek penalties to remove any economic gains that the company has realized as a result of its noncompliance. See "Incentives for Self-Policing: Discovery, Disclosure, Correction, and Prevention of Violations," 65 Fed. Reg. 19618 (April 11, 2000). Steve Herman considers this policy to be one of the signal achievements of his time in office. Interview with Steve Herman.

128. F.3d 894 (8th Cir. 1999).

129. For an analysis of those cases, see Joel A. Mintz, "Enforcement 'Overfiling' in the Federal Courts: Some Thoughts on the Post-*Harmon* Cases," *Virginia Environmental Law Journal* 21 (2003):425.

130. Interview with Gail Ginsberg.

131. Interviews with Ann Nutt, Allyn Stern, Steve Herman, John Rothman, Allan Zabel, Michelle Benson, Walter Mugdan, Tinka Hyde, George Hays, Nancy Marvel, Noël Wise, Kathleen Johnson, Gail Ginsberg, Eric Schaeffer, Sylvia Lowrance, Lois Schiffer, Bill Muno, David Nielsen, and Joe Boyle.

132. Interviews with several federal employees who preferred not to be identified. Another EPA attorney opined that the relationship varied from regional office to regional office. Interview with George Hays.

133. Interviews with Bruce Buckheit and Tinka Hyde. Buckheit told me: "[A]t times our relationship was contentious as we argued over things we were passionate about—usually about tactics rather than where to go. But that was never mostly the case. It was more like [we had occasional] differences within a family. We [at EPA] were never at war with the Department [of Justice]." Interview with Bruce Buckheit.

134. Interviews with Gail Ginsberg, Mimi Newton, George Czerniak, Eric Schaeffer, David Nielsen, Rett Nelson, Tom Bramscher, Allan Zabel, and Michelle Benson.

135. Interview with George Czerniak.

136. Interview with an EPA regional enforcement attorney who asked not to be identified by name.

137. Interview with Bill Muszynski. "DOJ's attitude was that they represent[ed] the United States, and not necessarily EPA. EPA's attorneys were more inclined to support the Agency's views. This caused some tension at times. Nonetheless, there was mutual respect." *Accord* interview with Larry Kyte.

138. Credit for EPA's good enforcement relationship with DOJ should also be given to John Cruden, a talented mid-level manager at DOJ. As Mike Walker put it, EPA-DOJ working relations in enforcement were "much improved, largely because of John Cruden. He's a wonderful man. He has sympathy for what it is like to be a client working for DOJ. He has done a great job." Interview with Mike Walker.

139. Interview with Steve Herman.

140. Interview with Lois Schiffer.

141. Interviews with John Cruden, Nancy Marvel, Kathleen Johnson, Mike Walker, Lois Schiffer, Tom Bramscher, John Rothman, Mimi Newton, David Buente, Bill Muno, and Allyn Stern. Part of the reason for this may have been the fact that U.S. Attorneys were (and are) not permitted to handle civil EPA enforcement cases without prior approval of DOJ headquarters. No such approval was (or is) required, however, as a prerequisite to their prosecuting environmental criminal cases. Interview with John Rothman.

142. Interviews with Nancy Marvel, David Nielsen, Eric Schaeffer, Rett Nelson, Mike Walker, Joe Boyle, Felicia Marcus. Tinka Hyde viewed that variation as being a function of the relative size and burdensomeness of the offices' caseloads. Interview with Tinka Hyde.

143. In particular, the U.S. Attorneys' offices in New York, Brooklyn, Las Vegas, Los Angeles, Chicago, Milwaukee, and San Diego were identified by people I interviewed as having been heavily involved in environmental enforcement cases, at one time or another, during the Clinton period. In all likelihood, this is an incomplete list.

144. Interview with David Nielsen. *Accord* interviews with Mike Stahl, Nancy Marvel, Walter Mugdan, and David Buente.

145. Interviews with Rett Nelson and John Lyons.

146. Interview with David Buente.

147. Interview with Kathleen Johnson.

148. Interview with Steve Herman.

149. Interviews with Gail Ginsberg, Eric Schaeffer, Steve Herman, Tinka Hyde, Mimi Newton, Allyn Stern, Bob Tolpa, Bill Muno, Bill Muszynski, Bob Kaplan, Rett Nelson, Sylvia Lowrance, Tom Bramscher, Ann Nutt, Walter Mugden, Nancy Marvel, and David Buente.

150. Interview with Steve Herman.

151. Interviews with Mike Stahl and Lois Schiffer.

152. Interview with Carol Browner. Browner indicated that her working relationships with the heads of other agencies and departments in the executive branch were generally cordial and mutually respectful.

153. Ibid.

154. Interview with Walter Mugdan.

155. Interviews with Sylvia Lowrance, Bob Tolpa, Gail Ginsberg, Steve Herman, David Nielsen, Ann Nutt, George Czerniak, Eric Schaeffer, Tom Bramscher, Tinka Hyde, Rett Nelson, Bruce Gelber, and John Cruden.

156. Interview with an EPA enforcement manager who asked not to be identified by name.

157. For example, in its enforcement investigation of the diesel truck industry, EPA found that the industry had developed and was using engine software that could run the vehicle clean when it was being tested by the Agency, but then triple the NOx emissions when the truck was on the highway (in exchange for much better engine fuel economy). That approach by the industry produced approximately one million tons per year of NOx air pollutant emissions that EPA had not previously inventoried. The industry's settlement agreement with the federal government resulted in over $1 billion in injunctive relief, and the payment of substantial penalties. Interview with Bruce Buckheit.

158. Interview with Bruce Buckheit. See also David Stout, "Seven Utilities Sued by U.S. on Charges of Polluting Air," *New York Times*, November 9, 1999, A1.

159. See Joel A. Mintz, "Treading Water," *Environmental Law Reporter 34* (October 2004): 10916–10919.

160. Interviews with Eric Schaeffer, Walter Mugdan, Joe Boyle, and Cheryl Wasserman.

161. Interview with David Nielsen.

162. Ibid.

163. Interview with Eric Schaeffer.

164. Interview with Gail Ginsberg.

165. Interview with Eric Schaeffer.

166. Interview with David Buente. *Accord* interviews with Mike Walker, Gail Ginsberg, and Lois Schiffer.

167. Interview with an EPA attorney familiar with the criminal enforcement program who preferred to remain anonymous. *Accord*, interview with David Buente.

168. Interview with David Buente.

169. Ibid.

170. Interview with Mike Walker.

171. Interview with Rett Nelson.

172. Interviews with Carol Browner, Lois Schiffer, Steve Herman, Bill Muno, Kathleen Johnson, Michelle Benson, and Bill Muszynski.

173. A number of these administrative reforms were subsequently codified by Congress in the Small Business Liability and Brownfields Revitalization Act of 2003.

174. Interview with Steve Herman. *Accord* interviews with Bill Muno, Lois Schiffer, Kathleen Johnson, and Bruce Gelber. As Bruce Gelber put it, "the Superfund administrative reform effort was a real credit to EPA. They listened and did what was necessary."

175. Some examples of SEPs may include monetary donations by the defendant for environmental scientific studies, dedications of tracts of land for local

public parks, and agreements by the defendant to restore damaged natural resources in a particular location.

176. Interview with Gail Ginsberg. *Accord*, e.g., interviews with Rett Nelson and Tom Bramscher.

177. Interview with Gail Ginsberg.

178. Interview with Bruce Gelber.

179. Interviews with George Czerniak and Gail Ginsberg.

180. Interview with Felicia Marcus.

181. Interview with Eric Schaeffer. At the same time, however, Schaeffer carefully noted that this approach to evaluating enforcement does raise a number of issues that must be addressed. He observed that "you can report a 'record year' for injunctive relief or pollution reduction by settling only very big cases" (e.g., with utilities or city wastewater plants).

182. Interview with Gail Ginsberg. *Accord* interview with Ann Lassiter. "This was a very, very tough job," Lassiter said. "There were always a lot of unknowns. . . . Over time we've gotten more systematic about doing it. But I still wouldn't take those numbers to the bank."

183. Interviews with Mimi Newton, David Nielsen, and Ann Lassiter. Newton also noted that measuring the amount of pollution cleaned up by enforcement cases tends to downplay the importance of some substances (such as nerve gas) which are extremely dangerous in small volumes.

184. Interview with Sylvia Lowrance.

185. See notes 152 to 153 above.

186. See notes 149 to 150 above.

187. See note 19 above.

188. See notes 116 to 135 above.

189. Interview with Gail Ginsberg. *Accord* interview with an EPA regional attorney who asked not to be identified by name.

190. Interview with an EPA manager who requested anonymity. *Accord* interview with Gail Ginsberg. Another person I interviewed, who declined to speak for attribution, stated that "under reinvention, excellence took a back seat. Form over substance was what prevailed."

191. Interview with Mike Stahl.

192. Interview with an EPA attorney who requested anonymity.

Chapter Eight

1. Interview with David Ullrich. *Accord* interview with Sylvia Lowrance.

2. Interview with Linda Fisher.

3. "EPA Budget Request Includes Staff Cut at Enforcement Office, Grants to States," *BNA Environment Reporter*, February 8, 2002, 286.

4. *Inside EPA*, August 31, 2001, 1, 16.

5. "Jeffords Announces New Investigation of Schregardus in Wake of EPA Report," *BNA Environment Reporter*, September 14, 2001, 1776; Katharine Q. Seelye, "EPA Faults Ohio Agency Headed by a Bush Nominee," *New York Times*,

September 5, 2001, A12; Katharine Q. Seelye, "EPA Enforcement Nominee Withdraws," *New York Times*, September 18, 2001, A16.

6. Interview with Gail Ginsberg.

7. Interview with Sylvia Lowrance.

8. See Douglas Jehl, "EPA to Abandon New Arsenic Limits for Water Supply," *New York Times*, March 21, 2001, A1. After embarrassing public criticism by environmental organizations and scientists, and a 97–1 vote in the Senate in favor of new arsenic standards, this decision was reversed by the Bush II administration several months later. See "Senate Backs New Standards for Arsenic Levels," *New York Times*, August 2, 2001, A16; Katharine Q. Seelye, "Arsenic Standard for Water Is Too Low, Study Concludes, *New York Times*, Sept. 11, 2001, A20; Katharine Q. Seelye, "EPA to Adopt Clinton Arsenic Standard," *New York Times*, November 1, 2001, A18.

9. See Douglas Jehl and Andrew C. Revkin, "Bush, In Reversal, Won't Seek Cut in Emissions of Carbon Dioxide," *New York Times*, March 14, 2001, A1; and Douglas Jehl, "Bush Defends Emissions Stance," *New York Times*, March 15, 2001, A23.

10. Interview with Linda Fisher. Fisher also noted that her SES rotation proposal was consistent with a previous suggestion of EPA's Human Resources Council, which had recommended that the Agency develop a workplace development strategy, including a senior executive succession planning component. For additional explanation of the SES rotation, see Memorandum from Linda Fisher to All SES Members, "Senior Executive Service Mobility Program," November 14, 2001.

11. Interview with Mike Walker.

12. Interview with Gail Ginsberg.

13. E.g., interviews with Mike Stahl ("If done in a fair way, I think it can actually be a positive for the organization"), Eric Schaeffer ("I didn't see [the SES rotation] as either political or a bad thing; on the other hand, you do need at least five years in a major office to have a major impact there"), and Walter Mugdan ("Among the SES, there was neither universal happiness nor universal skepticism with the rotation, especially after it was implemented").

14. Interview with Linda Fisher.

15. This NSR "reform initiative" and its consequences did not go unnoticed by investigative journalists. In the spring of 2004, the *New York Times* published two separate detailed accounts of it: Christopher Drew and Richard A. Oppel Jr., "How Industry Won the Battle of Pollution Control," *New York Times*, March 6, 2004, A1; and Bruce Barcott, "Changing All the Rules," *New York Times Magazine*, April 4, 2004, 38. In addition to the comments of those whom I interviewed, this section relies on the information gathered by those journalists. The accuracy of that information was independently confirmed by several EPA officials I spoke with who had read the newspaper analyses in question and had firsthand familiarity with the NSR reform dispute.

16. See 42 U.S.C. 7401 et seq., sub-chap. I, parts C and D.

17. The major exception to this was in EPA Region IX, where a number of NSR enforcement cases were initiated against power plants in the early 1990s and thereafter.

18. Interview with Bob Kaplan. *Accord*, interview with John Cruden ("Without question, Bruce Buckheit made a significant contribution to enhancing Clean Air Act enforcement of new source review requirements during his tenure as the head of the air enforcement program").

19. Interview with Bruce Buckheit.

20. Ibid.

21. Interview with Bob Kaplan.

22. In what later became a controversial tactic, the lawsuits included *all* violation counts found by EPA investigators, both minor and major. J. P. Suarez told me that he viewed that as a poor tactic that allowed opponents of the initiative to "distort" the debate regarding NSR. "If I were head of EPA enforcement at that time," he stated, "I would not have included a good one-third to one-half of the counts in the cases that were brought." Interview with J. P. Suarez. Bruce Buckheit later agreed with Suarez in the sense that "in hindsight, from a political standpoint," it would have been more advantageous only to file "the sexier claims" against utility defendants. Buckheit noted, however, that up to that point the filing of *all* viable, legally supportable claims against defendants in civil judicial enforcement cases was the usual practice of the DOJ and EPA. He also observed that, since it was unprecedented, OECA could not reasonably have anticipated political interference by the White House with any EPA cases or initiatives. Telephone conversation with Bruce Buckheit, August 3, 2004.

23. Interview with Bruce Buckheit.

24. Interview conducted "off the record" with an EPA official. I received similar comments in interviews with other EPA officials, including Bert Frey ("The NSR cases involved immense amounts of NOx and SOx emissions, often as much as 50,000 tons per year of excess emissions of S0x from one plant—those are huge amounts of pollution"); and George Czerniak (who said that the NSR initiative was aimed at "a significant part of the potential emissions that were there to be reduced").

25. Ibid.

26. Ibid.

27. Report of the National Energy Policy Development Group (May 2001).

28. Interview with Jeffrey Holmstead.

29. Ibid.

30. Ibid.

31. Ibid. See also David E. Sanger, "In Energy Plan, Bush Urges New Drilling, Conservation and Nuclear Power Review," *New York Times*, May 17, 2001, A1.

32. Interview with Bob Kaplan; Christopher Marquis, "EPA Power Plant Cases to Proceed, Ashcroft Says," *New York Times*, January 16, 2002, A12.

33. Barcott, "Changing All the Rules," 76–77.

34. See Katharine Q. Seelye, "White House Seeks a Change in Rules on Air Pollution," *New York Times*, June 14, 2001, A1. According to a DOJ attorney who preferred anonymity, EPA did not follow its typical procedure and formally consult with the DOJ prior to proposing and then promulgating this significant regulatory change.

35. Interview with J. P. Suarez.

36. Ibid.

37. See "Six Senate Chairmen Call on Whitman to Repropose Changes to Clean Air Program," *BNA Environment Reporter*, March 8, 2002, 526; "Whitman, Lieberman Spar over Future of Enforcement Actions against Utilities," *BNA Environment Reporter*, March 15, 2002, 575; "Senate Democratic Threatens to Block EPA Changes to Enforcement Program," *BNA Environment Reporter*, August 2, 2002, 1695; "Senators Press Whitman to Better Pursue NSR Enforcement Cases," *Inside EPA*, October 25, 2002, 19; "Bipartisan House Letter to EPA Chief Opposes Changes to Enforcement Program," *BNA Environment Reporter*, August 2, 2002, 1696. See also David Kocieniewski, "States to Fight Easing of Rules on Pollution by Power Plants," *New York Times*, August 29, 2003, B1; Richard A. Oppel Jr. and Christopher Drew, "Senators and Attorneys General Seek Investigation into EPA Rules Change," *New York Times*, November 7, 2003, A25.

38. The government's negotiating position was also harmed when Administrator Whitman, testifying before the Senate Committee on Government Affairs in March 2002, stated that, if she were an attorney for a utility defendant, she would not settle with the government until she knew the outcome of a challenge by the Tennessee Valley Authority to EPA's then-existing NSR rules. Though the statement appears to have been made without any intention of interfering with any ongoing negotiations, nonetheless it had the effect of discouraging utility industry settlement. Barcott, "Changing All the Rules," 73.

39. Ibid.

40. See Katherine Q. Seelye, "Top EPA Official Quits Criticizing Bush's Policies," *New York Times*, February 28, 2002, A15; and Jennifer Lee, "Three Top EPA Officials Say They Will Leave EPA," *New York Times*, January 6, 2002, A15.

41. See Katherine Q. Seelye, "Often Isolated, Whitman Quits as EPA Chief," *New York Times*, May 22, 2003, A1.

42. Christopher Drew and Richard A. Oppel Jr., "Lawyers at EPA Say It Will Drop Pollution Cases," *New York Times*, November 6, 2003, A1.

43. *New York v. EPA*, citation (December 24, 2003).

44. "EPA to File New Lawsuits for Violations of New Source Review, Leavitt Says," *BNA Environment Reporter*, January 27, 2004, 2435.

45. Interview with David Schultz and Louise Gross.

46. "Fiscal Years (FY) 2005–2007 National Program Managers Guidance—Supplement," undated memorandum of Marcus Peacock, deputy administrator, EPA (October 2005).

47. Interview with Adam Kushner.

48. Interview with Eric Cohen. Similar comments were made in interviews with George Czerniak and David Schultz.

49. *New York v. EPA*, 443 F.3d 880 (D.C. Cir. 2006).

50. Ibid., 887.

51. 549 U.S. 561 (2007).

52. Interviews with John Cruden, David Schultz, and Bruce Gelber.

53. Interview with David Schultz.

54. Interview with an EPA official who requested anonymity.

55. Interview with Steve Rothblatt.

56. Interview with Eric Schaeffer.

57. Interview with Bruce Buckheit.

58. Interview with J. P. Suarez.

59. National Academies Press, *Air Emissions from Animal Feeding Operations: Current Knowledge, Future Needs* (2003).

60. Interview with an EPA official who requested anonymity.

61. This controversy continued well into the second term of the Bush II administration. Ultimately, OECA and the Office of Water reached a draft compromise on the issue that paralleled an agreement that had been reached outside of the Agency between water utilities and environmental organizations. However, the interoffice compromise was later reviewed and rejected by the White House Council on Environmental Quality and the Office of Management and Budget. It was never finalized. Interview with Ben Grumbles.

62. Interview with an EPA employee who spoke off the record. This view was shared by a number of other EPA officials whom I spoke with, e.g., an EPA attorney who requested anonymity ("[The administration] is pro-energy and pro-industry. . . . Every time they can weaken the regulations they do so; they are trying to relax everything in sight"); Bill Muszynski ("There has been more engagement [in this administration] in the working pieces of the programs by political appointees; there seems to be more external pressure to make changes in EPA's regulations than had previously been true"); and another EPA lawyer who preferred not to be identified by name ("There is a tremendous lack of courage and convictions in the Agency overall, and there is very little support for decisiveness outside of this region").

63. Interview with Tom Bramscher.

64. Interview with an EPA regional enforcement attorney who spoke on condition of anonymity.

65. Interview with Cheryl Wasserman.

66. Interview with Mike Walker.

67. Interview with Tom Mintz.

68. Interview with an EPA employee who requested anonymity. See also "EPA Staff Morale Slumps amid Fears of Budget Cuts, Controversy," *Inside EPA*, November 22, 2002, 1. Notably, those kinds of perceptions were not unanimous. I was also told that "[m]orale in Region IX is not too bad" (interview with Ann Lyons) and Rick Duffy said, "I still think that what we do here is worth doing. I'm proud that I work here. I hope that we're able to do our job and make the world a better place for our kids." Interview with Rick Duffy.

69. Interview with an EPA official who requested anonymity.

70. 531 U.S. 159, 121 S.Ct. 675 (2001).

71. See "DOJ Opposes Appeal of the Wetlands Case Limiting EPA Authority," *Inside EPA*, May 17, 2002, 1.

72. 547 U.S. 715 (2006).

73. Toward the end of his tenure, J. P. Suarez initiated what appears to have been a useful review and restructuring of EPA's criminal enforcement program. In his words: "We made some changes that are very painful but nonetheless important changes in the criminal program. . . . I think you are [now] going to see a criminal enforcement program that is appropriately focused on its core mission. It will be better integrated and you will see leadership that is more involved with the day-to-day activities of EPA." Interview with J. P. Suarez.

74. Interview with two EPA attorneys who requested anonymity. Interview with George Czerniak.

75. See "GOP Support for Superfund Tax Raises Industry Fear on Energy Bill," *Inside EPA*, February 15, 2001, 1; "Bush Administration Reconsidering Superfund Tax Authorization," *Inside EPA*, April 12, 2002, 5; "With Trust Fund Depleting, Battle Brews over Whether to Reinstate Industry Taxes," *BNA Environment Reporter*, May 10, 2004, 1078; and "Democrats Press Unlikely Superfund Tax Reauthorization Bill," *Inside EPA*, February 21, 2003, 15.

76. Interview with Bill Muno. With regard to this trend, Kathleen Johnson perceptively observed: "From my perspective that is a bad cycle to get into. If we don't put sites on the NPL [National Priorities List], Congress will reduce its funding of the program, based on a perceived lack of need, and the program will spiral downward. I think that the reality is that there continues to be a critical need for the Superfund Program." Interview with Kathleen Johnson. In fact, there is some evidence that EPA increased the number of sites listed on the NPL during 2004.

77. Interview with Gail Ginsberg. During the second Bush II term the emphasis in the Superfund Program shifted. Greater emphasis was placed on the adequacy of financial assurance offered by PRPs and on institutional controls at already remediated hazardous waste sites. At the same time, the volume of "construction completions" at sites declined. Interview with Larry Kyte.

78. James R. May, "Now More Than Ever: Trends in Environmental Citizen Suits at 30," *Widener Law Review* 10 (2003): 1, 43.

79. "New Report Charges Enforcement Penalties Decline under Bush EPA," *Inside EPA*, November 8, 2002, 4.

80. "Dingell Targets Whitman in Attack on EPA Enforcement Decline," *Inside EPA*, February 7, 2003, 9.

81. "EPA Acknowledges Funding Pinch Has Slowed Superfund Cleanups," *Inside EPA*, February 8, 2002. These quantitative decreases in EPA enforcement outputs were widely reported in the press. See, e.g., Chris Bowman, "EPA under Bush Not as Aggressive," *Sacramento Bee*, May 25, 2003; "EPA Data Shows Drop in Administrative Enforcement Actions," *Inside EPA*, July 5, 2002, 1. Notably, some more recent enforcement statistics from the Bush II period are more positive. In FY03, for example, DOJ collected more than $300 million in penalties, a very high sum for a single year. Interview with John Cruden.

82. See text at notes 4 and 5 above.

83. See "Bush Nominates N.J. Gaming Official to Be Head of EPA Enforcement Division," *BNA Environment Reporter*, March 1, 2002, 484.

84. "Boxer Blocks Enforcement Pick over EPA Stalling on Superfund Data," *Inside EPA*, June 21, 2002, 1.

85. Interview with Linda Fisher.

86. Interview with Bob Tolpa. Similar comments were made by other EPA enforcement staff members and managers. From interview with Bob Kaplan: "J. P. is outstanding. He is first-rate. He is tough on enforcement and a strong voice. He is someone the career people are very happy with." From interview with Rick Duffy: "Suarez packaged and gave new impetus to some good things that were ongoing. He also came in with some new ideas." From interview with Cheryl

Wasserman: "J. P. Suarez is wonderful—a great guy. He really appreciates and cares about enforcement." From interview with Mike Stahl: "J. P. tried very hard to do the right thing, and in his heart he was in fact interested in enforcing the law. For the short time he was here, J. P. did a very nice job of identifying the appropriate strategic direction for the program. If you talk to the career staff, he would get very positive reviews for what he tried to do and the way he interacted with people."

87. "Industry Says EPA Enforcement Database May Violate Data Rules," *Inside EPA*, April 4, 2003, 10.

88. Interview with Mike Stahl. Regrettably, however, the Bush II administration consistently refused to allow the posting of data regarding industrial releases of toxic air pollutants to the atmosphere that had been submitted to the Agency by regulated companies under the Toxics Release Inventory (TRI) program mandated by the federal Emergency Planning and Community Right-to-Know Act. Interview with two EPA officials who requested anonymity.

89. Interview with J. P. Suarez.

90. In fact, a number of features of "Smart Enforcement" appear similar to the notion of "Focused Enforcement" that was in vogue at EPA during part of the Clinton administration.

91. Interview with J. P. Suarez.

92. For a more complete discussion of the notion of "Smart Enforcement," see "Environmental Results through Smart Enforcement," OECA Accomplishments Report, FY02, EPA-300-R-03-002 (2002).

93. See text at notes 34 to 42.

94. Interview with J. P. Suarez.

95. Ibid.

96. Katharine Q. Seelye, "Often Isolated," A1.

97. Through an aide, Whitman informed me that she has a "no interview policy" and that she would be unavailable to speak with me as I conducted research for this article. She did not, however, rule out the possibility of my interviewing her following the 2004 general elections. In press accounts at the time of her resignation from EPA, Whitman was described as "the odd woman out in the Bush administration." Katharine Q. Seelye, "Often Isolated," A1. She was also characterized as "a northeast Republican moderate" who "always seemed out of step with this conservative administration." Ibid., A27.

98. Interview with J. P. Suarez.

99. Ibid. In contrast, Suarez had high praise for the career staff in EPA's Office of Enforcement and Compliance Assurance ("Really some of the best, most dedicated, talented individuals I ever had the pleasure to work with"), and for Christine Whitman ("She was a fabulous leader and administrator"). A team player, he also complimented the Bush II White House ("I think it is important to say, politically, that an obstacle that was never before me was political resistance to what we wanted to do save one exception, and that was NSR").

100. According to press accounts, those other candidates included at least Idaho Governor Dirk Kempthorne, Florida Secretary of the Department of Environmental Regulation David Struhs, Region V Regional Administrator Tom Skinner, Josephine Cooper of the Alliance of Automobile Manufacturers, and

Deputy Secretary of Agriculture Jim Moseley. See "Whitman's Departure Sets Stage for Partisan Clash over Replacement," *Inside EPA*, May 23, 2003, 1; and "White House Facing Competing Pressures Picking New EPA Nominee," *Inside EPA*, May 30, 2003, 16.

101. "Senate GOP Moves to Head Off Bush Recess Appointment for Leavitt," *Inside EPA*, October 3 2003, 1.

102. Jennifer Lee, "After Long Delay, Senate Confirms Utah Governor as Head of EPA," *New York Times*, October 29, 2003, A20.

103. Interview with Tom Skinner.

104. Interview with Mike Stahl.

105. Interview with Tom Skinner.

106. Interview with an EPA official who requested anonymity.

107. See *Massachusetts v. EPA*, 547 U.S. 407 (2007).

108. These criticisms reached a crescendo in the spring of 2008, when Carl Pope, the executive director of the Sierra Club, wrote on his blog: "Time and again, Steve Johnson has shown that, whatever his personal views, and regardless of his oath of office to uphold 'the law,' he is entirely a creature of the whim of the president, the vice president, and other White House officials. . . . Steve Johnson has so fundamentally violated his duty that he simply needs to resign—now." "Activists Look to Congress to Bolster Push for Johnson Resignation," *Inside EPA*, March 21, 2008, 1, 15.

109. "Conflicts Raise Rhetoric over Johnson's Leadership," *Inside EPA*, March 7, 2008, 1, 5; "To Maintain Dialogue with EPA, Unions Snub Johnson Resignation Call," *Inside EPA*, June 20, 2008, 1, 14, 15.

110. For example, one EPA headquarters enforcement official told me that Johnson was "extremely disappointing in his work habits and his integrity. He was the worst person for the Agency. It was really bad." Interview with Cheryl Wasserman. Another longtime EPA employee from the Agency's Midwest regional office opined that Johnson was even "less beneficial" to the EPA's mission than Anne Gorsuch had been. He stated: "When Gorsuch came in she was the outsider. Most of the Agency, including middle management, resisted her programs. [In contrast], Johnson was sold as 'one of our own coming through the ranks,' and the middle management were not as resistant to some programs he instituted that were contrary to the Agency's mission." Interview with Charles ("Chuck") Orzihoskie.

111. Interview with Ben Grumbles.

112. Interview with Grant Nakayama.

113. Interview with Gary Jonesi. His first encounters with the Agency's enforcement staff left Nakayama impressed as well. He stated: "I can't say enough about the people in OECA, they are tremendous. I really enjoyed working there. It was one of the most fulfilling things I have ever done." Interview with Grant Nakayama.

114. Interview with Grant Nakayama.

115. Nakayama had a small number of detractors, who criticized his decisions to replace longtime civil servants with his own appointees in certain management positions in his office (all of whom preferred not to be identified by name). However, most enforcement staff members whom I interviewed were fulsome in their

praise of Nakayama's work at EPA. Interview with Eric Cohen: "Nakayama was a beacon out there for enforcement." Interview with George Czerniak: "Nakayama really pushed the enforcement program as far as it could be pushed. I was really pleased to work under his leadership." Interview with Adam Kushner: "Grant had wisdom, institutional knowledge, and wherewithal. He spoke softly but carried a big stick. He kept his head down, called it straight and did his work." Interview with Cheryl Wasserman: "Grant Nakayama was known for his support for enforcement. He went after [violators] and continued to go after them." Interview with Jonathan Libber: "Grant Nakayama was probably the best [assistant administrator] for enforcement we ever had, and I've seen a lot of them. He was phenomenal in his commitment to the environment, a quick study, and a real advocate for our position." Interview with Richard Emory: "My impression is that he was about as good as [we] could get for enforcement in those times. He was a man of integrity and mental rigor." Interview with Michael Stahl: "Grant ran interference for the [enforcement] program very effectively. . . . He went to bat many times on substantive issues between enforcement and other parts of EPA. I think he deserves a lot of credit for that, and for steering the program through what would otherwise have been a difficult time." Interview with Catherine McCabe: "He was a brilliant man, a great leader, a wonderful boss, and truly dedicated to doing the right thing. He stood up for enforcement." Nakayama also won praise from the Department of Justice (interview with John Cruden) and from the EPA deputy administrator whom he reported to (interview with Marcus Peacock).

116. Interview with Grant Nakayama.

117. One particularly effective partnership was developed with Wayne Nastri, the regional administrator in EPA Region IX. Like Nakayama, Nastri was also a strong proponent of enforcement, who was respected and liked by the EPA enforcement personnel in his regional office. Interviews with Nancy Marvel and an EPA attorney who preferred to remain anonymous.

118. Under EPA's internal procedures where at least two Agency offices, including regional offices, object to a proposed new rule, EPA's deputy administrator must arbitrate the dispute. Interviews with Grant Nakayama and Marcus Peacock.

119. Interviews with Mike Stahl, George Czerniak, Marcus Peacock, and Lisa Lund. "Global settlements" are cases that involve particular companies that have violations at multiple facilities.

120. Interviews with David Buente, George Czerniak, Nancy Marvel, Bruce Gelber, John Cruden, Jonathan Libber, Catherine McCabe, Bert Frey, Tom Skinner, Mike Walker, and Rett Nelson.

121. Interviews with Catherine McCabe, Nancy Marvel, Bert Frey, Rett Nelson, Tom Skinner, and Bruce Gelber. CSOs are facilities in which rainwater runoff from streets and roads is collected in the same pipe as domestic sewage and liquid industrial wastes. SSOs, which are designed only to collect sewage, sometimes overflow where the sewage system has inadequate capacity or where it is operated or maintained inadequately.

122. Interview with Jonathan Libber.

123. Interview with Grant Nakayama; "New EPA Website to Report Violations Will Strengthen Program, Nakayama Says," *BNA Environment Reporter*,

December 8, 2005, 2502; "EPA Creates Website Listing Violators of Environmental Law Fleeing Prosecution," *BNA Environment Reporter*, December 12, 2006, 2462.

124. Interview with Bill Wehrum.

125. Ibid. Jeff Holmstead took a similar view in our interview, stating, "You undercut the government's ability to deal fairly with the regulated community if you give enforcement folks a rolling mandate to bring lawsuits based on exploiting uncertainties and confusion in the law." Interview with Jeff Holmstead.

126. Interview with Bill Wehrum.

127. Interview with Grant Nakayama.

128. Interview with Jeff Holmstead.

129. Interview with George Czerniak.

130. Interview with Ben Grumbles.

131. Interview with an EPA official who did not wish to be identified by name.

132. "Program Description of National Environmental Achievement Track," 55 Federal Register, 41655–41663 (July 6, 2000).

133. Some EPA officials referred to Performance Track as "the gold standard" among its partnership programs with the regulated community.

134. U.S. EPA, National Environmental Performance Track, North Central Texas EMS Work Group Meeting, Briefing Document by Craig Weeks and Israel Anderson, EPA Region VI, Arlington, TX, March 2, 2007, and interview with an EPA employee who requested anonymity.

135. Ibid.

136. Interview with an EPA employee who asked to remain anonymous.

137. Interview with Marcus Peacock.

138. U.S. EPA Office of Inspector General, "Performance Track Could Improve Program Design and Management to Ensure Value," Report No. 2007-P-00013, March 29, 2007. Performance Track was later criticized sharply in the press as well. See John Shiffman and John Sullivan, "Green Club an EPA Charade," *Philadelphia Inquirer*, December 3, 2008.

139. Interview with Marcus Peacock.

140. Interview with an EPA official who requested anonymity. *Accord*, interviews with Bob Tolpa, Rett Nelson, Kathleen Johnson (as to Superfund enforcement), and Mimi Newton (as to RCRA underground storage tank enforcement on tribal lands). See also "EPA Budget Request Includes Staff Cut at Enforcement Office, Grants to States," *BNA Environment Reporter*, February 8, 2002, 286; "EPA Officials Brace for Cuts in Stripped Down FY04 Spending Bill," *Inside EPA*, July 25, 2003, 1.

141. Interview with Tinka Hyde.

142. Interview with Bert Frey. This office was able to hire eleven new attorneys in FY03. However, even this addition to its staff left it short of previous higher levels of staffing. Ibid. From FY96 to FY04, the number of full-time employees in Region V's regulatory enforcement programs fell from 367 to 268. Interview with Tinka Hyde.

143. Interview with Tinka Hyde.

144. Interview with J. P. Suarez.

145. Interview with Adam Kushner. Other EPA enforcement officials made similar observations following the Bush II period. Interview with Grant Nakayama: "It was a really tough budget environment. We were very prudent with our budget . . . [but] we could always have done more with more money." Interview with Mike Stahl: "OECA was getting squeezed to the point where extramural dollars were a real problem. . . . OECA was in a pretty hard place to find where it could cover its on-board staff and still have a viable program." Interview with Gary Jonesi: "We can use more resources. It is tough to do the job when we're a small agency and enforcement is a small outfit." Interview with Jonathan Libber: "Resources are a real problem around here. We really do not have the resources we need to do the job in front of us."

146. Interviews with Larry Kyte (who noted delays in cleanups at "orphan sites" as a result of funding shortfalls) and Grant Nakayama (who observed that with more adequate funding EPA could have hired more civil investigators to identify PRPs in certain Superfund cases).

147. Interviews with two EPA employees who asked not to be identified by name. Those individuals made note of the fact that during the Bush II administration, the Agency failed to have the full complement of two hundred criminal investigators required by Congress in the Federal Pollution Prevention Act.

148. Interviews with Adam Kushner (who cited a particular need to update EPA's electronic TRI data system) and Lisa Lund, who said, "We don't get a lot of resources to modernize our [data management] systems or to do some of the things that new technology now allows you to do. We are constantly playing catch-up with that and trying to address crises instead of being able to get out ahead and prevent crises."

149. Interview with Mike Stahl.

150. Interviews with Mimi Newton ("[In RCRA enforcement] we need more attorneys, we need more inspectors, we need more equipment, and we need more training") and Richard Emory, who noted that EPA has numerous import-export programs scattered throughout the Agency, each of which has its own record-keeping system. This internal disorganization has made it especially difficult for EPA to coordinate its efforts to enforce the export requirements of RCRA 3017 with U.S. Customs.

151. See "Resource Limits Slow DOJ's Enforcement Early in FY03," *Inside EPA*, April 4, 2003, 1.

152. Interview with David Buente. *Accord* interview with Nöel Wise.

153. Interview with George Czerniak.

154. For example, in EPA Region IX, headquartered in San Francisco, Regional Administrator Wayne Nastri directed that the regional office issue a press release for every major formal enforcement action other than the issuance of a notice of violation. Interview with Kathleen Johnson.

155. Interview with Catherine McCabe. EPA did issue a press release following its landmark settlement with American Electric Power Company. However, this settlement did little to change EPA's poor public image regarding enforcement.

156. See, e.g., Rita Boamish, "Number of Environmental Cops Decreasing," *USA Today*, July 26, 2007; Seth Borenstein, "Pollution Regulation Weak-

ens," *Detroit Free Press*, September 9, 2003; Seth Borenstein, "Pollution Citations Plummet under Bush," *Philadelphia Inquirer*, December 9, 2003. A particularly scathing picture of EPA enforcement (and regulations) was provided in a series of four articles by John Shiffman and John Sullivan in the *Philadelphia Inquirer*, which appeared on December 17–20, 2008, titled "Smoke the Mirrors: The Subversion of EPA."

157. Interview with George Czerniak ("There were some significant morale problems").

158. Interview with Mike Walker.

159. Interview with an EPA enforcement official who requested anonymity.

160. Interview with David Schultz.

161. Interviews with David Schultz, Bart Frey, Jonathan Libber, Gary Jonesi, Kathleen Johnson, Eric Cohen, Mike Stahl, Rett Nelson, Adam Kushner, and George Czerniak.

162. Interview with Mike Walker.

163. Interviews with Louise Gross and Lisa Lund.

164. Interview with Mimi Newton.

165. Ibid.

166. Interview with Bill Muszynski.

167. Interviews with Bill Muno, Larry Kyte, and Kathleen Johnson.

168. Interview with Kathleen Johnson.

169. Interview with Eric Schaeffer.

170. Interview with David Nielsen. *Accord*, interviews with Grant Nakayama, Tom Skinner, and Arthur Horowitz.

171. Interview with Adam Kushner.

172. E.g., interviews with Eric Cohen, Ann Strickland, Gary Jones, Bert Frey, Kathleen Johnson, and Mike Walker.

173. On the other hand, a few individuals I spoke with noted tensions in this relationship. Interviews with Joseph Boyle and Mike Stahl. Another EPA official noted that there are generally more tensions among professional disciplines in EPA regions where attorneys and technical people are in separate offices and answer to separate bosses. Interview with Catherine McCabe.

174. Interviews with Sylvia Lowrance, George Czerniak, and Tom Bramscher. Notably, EPA's oversight of state performance during the first term of the Bush II period was criticized harshly by the Agency's Office of Inspector General (OIG). See, e.g., "EPA Region 6 Needs to Improve Oversight of Louisiana's Environmental Programs," Final Report 2003-P-00005, U.S. EPA Office of the Inspector General, February 3, 2003.

175. Interviews with Bert Frey, Jonathan Libber, John Cruden, Arthur Horowitz, and Rett Nelson.

176. Interview with John Cruden.

177. In June 2003, Bob Kaplan, an EPA headquarters manager who had previously served as a senior attorney at the Department of Justice told me: "There is a massive budget crisis at the Department going on right now. There are no travel funds and no deposition funds. . . . They are just going on fumes. It is a desperate situation. It has affected morale." Other EPA employees I spoke with also made

note of the Justice Department's paucity of resources. Interviews with Nancy Marvel and Kathleen Johnson. Nancy Marvel also perceptively observed, "I don't think anyone has ever looked at the ratio between the resources EPA is expending to generate enforcement cases and the resources available at main Justice to handle them." Interview with Nancy Marvel.

178. Interview with J. P. Suarez. Suarez also took the position that the DOJ tends to "overstaff" some enforcement cases and to make them "overly complex," a practice that makes it difficult to get the cases brought to conclusion.

179. The U.S. Attorneys' offices that handle civil judicial enforcement cases on behalf of EPA typically tend to be located in large cities, e.g., New York, San Diego, Chicago, Los Angeles, and Las Vegas.

180. Interview with Catherine McCabe.

181. Interviews with Gail Ginsberg ("There were always conflicts with the Corps of Engineers over wetlands issues") and Sylvia Lowrance ("The Army Corps of Engineers makes no pretense of working with the EPA").

182. Interview with Bob Tolpa ("We have had a good rapport with the Corps of Engineers"); Tom Bramscher ("There has generally been a good relationship with the Corps"); and an EPA regional official who spoke on condition of anonymity ("The Corps of Engineers' cooperation in 404 cases varies from Corps district office to Corps district office. Our relationship with them depends upon the identity of the district engineer and the size of the district office's staff").

183. Interview with Bob Kaplan.

184. Interview with Grant Nakayama.

185. Interview with Ben Grumbles.

186. Deputy Administrator Marcus Peacock remarked, "If [the White House] was involved it was probably on NSR. They wanted to make sure that the NSR policy of the White House was being executed." Interview with Marcus Peacock.

187. Interviews with an EPA lawyer who asked not to be identified by name ("The White House, through OMB, has been involved in the development of policies usually, with rare exceptions, from an industry point of view"); another EPA attorney who spoke off the record ("I have a clear sense that EPA's assistant administrators have been given clear direction as to what they must do from the White House"); a senior EPA enforcement official who spoke upon condition of anonymity ("I do get the feeling that the Agency is much more under the thumb of the White House than it was under other administrations"); an EPA supervisor who asked for anonymity ("The assistant administrators and regional administrators talk directly with people in the White House; there is more control at higher levels than there used to be; we are not as independent as we may have been a while back"); and Gail Ginsberg ("I think clearly now the White House controls everything in the Bush administration"). Compare interview with J. P. Suarez: "My relationship with the White House was very good, very respectful. I appreciated their support."

188. Interview with Bruce Buckheit. I received similar observations during interviews with Nancy Marvel, Catherine McCabe, Grant Nakayama, George Czerniak, Adam Kushner, David Schultz, and Tom Skinner.

Chapter Nine

1. Beyond the selected works summarized and discussed below, the regulatory activities of EPA have also been considered in such writings as Marc K. Landy, Marc J. Roberts, and Stephen R. Thomas, *The Environmental Protection Agency: Asking the Wrong Questions* (Oxford: Oxford University Press, 1990); Bruce Ackerman and William Hassler, *Clean Coal/Dirty Air* (New Haven: Yale University Press, 1981); Alfred Marcus, "The Environmental Protection Agency," in *The Politics of Regulation*, ed. James Q. Wilson (New York: Basic Books, 1980); Alfred Marcus, *Promise and Performance: Choosing and Implementing an Environmental Policy* (Westport, Conn.: Greenwood, 1981); Christopher T. Bosso, *Pesticides and Politics: The Life Cycle of a Public Issue* (Pittsburgh: University of Pittsburgh Press, 1987); Richard A. Harris and Sidney M. Milkis, *The Politics of Regulatory Change: A Tale of Two Agencies* (Oxford: Oxford University Press, 1989); David Doniger, *The Law and Policy of Toxic Substances Control* (Baltimore: Johns Hopkins University Press, 1978); R. Shep Melnick, *Regulations and the Courts: The Case of the Clean Air Act* (Washington, D.C.: Brookings Institution, 1983); Rosemary O'Leary, "The Impact of Federal Court Decisions on the Policies and Administration of the U.S. Environmental Protection Agency," *Administrative Law Review* 41 (1989): 549; Walter A. Rosenbaum, *Environmental Politics and Policy*, 2nd ed. (Washington, D.C.: CQ Press, 1991); and B. Dan Wood, "Principals, Bureaucrats and Responsiveness in Clean Air Act Enforcements," *American Political Science Review* 82, no. 1 (March 1988).

2. Keith Hawkins and John M. Thomas, eds., *Enforcing Regulation* (Boston: Kluwer-Nijhoff, 1984).

3. Keith Hawkins and John M. Thomas, "The Enforcement Process in Regulatory Bureaucracies," in ibid., 113–115.

4. U.S. Environmental Protection Agency, *The Nation's Hazardous Waste Management Program at a Crossroads: The RCRA Implementation Study*, EPA/530-SW-90-069 (July 1990), 56.

5. See Cheryl E. Wasserman, "An Overview of Compliance and Enforcement in the United States: Philosophies, Strategies and Management Tools," in U.S. Environmental Protection Agency and Netherlands Ministry of Housing, Physical Planning and Environment, *International Enforcement Workshop Proceedings* (Utrecht, Netherlands, May 8–10, 1990), 26.

6. Personal communication with two EPA regional attorneys who preferred not to be identified.

7. Steven Shimberg, "Checks and Balances: Limitations on the Power of Congressional Oversight," in Christopher H. Schroeder and Richard J. Lazarus, eds., "Assessing the Environmental Protection Agency after Twenty Years: Law, Politics and Economics," *Duke Journal of Law and Contemporary Problems* 54 (Fall 1991), 247.

8. Joel D. Auerbach, *Keeping a Watchful Eye: The Politics of Congressional Oversight* (Washington, D.C.: Brookings Institution, 1990), 195.

9. See Richard J. Lazarus, "The Tragedy of Distrust in the Implementation of Federal Environmental Law," and Richard J. Lazarus, "The Neglected Question of Congressional Oversight of EPA: *Quis Custodiet Ipsos Custodes* (Who Shall

Watch the Watchers Themselves?),” in Schroeder and Lazarus, eds., “Assessing the Environmental Protection Agency,” 311–374.

10. Auerbach, *Keeping a Watchful Eye*, 1198.

11. Steven A. Cohen, “EPA: A Qualified Success,” in *Controversies in Environmental Policy*, ed. Sheldon Kaminiecki, Robert O’Brien, and Michael Clarke (Albany: SUNY Press, 1986), 1174.

12. Donald E. Mann, “Democratic Politics and Environmental Policy,” in ibid., 4.

13. U.S. General Accounting Office, *Environmental Protection Agency: Protecting Human Health and the Environment through Improved Management*, GAO/RCED-88-101 (August 1988), 2116.

14. K. Gaynor, “Too Many Cooks,” *Environmental Forum* (January/February 1989): 9, 10.

15. Interview with David Buente.

16. Interviews with Julie Becker, Phil Cummings, and Thomas Gallagher.

17. Lazarus, “The Neglected Question,” 228.

18. Ibid., 229.

19. Interviews with Thomas Adams and Julie Becker. Somewhat surprisingly, in his reply to Lazarus, Steven Shimberg appears to concede Lazarus’s point. See Shimberg, “Checks and Balances,” 244 (“Congressional oversight *does* divert valuable, scarce Agency resources” [emphasis in original]). My own research, however, does not indicate that such a diversion has created serious obstacles for EPA enforcement efforts.

20. Interviews with Anne Allen, Scott Fulton, Thomas Gallagher, Norm Niedergang, and Elaine Stanley.

21. See Lazarus, “The Neglected Question,” 212–213, 232–234.

22. Ibid., 230.

23. Shimberg, “Checks and Balances,” 244.

24. Lazarus, “The Neglected Question,” 227.

25. See, e.g., Matthew D. McCubbins and Thomas Schwartz, “Congressional Oversight Overlooked: Police Patrols and Fire Alarms,” *American Journal of Political Science* 28 (February 1984): 165; and Auerbach, *Keeping a Watchful Eye*, 121.

26. My research has not always revealed this to be the case. For example, Phil Cummings, formerly chief counsel to the Senate Committee on Environment and Public Works, candidly told me: “I was involved for so long in the business of putting pressure on [EPA] to do more that it’s hard for me mentally to give them credit for doing anything.” Interview with Phil Cummings. Another congressional staff member, who asked not to be identified by name, stated: “[In overseeing EPA enforcement] it’s the sore thumbs that get attention. You don’t really ever have a feeling of what else is out there.”

27. Lazarus, “The Neglected Question,” 230.

28. Interview with Lloyd Guerci.

29. Interview with Steven Leifer. Thomas Adams and Julie Becker were also largely critical in their assessments of congressional oversight performance.

30. Interviews with Thomas Gallagher, Elaine Stanley, Norm Niedergang, Anne Allen, and Scott Fulton. One of Fulton’s comments was reasonably typical of their views: “By and large [congressional oversight of the agency] is construc-

tive, even though it's been a pain to deal with. . . . At times, oversight has helped us focus and to identify where our weaknesses are so we can respond to them. Sometimes, when you're in the middle of it, you don't see your weaknesses as readily as someone more objective."

31. Lazarus, "The Neglected Question," 231.

32. Some observers have opined that statutory fragmentation has limited EPA's abilities to deal comprehensively with broad, cross-program environmental challenges. See, e.g., Alfred A. Marcus, "EPA's Organizational Structure," in Schroeder and Lazarus, eds. *Assessing the Environmental Protection Agency*, 39 ("[M]icro-management by Congress severely constrains EPA from balancing the costs and benefits of its many activities and from coming up with a rational calculus of what it should and should not do").

33. Jeffrey G. Miller, "Federal Enforcement," in Sheldon Novick, ed., *Law of Environmental Protection* 1, § 8.01 (1990), 8–16.

34. Lazarus, "The Neglected Question," 230.

35. This quotation appears in Cohen, "EPA: A Qualified Success," in Kaminiecki, O'Brien, and Clarke, eds., *Controversies in Environmental Policy*, 179.

36. *Observations on the Environmental Protection Agency's Budget Request for Fiscal Year 1992*, statement of Richard L. Hembra before the Senate Committee on Environment and Public Works, GAO/T-RCED-91-14, March 7, 1991. Hembra's testimony is consistent with a careful, scholarly study of the Agency's budget. James L. Regens and Robert W Rycroft, "Funding for Environmental Protection: Comparing Congressional and Executive Influences," *Social Science Journal* 26 (1989): 289–301.

37. Interviews with Norm Niedergang and Rick Duffy. See also Nancy Firestone, "Regulating Solid and Hazardous Wastes: Has Federal Regulation Lived Up to Its Mandate or Can the States Do a Better Job?," *Environmental Law Reporter* 22 (January 1992): 10039 (describing problems caused by budget shortages for implementation of the RCRA) and Environmental Law Institute, *Toward a More Effective Superfund Enforcement Program* (Washington, D.C., March 1989), 69.

38. Interviews with Thomas Adams, Julie Becker, David Buente, Maria Cintron, Scott Fulton, Steven Leifer, Rett Nelson, Eric Olson, Joyce Rechtschaffen, and Deborah Woitte.

39. Interview with Carrie Apostolou.

40. Interview with Michelle Burkett.

41. Ibid.

42. Interview with Stephanie Clough.

43. U.S. Senate Committee on Appropriations, *Department of Veterans Affairs and Housing and Urban Development and Independent Agencies Appropriations Bill*, 1991, no. 101-474, September 1990, 84–98.

Chapter Ten

1. Marver H. Bernstein, *Regulating Business by Independent Commission* (Princeton: Princeton University Press, 1955; reprinted in 1977 by Greenwood Press). All references in this chapter are to the Greenwood edition.

2. Ibid., 74–102.

3. See, e.g., Sam Poltzman, "Toward a More General Theory of Regulation," 19 *Journal of Law and Economics* 211 (1976); Richard A. Posner, "Theories of Economic Regulation," 5 *Bell Journal of Economics and Management Science* 335 (1974); George J. Stigler, "The Theory of Economic Regulation," 2 *Bell Journal of Economics and Management Science* 3 (1971); Barry M. Mitnick, *The Political Economy of Regulation* (New York: Columbia University Press, 1980); Grant McConnell, *Private Power and American Democracy* (New York: Vintage Books, 1970); John E. Chubb, *Interest Groups and the Bureaucracy* (Palo Alto: Stanford University Press, 1983); Lawrence S. Rothenberg, *Regulation, Organization and Politics: Motor Freight Policy at the Interstate Commerce Commission* (Ann Arbor: University of Michigan Press, 1994); Philip Selznick, *TVA and the Grass Roots: A Study in the Sociology of Formal Organization* (New York: Harper Torchbooks, 1966); James Q. Wilson, *Bureaucracy: What Government Agencies Do and Why They Do It* (New York: Basic Books, 1989); Roger G. Noll, *Government Regulatory Behavior: A Multidisciplinary Survey and Synthesis*, in *Regulatory Policy and The Social Sciences*, ed. Roger G. Noll (Berkeley: University of California Press, 1985); Michael E. Levine and Jennifer L. Forrence, "Regulatory Capture, Public Interest and Public Agenda: Toward a Synthesis," 6 *Journal of Economics and Organizations* 167 (1990): 167; William Gormley, "A Test of the 'Revolving Door' Hypothesis at the FCC," 23 *American Journal of Political Science* 665 (1979); William R. Freudenberg and Robert Gramling, "Bureaucratic Slippage and Failures of Agency Vigilance: The Case of the Environmental Studies Program," *Social Problems* 41 (1994): 214; Paul Sabatier, "Social Movements and Regulatory Agencies: Toward a More Adequate—and Less Pessimistic—Theory of 'Clientele Capture,'" 6 *Policy Sciences* 301 (1975); James Q. Wilson, "The Politics of Regulation," in *Social Responsibility and the Business Predicament*, ed. James W. McKie (Washington, D.C.: Brookings Institution Press, 1974), 135; and Gabriel Kolko, *The Triumph of Conservatism: A Reinterpretation of American History, 1900–1916* (New York: Free Press, 1963).

4. See e.g., Matthew D. Zinn, "Policing Environmental Regulatory Enforcement Cooperation, Capture and Citizen Suits," *Stanford Environmental Law Journal* 21 (2002): 81; Clifford Rechtscheffen, "Promoting Risk Regulation: Is Enforcement Discretion the Answer?" *Kansas Law Review* 52 (2004): 1327.

5. Bernstein, *Regulating Business*, 7.

6. Those agencies were the Interstate Commerce Commission, the Civil Aeronautics Board, the Federal Power Commission, the Federal Communications Commission, the Federal Trade Commission, the National Labor Relations Board, and the Securities and Exchange Commission, ibid., 8–9.

7. Ibid., 7.

8. Ibid., 13–73.

9. Ibid., 129.

10. Ibid.

11. Ibid.

12. Ibid., 114–116.

13. Ibid., 117.

14. Ibid., 119.

15. Ibid., 144.

16. Ibid., 144–145, 147.

17. Ibid., 274–275.

18. Ibid., 281.

19. Ibid., 166.

20. Ibid., 81.

21. Ibid., 277.

22. Ibid., 74–77.

23. Ibid., 80.

24. Ibid., 79–82.

25. Ibid., 82–83.

26. Ibid., 86–89.

27. Ibid., 91–95.

28. Ibid., 74.

29. Ibid., 154.

30. Bernstein reiterates the latter point frequently. See ibid., 2, 20, 25, 28, 32, 38, 39, 41. Louis Jaffe, "The Illusion of Ideal Administration," *Harvard Law Review* 86 (1973): 1183, 1198 (agencies cannot function absent widespread political support).

31. Bernstein, *Regulating Business*, 265–266.

32. Ibid., 217.

33. Ibid., 224.

34. Ibid., 232.

35. Ibid., 217–218.

36. Ibid., 220.

37. Ibid., 229.

38. Ibid., 235.

39. Ibid., 220.

40. Ibid., 240.

41. Ibid., 236.

42. Ibid., 223, 229.

43. Ibid., 244.

44. Ibid., 249.

45. Sidney Shapiro and Robert Glicksman, "Congress, The Supreme Court, and the Quiet Revolution in Administrative Law," *Duke Law Journal* (1988): 819.

46. Ibid., 828.

47. Ibid., notes 87–88 and accompanying text.

48. Ibid., note 41.

49. See, e.g., the 1984 amendments to the Resource Conservation and Recovery Act (RCRA), 42 U.S.C. § 6924(c)(2) (1982 and Supp. IV 1986); the 1986 amendments to the Comprehensive Environmental Response, Compensation and Liability Act (CERCLA), 42 U.S.C. 9605(b)-(c); 9604(i)(2)-(3); 9602(a); and 9616(b)-(e) (1982 and Supp. IV, 1986); the Safe Drinking Water Act, 42 U.S.C. § 200g-1(b)(1) and 300(h)-5(a) 1982 and Supp. IV 1986; the Toxic Substances Control Act, 15 U.S.C. § 2643(a) (Supp. IV 1986); the 1987 amendments to the Clean Water Act, Pub.L. No. 100-4 § 301(F); 33 U.S.C. § 1314(m) (West Supp. 1988); § 1342(p)(4) and § 1342(p)(6) and 1342(d)(2)(A)(I); and the 1988 amendments to the Federal Insecticide Fungicide and Rodenticide Act, Pub.L. No. 100-532, § 102(a) § 3 A.

50. E.g., the standards imposed on EPA regarding establishment of Clean Air Act National Ambient Air Quality Standards (NAAQS), 42 U.S.C. § 109.

51. See, e.g., 33 U.S.C. § 1311(g)(4) (West Supp. 1988); 42 U.S.C. § 11, 023(e) (Supp. IV, 1986).

52. See, e.g., 42 U.S.C. § 7604; 33 U.S.C. § 1365; 15 U.S.C. § 2619; 42 U.S.C. § 300j-8; 42 U.S.C .§ 6972; and 42 U.S.C. § 9659a.

53. Thomas W. Merrill, "Capture Theory and the Courts: 1967 to 1983," 73 *Chicago-Kent Law Review* 1039 (1997).

54. Richard B. Stewart, "The Reformation of American Administrative Law," 88 *Harvard Law Review* 1669 (1975).

55. Ibid., note 66.

56. Ibid., 1723–1747.

57. Ibid., 1748–1756.

58. Ibid., 1756–1760.

59. Howard Latin, "Regulatory Failure, Administrative Incentives and the New Clean Air Act," 21 *Environmental Law* 1647 (1991).

60. Ibid., 1673.

61. Latin's "laws" are as follows: 1) in conflicts between political considerations and technocratic requirements, politics usually prevails, 2) agencies avoid making regulatory decisions that would create severe social or economic dislocation, 3) agencies avoid resolving disputed issues unless they can render scientifically credible judgments, 4) agencies will not meet statutory deadlines if budget appropriations, personnel, information, or other resources are inadequate, 5) regulators are influenced by disciplinary norms that may conflict with statutory mandates, 6) bureaucrats are conditioned by criticism or other forms of negative feedback, 7) agency behavior is partly conditioned by manipulated tactics of regulated parties, and 8) administrators of multi-purpose statutes usually "simplify" the decisional process to emphasize only one or two statutory goals. Ibid.

62. Mark Seidenfeld, "Bending the Rules: Flexible Regulation and Constraints on Agency Discretion" 51 *Administrative Law Review* 429–459 (1999).

63. Ibid., 462–464, note 71.

64. Ibid.

65. Daniel C. Esty, "Toward Optimal Environmental Governance," 74 *New York University Law Review* 1495, 1547, 1548–1549 (1999).

66. Matthew D. Zinn, "Policing Environmental Regulatory Enforcement: Cooperation, Capture and Citizen Suits," 21 *Stanford Environmental Law Journal* 81 (2002).

67. Ibid., 126, note 78.

68. Ibid., 126.

69. Ibid., 126–127.

70. Clifford Rechtschaffen, "Promoting Pragmatic Risk Regulation: Is Enforcement Discretion the Answer?," 52 *Kansas Law Review* 1327 (2004).

71. Ibid., 1353, note 82.

72. Bernstein, *Regulating Business*, 232, note 1.

73. Paul J. Quirk, *Industry Influence in Federal Regulatory Agencies* (Princeton: Princeton University Press, 1981), 4.

74. Ibid., 31.

75. Ibid., 51–59, 79–83, 85–88, 87–99.
76. Ibid., 31.
77. Tom Konda, Letter to the Editor, *New York Times*, November 1, 1993, A8.
78. Quirk, *Industry Influence*, 35–39.
79. Bernstein, *Regulating Business*, 88.
80. See, e.g., 33 U.S.C. § 1368 and 42 U.S.C. § 7606.

Chapter Eleven

1. Paul C. Light, *A Government Ill-Executed: The Decline of the Federal Service and How to Reverse It* (Cambridge: Harvard University Press, 2008).
2. Ibid., 4.
3. Ibid., 9.
4. Ibid., 32–38.
5. Ibid., 38.
6. Ibid., 53.
7. Ibid., 67.
8. Ibid., 83.
9. Ibid., 128.
10. Ibid.
11. Council for Excellence in Government, *Within Reach . . . but Out of Synch: The Possibilities and Challenges of Shaping Tomorrow's Government Workforce and the Gallup Organization* (Council for Excellence in Government, 2006), 1.
12. Light, 131–162.
13. Interviews with David Buente and Adam Kushner.
14. Light, 165–166.
15. Ibid., 177.
16. Ibid., 187.
17. Ibid., 189.
18. Ibid., 190.

Index